The Assault on PELELIU

Major Frank O. Hough, USMCR

Foreword

Many factors combined to make the assault on Peleliu one of the least understood operations of World War II. Yet it was one of the most vicious and stubbornly contested, and nowhere was the fighting efficiency of the U. S. Marine more convincingly demonstrated.

At Peleliu the enemy proved that he had profited from his bitter experiences of earlier operations. He applied intelligently the lessons we had taught him in the Solomons, Gilberts, Marshalls, and Marianas. At Peleliu the enemy made no suicidal *banzai* charges to hasten the decision; he carefully concealed his plans and dispositions. He nursed from his inferior strength the last ounce of resistance and delay, to extract the maximum cost from his conquerers. In these respects Peleliu differed significantly from previous campaigns and set the pattern for things to come: Iwo Jima and Okinawa.

Because the operation protracted itself over a period of nearly two and a half months, it is easy to lose sight of the fact that the strategic objective was accomplished within the first week: neutralization of the entire Palaus group, and with this, securing of the Philippines approaches.

C. B. CATES,

GENERAL, U. S. MARINE CORPS,

COMMANDANT OF THE MARINE CORPS.

Preface

THE ASSAULT ON PELELIU is the seventh in a series of operational monographs, based on official sources and documented in detail, being prepared by the Historical Division, Headquarters, U. S. Marine Corps. The purpose of these monographs is to afford the military student as well as the casual readers a factually accurate study of the several Marine Corps operations in World War II. Upon completion of the series, it is planned to edit the individual pieces into a complete operational history of Marine campaigns in the Pacific.

As initially conceived, seizure of Peleliu would constitute only one phase of a many-sided operation (designated STALEMATE) against the western Carolines, embracing at one time or another capture of all the Palaus group, Yap and Ulithi. Subsequent revisions of the original plan, however, raised Peleliu from a secondary target to the primary one, precipitating one of the most bitterly contested campaigns in the entire Pacific war, beside which the concurrent seizures of Angaur and Ulithi were largely incidental. Because Marine assault echelons were committed nowhere else, operations on Peleliu are discussed in fine detail, whereas those elsewhere are merely summarized to round out the strategic picture as a whole.

This manner of treatment is complicated somewhat by the participation of U. S. Army elements, especially the 81st Infantry Division. Believing that Army agencies are better qualified to deal with strictly Army operations, and would prefer doing so, we have described these herein only in sufficient detail to reveal their essential nature. An exception is made in those instance when Army units fought directly beside the Marines, attached operationally under over-all Marine command, as was the case with Regimental Combat Team 321 on Peleliu.

Many individuals and agencies contributed to the compilation of this monograph. To the more than 100 participants in the actual operation who furnished comment, corrections and elaborations, grateful acknowledgment is made herewith. Special gratitude is extended to Office of Naval History, Naval Records and Library, and Office of the Chief of Military History, Department of the Army: in particular Dr. Philip A. Crowl and Mr. Robert R. Smith of the Pacific Section. Maps were prepared by Reproduction Department, Marine Corps Schools, Quantico, Virginia. Official U. S. Marine Corps photographs have been used except as otherwise noted.

BRIGADIER GENERAL, U. S. MARINE CORPS,
DIRECTOR OF MARINE CORPS HISTORY.

Contents

PAGE

BACKGROUND 1
   Strategic Situation, 1944, *p.* 1.
   Concept at Top Level, *p.* 3.
   Some Geography and History, *p.* 4.

PLANNING AND PREPARATION 10
   Higher Level Plans, *p.* 10.
   Planning on Division Level, *p.* 13.
   Intelligence Phase, *p.* 14.
   Operational Planning, *p.* 18.
   Logistics, *p.* 20.
   Preliminary Bombardment, *p.* 24.
   Troop Training Program, *p.* 25.
   Shortage of Equipment, *p.* 29.
   Loading and Mounting Out, *p.* 34.

D-DAY ON PELELIU 36
   The Fight on the Left, *p.* 38.
   In the Center, *p.* 41.
   The Southern Zone, *p.* 45.
   The Japanese Strike Back, *p.* 49.
   The Command Situation, *p.* 54.

SECOND OPERATIONAL PHASE: D-PLUS 1—D-PLUS 7 59
   Clean-up in the South, *p.* 62.
   Advance of the 5th Marines, *p.* 67.
   Difficulties of 1st Marines, *p.* 74.
   Irresistable Force Versus
     Immovable Object, *p.* 83.

"A HORRIBLE PLACE" 94
   Supporting Arms and Auxiliary
     Elements, *p.* 98.
   Summary, *p.* 103.

PAGE

THIRD OPERATIONAL PHASE: D-PLUS 8—D-PLUS 15 104
   The 81st Division on Angaur, *p.* 106.
   Isolation of the Umurbrogol, *p.* 109.
   Drive to the Northward, *p.* 116.
   Ngesebus to Radar Hill, *p.* 123.
   Further Operations of RCT 321,
     p. 129.
   Other Developments and First
     Reliefs, *p.* 133.

THE UMURBROGOL POCKET: D-PLUS 14—D-PLUS 30 136
   Operations of the 7th Marines, *p.* 143.
   Final Drive of the 5th Marines,
     p. 154.
   Relief and Departure of 1st Marine
     Division, *p.* 167.

THE WILDCATS TAKE OVER 171

CONCLUSION 179

APPENDICES 184
   A. Bibliography, *p.* 184.
   B. STALEMATE II, and the
     Philippines Campaign, *p.* 190.
   C. Japanese Defensive Concept,
     p. 192.
   D. Japanese Caves, *p.* 194.
   E. Aviation at Peleliu, *p.* 198.
   F. The Mysterious Mission of
     Murai, *p.* 200.
   G. Marine Order of Battle for
     Peleliu, *p.* 203.
   H. Command and Staff, *p.* 205.

CHAPTER I

Background

Seizure of the southern Palaus, with resultant neutralization of this entire island group, was the most important concrete achievement to stem from the elaborate strategic plan designated OPERATION STALEMATE (subsequently STALEMATE II—see Chapter II). The campaign resulting in this seizure was an exceedingly difficult and costly one. The late General Roy S. Geiger, whose judgment in such matters can hardly be described as unsophisticated, declared repeatedly that the battle for Peleliu was the toughest in the entire Pacific war, an estimate corroborated by at least one disinterested authority.[1] Because benefits gained were not immediately perceptible, and because the operation itself was largely overshadowed in the public mind by events taking place elsewhere simultaneously or shortly following, there has been a widespread tendency to discount its importance, even to question the necessity for staging it at all.

In early 1944 the Palaus stood as one of the key strongholds in Japan's second line of defense: her first line, once New Guinea and the Marshalls had been eliminated and the central Carolines successfully by-passed; and the most powerful and most strategically placed stronghold remaining in that line following the fall of the Marianas. It lay squarely on the flank of any attack aproaching the Philippines from the southeast, only some 500 miles off Mindanao, and too distant from any U. S. bases, actual or potential, to make permanent neutralization by air or sea attack practicable.

Whether General Douglas MacArthur could have invaded the Philippines successfully with the Palaus still in Japanese control is a matter for speculation now. He did not think so at the time, and neither did Admiral Nimitz nor the Joint Chiefs of Staff.[2] Whatever might have been, the Marines hit the Peleliu beaches on 15 September 1944, and history records that nine days after the assault phase was declared at an end, MacArthur invaded Leyte. For better or for worse, his flank had been secured, and with the action which followed the Pacific War entered a new and decisive phase.

STRATEGIC SITUATION, 1944

The South Pacific Theater had been pinched out as an area of active operations

---

[1] Fletcher Pratt, *The Marines' War* (Sloane Associates, 1948), Chap. 20; "Peleliu: The Hardest Battle."

[2] It is scarcely conceivable that the operation would have been planned and carried through had it been otherwise. The only high officer to go on record against it in advance was Admiral W. F. Halsey. See Appendix B.

by early 1944, following the invasion of the northern Solomons and completion of air facilities which insured the neutralization of Rabaul. In the Central and Southwest Pacific Theaters the first tentative steps had been taken on the twin drives to the westward which were to end the war, but not on such a scale as to reveal their full significance. In other words, the handwriting was already on the wall, but the Japanese as yet had been unable to interpret it.

Both Central and Southwest Pacific were under direction of the Joint Chiefs of Staff. The latter was an Allied theater in that its participants included Australian and Dutch [3] in addition to the greatly predominant U. S. forces, under the command of General Douglas MacArthur. Central Pacific was a U. S. joint theater, one component (together with the no longer active North and South Pacific) of the vast expanse designated Pacific Ocean Areas. Here Admiral Chester W. Nimitz commanded as CinCPac-CinCPOA.[4]

Thrown on the strategic defensive after Guadalcanal, Japan had reason to consider her strategic position excellent. The war was thousands of miles away from the homeland, and from her major conquests: the Philippines, Netherlands Indies, Malaya, Burma and Indo-China. Hopping from island to island following Guadalcanal, the Americans had required a year merely to secure the Solomons. MacArthur had slugged his way along the coast of northeastern New Guinea only as far as Finschhafen at the beginning of 1944. Her outermost line of defense had been barely dented at Tarawa, and even this loss could be viewed with complacency: if every fortified Japanese position in the Pacific had to be reduced at comparable cost, it was improbable that U. S. troops, the U. S. Treasury or the U. S. public could or would stand the strain.

Her disillusionment was abrupt and startling. The day after Christmas, 1943, MacArthur hurled the 1st Marine Division against the Japanese airfield and staging area at Cape Gloucester, western New Britain, thereby closing in on Rabaul from the south. With his flank thus secured, his forces seized the important Admiralty Islands and commenced a series of amphibious leapfrogging operations westward along the New Guinea coast, by-passing enemy strongpoints to isolate them or take them in flank or rear: Madang, Wewak, Hollandia, Aitape. In February Nimitz's forces struck in the heart of the Marshalls—Kwajalein and subsequently Eniwetok—by-passing the strongly fortified islands of Mille, Jaluit, Wotje, and Maloelap, thus gaining control of the entire group at a stroke. And the Imperial High Command awoke to the fact that the Joint Chiefs of Staff had no intention of fighting the war on Japan's terms. Supposedly powerful Truk, instead of being subjected to costly assault, had been successfully neutralized in a fraction of the time, and with an even smaller fraction of the effort, which had been required to neutralize Rabaul.

This situation had to be reassessed, and quickly. In something like a frenzy, the enemy high command began pouring weapons and fortification materials into the second line of defense and reinforcing the garrisons with veteran troops from the crack Kwantung Army. There was a limit to the time and means available, and the problem was not simplified by the unfortunate proclivity of U. S. submarines for torpedoing transports and supply ships. Thus, when the Marines struck the Marianas, beginning 15 June, they found the fortifications in an early stage of development and many of the new weapons not even mounted.

Saipan fell with a crash that carried the Tojo Cabinet down with it. Tinian and

---

[3] As did Seventh Fleet, attached to this area command. Occasionally British naval units also operated here as well.

[4] Commander-in-Chief Pacific Fleet, and Commander-in-Chief Pacific Ocean Areas. The former title represented Nimitz's naval command, the latter his over-all command under the Joint Chiefs of Staff. As his opposite number, MacArthur held the title of CinCSoWesPac: Commander-in-Chief Southwest Pacific Area, later shortened to CinCSWPA. His official JCS title was actually Supreme Commander, Southwest Pacific Area, but this never was used in this area.

Guam followed, and the Rota garrison and airfield were neutralized. And with B–29's operating from Marianas airfields, Tokyo itself began to come under long range air attack.

In the Southwest Pacific, MacArthur had continued to parallel the advance in the Central Theater, reaching Cape Sansapor, at the western end of New Guinea, on 31 July. By now his supply line had been stretched so far that logistics loomed as a major problem. So here he paused before mounting his assault on the Philippines until sufficient shipping should be available and Central Pacific forces could secure his right flank.

The turn of the western Carolines had come.

CONCEPT AT TOP LEVEL

As viewed in relation to the strategic concept of the Pacific offensive as a whole, the seizure of the western Carolines constituted a more or less routine step in gaining control of the approaches to Japan proper: bases from which further attacks, ever closer in, could be mounted.

The direction of advance in the Pacific had been discussed on the highest strategic level as early as the Casablanca conferences in January 1943. The two-pronged drive through the Central and Southwestern Pacific Theaters previously described began to assume definite form in the planners' minds in November-December of that year.[5] This occurred during a series of meetings of the Combined Chiefs of Staff,[6] in connection with the SEXTANT conference, held in Cairo, Egypt, and attended by President Roosevelt, Prime Minister Churchill and Generalissimo Chiang Kai-shek, together with their principal advisors. These consultations, of course, were concerned with matters on a global scale, many of which have no pertinence to this narrative. So far as the offensive westward across the Pacific was concerned, the planners not only defined the strategic concept, but set up a tentative time schedule for its execution.

That time schedule, contained in a report entitled "Specific Operations for the Defeat of Japan,"[7] makes odd reading today. It must be remembered that in late 1943 progress of the war in the Pacific had not been such as to give any very clear indication of developments to come. Hence, the schedule included a number of operations which were never executed, for a variety of excellent reasons, and omitted some which were executed, including the western Carolines. That no one was inclined to over-optimism is indicated by the fact that the original date set for attacking the Marianas was 1 October 1944.[8]

But there was no intention of laying down anything resembling a hard and fast schedule. Rather, it was wished to set up a mark to shoot at: a tentative program for planning purposes which would be kept flexible for swift adaptation to drastic short cuts should unforeseeable developments permit. As envisioned at the time, the most important of these might be:

a. Early defeat of the Japanese Fleet.

b. Sudden withdrawal of Japanese forces from occupied areas.

c. Increase in our means such as by acceleration of the assault ship building program and by an earlier defeat of Germany than by 1 October 1944.

d. The early collaboration of the U. S. S.R. in the war against Japan.[9]

As has been seen, it was none of these factors that provided the first swift accele-

---

[5] "Over-all Plan for the defeat of Japan," CCS 417 and 417/1.

[6] CCS comprised the U. S. Joint Chiefs of Staff (JCS) and British Combined Chiefs of Staff (or their representatives) meeting together. American representatives at this meeting were Admirals King and Leahy, and Generals Marshall and Arnold. British: General Brooke, Air Chief Marshall Portal, and Admiral Cunningham.

[7] Report to the President and Prime Minister, CCS 426/1.

[8] Admiral Nimitz's Campaign Plan GRANITE based on the foregoing concept, set 15 November as date securing the Marianas should be completed.

[9] Enclosure to CCS 397 (revised).

ration of the Pacific offensive,[10] but the surprising ease with which it proved practicable to by-pass enemy strongholds both in the Marshalls and along the coast of New Guinea. Perhaps even more astonishing was the revealed vulnerability of fabulous Truk, which rumor and legend, and no doubt self-delusion which the Japanese did nothing to discourage, had built up in American minds to something resembling a Pacific Gibraltar. There could be no more striking testimony to the flexibility of that tentative schedule than the promptness with which it was adapted in the light of these factors to put U. S. troops in the Marianas three and one-half months sooner than had been contemplated originally.

The first major revision designed to step up the speed and scope of the Pacific offensive was issued on 12 March, largely as a result of the swift success of operations in the Marshalls. This document also contained the first mention of the western Carolines as a specific target with a directive to Admiral Nimitz to: "Occupy the Marianas-Palaus line."[11] The target date for the Palaus phase of this mission was subsequently set for 8 September 1944.[12]

It was designated OPERATION STALEMATE.

SOME GEOGRAPHY AND HISTORY

The Carolines comprise the most extensive island chain in the world, spanning 33 degrees of longitude just north of the Equator: westward from the Gilberts and Marshalls to within 500 miles of the southern Philippines. An idea of the smallness of the individual islands (mostly coral atolls) is conveyed by comparative statistics:[13] although eight times more numerous than the Marianas, the Carolines contain only slightly more than two-thirds the land area of that neighboring group, members of which, in turn, are unimpressive as compared to islands in Melanesia and Polynesia.

American strategic thinking in late 1943–early 1944 divided the Carolines roughly into three groups. Truk itself lay in the central group. Serving as outlying defenses for that major base were three islands in the eastern group, believed strongly held: Kusaie, Ponape, and Pingelap.

Each of these had been designated a target for U. S. attack during one phase or another of the early planning, to be abandoned as such with the neutralization of Truk itself.

The western Carolines contained three targets considered potentially profitable, their geographical positions forming a rough arc in southwesterly projection of the line achieved with the securing of the Marianas. From northeast to southwest these were: Ulithi, a large atoll whose unusually deep and extensive lagoon provided a fine fleet anchorage; Yap, an air base made up of a compact group of four small islands which had long enjoyed some international importance as a center of the Pacific cable network; and the much larger group known as the Palaus. Since the spotlight of immediate history was to focus almost exclusively upon the latter, they will be dealt with in greater detail.

The Palaus (or Pelews) are the westernmost of the Caroline Islands, so far removed from the main body of that chain that, until the Japanese assumed jurisdiction, most geographers regarded them as a separate formation. The group includes 100 to 200 separate islands (depending on the definition of what constitutes an "island"), lying on a generally northeast-southwest axis, neatly bisected by the meridian 134° 30′ East

---

[10] Japanese forces withdrew only in the strategically unimportant Aleutians, Germany did not surrender during this interval, and U.S.S.R. very definitely failed to "collaborate." However, acceleration of the ship building program and subsequent defeat of the Japanese Fleet in the Philippines Sea (19 June) had important effects in the speeding up of later operations.

[11] JCS 713/4, 12 March 1944.

[12] Campaign Plan GRANITE II, 3 June 1944. Issuance of this document followed preliminary planning steps by Admiral Nimitz which had already set this tentative target date. See Chapter II.

[13] *Pacific Islands Handbook*, 1944.

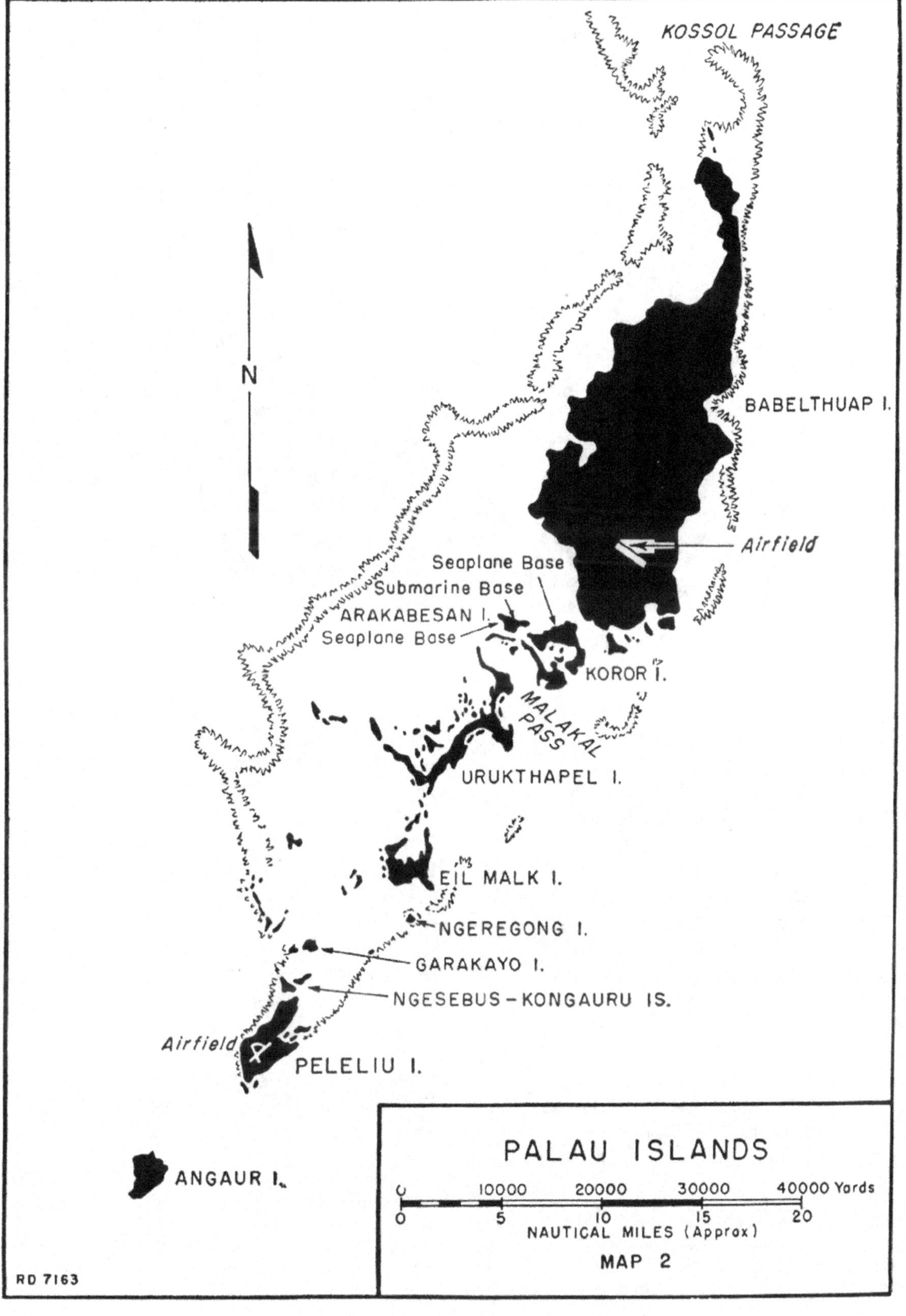

KOSSOL PASSAGE
N
BABELTHUAP I.
Airfield
Seaplane Base
Submarine Base
ARAKABESAN I.
Seaplane Base
KOROR I.
MALAKAL PASS
URUKTHAPEL I.
EIL MALK I.
NGEREGONG I.
GARAKAYO I.
NGESEBUS - KONGAURU IS.
Airfield
PELELIU I.
ANGAUR I.
PALAU ISLANDS
10000   20000   30000   40000 Yards
0   5   10   15   20
NAUTICAL MILES (Approx)
MAP 2
RD 7163

PHOSPHATE LOADING PIER ON ANGAUR. This pre-war photograph, collected by ONI, was typical of meager U. S. intelligence of the Palaus prior to carrier strike in late March 1944.

Longitude. Latitude 7° North lies almost midway across Peleliu, next to the most southerly of the chain.

The nature of the islands varies from typical flat coral atolls in the north to the higher, more rugged results of submarine volcanic action in the central and southern Palaus.[14] The formation of the group as a whole is unusual in that all the members, with the exception of Angaur, the southernmost, are included within a complex of fringing and barrier reefs to comprise, by a certain stretching of that term, a single enormous atoll.

The natives of these islands are more or less typical Micronesians, or "Kanakas," as they were called by the Japanese and others before them to distinguish them from the Chamorros of the Marianas: a blend of Polynesian and Melanesian stock, with an increasing infiltration of Malay blood to the westward. This latter influence, stemming from the comparative proximity of the Netherlands Indies, was apparent also in the speech of the Palau Islanders, a dialect outlandish even to other Micronesians, with the frequent occurrence of the characteristically Malay digraph "ng" at the beginning of many place names (Ngesebus, Ngarmoked, etc.) which baffled forthright Americans from places with such honest U. S. names as Nacogdoches, Texas and Pottawatomie, Kansas.[15]

Their remoteness from the rest of Micronesia had a direct bearing on the history and

---

[14] The terrain of the southern Palaus is described in detail as it affected operations there. As the northern islands never entered strategic or tactical consideration, they are omitted from this discussion.

[15] Most Americans came to pronounce the digraph as though it were a syllable: "neg" ("Negesebus"). A closer, but not too close, approximation would be "n'y": "N'yesebus," much in the manner of that non-Malay city on Manhattan Island, known to its natives as "N'York."

development of the Palaus. They were among the last of the islands to be discovered by white men. Although some authorities credit their discovery to the Spanish explorer Villalobos in 1543, the first authenticated visit occurred in 1712: by Spanish missionaries who had long been established in the Marianas. And history contains no further reference to them until 1783.

Spain professed shadowy claims to possession of the Palaus, along with all the Carolines and Marianas, but showed little interest in their development for more than a century. By 1885 her jurisdiction had become so tenuous that colony-hungry Germans had no hesitation in hoisting their flag on Yap and laying claim to the entire area in the name of the new German Empire. Their claim was disallowed at that time. However, in 1899, following disasters suffered in the Spanish-American War, Spain determined to withdraw from the Pacific altogether and found in Germany a ready cash customer [16] for all her remaining possessions (Guam and the Philippines had been seized by and ceded to the United States in 1898).

Vigorous German exploitation had made substantial progress in developing the economic possibilities of the islands prior to 1914. With the outbreak of World War I, however, Japan, ever the opportunist, grasped the chance to join the nations allied against the Central European powers and set about seizing everything within reach. That nation's title to all former German Pacific colonies north of the Equator was legitimized, more or less, by League of Nations Mandate in 1920. So far as the Palaus were concerned, this title remained undisputed, even after Japan withdrew from the League in 1935, until a certain morning in September 1944.

Japanese economic development followed in general the lines begun by the Germans. In the Palaus, where physical conditions prohibited agricultural development on any large scale,[17] this took the form of exploitation of mineral resources. The Germans had discovered rich phosphate deposits on Angaur and had already placed that industry on a profitable basis prior to their ousting. Their successors not only expanded operations there, but discovered additional deposits on neighboring Peleliu and built a refinery on that island to exploit them. This attempt was less successful, however, and both mining and refining had been abandoned some time prior to the U. S. invasion.[18]

But it was governmental rather than commercial activity that gave the Palaus their greatest importance, especially in American eyes.

Under the Japanese, administrative headquarters for all of the mandated territory, including the Carolines, Marianas and Marshalls, was set up at Koror, a pleasant little town situated on a small island of that name in the central Palaus. This was, of course, strictly a civilian agency, but with the Japanese it was difficult to tell where civilian functions left off and the military began— if, indeed, there were any clear-cut line of demarkation. Under the terms of the Mandate, they were specifically prohibited from fortifying any of the territory entrusted to them, but the extreme secrecy with which the Japanese imediately cloaked all their activities and the pointedness with which they attempted to exclude all foreigners soon gave rise to lively suspicions that they were doing so, regardless. It was in an ambitious one-man effort to penetrate this precursor of the Iron Curtain that the Marine Corps' somewhat fabulous Lieutenant Colonel Earl H. Ellis lost his life in 1923.

---

[16] The price was $4,000,000. *Pacific Islands Handbook*, 1944.

[17] Much of the surface of the larger islands is rough and broken, the soil shallow and not very fertile above coral limestone bedrock pushed up from the floor of the ocean by the volcanic action which had brought the islands themselves into being. In many places even the jungle failed to attain any great luxuriance.

[18] Deposits of low-grade bauxite ore had recently been discovered on Babelthuap, but no attempt to exploit this had been started.

KOROR WAS A PLEASANT LITTLE TOWN before the war. Another early ONI photograph, undated.

Ellis died at Koror under circumstances which are still shrouded in mystery. His is an unusual and dramatic story,[19] but it is pertinent to this narrative only in that he did not return alive to report what he may have discovered. No one else attempted the mission during the duration of the Mandate, and with Japan's withdrawal from the League of Nations, in 1935, even theoretical higher control ceased to exist over the territory she refused to relinquish. Thus, when they first began to figure in U. S. strategic deliberations, the Palaus, which had never previously been considered of much importance to anybody, came very close to being a complete enigma.

The only existing sources from which information could be derived were scattered and fragmentary: old navigational charts, a few reports made during the German occupation (all dating prior to 1914), and a little very incomprehensive material which had leaked out of Japan, supplemented by some more or less random aerial observations made earlier in the war.[20] What these disclosed can be summarized briefly.

The principal island extends northward from approximately the center of the group: Babelthuap (sometimes called Palau Island) a "limited land mass" in the military sense, larger (roughly 20 miles by five miles) than

[19] The most complete extant account of Ellis' adventure, compiled entirely from official sources, appears in *Saturday Evening Post*, 23Nov46: "The Marines' First Spy", by Major John L. Zimmerman, USMCR, formerly a member of Historical Division, U. S. Marine Corps. This has been substantiated and somewhat supplemented by new material now in possession of Marine Corps Historical Division.

[20] Compiled in Joint Army-Navy Intelligence Study (JANIS) #103.

either Saipan or Tinian and second in size only to Guam in all Micronesia. Surrounded by wide fringing reef, its terrain rugged and jungled, Babelthuap was an ideal base for ground troops in large numbers and formidable defenses, but boasted only a single, not very prepossessing air strip still under construction.

Immediately to the south lay a complex of small islands, including Koror, where there were some sea plane facilities and AA defenses. A deep-water lagoon provided limited anchorage facilities, but the approaches were tortuous through a maze of reef channels. A larger and more useful anchorage, Kossol Passage,[21] sheltered from the sea by islands to the north of Babelthuap, constituted the most important tactical feature from a naval point of view.

The principal air installations were situated on Peleliu (described in detail subsequently), the southern-most island within the reef system: a two-strip, hard-surfaced bomber-fighter field with complete servicing facilities, on Peleliu proper, and an auxiliary fighter strip building on the smaller island of Ngesebus, off-lying to the north. And seven miles still farther south lay Angaur, center of the phosphate industry, a comparatively level island except for its northwest quarter suitable for the development of additional air installations.

Earliest wartime intelligence indicated that the Palaus were being used mainly as a staging area and replacement center for troops, aircraft and naval units destined for the Netherlands Indies and New Guinea, much in the capacity that Saipan served Truk, Rabaul and their dependencies. And as was subsequently proved, the Palaus garrison, prior to the frantic Japanese reinforcing activities which followed the fall of the Marshalls, consisted mainly of the rear echelons of units engaged in those areas.

These things, and not much more, were known to U. S. strategists on the highest level at the time the Western Carolines operation was determined upon and the responsibility for formulating definite plans was passed along by the Joint Chiefs of Staff to the top echelon in the Central Pacific.

---

[21] Described as a "reef-and-land-protected anchorage of considerable size." Third Fleet *Action Report Palaus, Ulithi, Morotai*, 5, hereinafter cited as 3d Flt *AR*. Kossol Passage proved to be swept by a heavy swell during foul weather, which limited its over-all value, though it was useful in many ways during the immediate operation. Commander Amphibious Group Five (CTF 32) *Report of Amphibious Operation to Capture Peleliu and Angaur*, hereinafter cited as CTF 32 *OpnRpt*.

CHAPTER II

Planning and Preparation

HIGHER LEVEL PLANS

Admiral Nimitz issued CinCPOA "Joint Staff Study, Revised," for Operation STALEMATE (seldom was a more appropriate code name applied to any operation) under date 10 May. This designated Commander Third Fleet as over-all commander; Commander III Amphibious Force as Joint Expeditionary Forces Commander; and Commanding General III Amphibious Corps as Commanding General Joint Expeditionary Troops. Target date was set tentatively as 15 September.

These echelons commenced preliminary study at once, handicapped by the previously noted lack of reliable information. The regular staff of III Amphibious Corps was already committed to the Guam phase of the Marianas operation, plans for which had assumed virtually final form. Thus, it was necessary to set up a separate provisional staff when, on 18 May, a dispatch arrived from ComSoPac directing Corps to send a staff planning representatives to Noumea, New Caledonia, to confer with Commander Third Fleet.[1]

As a result of this conference, Commander Third Fleet issued a Warning Order for the operation on 26 May. The following day, however, he was obliged to cancel this upon notification by CinCPOA Dispatch that the order was to be issued by that headquarters. Thus, the staff representatives of III Amphibious Corps returned to Guadalcanal with nothing definite accomplished, though much miscellaneous information had been compiled and a tentative scheme of maneuver worked out. In accordance with a CinCPOA dispatch dated 23 May this planning group was ordered to proceed to Pearl Harbor upon departure of CG, IIIAC for the Marianas.[2]

The CinCPOA Warning Order, in favor of which Halsey's had been cancelled, was issued on 29 May. This envisioned seizure of the entire Palau group in an operation on a larger scale than either Saipan or Guam, and nearly as large as the two combined, with 8 September designated as the target date. Major General Geiger, CG,-IIIAC, was designated also Commander Expeditionary Troops and Landing Force. Four divisions, organized into two corps, were to be employed. The IIIAC, consisting of the 1st Marine Division and 81st Infantry Division, was to assault the southern islands of Peleliu and Angaur. Simultaneously, the XXIV Corps, U. S. Army, 7th and 77th Infantry Divisions, would assault the

---

[1] At this time Admiral Halsey held both of these titles as a dual command. VAdm J. H. Newton relieved him as ComSoPac on 15 June, and Halsey removed headquarters, Commander Third Fleet, to Pearl Harbor on the 17th.

[2] III Amphibious Corps *Report on Palaus Operation*, hereinafter cited as IIIAC *OpnRpt;* Enc. A, 1.

main island of Babelthuap, second largest in all Micronesia. Still another Army division, the 27th, was designated to stand by in reserve on New Caledonia.[3]

Once Third Fleet and IIIAC planning staff arrived at Pearl Harbor,[4] the project began to shape up in earnest. XXIV Corps was already in the area, so the several staffs could work in close conjunction, and 1st Marine Division sent a representative (Lieutenant Colonel L. J. Fields, D–3) to join the conference on 1 July. Joint Army-Navy Intelligence Service (JANIS) prepared hydrographic-geographic surveys of the target area. Aerial and submarine photographs were made, and the providential capture on Saipan of the Japanese order of battle for the entire 31st Army area greatly simplified the intelligence problem.

Yet the plan soon began to run into trouble. The 27th Infantry Division, designated as general reserve, was removed from the picture by being committed on Saipan. Then came the long delay in the Guam operation,[5] to which both IIIAC and the 77th Infantry Division had been committed. Nor was there any visible solution to the transportation problem, that perennial limiting factor in all Pacific operations, especially acute here because of the large commitments of shipping in the Marianas.

Other factors were developing which tended to throw a different light upon the whole Western Carolines operation as conceived in the 30 May order.[6] Additional intelligence cast serious doubt on the advisability of attacking Babelthuap at all. The big island was known to be strongly garrisoned and probably very powerfully fortified, whereas the terrain was so rugged as to offer limited possibilities for the development of air facilities. In contrast, Peleliu boasted a fine airfield long in operation, with an auxiliary strip building on the off-lying small island of Ngesebus which, once in our possession, would make neutralization of all forces and facilities on the big island a simple matter.

As a result of these several factors, on 7 July CinCPOA issued a second warning order, cancelling the previous one and setting forth a new concept under the designation STALEMATE II. This substituted the 96th Infantry Division for the 77th in the XXIV Corps, and set the target date for the southern Palaus back to 15 September.

Major General Julian C. Smith was placed at the head of the planning group which had been detached from IIIAC and which was now designated X-Ray Provisional Amphibious Corps, to exercise command over the 1st Marine Division and 81st Infantry Division. At this time General Smith was Deputy Commander, FMFPac, and he continued to function in both capacities until his appointment as Commander Expeditionary Troops and Landing Force for STALEMATE II, vice General Geiger, whose continued absence on the Guam operation had left this important post unfilled.[7]

STALEMATE II split the over-all operation into two phases, to be carried out by two separate attack forces. Plans for the southern Palaus were retained intact, but

---

[3] Third Amphibious Force (CTF 31) *Report on STALEMATE 2 Operation*, 1, 2, hereinafter cited as CTF 31 *Rpt*.

[4] This group was then headed by Col Dudley S. Brown. It was detached from IIIAC on 30 May in accordance with Corps Special Order #25–44 and was operative at Pearl Harbor on 12 June. It was subsequently designated X-Ray Provisional Amphibious Corps (see below) and still later Expeditionary Troops Third Fleet, under which title its *Report Palau Operation* was issued. Hereinafter cited as ExpTrps *OpnRpt*. Source of above material is Enc B, 2, of this report.

[5] Result of unexpected difficulties on Saipan and sortie of the Japanese fleet, culminating in First Battle of the Philippine Sea. Attack originally scheduled for 18 June did not take place until 21 July, and Guam was not declared secure until 10 August.

[6] As early as 13 June a dispatch arrived from the Joint Chiefs of Staff requesting the views and recommendations of top Pacific echelons on the feasibility of by-passing the Western Carolines and other intermediate targets in order to advance the date for striking major objective closer to Japan, notably Formosa. See Appendix B.

[7] CTF 31 *Rpt*, 2, 3. IIIAC *OpnRpt*, Enc A, 2. ExpTrps *OpnRpt*, 2, 3. Interview LtGen J. C. Smith, 23Nov49, hereinafter cited as *J. C. Smith Interview*.

the objectives of the XXIV Corps were shifted from Babelthuap to Yap and Ulithi, with target date tentatively set for 5 October.

Here is the command set-up as then designated:

THIRD FLEET—Admiral Halsey

CTF 31: Third Amphibious Force—VAdm Wilkinson.
CTF 36: Expeditionary Troops and Landing Force MajGen Julian C. Smith.

PHASE I

CTF 32: Western Attack Force—TG 36.1: Western Landing Force (III AC). RAdm Fort.
TG 32.1: Peleliu Attack Force—TU 36.1.1: Peleliu Landing Group (1st MarDiv).
TG 32.2: Angaur Attack Force—TU 36.1.2: Angaur Landing Force (81st InfDiv).

PHASE II

CTF 33: Eastern Attack Force—TG 36.2: Eastern Landing Force (XXIV Army Corps). VAdm Wilkinson.
TU 36.2.1: 7th InfDiv.
TU 36.2.2: 96th InfDiv.

The 77th Infantry Division was designated Floating Reserve, to be embarked at Guam, while the newly arrived 5th Marine Division was to be held as General Reserve in Hawaii.[8]

As far as concerned Phase I, this organization remained till D-Day, with only one major change. Upon completion of the Guam operation, General Geiger was ordered back to Guadalcanal where, on 13 August, he and his staff from IIIAC relieved General Julian Smith in command of Western Landing Forces (TG 36.1), X-Ray Provisional Amphibious Corps, as such was deactivated, but most of the staff was retained by General Smith who continued in command of the higher echelon (CTF 36), now designated Expeditionary Troops Third Fleet.[9]

As had become standard practice long since in amphibious assaults, over-all plans paid due attention to all off-lying Japanese bases and facilities which might conceivably interfere with the attack on the target islands. One part of Third Fleet's mission was defined thus:

Seek out and destroy hostile air and naval forces which threaten interference with STALMATE II operations, in order to inflict maximum damage on the enemy and to protect our own forces.[10]

Accordingly, the plan called for powerful strikes against the Bonins (Iwo Jima and Chichi Jima) on 31 August–2 September, Yap on 7–8 September, and Mindanao 9–14 September. Because of the astonishing success of the initial attack against the latter island, and the weakness of resistance encountered, the follow-up strikes originally planned were hurriedly shifted from there to the central Philippines, where the Visayas were hit on 12 September with even more devastating results.[11]

Because these unexpected developments were destined to have a profound effect on the operation immediately under discussion, it may be well to step out of strict chronology here in order to discuss briefly what actually happened in that connection.

The Western Attack Force completed its preparations on schedule and was en route to the target when, on D-minus 1 (14 September) the command ship intercepted a message from CinCSoWesPac to CinCPOA carrying the rather startling implication that abandonment of the attack on Yap was under serious consideration (see Appendix B).

On the morning of 16 September, while Marines of the 1st Division were fighting desperately for Peleliu, Admiral Wilkinson was alerted by commander Third Fleet to be prepared to use the one regimental combat team which comprised the corps reserve for the seizure of Ulithi. This was substantiated that evening by orders from the same source to carry out this mission ". . . as early as practicable . . . with resources at hand." Then, as though to make all this official—and explicable—Admiral Halsey arrived in

---

[8] CTF 31 *Rpt*, 4.
[9] ExpTrps *OpnRpt*, Enc B, 4.

[10] Hq Commander Western Pacific Task Forces, Operation Plan 14–44, 1Aug44.
[11] 3d Fl *AR*, 3, 4.

person the following day aboard his flagship, USS *New Jersey*.[12]

In brief, the decision had been made to cancel entirely the second phase of STALEMATE II as originally planned in favor of a new and daring conception of the Philippines campaign.[13] The Eastern Attack Force, designated for the Western Carolines, reached its advance staging area, Eniwetok, only to be ordered immediately to report to General MacArthur's command at Manus in the Southwest Pacific. Thus, the XXIV Corps sailed right out of the plan and out of the theater; and IIIAC, at grips with the enemy on Peleliu and Angaur, found the only reserve on which it had been led to think it could count committed to the seizure of Ulithi, hundreds of miles away—with results discussed subsequently as they apply chronologically.

PLANNING ON DIVISION LEVEL [14]

This planning by the higher echelons was largely generalized in nature and concerned mainly with top level strategic considerations. Because of the improvised nature of the X-Ray staff and the absence of IIIAC on the Guam operation, the actual detailed, down-to-earth planning developed upon the fighting echelons to a degree perhaps unprecedented since Guadalcanal: the 1st Marine Division and the 81st Infantry Division as concerned the Western Phase (because of its subsequent cancellation, discussion of the Eastern Phase has no place in this narrative). The 81st, based in the Hawaiian area, was able to work in close conjunction with the other echelons, but the isolated 1st Marine Division was largely on its own.

This unit was in something less than the best condition, physical and mental, of its distinguished career. Following the long and exhausting, if not especially bloody, Cape Gloucester campaign, it had been removed from New Britain early in May to Pavuvu, in the Russell Islands, about sixty miles northwest of Guadalcanal. The purpose of this move was officially given out as "rest and rehabilitation," terms whose implications became increasingly ironic as all hands grew acquainted with the more salient attractions of that rat-infested mudhole.[15] Also, more than two-thirds of the personnel had been in the Pacific in excess of twenty-four months, had served through two exhausting jungle campaigns, and had been led to expect early relief under the new rotation of service plan. To assure that ample replacements were received in plenty of time, the division commander, Major General William H. Rupertus, and Colonel John T. Selden, chief of staff, obtained orders to proceed Stateside to place their needs before Headquarters Marine Corps, and hence were absent during the initial planning phases.

CinCPOA warning order of 29 May reached the Division on 2 June. Brigadier General Oliver P. Smith, Assistant Division Commander, put the division staff to work immediately, to such good effect that a complete study with two alternate schemes of maneuver was ready for submission to the commanding general upon his return on 21 June. The alternative determined upon then became the division plan. Since the new conception of STALEMATE II (CinCPOA warning order dated 7 July) did not affect the operations on either Peleliu or Angaur, this same plan was approved in turn by Commander Western Attack Force (CTF

---

[12] CTF 31 *Rpt*, 8.

[13] 3d Flt *AR*, 4. For further detail regarding this dramatic change in plans, and the thinking that led up to it, see Appendix B, this monograph.

[14] Discussions of one phase or another of planning and preparation occur in reports of all the higher levels of command previously cited. In accordance with the policy of this monograph of drawing on the echelon most directly concerned, this account, except as otherwise noted, derives mainly from 1st Marine Division *Special Action Report, Palau Operation*, hereinafter cited as 1st MarDiv *SAR*. This work is divided into two parts: Phase I—Planning and Training (Annexes A to E inclusive); Phase II—Operational Phase (Annexes A to L inclusive).

[15] A graphic and accurate description of life on Pavuvu appears in 1st MarDiv unit history: *The Old Breed*, by George McMillan (Infantry Journal Press, 1949), Chap. 16. Hereinafter cited as *The Old Breed*.

AKARAKORO POINT, northern tip of Peleliu, was separated from Ngesebus by reef in foreground and from the northeast peninsula (background) by a reef-floored arm of the sea which tapered off into dense mangrove swamps. On shore at right is phosphate plant before its destruction. Photo taken during carrier strike, 31 March 1944.

32—Rear Admiral George H. Fort), and by CG, IIIAC upon General Geiger's return from Guam to resume command on the corps level [16] (TG 36.1—Western Landing Force) on 13 August.

Description of this plan in essential detail follows.

INTELLIGENCE PHASE

Earliest reports on Peleliu showed the island to be about six miles long, shaped roughly like the claw of a lobster, and surrounded by a fringing reef up to 1000 yards in width. The southern portion where the airfield lay, below what might be called the hinge of the claw, achieved a maximum width of about two miles. The whole was described as "low and flat", a definition which persisted throughout these surveys although even the early charts showed estimated elevations up to 260 feet [17] (in contrast to "low, flat" Tarawa where maximum elevation reaches perhaps 20 feet above high tide).

First systematic aerial photographic coverage occurred during the devastating strike of the Fast Carrier Task Force (TF 58) against the Palaus on 30–31 March, 1944, as one of the covering actions for the Hollandia operation in New Guinea. This attack proved to be even more successful than its perpetrators could appreciate at the time: the Palaus were permanently crippled as a naval base of real importance, and an esti-

---

[16] As previously noted, General Julian Smith retained command of the next higher echelon: Expeditionary Troops Third Fleet, which included both IIIAC and XXIV Corps until removal of the latter from the area with cancellation of Phase II of STALEMATE II.

[17] JANIS #103.

mated 160 Japanese planes were destroyed in the air or on the ground.[18]

Photographic coverage, however, was incomplete and generally unsatisfactory for planning purposes. To supplement this material and keep it up to date, subsequent sorties were flown at behest of X-Ray staff, starting 2 July and continuing until late August, by both Navy carrier planes and New Guinea-based planes of the Army's Fifth Air Force, taking both vertical and oblique shots. Between 23 and 28 June the submarine USS *Seawolf* lay off Peleliu and photographed the profiles of all possible landing beaches. From this material a workable and generally accurate [19] map was compiled by 64th Engineer Topographical Battalion, USAFICP, on scale 1:20,000. This, with a target area grid superimposed, was the standard map used throughout the operation, special portions being blown up to 1:10,000 and 1:5000 for the benefit of unit commanders operating ashore.[20]

Complete as this photographic coverage was, it fell short of entire adequacy. The division aerial photographic interpreters were able to spot many ground installations —but not nearly so many as the size of the garrison and length of enemy occupancy would give reason to believe existed. And a number of installations spotted could not be identified.[21]

The map as finally issued showed the southern part of Peleliu to live up generally to the JANIS description: "low and flat" (though even this proved to be a considerable over-simplification). The same could be said of the northeastern peninsula, or shorter prong of the lobster's claw. Here in a small village with the jaw-breaking name of Ngardololok the Japanese had a radio direction finder, power plant and lesser utilitarian installations, all in the open and tastefully landscaped. Beyond this the terrain of the peninsula deteriorated into a series of smallish islands, separated from each other and from the longer northwestern peninsula by a complex of swamps and shoal coral, some of it dry at low tide.

The airfield was an unusually good one, with bomber and fighter strips of hard-packed coral, served by ample taxiways, dispersal areas and turning circles. Immediately to the north of it lay a sizeable area of utilitarian rather than defensive installations: barracks, hangars, large water cisterns, machine shops, another power plant, a radio station, a large two-story administration building of the type encountered previously on well developed Japanese air bases. Just beyond this area jungle masked the details at what appeared to be the base of rising ground. A dense mangrove swamp bordered the airfield to the east, while to the west and south lay scrub jungle liberally interspersed with wild coconuts and occasional grass-grown clearings.

"There was never any question in the minds of the 1st Division planners but that the high ground north of the airfield was the key terrain feature of the island," declared the officer who headed those planners during the early stages.[22] By this, he referred to the northwestern peninsula, or longer pincer of the lobster claw. That this was high ground had been noted in the early JANIS studies. Profile photographs taken by the

---

[18] *Interrogations of Japanese Officials*, U. S. Strategic Bombing Survey (Pacific), Vol II, 432.

[19] Shortcomings of this map in one particularly important small area led to criticisms which have tended to obscure the fact that for the greater part of the island it was excellent.

[20] ExpTrps *OpnRpt*, Enc B, 5, 6.

[21] To facilitate such identification in future operations, the chief API officer, Captain Jerome J. Foley, set up two special teams whose mission after landing was to photograph, sketch and describe fully all enemy installations immediately after they were captured. These teams were made up of trained intelligence personnel, with photographers specially attached from the Public Relations Section. The result was a remarkably complete coverage of enemy installations and weapons showing them both as they appeared on the ground and as they looked in the aerial photographs from which

identification must be made, issued under title "Peleliu: Its Terrain and Defenses".

[22] BrigGen O. P. Smith in special Memorandum, Marine Corps Schools, Quantico, dated 4 February 1947.

SOUTHERN NGESEBUS, with its air strip and causeway connecting to Peleliu, as it appeared on 25 July, 1944.

submarine substantiated this, but without providing reliable means of estimating how high or how rugged it might be. Vegetation cloaked the slopes; sparse, scraggly vegetation, as it turned out, but sufficient to mask the contours from aerial observation. Not a single defensive installation of any importance was spotted in this region, although previous experience with the Japanese in similar situations indicated that there were doubtless many such.

As finally drawn up, the map indicated the high ground to be a single more or less continuous ridge system running about two-thirds of the way up the peninsula, flanked by a good road on either side. Here the ground flattened out briefly, and the East Road angled through a wide draw to converge with the main, or West Road, which continued past another Japanese radio station to the phosphate refinery which had constituted the island's principal industry. Inland from these rose a narrower ridge and several abrupt, more or less isolated hills, one of them mounting a radar installation. About 500 to 700 yards beyond the northwestern tip of the peninsula, and connected with it by a wooden causeway across the shallow reef, lay the semi-joined smaller islands of Ngesebus and Kongauru where the auxiliary airstrip was building.

With this somewhat speculative intelligence, the planners had to be content, since it would be manifestly impossible to send pre-invasion patrols ashore on a land mass so small and so strongly held. For detailed data concerning reef and beach conditions they must wait on the operations of the underwater demolition teams on D-3, D-2 and D-1.[23]

From the foregoing it may be seen that, while the terrain of southern Peleliu might possibly be compared with an atoll island of the Tarawa type, there was a second school of thought which uneasily sought other comparisons for that northwestern peninsula. The most immediate possibility was Saipan,[24] and officers from the division were dispatched to interview anybody they could find who had fought on that island. But the two operations followed one another too closely to permit compilation of a thorough intelligence study of Saipan, and the little information obtained came mostly from men wounded there and evacuated to hospitals within reach.[25]

And there was another difference between Tarawa and the Palaus. Betio had been garrisoned by 4,836 Japanese, with no other substantial enemy forces within reach. Even the notably low early estimates placed 9,000 Japanese on Peleliu, and in estimating the

---

[23] Work of the UDT's at Peleliu was especially fine: reporting on reef conditions, destroying obstacles and mines, and scouting approaches to the beaches themselves. IIIAC *OpnRpt*, Enc C, 2. An earlier attempt had been made in mid-July by volunteer UDT men operating from a submarine, but they were able to reconnoiter one beach only. In a similar attempt at Yap three UDT men were lost and subsequently discovered to have been captured by the Japanese. CTF 31 *Rpt*, Enc A, 1.

[24] Actually a closer parallel was Biak (17 May 26-Jul44), in the Southwest Pacific, where the 41st Infantry Division had to cope with terrain problems strikingly similar to those encountered on Peleliu. That could not be foreseen in advance, however, and there was insufficient time for thorough evaluation of the lessons learned in that operation.

[25] Oral statement to the author by MajGen O. P. Smith, 13Jan49. General Smith added, in effect, that while he did not think that many responsible officers of the division gave much weight to the Tarawa comparison, certainly even fewer, himself included, ever imagined that Marines would still be fighting on Peleliu a month after the landing.

enemy's potential the Division Intelligence Section was acutely aware that upward of 25,000 additional troops were posted on islands within practicable reinforcing distance.

Our preliminary knowledge of the enemy's strength resulted from one of those providential accidents of war which might be considered as bordering on the miraculous in the case of any enemy other than the security-unconscious Japanese, with their predilection for keeping voluminous records and then letting them lie around. Saipan had been headquarters of the 31st Army, and with its fall U. S forces captured a considerable part of that echelon's files,[26] together with a Japanese intelligence officer to help interpret it.

This remarkable combination of related documents designated the units stationed in the Palaus and listed the approximate strength of each, but did not indicate definitely their disposition. There were sufficient clues, however, to provide competent intelligence officers with the means for shrewd analysis. X-Ray Intelligence handled most of this work, passing its findings along to the division, modified from time to time as additional information became available. These estimates proved remarkably accurate from the first in the case of Peleliu, where a final check at the end of the operation disclosed discrepancies of only three minor units not identified on the preliminary estimates.[27] The fact that more Japanese were encountered on the island than the estimates indicated resulted from their partially successful efforts to reinforce the garrison by barge from the large reservoir of troops on Babelthuap.

The backbone of the force defending the Palaus was the 14th Division, Imperial Japanese Army. This was one of the oldest and best units in all of the enemy's armed forces, with a history dating back to the Sino-Japanese War (1894–95) and an outstanding record in the Russo-Japanese War (1904–05). Formerly a part of the famed Kwantung Army, the division had been rushed to the Pacific in the spring of 1944 when the fall of the Marshalls had awakened Japan tardily to the peril facing her second line of defense. Its component infantry regiments were the 2d, 15th and 59th. Also on hand were the 53d Independent Mixed Brigade, and the usual miscellany of smaller units so dear to the Japanese military mind, together with sizeable contingents of naval personel, both combatant and construction.

Commander of the Palaus Sector Group, which included all the Palaus and the island of Yap to the northeast, was Lieutenant General Sadae Inoue, who was also commanding general of the 14th Division. His headquarters were at the town of Koror, on the small centrally located island of that name, pre-war administrative capital of western Micronesia. The greater portion of the troops, estimated upward of 25,000, were on the big island of Babelthuap, immediately to the north. This force included the Sea Transport Units of the 1st Amphibious Brigade, 1,349 men. Since many of the assault elements were known to have received special training in counterlanding operations, the potential of the enemy for reinforcing the Peleliu garrison appeared very real indeed.

Early reports had Angaur, the southernmost island and objective of the 81st Infantry Division, garrisoned by some 4,000 Japanese. Subsequent intelligence scaled this figure down to include only one reinforced battalion of the 59th Infantry, an independent AA artillery company and a few smaller units: an estimated total of 1,400–2,100 combat troops.[28]

---

[26] ExpTrps *OpnRpt*, Enc B, 4.

[27] These were a temporary mortar company, a machine cannon company and some sort of a heavy rocket unit about which nothing definite was ever learned. All three are believed to have been improvised on the spot from personnel detached from the infantry units.

[28] The lower figure squares neatly with the final estimate of the 81st Division, which reported 1,338 Japanese killed on Angaur, 59 taken prisoner. 81st Infantry Division *Operation Report*, Phase I, 69; hereinafter cited as 81st *OpnRpt*.

Since this monograph is concerned mainly with the action on Peleliu, presented herewith is a detailed breakdown of the final preinvasion intelligence estimate of the Japanese forces on that island and semi-joined Ngesebus, which proved so accurate.[29]

Army

14th Div.

2d Inf Reg including 1 Arty Bn	3,283
One Bn 15th Inf [30] including one Arty Bty (4x75mm) and one Mortar Co. (10x81mm)	1,030
Tank Unit, less 1 Plt (12 tanks)	100
Sig Unit, 1 Radio Squad	10
Intendance Duty Unit	30
Fd Hosp	250
53d Ind Mixed Brig	
One Ind Inf Bn [31]	685
	5,388

Navy, Combatant

45th Guard Force Det	200–400
114th and 126th AA Units	600
	800–1,000

Navy, Labor

204th and 214th Const Bns	
Elements of 43d and 235th Const Bns	2,000–2,200

Navy, Airbase Personnel

PELELIU	1,270
NGESEBUS	950
	2,220

Recapitulation

Army, Combatant	5,300	
Navy, Combatant	800–1,000	
	6,100–6,300	6,100–6,300
Navy, Labor		2,000–2,200
Navy, Airbase Personnel		2,220
		10,320–10,700

[29] Above tabulation transcribed literally from F–2 report dated 28Aug44. ExpTrps *OpnRpt*, Enc B, Appendix 10, 1.

[30] Further identified subsequently as 3d Bn, 15th Infantry. 2d Bn same regiment also participated in defense of Peleliu though not on the island on D-Day. See Chap V.

[31] Further identified subsequently as 346th Independent Infantry Battalion.

The Japanese over-all commander on Peleliu was reported to be Major General Kenjiro (or Gongiro) Murai. Precisely what part this officer played in the campaign remains a mystery to this day. Not until after his death was tangible evidence found that he was even on the island (see Appendix F). The one undisputable fact is that all important captured orders concerned with one of the most stubborn defensive actions in history were signed by Colonel Kunio Nakagawa, commanding officer of the 2d Infantry, Imperial Japanese Army. And a dangerous and resourceful opponent he proved to be.

OPERATIONAL PLANNING

On Peleliu there was no dearth of wide sand beaches suitable for landing operations. The width of the fringing reef made it apparent that the landing technique developed in the Marshalls and Marianas would have to be adapted here, and this premise was accepted in all studies concerned with working out the scheme of maneuver.

Four sets of beaches were taken into consideration.

(1) Beach Purple presented the greatest natural advantages. The reef here was nowhere more than two hundred yards wide, while at one short stretch it appeared practicable (with some improvements, this later proved to be the case) to bring vessels as large as LST's directly to the beach. However, these advantages were equally obvious to the Japanese, and their strongest defense system was set up here. The real clincher in rejecting such a landing was the presence a short distance inland of a dense mangrove swamp which in two places narrowed ingress to the main part of the island to a corridor barely wide enough to accommodate a road: a double bottleneck ideal for defense which the Japanese could be depended upon to exploit to the limit.

(2) A projected landing on the Scarlet Beaches, including and overlapping the southern promontories, in conjunction with a coordinated landing on the Orange Beaches on the opposite (southwestern) shore was discarded because of the tactical disadvant-

ages of assault elements converging on each other, plus the fact that late photographs showed the southern faces of the promontories to consist of coral ledges exposed to the surf and the inlet between them to be choked with concrete tetrahedrons.[32]

(3) Beach Amber lay along the northwestern peninsula where the reef is widest, the northern flank enfiladed by the off-lying island of Ngesebus, known to be strongly held. Inland of the beach, a comparatively level shelf was dominated by high ground at ranges of 100–300 yards. A successful assault here would have the advantage of placing what was recognized as the key terrain in the division's hands at the outset. But failure of the initial momentum to carry the ridge line would leave the troops on the constricted low ground without room to maneuver or to emplace artillery, with the enemy "looking down their throats."

(4) A landing on the White and Orange Beaches followed by a drive straight across the island to seize the airfield and split the defenders was the scheme of maneuver ultimately determined.[33]

The soundness of this decision is best attested by hindsight. Officers who participated in the operation, reviewing it in the light of much more thorough knowledge of the island's terrain and defenders, are unanimous in the opinion that the course chosen was the best one.[34]

The plan as finally formulated called for the landing of the division's three infantry regimental combat teams abreast. The 1st Marines (coded "Spitfire") would put ashore one battalion in assault on each of the White Beaches, with the remaining battalion in regimental reserve. Their mission was to drive inland through the barracks area to a predetermined point, then wheel left and attack the nose of the ridge which extended up the northwestern peninsula.

The 5th Marines ("Lonewolf"), in the center, would land in similar formation on Beaches Orange 1 and 2, the battalion on the left tying-in with the 1st Marines, the other driving straight across to Peleliu's eastern shore. The support battalion, landing at H-plus one hour, would move in between the other two, attack across the lower end of the airfield, and then participate in the turning movement to the northward. Following securing of the airfield, the regiment's mission became seizure of the comparatively flat northeastern peninsula and its outlying islands.

The 7th Marines ("Mustang"), less one reinforced battalion to be kept afloat as the division reserve, would land in column of battalions on Beach Orange 3, drive across to the eastern shore on the flank of the 5th, then wheel right and mop up the now isolated enemy contingents in a drive to the southern tip of the island.

The advantages of this scheme of maneuver were obvious; the disadvantages during the planning phase, somewhat less so.

On the credit side, it would be possible to land on a wide front, with a straight and clear approach to the beaches across a not-too-bad reef which attained a maximum width of about 700 yards. The airfield and comparatively open ground immediately to the south of it was suitable for tank operations, and it was anticipated that the drive across the island could be completed in short order. This would not only provide elbow

---

[32] This figured in the planning for some time, nonetheless, and was to be the last alternative discarded. From enemy dispositions on D-Day, there is reason to suspect that they may have got wind of it: Whereas elsewhere on the island, Japanese sector defense units displayed a high degree of mobility, on southern Peleliu they allowed a strongly reinforced battalion to be cut off and annihilated. MajGen O. P. Smith, interviewed 4Apr50.

[33] A detailed and scholarly analysis of the many factors considered in the several alternatives was prepared by BrigGen O. P. Smith in a special memorandum dated 4Feb47.

[34] As evidenced by the following studied opinion: "None of the remaining beaches which might permit a landing in force would allow the rapid development of an adequate beachhead which is so essential in a landing operation. . . . The correctness of the decision to land on the White and Orange beaches

is hardly open to question." Ltr BrigGen W. A. Wachtler to CMC, 1Mar50, hereinafter cited as *Wachtler*.

room for emplacing artillery, but should enable the 5th Marines to take Beach Purple in the rear, potential typhoon conditions making it imperative that beaches on both shores be secured as soon as possible to facilitate the continuous flow of supplies.

The disadvantage of driving across open, "flat" (more or less) terrain commanded by the high ground to the north was clearly —if perhaps not fully—realized. Although the contours of this high ground were still hidden by the vegetation, past experience made it a foregone conclusion that the Japanese would have plenty of heavy weapons emplaced there. It was understood, too, that in having this high ground as its objective the 1st Marines had drawn by far the toughest assignment. But it was anticipated that the 7th would complete its initial mission the first day and become available to regroup in support of the 1st, so that the striking power of two combat teams would be concentrated against the key terrain within a short time. In the meanwhile, it was planned to support the 1st Marines with a maximum concentration of air, naval gunfire, artillery and tanks.

And, according to the original over-all plan, there was what appeared to be an ample margin of safety: the 81st Infantry Division was not to be committed on Angaur until the situation on Peleliu was well in hand.[35]

LOGISTICS

The problem of transporting the troops to the target, putting them ashore across coral reef, and supplying them while there

followed the general pattern resulting from the lessons learned at Tarawa and further developed during operations in the Marshalls and Marianas. This well known technique need be reviewed here only as it applied particularly to the Palaus operation.

Every type of vessel which had proved its value in such an operation was to be utilized, and in the manner it had previously proved most useful. As had become standing operating procedure by now, the foremost assault waves and the amphibian tractors (LVT's) which were to carry them in across the reef were loaded on LST's, as were the armored amphibians (LVT(A)'s) which had been designated to serve as an advance wave and lead ashore the waves carrying assault troops. Development of the new LVT(4) with integral ramp astern (first used at Saipan) made it possible to land 75mm pack howitzers fully assembled and ready for action, and an adequate number of these vehicles were assigned to the artillery for their initial mission. So were the Army amphibious trucks (DUKW's) equipped with an A-frame unloading device capable of handling a 105mm howitzer, a method developed by the 7th Infantry Division at Kwajalein.

The tanks and their crews traveled aboard LSD's, the big, seagoing, drydock vessels originally designed to effect repairs on smaller craft at sea but now adapted to assault purposes. The tanks would be preloaded in LCT's which would move under their own power into the flooded drydock compartment. This would then be pumped dry for the run to the target area, there to be flooded once more and the capacious maw opened to emit its occupants in the transport area. The LCT's would then run in to the reef's edge and there discharge their tanks, waterproofed for the purpose, to get the rest of the way to the beach under their

---

[35] The original plan drawn up by X-Ray staff called for operational attachment of one regimental combat team of the 81st Division to serve as division reserve, all three Marine regiments to land in assault. From the first General Rupertus displayed that marked reluctance to use Army troops which was to color the first week of the operation. Accordingly, the division plan called for landing three regiments abreast, less one BLT which would be the sole division reserve. This was predicated on

the presumed availability of at least some part of the 81st Division, one RCT of which had been designated corps reserve. *J. C. Smith Interview.*

PELELIU'S REEF, up to 700 yards wide in the landing areas, required that supplies be manhandled or carried in amphibian vehicles until pontoon causeway was built.

own power, guided by specially assigned LVT's.[36]

The remainder of the troops and their supplies would make the journey in the more conventional types of assault transports:

APA's (personnel) and AKA's (cargo), combat loaded as it should go without saying. Admiral Fort and Generals Geiger and Julian Smith, with the staffs of the higher echelons, would be embarked in USS *Mount McKinley*, one of the specially designed command ships (AGC's) which had proved so useful; General Rupertus and the bulk of the division staff in USS *DuPage*, an APA equipped (somewhat sketchily) to serve as an auxiliary command ship; and General

---

[36] This highly successful innovation was tried first at Peleliu, as a result of tank casualties and landing delays in the Marianas. An officer of the 1st Tank Bn explains it as follows: "An LVT was placed on each LCT to lead the tanks ashore. These LVT's were used to test the depth of the water, and as long as they propelled themselves along the bottom the tanks would follow, but if the LVT's became waterborne the tanks would stop until the LVT's could reconnoiter a safe passage. . . . Fuel, ammunition and maintenance supplies were loaded

on these LVT's which enabled the tank units to have a mobile supply dump available to them upon reaching the beach." Ltr Capt G. E. Jerue to CMC, 2Mar50, hereinafter cited as *Jerue*.

SEABEES AND ENGINEERS, working under fire, had this causeway fully operative by D-plus 6 to bridge the reef. Angaur Island in background.

From here they would continue in formation to the transfer control line, just beyond the reef's edge, to rendezvous with the returning LVT's and DUKW's which would shuttle the men and cargo in across the coral. Patrol craft and submarine chasers were stationed along both the line of departure and transfer control line to coordinate boats and vehicles in the ship-to-shore movement and to facilitate communications from ship-to-shore and among the various landing elements involved.

The methods of getting equipment and supplies ashore in the wake of the troops presented a few more or less novel aspects, which were to prove satisfactory in varying degrees. The amphibious trailer was used in quantity at Peleliu for the first time. Equipped with wheels and a metal cover which could be bolted down to make it water-tight all around, this vehicle was of a size which could be handled conveniently by a ship's crane. Hoisted from the hold of a transport and lowered over the side, it floated low in the water and could be towed as far as the reef's edge by any powered craft available, and lugged across the coral and on shore by an amtrack or DUKW, or even a tank or bulldozer.

O. P. Smith and remainder in a similar vessel: USS *Elmore*. Two APH's (hospital transports) armed and claiming no immunity in combat, would be on hand to care for the wounded, four regular hospital ships to arrive as early as practicable.[37]

The formation of the assault was also conventional, following the general pattern set in the Marshalls and Marianas. The LST's would discharge leading echelons in their launching area, from whence the vehicles would proceed to the line of departure where they would be formed into waves and advance successively to the beach. Troops from the transports would move to the line of departure in landing craft (LCVP's and LCM's) where the waves would be formed.

Some 60 of these trailers were used. Apportioned among the infantry battalions, regimental headquarters, the artillery and division headquarters units, they were loaded with high expenditure rate items: mortar and machine gun ammunition, flame-thrower fuel, medical supplies, signal equipment and other technical gear easily damaged. The light artillery brought in their first unit of fire in them. As a means of bridging the gap in time between arrival of assault elements at the beach and establishment of the shore party ashore, the amphibious trailer proved its worth, for there were supplies at hand, drawn into cover on the beach and available if needed, with no shore party assistance required. True, the hitch provided was valueless while waterborne, but this was cured by a towing bridle of manila line that could be passed readily from boat to trailer

---

[37] Each APA on the scene was also prepared to care for a limited number of wounded (average 25) who would be carried out direct from the beach until adequate hospital facilities could be set up on shore. See Chap. IV.

and could be cut should the trailer be hit, and such an arrangement did not affect the amphib's maneuverability. While a one-shot item of equipment, for re-loading at ship's side proved impractical due to low freeboard, the amphibian trailer did permit immediate response to a unit's need for supplies.

The use of pallets was another Army innovation, tried first at Kwajalein. The pallet was simply a heavy sled, measuring four by six feet, with wooden runners. Pallets were to be loaded in the staging area not to exceed limits of 3,000 pounds weight and three feet in height, the load being lashed down firmly with 1¼ inch steel strapping. The division used some 2200 at Peleliu to palletize a representative portion of all elements of the bulk cargo load. While results were generally satisfactory, the conclusion was reached that only barbed wire, screw pickets, and heavy shell lifts, or items not readily transportable in a cargo net, would thereafter be palletized. The objection lay in the requirement for a fork lift to handle pallets in each hold where they were to be stowed aboard ship, unless square-of-the-hatch space was used; and this space, generally, had to be held for high-priority vehicles and equipment.

The plan for handling supplies was based on all bulk cargo moving from ship to dump either in cargo nets or on pallets with cranes to be used at all points where the net or pallet had to be loaded, transferred, or unloaded. Commodore Buchanan, the Transron Commander, in one high-powered raid on the Advance Base Construction Depot on Banika, procured 36 Trackson cranes and six P&H five-ton crawler cranes for the division. At Guam crawler cranes had been placed on the reef. There they presented relatively stationary targets and some were knocked out. The division's veteran pioneers had used a crane mounted on a barge as far back as Guadalcanal and found it good. So why not mount cranes on self-propelled barges to establish a cargo transfer line 1,000 yards or so off the reef? The barges could move in or out depending on fire received from the beach; and so another shore party technique was born.

Pontoon barges were seven cells long by three wide, bolted together to form a single unit powered by an outboard motor. They were to be carried to target secured to the sides of LST's, from which they could be launched simply by cutting the lashings. Under their own power, each was to proceed to a designated ship to receive its crane. Special hold-downs were prepared in advance, and the crane's boom was rigged as the barge chugged to its appointed station. A landing craft loaded with netted or palletized cargo came along one side, a DUKW or LVT along the other, and the crane swung the load from the boat to the vehicle which carried it across the reef and to the dump where the load was picked out by crane. Nine barges were used at Peleliu with excellent results.

Six other LST's would arrive on the scene with pontoon causeways attached, one to each side. These were made up of 2x30 pontoon cells to a length of 175 feet. Once the beach had become sufficiently secure, they would be assembled to build a dry roadway across the reef from the shore to deep water where trucks could load direct from LST's.

Supplying water to the troops ashore constituted a particularly acute problem in the case of this operation. Peleliu had no surface water, and the heat was known to be peculiarly enervating. The Japanese used large cisterns to collect the frequent rain, but until the Marines should have facilities for collecting or otherwise producing drinking water, it would be necessary to supply all requirements from the ships. Five-gallon combat cans were gathered in quantities to be rushed ashore, and a reserve supply was put into 55-gallon oil drums which had been scoured out for that purpose. The latter expedient proved unsatisfactory; too often the scouring was insufficient to make the water palatable, and it was found that unless the drums were filled entirely flush the inside would rust and pollute the water.

Fortunately, it was discovered soon after landing that even shallow holes scooped in

PONTOON BARGES transshipping cargo from boats to amphibian vehicles near reef's edge.

the sand near the shore would yield drinkable water, and with the drilling of real wells and setting up of distillation apparatus, the problem passed the critical stage within a few days.

PRELIMINARY BOMBARDMENT

Fast Carrier Task Forces had attacked the Palaus as early as 30 March, and they struck again in July and August. They were also to participate in the pre-D-Day bombardment and to furnish close air support for the landing. The Escort Carrier Groups, whose initial mission was to protect the transport convoys en route to the target, were to join in the close support for the landing. Once the assault troops were ashore, all naval aircraft in the area were to be available for special support missions on call.

The pre-landing naval gunfire objectives were the conventional ones: to soften up the target by knocking out enemy aircraft and artillery installations, and destroying as many strong points as possible. Because of the nearness of large enemy ground forces, a third naval gunfire mission assumed unusual importance: to destroy all ships, barges and sampans to be found among the islands to the northward, and to be prepared to intercept any attempts to reinforce the garrison from that direction.

24

The original plan called for only two days of pre-landing bombardment. Subsequent intelligence caused this to be revised upward to three days. Not all of this was fired, however. Although events were to prove the naval gunfire preparation at Peleliu the least adequate for its purpose of any Pacific operation with the possible exception of Tarawa, before the morning of D-Day Admiral Oldendorf, Commander Western Gunfire Support Group (TG 32.5), was complaining that he had run out of profitable targets.[38]

This view was justified to the extent that gunfire had demolished most of the more conspicuous aboveground installations: barracks, hangars, utility and administrative buildings, larger guns in open emplacements —most of which had already been damaged to varying degrees by previous air strikes. Also, it had sheared a large part of the jungle from the northwestern ridges. But the Japanese, with ample shell-proof cover and operating according to a new tactical concept designed to cope with naval gunfire, suffered negligible casualties. And the sad truth is that the effect of this vast expenditure of ammunition was disappointing, insofar as disrupting Peleliu's basic defense system was concerned, (see Appendix C).

A more immediate factor contributed to this inadequacy. Unlike units which had been operating in the Central Pacific, the 1st Marine Division had never had to cope with this peculiar problem before and had no Naval Gunfire Officer organic to the organization.[39] At the last moment Lieutenant Marvin P. Morton, USN, was flown in from Pearl Harbor to take over this function and performed excellently once the troops were ashore and liaison was all-important in controlling call fires. But the lack of an experienced officer in the post proved a severe handicap during the planning and preparatory stages.

Essentially the schedule and control of naval gunfire adhered to the pattern which had become standard long since. Pre-landing fire on D-Day morning would be concentrated on the beaches, shifting inland, then to the flanks, as the leading waves approached the shore. Special missions would be fired on call once the troops were safely landed. Eighteen LCI gunboats mounting rocket launchers were to blanket the beaches immediately ahead of the assault elements, while four other LCI's mounting 4.2" mortars were to concentrate on the rugged ground on the left flank and inland of the northern beaches from which trouble was anticipated, beaching on the reef if necessary to steady their aim.

TROOP TRAINING PROGRAM

Training of the 1st Division for the new operation proceeded along conventional lines, handicapped by certain complications which were something less than conventional.

One of these had to do with personnel. The division had withdrawn from Cape Gloucester to Pavuvu in May following an exhausting campaign which had protracted itself throughout the entire inhospitable northwest monsoon season on New Britain. Now all hands found themselves dumped on a rain-soaked, rat-infested hunk of real estate where virtually nothing had been done to prepare for their arrival.[40] Thus, instead

---

[38] "I recall vividly the reaction of General Rupertus and LtCol Fields upon hearing CTG 32.5's plain-language voice transmission to the effect that he had run out of targets. Their reaction was that of incredulity." Ltr LtCol F. A. Ramsey, Jr., to CMC, 28Feb50, hereinafter cited as *Ramsey*. "The dispatch sent by Adm Oldendorf was not only a surprise but was not understood by any of us on the Division Staff in view of the study and requirements we had submitted, and the plans which had been so carefully prepared and agreed to as essential." Ltr LtCol L. J. Fields to CMC, 17Mar50, hereinafter cited as *Fields*. See also Chaps. III, IV, VIII, this monograph.

[39] 1st MarDiv *SAR*, I, Annex K.

[40] It was General Geiger's idea to base the division in the Russells in order to avoid its having to furnish large working details, as was the rule on Guadalcanal (average of 1,000 men a day had been the case with the 3d Division), which would inter-

of the "rest and rehabilitation" upon which a vigorous training program should be predicated, all hands were obliged to turn to on the construction of roads and camp facilities; and, as many men will never forget, the disposal of mutiple tons of fallen coconuts and palm fronds which had accumulated in the long-neglected plantations [41]— and which would continue to fall, as many a dented skull would testify.

The incidence of sickness shot upward, while morale plummeted to the lowest point it ever reached during the Pacific service of this elite outfit. The food situation was only one of several causes, but by no means the least cogent. Rations had been bad throughout the protracted Cape Gloucester operation, as is to be expected in an active combat area. At Pavuvu, the amply stocked 4th Base Depot on neighboring Banika was only ten minutes away by cub plane, the big base at Guadalcanal only about 60 miles, yet any change for the better was purely coinciden-

tal. Fresh meat was available for only one meal a week on the average, fresh eggs twice during this four-month stay.[42]

Casting about for indigenous sources of fresh food led to the discovery of large herds of cattle on this and neighboring islands which had been used by the departed planters to graze in the groves in order to keep the ground at the base of the coconut palms free of undergrowth. A call was sent out for all men experienced as cowboys and butchers. A roundup was held and a slaughterhouse constructed at cost of considerable labor and expense which was capable of supplying all hands with fresh beef two days a week. But just as this got into full production, as General Smith puts it in his *Personal Narrative:* "The Australians decided they did not want to engage in that type of reverse lend-lease operations and we were directed to cease."

Efforts of enterprising individuals to supplement their diet with alligator steaks had to be curtailed when the hunters lost direction in the dark (this was purely a nocturnal sport) and shots began falling in the bivouac areas. Fishing the lagoons with hand grenades and TNT was likewise forbidden after several men had been severely injured. The giant clam, captured in its prime, would feed a dozen men, but its meat proved no great improvement over the uninterrupted diet of spam and dehydrated potatoes twice a day, varied by powdered egg and an occasional can of C-Ration.

While the service troops on Banika and Guadalcanal had a reasonably adequate supply of beer with which to sustain their sagging spirits, there was none at all on Pavuvu

---

fere seriously with the training program. Reconnoitering for a suitable spot in the immediate area, the general selected Pavuvu, where there was a battalion of Seabees to prepare facilities. Unfortunately, his reconnaissance was made by air and failed to disclose the more serious terrain difficulties. And the Seabees, who were due for early transfer Stateside, apparently misunderstood their orders. They had commenced construction of an excellent steel pontoon pier and laid out a rudimentary road, but that was about all.—Oral statement, BrigGen J. T. Selden, 4Mar49. This is corroborated by Gen. O. P. Smith who adds that when the true situation became known, General Geiger offered to have the division transferred to the 3d Division's camp on Guadalcanal upon that unit's departure for Guam. However, there was a dearth of shipping available to effect such a transfer, and by that time many of the difficulties on Pavuvu had been overcome. Thus, it was felt that another move would serve only further to retard the training program. BrigGen O. P. Smith *Personal Narrative,* hereinafter cited as O. P. Smith *PerNar.*

41 The plantations had been abandoned for nearly three years and many of the nuts were in advanced stages of decay, pervading the island with a faint odor of rot which is difficult to describe and equally difficult to forget. Many a veteran of Pavuvu remains allergic to coconuts to this day.

42 "The men were not in very good physical condition. The purpose of the move to the Russell Islands was to rehabilitate the Division for future operations. Authority was granted to increase the ration twenty-five per cent. It was assumed that fresh provisions in reasonable quantities would be furnished. We built reefer boxes on the beach to receive these stores but the reefer boxes were generally empty." O. P. Smith *Op. Cit.*

during the first weeks.[43] Even after a regular ration was instituted, men considered themselves lucky to average three cans a week. Motion pictures were limited mostly to the poorest "B" films which troops in the rear areas, who had some choice in the matter, could not be bothered showing for themselves. The only USO show to reach this miserable hole was not scheduled to come at all; it arrived only by dint of the personal efforts of Bob Hope and at considerable inconvenience to his troupe, who managed to sandwich in a morning performance between rear echelon engagements shortly before the division shoved off for Peleliu.

Conditions were especially disheartening to the 24-months men, who still comprised a sizeable majority of the division, and who had been led to hope for early relief under the rotation plan, or at worst a return to Australia. By the end of July, a total of 4,860 replacements[44] had arrived, making it possible to relieve slightly more than half the two-year veterans, which was very cheering to those actually returning to the U. S., but did little to raise the spirits of those left behind, many of them key specialists for whom competent replacements might never be available. And the new men, fresh from the amenities of Stateside life and requiring intensive special training, were poorly conditioned for the wretched life into which they had been so rudely pitchforked.

Yet, despite all the discouragements and handicaps, such was the spirit and resiliency of this veteran combat outfit, passed on by the old-times to the infusion of new blood, that morale rebounded progressively as the prospect of going into action again became more imminent. Or perhaps, as many firmly believed, all hands were simply so disgusted with Pavuvu that they welcomed the opportunity to vent their resentment on the Japanese.[45] Whatever the case, the number of sick in hospital had been reduced to 150, and the spirit of the division left little to be desired in the matter of fighting edge when the time came to embark for the operation.

A second factor hampering the training program was terrain: both its nature and extent.[46]

Except for fringing reef, Pavuvu shared practically no features in common with Peleliu. From the time of arrival it had been apparent that the island simply lacked the area of suitable ground necessary for the training of a unit the size of a reinforced division, and the weeks spent in making the place habitable (more or less) emphasized this feature as well as cutting seriously into actual training time. Units as small as battalions, maneuvering over terrain supposed

---

[43] There were a few exceptions where individual officers were able to get over to the base depot and persuade the powers there to let them buy out of their own means enough to furnish all hands within their own commands a token drink. This was the first beer most of the men had tasted since their departure from Melbourne nearly nine months before.

[44] As the division was finally shaken-down for the Peleliu operation, approximately 30% of the men had been in the Pacific in excess of 24 months and served through two debilitating jungle campaigns; another 30% had 12 months and one campaign under their belts, while the remainder were replacements in various stages of seasoning. As embarked, the division was about 5% above T/O strength. 1st MarDiv *SAR*, I, Anx. A.

[45] The theory is held in some military circles that good treatment only softens first rate assault troops; that the rougher they get it when not in combat, the tougher they will be when they are in combat. Thus, the belief prevailed among many of the officers and men of the 1st Division that the ubiquitous discomfort and privation which fell their lot was the result of deliberate policy, rather than neglect and/or callous indifference. It was certainly true that other Marine combat units had enjoyed comfortable base camps in such pleasant places as New Zealand and the Hawaiian Islands, and even the comparative civilization of New Caledonia and Guadalcanal; whereas the 1st Division, except for the interlude of its happy sojourn in Australia, never got out of the boondocks from the beginning to the end of the war.

[46] "It took no great discernment to see, even from the air, that the place was entirely unsuitable. . . . With the exception of an overgrown and abandoned coconut grove, the island was a veritable jungle in which a troop unit even as small as a platoon would have great difficulty maneuvering." *Wachtler.*

PACK HOWITZERS, first artillery emplaced on D-Day, were landed and supplied by amphibious vehicles.

to simulate the target, found themselves dodging among heads and mess halls and tripping over the guy ropes of their own tents. Conditioning hikes, so useful in hardening the men physically for the ordeal to come, were possible only by marching the troops monotonously around in constricted circles, usually colliding with other units doing the same thing. Weapons and combat ranges were constructed which were adequate in themselves, but neither large enough nor numerous enough to serve adequately the number of men who had to use them.

If Pavuvu was inadequate for infantry training, it was something worse than that for the supporting arms with bulky equipment. Yet despite handicaps of space, the 1st Tank Battalion spent a full day with each infantry battalion, during which time each squad practiced coaching movement and fire by tank-infantry telephone and visual signals, an expedient which went far to foster mutual understanding, cooperation and esteem.[47] But the artillery "was reduced to the pitiful expedient of firing into the water with the observers out in a boat or DUKW."[48]

Altogether, the situation was one calling for all the resourcefulness and ability at improvisation for which the Marine Corps is

---

[47] Ltr LtCol A. J. Stuart to CMC, 25Apr50, hereinafter cited as *Stuart*.

[48] Ltr LtCol L. F. Chapman, Jr. to CMC, 5Mar50.

noted. When large unit training proved unfeasible, the emphasis was placed on small unit exercises until transportation could be obtained for rehearsals on more suitable terrain elsewhere (see below). Intensive schooling was instituted for junior officers and NCO's. Congestion of the ranges was largely solved by adhering to an exceedingly tight schedule calculated to wring out the last ounce of usefulness from the limited facilities.

That a division containing 40% replacements should emerge even half trained under the circumstances would have been a minor wonder. That actually the ground training of all hands proved something more than merely adequate constitutes a high tribute to the efficiency and cooperation of officers and men of all units on all levels.

SHORTAGE OF EQUIPMENT

The amphibious phases of training, in particular, were further handicaped by a sad lack of practically everything necessary to carrying them out; shortages which, constituting a mere retarding factor at the beginning, grew to be a matter of major concern as the time for action approached.

Between the jungle and the monsoon, the four-months Cape Gloucester operation [49] had been especially debilitating to the 1st Marine Division's rolling stock, tracked vehicles and communications equipment; [50] and many expendable items had been left on New Britain under an exchange arrangement

with the Army. This plan proved to be something less than a boon to the division since many of these items proved later to be in short supply in Army depots at Guadalcanal. The demands of the long-drawn-out Marianas campaign further delayed the acquisition of replacement equipment interminably, or so it seemed to the division's worried officers.

Yet once more energy and resourcefulness overcame all obstacles—or a good many of them, anyhow. Few deficiencies in equipment or technique were apparent on D-Day and the critical days that followed.

It should be remembered that up until this time the 1st Marine Division had never made an assault landing across a wide fringing reef. Although most of the veteran personnel were familiar with the various landing craft and vehicles employed in such an operation, considerable training was required in the specialized adaptation of these to this particular problem: launching of amphibian tractors and DUKW's from LST's at sea, transfer of troops from landing craft to vehicles in deep water, advance in waves across the coral, and quick formation of the land assault once disembarked. Thus, the shortage of all this equipment presented a serious problem. Its solution involved a striking example of that improvising on which the Marine Corps has had to depend so often.

The 1st Amphibian Tractor Battalion was still organic to the division [51] upon arrival in the Russells, but it had few LVT's still operative. To supplement these, IIIAC sent over Army DUKW's. In mid-June 40 LCVP's arrived from Tulagi. These were surveyed craft but adequate for their present jobs, however inadequate in numbers. No LST's became available until August, but with this skeleton set-up the division undertook a program of piecemeal training of

---

[49] This operation had lasted throughout the entire season of the northwest monsoon, when rainfall up to nine inches was recorded for a single 24-hour period. In addition to vital combat equipment, nearly everything the division owned had been ruined, including canvas tentage, field kitchens and clerical gear.

[50] As a component of the VI Army, the division had operated at Gloucester under Army communication plans and instructions. Not only were its officers wholly unfamiliar with the Central Pacific Communications Plan prescribed for the Peleliu operation, but because of the division's isolation from its higher echelons there was a long delay in obtaining copies of this plan for instructional purposes. *Ramsey.*

---

[51] The 1st Division reorganized under the new T/O while at Pavuvu. This decreed, among other provisions, that amphibian tractor battalions should be detached from the divisions and pass under corps control.

all personnel in operations across reef.[52] It was while observing such a landing drill that the commanding general fell from an amtrack and sustained the severely fractured ankle which nearly caused him to be left behind on the operation.[53]

Then, to complicate this makeshift set-up even further, in early July the 1st Division was directed to form two provisional amphibian tractor battalions within the organization: the 3d Armored Amphibian Battalion (Provisional) and 6th Amphibian Tractor Battalion (Provisional), "utilizing personnel of the 1st Amphibian Tractor Bn., augmented by personnel from units of the division." [54]

Here was a task of daunting magnitude. The only trained LVT men available were those of the single unit already in existence; thus the 1st Amphibian Tractor Battalion was obliged to divide itself into thirds, so to speak, in order to furnish each of the new units with a cadre of experienced officers and men, and at the same time retain a similar cadre for itself. Utilizing "personnel from units of the division" to build the three battalions up to strength was easier said than done: units preparing for combat are not prone to part with any of their men without a fight. And even when sufficient personnel had been obtained for all three battalions, it would be necessary to train them in a number of vehicles grossly insufficient for a single battalion and already working full time on the landing exercises of the assault troops.

Sufficient LVT's were obtained in time for the operation, but competent personnel remained a problem throughout. Because of the comparatively small size of the target, it was not anticipated that transportation on shore would constitute a major problem; hence only one company (Company A) of the 1st Motor Transport Battalion was to bring in its organic equipment, including trucks and repair facilities. This made it possible to detach Company C in toto and assign its men to the 1st Amphibian Tractor Battalion, in which connection they served throughout the operation.[55] But even with the addition of this manpower, the latter unit was still so under strength that it proved necessary to reduce the basic crew of each vehicle from three men to two.[56]

Thus, the new amtrack crews were being broken in at the same time that the infantrymen were being trained for beach assault, and in the same vehicles. And such were the demands on this overworked and insufficient equipment that the artillery had a minimum of time to practice their own new assault technique: loading and unloading of their 75mm and 105mm howitzers in LVT–4's and DUKW's, respectively; also, the loading and unloading of radio jeeps in DUKW's, using the A-frames.

The problem of organizing the armored amphibian battalion multiplied these complexities. The LVT(A), or "amphibian tank," was a newly developed vehicle which had been used in combat heretofore only in the Central Pacific. Few officers of the 1st Marine Division had so much as laid eyes on one.[57] And at the outset none were avail-

---

[52] A further handicap here was that the DUKW is by no means an adequate substitute for the amtrack in reef crossing. It is easily stopped by rugged coral and must pick its way ashore with great care, thus breaking the wave formation and falling more or less automatically into column.

[53] "General Geiger visited me at the CP during the first rehearsal (27 August). He had not realized that General Rupertus was unable to make the trip ashore and was somewhat concerned about him going on the operation. I assured General Geiger that in the two weeks remaining before the landing I felt General Rupertus' ankle would mend sufficiently to permit him to carry on." Smith *PerNar.*

[54] 1st MarDiv *SAR*, I, 5.

[55] Company B personnel served as stretcher bearers and relief drivers. Ltr Maj R. B. McBroom to CMC, 13Mar50. Ltr Maj G. J. DeBell to CMC, 20Mar50, hereinafter cited as *DeBell.*

[56] Ltr Maj A. F. Reutlinger to CMC, 10Mar50, hereinafter cited as *Reutlinger.* This letter contains a wealth of graphic detail regarding the problems encountered in this reorganization.

[57] "His (the CO's) only knowledge of the vehicle he was to fight was a picture seen in ONI 226." LtCol K. H. Boyer, monograph prepared at Marine Corps Schools, March 1947, hereinafter cited as *Boyer Mono.*

able here even for demonstration purposes. Thus, not only must sufficient personnel be obtained, but these must be trained initially from blueprints in the operation of a vehicle they would be called upon to take into battle.

The man appointed to this seemingly insuperable task was Lieutenant Colonel Kimber H. Boyer, until then commanding officer of the 1st Motor Transport Battalion. For the first ten days his entire officer complement consisted of one first lieutenant and two warrant officers, and to initiate training he had to borrow a weapons expert from the 7th Marines.[58] His personnel arrived in driblets from various sources: rear echelons of other armored amphibian battalions and tank battalions, and men shipped out from the Tracked Vehicle School in the United States. Few had had any combat experience at all; of the 36 officers and 800 enlisted men who finally comprised the battalion, only approximately 50 had ever fought an LVT(A).

Intensive training began with delivery of the first six vehicles: LVT(A)(1)'s. By the first week in August the battalion had acquired 50 per cent of its machines and 60 per cent of its personnel, when disturbing word arrived that its remaining quota of vehicles would be of a different model: LVT(A)(4)'s, mounting 75mm howitzers in place of the 37's with which the men had been trained up to this point, with embarkation only about three weeks away. That the battalion should turn in an outstanding performance after such unpropitious beginnings might well rank as one of the minor miracles of the campaign.[59]

---

[58] This was Maj J. E. Buckley, CO Wpns Co, 7th Marines. In a letter to CMC, 10Mar50, LtCol Buckley (Ret.) wrote: "Kimber Boyer did one of the greatest training jobs I ever saw or heard of."

[59] Col Boyer himself viewed the "miracle" in a somewhat different light: "It would be an insult to the intelligence of a military minded reader to say that the Battalion was sufficiently trained and indoctrinated to carry out its mission. It can be considered some sort of a miracle that the initial phase of the Operation was not seriously disrupted." *Boyer Mono*, **17.**

Shortages of critical equipment were not limited to heavy assault vehicles. They embraced everything from tank spare parts and communications equipment to bazookas, BAR's, and spare machine gun barrels, to such a degree as not only to hamper training but to cause serious concern over the forthcoming operation. This was notably true in the case of the pack type flamethrowers which arrived too late to be distributed according to plan. Final allotments in many categories arrived barely in time to be combat loaded, and a few had to be crammed aboard the transports after the troops had embarked.[60]

In general, it may be said that the only items in which shortages did not exist were the basic arms of the individual Marine. And even here there was some minor difficulty: the decision to replace carbines in infantry units with rifles and submachine guns could not be implemented immediately for lack of the latter weapons.[61]

The equipment finally delivered was the most up-to-date available, much of it improved over earlier models with which the 1st Division was familiar.[62] Only two en-

---

[60] A full allowance of new dry cell batteries for the vital TBX radios, issued at the last moment, were discovered to be essentially all dead. Fortunately, 4th Base Depot was able to duplicate the issue the same day. *Ramsey*. "Belts of machine gun ammunition had rotted . . . powder rings on mortar ammunition were disintegrating and bourrelets rusted, shotgun shells swollen or if brass corroded. All ammunition had to be unstowed, inspected and in large part replaced and restowed at the last minute." Ltr LtCol S. S. Berger to CMC, 19Mar50, hereinafter cited as *Berger*.

[61] "Carbines were retained generally by personnel assigned to crew-served weapons and others who formerly carried a pistol. The attitude of the battalions was that the carbine without bayonet was an adequate substitute for a pistol, but not for an M-1 rifle with bayonet." 1st MarDiv *SAR*, I, 5. "M-1's and TSMG's were substituted in 2/7 for carbines. Machine gun squad leaders carried TSMG's." *Berger*.

[62] The 1st Tank Bn, for instance, which had begun the war with gas-engine light tanks and subsequently acquired one company of gas-engine mediums for the Cape Gloucester operation, now found itself equipped entirely with diesel-engine mediums. *Stuart*.

tire.y new items worthy of mention were issued at this time.

Most notable was the Navy Mark I flamethrower, an experimental weapon developed by the Seabees at Pearl Harbor, which was capable of throwing a stream of blazing Napalm up to 150 yards. The first three of these were furnished the division in July, together with four LVT–4's on which to mount them. Their primary function was thought to be immediate action against beach pillboxes in support of the assault waves, though actually they proved their greatest usefulness in subsequent developments farther inland. The flame units were installed on three of the LVT–4's as prescribed, the fourth amtrack being adapted as a supply carrier to service them in the field.

The second new weapon was the 60mm shoulder mortar, a standard mortar adapted to a light machine gun mount for direct, flat-trajectory fire against caves and pillbox openings. Some of its parts proved not rugged enough for sustained use and had to be replaced nearly as often as the poor devils who were obliged to fire the contraption from their shoulders. Essentially its functions duplicated those of the bazooka, and its adoption resulted from the frequent failure of bazooka rockets to detonate in the soft mud of Cape Gloucester. However, there proved to be very little soft ground amid

LONG RANGE FLAME-THROWERS were first used at Peleliu.   LVT mount was thereafter replaced by tank.

FINAL CRITIQUE, following last rehearsal at Guadalcanal. Assembled Marine and Navy Officers are here addressed by First Division chief of staff. Front row: Generals O. P. Smith and W. H. Rupertus, and Captain T. B. Brittan, USN, commander of the transport group.

the coral of Peleliu and, although the shoulder mortar was used effectively, it came to be considered less practical all around than the weapon it had been designed to replace.[63]

The training program culminated in two full-scale rehearsals, held on 27 and 29 August respectively, in cooperation with Task Force 32.1 (Peleliu Attack Force). By this time the assault troops were all embarked on the vessels which were to carry them to the target (see below) and standing by off Guadalcanal, and the terrain selected for these maneuvers was the Tassafaronga region of that island.

No coral reef exists here, but this was readily simulated by setting up an arbitrary transfer control line at the proper distance from the beach where the landing craft carrying the later waves halted to rendezvous with the returning LVT's which shuttled the men in from there. Once ashore, the assault units moved out at once on a reasonably accurate facsimile of their missions, and an

---

[63] "As presently constructed, they (shoulder mortars) are too heavy and certain parts are too weak. . . . After firing two to four rounds, it is necessary to replace the gunner. Units feel that the shoulder mortar as now constructed is not of sufficient value to include it in the authorized weapons." 1st MarDiv *SAR*, II, Annex A, 5.

advance division command post was set up to coordinate their movements.

The first of these exercises had been described as a "pre-dress rehearsal."[64] Naval gunfire and air support units went through their respective motions, but there was no firing. Everything progressed with pleasing smoothness up to the point where the division command post attempted to establish communication with the regiments. This was eventually achieved by field telephone but the radio proved useless, the new equipment having arrived too late to be calibrated accurately and set up in accordance with the plan.[65] This was quickly rectified, however, to such good effect that the second rehearsal, using token quantities of live ammunition, aerial bombs and rockets, came off so well that a critique held the following day at IIIAC headquarters produced little that was constructive because "everyone was pleased with everyone else."[66]

A shore party exercise at Tetere Beach on 3 September, mainly to perfect the setting up of communications, completed the training phase. For better or for worse, the 1st Marine Division and its reinforcing troops were as ready for combat as they would ever be.

LOADING AND MOUNTING OUT

Availability of shipping had always been one of the critical controlling factors in the U. S. Pacific offensive, involving as it did such vast distances between base and target. Not since the early stages of the war, when ships in sufficient numbers simply did not exist, was the shortage felt so acutely as just prior to the Peleliu operation. Again, responsibility could be attributed to the long delay in the Guam invasion. The sortie of the Japanese Fleet into the Philippines Sea might be rated as a major enemy disaster on the strategic level, but as a means for providing headaches for the 1st Marine Division it proved an unqualified success.

Nobody knew when the necessary shipping would arrive, except that it became increasingly apparent that this was not going to be until the last moment. The elaborate loading plans on which such an operation is predicated were meticulously worked out on the general level, but detailed planning was impossible in advance owing to lack of knowledge as to exactly which ships would be available and the individual capacities and peculiarities of each. And the inevitable misunderstandings among the diverse elements in this highly complicated business necessitated changes, compromises and improvisations up to the last minute.

The problem was not simplified by the fact that loading operations had to be conducted at five widely separated points: Pavuvu, Banika, Guadalcanal, Tulagi, and Espiritu Santo (New Hebrides), the last named being the base of the Marine air squadrons designated to operate from the field on Peleliu once it had been secured. Several of the ships, indeed, were scheduled to pick up portions of their cargo at two or more of these separated points. Careful coordination was necessary to avoid wasted effort and backtracking. Especially at Pavuvu and Banika, beaches, lighters and dockage facilities were insufficient to load more than a few vessels at a time; thus, when most of them appeared simultaneously with little time to spare, they were obliged to take their turns in accordance with an exceedingly tight schedule and keep out of each other's way while doing so.

It was a step by step process, entailing close coordination and prodigious labor. The LST flotilla had to be assembled from several areas of the Central Pacific, and the first units did not begin arriving until 15 August. The last ones appeared only on the 26th, by which time the troops had been embarked in preparation for their landing exercises. Despite this, all 30 LST's, in addition to 17 transports and two LSD's, had been combat loaded by the 31st.

---

[64] O. P. Smith *PerNar*.

[65] 1st MarDiv *SAR*, I, Annex E. For amplification see *Ramsey*.

[66] O. P. Smith, *op.cit.*

Following the rehearsals, the convoy stood by off Tetere Beach while the 81st Infantry Division, which had assembled in the area by 26 August, took over Tassafaronga for its own final rehearsals for the assault on Angaur. While awaiting completion of these, the Marines were landed daily for recreation and small unit exercises, and the transports moved by turn over to Tulagi for fueling.

With everything in readiness at last, the slower moving tractor groups of the two divisions, aboard LST's (average speed, 7.7 knots), departed Guadalcanal with their respective screening forces early on the morning of 4 September. The faster transports and LSD's (averaging 12.1 knots) left on the 8th to rendezvous with them during the early hours of D-Day off the target which the fire support group would have been softening up for three days by then. Their course took them northwestward through the Solomons, then across the Equator on an approach generally parallel to the northern coast of New Guinea: a distance of approximately 2,100 miles. The sea was smooth throughout, the run uneventful—and miserably uncomfortable for the men, as such trips inevitably are in the tropics.

Previous to departure from Guadalcanal, a sealed envelope had been issued to each of the civilian news correspondents assigned to cover the expedition, and to the troop commanders aboard several of the ships, marked with explicit instructions that it was not to be opened until D-minus 1, at which time the contents was to be broadcast to all hands. On the morning of 14 September, therefore, the seals were broken and the recipients learned, to the considerable astonishment of many of them,[67] that the division's commanding general expected the operation to be very tough but very short, comparable to Tarawa, and that Peleliu should be secured within four days: perhaps the most striking manifestation of that preoccupation with speedy conquest at the highest division level which was to color tactical thinking ashore for a month to follow.[68]

---

[67] "I doubt that anyone with the possible exception of the Chief of Staff was consulted before the letter was written and distributed. . . . I was given a complete rough draft of the letter and merely supervised its reproduction." Ltr LtCol W. E. Benedict (D–1) to CMC, 27Feb50, hereinafter cited as *Benedict*.

[68] Most officers believed this unusual document intended in the nature of a "pep talk." This was not its effect on the news correspondents, however: many of the 36 accredited to the division did not come ashore at all, and only six (one of whom was killed) chose to stay through the critical early phases. Hence, news coverage of the operation was sketchy, often misleading, and, when quick conquest failed to materialize, tinged with biting criticism.

CHAPTER III

D-Day on Peleliu

Beginning with its first amphibious assault, the 1st Marine Division had built up a tradition of extraordinary good luck in making its initial landings against the enemy. At Guadalcanal a low overcast had covered the approach of the convoy, tactical surprise had been complete, and landing conditions perfect. At Cape Gloucester, again tactical surprise was achieved in the selection of the beaches, and D-Day provided virtually the only clear, calm morning which occurred during the entire monsoon season. The sea was placid at Peleliu, too, and the temperature the least debilitating that would be encountered in weeks to come. But beyond this point, any resemblance to the "landing luck" of Guadalcanal and Cape Gloucester was purely coincidental.

Everything that was, or appeared, practicable had been done in preparation. Naval gunfire and air strikes had, presumably, softened up the defenders for the past three days. The underwater demolition teams had cleared the approaches and scouted the reef as well as conditions would permit—and done a satisfactory job, as things turned out. At 0800 direct supporting fire was commenced with high explosive to knock out beach defenses and white phosphorous smoke shell farther inland to screen the approach by blacking-out observation from the high ground north of the airfield. Under this cover the personnel assault waves moved toward the shore behind the "amphibian tanks" of the newly improvised provisional 3d Armored Amphibian Battalion, the naval gunfire moving forward and toward the flanks according to schedule as they drew nearer, and carrier-borne planes coming in to strafe and dive-bomb directly to their front.

All this was as had been planned and rehearsed; a school problem. But presently the Japanese began revising "The Book."

As the leading waves entered the zone between the transfer line and the reef's edge, shells began to fall among the vehicles, throwing geysers of water skyward. This did not appear to be aimed fire, but rather a protective curtain of some intensity which moved shoreward with the approach of the vehicles.[1]

The smoke screen drifted seaward to obscure the beach and its approaches, dissipating lanquidly in the windless air. And when at last visibility was possible again, watchers still aboard the ships off-shore were appalled to discern smoke of another sort: burning amtracks and DUKW's littered across the length and breadth of the reef.[2]

---

[1] 1st Marines *Regimental Narrative,* hereinafter cited as 1st *MarNar.*

[2] LtCol H. C. Tschirgi, D–4, viewed this scene from the deck of a transport. "I'd never seen combat before," he recalled later, "and the first thing that struck me was that this was a hell of a way to treat $40,000 equipment." Interview with Col Tschirgi, 26Jan49.

Taking their losses in stride, the assault waves pressed on. The LVT(A)'s in the lead, hit the beach at approximately 0830,[3] heaved themselves up out of the water and led the inland advance of the infantry through a mounting volume of artillery and mortar fire, picking a gingerly way among the mines thickly seeded on the beach and for an average depth of a hundred yards inland.[4] Only scattered enemy infantry had remained in the beach positions throughout the heavy shelling, but resistance developed rapidly as the advance progressed.

Sherman medium tanks began to arrive simultaneously with the fourth wave to take over from the much more vulnerable amphibians. This was much earlier than in any previous Marine operation, as a result of well worked planning. Thanks to excellent water-proofing and the efforts of the under-water demolition teams in clearing away the worst of the obstacles, they were guided across the reef without major physical difficulties. However, so slowly did they have to pick their way and so intense was the enemy fire, that all but one of the 18 machines assigned to support the 1st Marines were struck by high explosive shells before reaching shore.[5] Only three were knocked out of action, fortunately, some explosions occurring below the surface where the depth of the water prevented serious damage.

MARINES going into battle.

The tractor-borne waves continued to push in on schedule, taking their losses grimly, and thus the initial momentum was sustained. But subsequent elements were delayed increasingly at the transfer control line as the mounting shortage of LVT's made itself felt.[6] The destruction was comparatively light in the center where only artillery and mortar fire was encountered. The flanks, however, were enfiladed by high velocity weapons: emplaced on Peleliu's southwestern promontory and a small unnamed island offshore a few hundred yards below Beach Orange 3; and to the north on a point of high ground projecting about 25

---

[3] Exact time of first landing recorded as 0832. 1st MarDiv *SAR*, II, 2.

[4] Many mines were improvised from aerial bombs buried up to the nose in the sand, to supplement land mines of the conventional type and horned anti-invasion mines. Many of the latter were not armed and failed to detonate. It is believed that most of them were set out hurriedly during the night, as the UDT's did not spot them in large numbers the previous day, which would help to explain an otherwise almost incomprehensible piece of carelessness on the enemy's part.

[5] This unit was Co. A, 1st Tank Bn. Six more of its machines were knocked out by enemy action during the next few hours, and by the end of the second day it had only five machines operative. 1st Mar *Nar*. Of the division's total of 30 tanks "over half . . . received from one to four hits during the 10 minutes reef crossing." 1st MarDiv *SAR*, II, Anex J.

[6] Only 26 LVT's were reported actually destroyed on D-Day. *Ibid.*, Annex F. Yet an air observer on one occasion reported 38 burning simultaneously and unofficial estimates by assault unit commanders bring the total knocked out at least temporarily in excess of 60. Partly accounting for the apparent discrepancy might be "the extreme reluctance, short of complete demolition or submersion in over 10 fathoms, of any crew chief to regard his vehicle as destroyed"; also, DUKW'S and LVT(A)'s were being hit and were not readily distinguishable from the air. *Reutlinger*. Contributing perhaps even more to the growing shortage was the necessity for repair and refueling, and the practice of evacuating the more seriously wounded all the way to the transport area in the slow-moving amtracks.

LVT(A)'S LED THE ADVANCE across the beach. Wrecked LVT (left background) is one of many knocked out in the first onslaught.

yards to seaward just beyond the ultimate boundary of White 1.[7]

As has been noted, the scheme of maneuver assigned a particular mission to each of the regimental combat teams. Because these missions varied, and encountered varying fortunes, they are best discussed individually.

THE FIGHT ON THE LEFT [8]

The 1st Marines had as its target the White Beaches, and the assault waves hit these approximately on schedule: 2d Battalion on the right, 3d on the left, with the 1st Battalion to come in behind them at about 0945 as regimental reserve, prepared to participate in the left turn to the north by attacking through the center of the regiment and seizing the high ground to the north of 0–2.[9]

On White 2, the 2d Battalion drove inland against resistance described as "moderate".[10] Utilizing all organic regimental weapons and supported by the surviving armored amphibians until the Sherman

---

[7] That positions of such obvious tactical importance had not been demolished by naval gunfire and close air support was the subject of much bitter comment by the troops who had to put them out of action after being obliged to land through their fire. But most of these installations were proof against anything short of a direct hit and so well camouflaged that their precise positions could not be spotted; and "The idea . . . of just firing at an island is an inexcusable waste of ammunition." Ltr RAdm G. H. Fort to BrigGen C. C. Jerome, 20Mar50, hereinafter cited as *Fort*. "My surprise and chagrin when concealed batteries opened up on the LVT's can be imagined." Ltr Adm. J. S. Oldendorf to BrigGen C. C. Jerome, 25Mar50, hereinafter cited as *Oldendorf*.

[8] Wherever possible, this monograph's accounts of regimental actions are drawn from reports submitted at regimental or battalion level, supplemented as practicable by higher echelon reports, personal consultations, letters and private memoirs. Basic sources on 1st Marines are: *History of 1st Marine Regiment, 1st Marines Regimental Narrative* (context of these two works almost identical, latter being a later rewrite of material prepared during and immediately following the operation), *1st Battalion Unit History*, and *3d Battalion Record of Events*.

[9] Ltr LtCol R. G. Davis to LtCol G. D. Gayle, 4Nov49; hereinafter cited as *Davis*.

[10] 1st Mar *Nar*.

MEN OF 1st MARINES advance around unexpected coral ridge inland from White Beaches.

tanks should come up, this unit reached the 0–1 phase line—approximately 350 yards through heavy woods—by 0930: an excellent achievement, though not without cost. Here, facing the airfield and building area from the far side of the woods, the battalion tied in with the 5th Marines on its right; and, perforce, was ordered halted and held up pending solution of the problem facing the 3d Battalion.

By this time the 3d Battalion was in very serious trouble indeed. From the moment of landing this unit had run into opposition of the most stubborn and violent kind from strongly emplaced Japanese who added small arms and automatic weapons fire to the brutal artillery and mortar shelling which was blanketing the whole area. What was worse, the leading elements had not advanced a hundred yards inland before they found themselves confronted by a most formidable natural obstacle which showed on none of the advance maps or intelligence reports: a long, rugged coral ridge about 30 feet in elevation, its precipitous face honeycombed with caves and dug-in positions. All initial assaults were repulsed, even after the tanks had been brought up. Troops attempting to storm the northern portion stumbled into a wide, deep anti-tank trench, dominated by the ridge itself and cleverly enfiladed, where many of them remained pinned down for hours.

Company A of the reserve battalion was committed early in the day in support of the 3d Battalion and Company B late in the afternoon, but their most determined efforts failed to close the gap which had occurred over toward the left (see below). Late in the afternoon the securing of a precarious foothold on the southern sector of the ridge top improved the position somewhat but gave cause for little optimism.[11]

More than eight hours of some of the fiercest and most confused fighting in the Pacific war had produced two major gaps in the line so serious as to imperil the position of the entire division. All the men in reach who could possibly be spared, including headquarters personnel and 100 men from the 1st Engineer Battalion,[12] were brought up to form a defense in depth against the threat of a counterattack in force along the corridor between the ridge and the sea which might well roll up the line and sweep down the landing beaches, now congested with gear and supplies owing to the shallowness of the inland penetration.

Fortunately, this particular attack did not materialize. No doubt, the tactical situation was as obscure to the Japanese as it was to the invaders, for their communications system must have been badly battered. Furthermore, the unusually elaborate plans for the defense of Peleliu, as was later discovered, did not envision a major counterattack in this particular sector. Never overgifted with the resourcefulness to regroup quickly in order to capitalize a fluid tactical situation, the Japanese were in no position to do so now. Grimly they went ahead with their preconceived plans and, as happens so often in the confusion of battle, the golden opportunity slipped through their fingers.

To complete the 3d Battalion picture, Captain George P. Hunt's Company K was writing an epic of small unit combat on the extreme left; an action which, owing to the course of events, became in effect a solo performance.[13]

Company K's position was on the extreme left of the 3d Battalion, thus responsible for securing the flank of the entire division. The most important objective in this zone was the point just to the north, previously mentioned, from which destructive enfilading fire was being poured the length of the White Beaches. The threat this position presented to the entire landing operation was self-evident. Its formidability is best described in Captain Hunt's own words:

The Point, rising thirty feet above the water's edge, was of solid, jagged coral, a rocky mass of sharp pinnacles, deep crevasses, tremendous boulders. Pillboxes, reinforced with steel and concrete, had been dug or blasted in the base of the perpendicular drop to the beach. Others, with coral and concrete piled six feet on top were constructed above, and spider holes were blasted around them for protecting infantry. It surpassed by far anything we had conceived of when we studied the aerial photographs.[14]

There was no evidence that naval gunfire had had any effect whatever on these installations.

The point was unassailable from the beach. The rifle platoon assigned to deal with it was obliged to fight inland, then execute a turning movement to take it from the landward side. In so doing this platoon lost contact with the other assault platoon which, as it turned out later, had lost its leader, killed, and had been caught in the tank trap where it was pinned down for some time.

Resistance was fierce and stubborn, and Captain Hunt was obliged to commit his support platoon. The ensuing fire fight lasted nearly two hours. During this time most of

---

[11] Five LVT's carrying the 1st Marines' command group had been badly hit while crossing the reef with the resultant loss of most of its communications equipment and expert operators. Not until much later did the division command have any accurate conception of the precariousness of the 1st Regiment's position. O. P. Smith *PerNar.*

[12] 1st Mar *Nar.*

[13] Captain Hunt, a professional writer in civilian life, has described this action fully in an excellent small book: *Coral Comes High*, Harper, 1946, from which many of the substantiated details of this account have been drawn.

[14] Hunt *op.cit.*, 58.

the enemy infantry protecting the installations were killed, and at 1015 what was left of the two platoons stormed the point, driving off the remainder and annihilated the pillboxes[15] by taking advantage of their blind spots.

The principal installation proved to be a powerful reinforced concrete casemate built into the coral near the base of the cliff and mounting the 47mm antitank-antiboat gun which had been playing such havoc by enfilading the beach all morning. This was taken by creeping down on it from above. Lieutenant William L. Willis, the surviving platoon leader, managed to drop a smoke grenade just outside the embrasure to cover the approach, whereupon Corporal Anderson launched a rifle grenade into the firing aperture. This struck the gun barrel, knocking the weapon out of action, and ignited "something inflammable".[16] There was a big explosion, and the whole interior of the casemate was swept by flame. Screaming Japanese, the ammunition in their belts exploding like firecrackers from the intense heat, fled out the rear exit where they were mowed down by a squad of Marines placed there for that express purpose.

So Captain Hunt was on the point with the 30-odd men of the two platoons who had survived the assault. And there he remained isolated for thirty hours as the Japanese, discovering the gap in Company K's lines, moved into the area in force. Repeated efforts by elements of the reserve battalion failed to close the gap, and at nightfall it was necessary to establish a second line of defense to protect the division flank, leaving Hunt and his men to hold the point as best they could against the series of sharp counter-attacks which developed.

Later it proved possible to send in water, food and ammunition, and to evacuate the wounded, by amtrack. But it was such a narrow thing that at one stage during the first night Hunt was holding the point with 18 men and leaning heavily on a captured Japanese machine gun to stave off annihilation.[17]

IN THE CENTER [18]

The 5th Marines, in the center, fared somewhat better. The deadly antiboat fire which played such havoc with the landing vehicles operating against the flank beaches was less effective (though not wholly ineffective) in this regiment's zone, with the result that the assault waves suffered comparatively smaller losses, mainly from artillery and mortar fire in crossing the reef. Nor was the ground to the front so strongly defended.

This regiment also landed two battalions in assault: the 1st on Beach Orange 1, the 3d on Orange 2. They met only scattered resistance on the beaches and not much more immediately inland. The terrain here was favorable for maneuver, coconut groves providing cover with little obstruction, and contained no such natural obstacles as the formidable coral ridge which was causing the 1st Marines so much trouble. Thus, the 1st Battalion drove through without undue difficulty to the 0–1 phase line and there tied-in firmly with 2/1 [19] on the left. And,

---

[15] There were five billboxes altogether, four mounting heavy machine guns, the fifth the 47mm. The spider trenches were manned by riflemen and light machine gunners. 3d Bn, 1st Mar *Record of Events*, hereinafter cited as 3/1 *RofE*.

[16] Lt. Willis quoted by Hunt, *op. cit.*, 65. A subsequent intelligence report attributed the knocking out of this casemate to the use of a flame thrower, a weapon which the platoon did not have available at that particular time, though the end effect was very similar. What the grenade set off was probably stacked up 47mm ammunition.

[17] *History of 1st Marine Regiment*, 7; hereinafter cited as *Hist 1st Mar*.

[18] Except as otherwise cited, this monograph's accounts of all operations of 5th Marines derive from the following basic documentary sources pertaining to that regiment: *Regimental Narrative, War Diary, R-2 Reports, 1st Battalion Bn-3 Journal, 2d Battalion Journal, 3d Battalion Record of Operations, 5th Regiment Unit Reports*.

[19] This short form designates 2d Battalion, 1st Marines: the battalion numeral preceding that of the regiment. Such abbreviations appear in most contemporary reports of the period under discussion, though occasionally appearing in hyphenated form (3–1), and are used throughout this mono-

1st LIEUTENANT CARLTON R. ROUH received the Medal of Honor for placing his body between a Japanese grenade and two comrades to absorb the full force of the explosion himself.

as with that battalion, here the companies were obliged to remain, owing partly to the inability of the 1st Marines to advance on the extreme left and partly to the murderous artillery and mortar fire from the high ground to the north which now swept the open airfield to their front.

---

graph. Companies are sometimes similarly designated: E/5 (Company E, 5th Marines). It should be understood as standing for a reinforced infantry unit, but the terms BLT (battalion landing team) and RCT (regimental combat team) had not come into general use in the Marine Corps at this time and occur with comparative infrequency.

The story of the 3d Battalion on the right developed differently, however. This unit was commanded by Lieutenant Colonel A. C. Shofner, who had previously distinguished himself by escaping from a Japanese prison camp where he had been confined following the fall of Corregidor. His executive officer, Major Robert M. Ash, was killed within a few moments of hitting the beach, and the LVT carrying most of the battalion's field telephone equipment and personnel was destroyed on the reef,[20] thereby complicating a control problem which was difficult enough to begin with.[21]

According to plan, Company I landed on the left, Company K on the right, with Company L coming in immediately behind the assault waves. On the left all went well, or as well as can be reasonably expected in battle: Company I made contact with the 1st Battalion and, advancing abreast, reached 0–1 simultaneously with that unit, at about 0930.

Company K, however, ran into trouble at once owing to circumstances which caused many assault elements of the 7th Marines to be landed on the southern zone of Beach Orange 2 rather than on Orange 3 as prescribed. (See following sub-chapter.) This not only caused confusion on the beach but also delayed the company's advance while its unexpected guests were trying to extricate themselves and make their way to their own designated sector. Further hampered by an enemy mortar barrage, Company K

---

[20] Ltr LtCol A. C. Shofner to CMC, 9Mar50, hereinafter cited as *Shofner*.

[21] Considerable confusion exists as to what really happened to 3/5 during D-Day. Only extant official reports from 5th Marines bearing on the subject are Regimental *War Diary* and 3/5 *Record of Operations*, which do not agree on all points and frequently conflict with reports of 7th Marines (see sub-chapter following). This account supplements these basic sources with carefully screened material recently obtained from surviving officers who were on the scene. In view of the fallibility of the human memory five years after the event, allowance must be made for a certain amount of conjecture.

did not draw abreast of Company I until about 1000.[22]

But if the situation in the 3d Battalion zone could be said to be fairly stabilized at this point, it was not destined to remain so for long. Company K's line of advance lay through dense scrub jungle which, while slowing progress somewhat, provided concealment from the heavy shelling which was holding up those elements facing the open airfield. Thus, no sooner had the eastward push been resumed (at 1030) than contact was broken with Company I on the left, which had the responsibility for remaining tied-in with the 1st Battalion.

Company L was committed in an effort to close this gap, but the line remained dangerously extended. Fortunately, the 5th Marines Operations Plan called for Major Gordon D. Gayle's 2d Battalion, in regimental reserve, to come in close on the heels of the assault waves and be committed on the right of the 1st Battalion. Advance elements of this unit began landing at 0935, and the battalion as a whole was in position on the 0–1 line by 1130.[23] Here it relieved Company I, which was ordered to pass around the right of Company L and tie in between that unit and the left of Company K which reported its position as along a trail about halfway across the island.

The 2d Battalion now began a strong drive eastward, described subsequently, preparatory to a turning movement toward the north. Because contact had to be maintained with the 1st Battalion, still on the 0–1 line, the completion of this maneuver found 2/5 deployed completely across the southern edge of the airfield.[24] Company L, keeping pace, succeeded in reaching Peleliu's eastern shore, thus cutting the island into two parts in accordance with the operations plan, but in accomplishing this eventually lost contact with the rest of its own 3d Battalion.[25]

Shortly after noon, strong resistance from a nest of pillboxes halted the advance of Companies I and K. By the time this was overcome with the aid of tanks, it was discovered that contact had been lost with 3d Battalion, 7th Marines, on the right.[26]

Radio communication was established between the two battalions, and 3/5 gave the location of its right flank as along a diagonal north-south trail in Target Square 125–P. Taking stock of its own situation, 3/7 reported its left on a similar trail approximately 200 yards farther forward.[27] Thereupon, Shofner's battalion pressed on to the designated spot and, when unable to make contact there, continued the advance to the main north-south road. Here, at about 1600, a subsequent radio message was received from 3/7, stating that the previous location given for that battalion's position was incorrect and that its left actually lay on the trail in "the lower corner of target square 125–P".[28]

This unfortunate miscalculation is indicative of the difficulties of operating in unfamiliar, sketchily mapped terrain cloaked with scrub jungle and infested with the enemy. The two trails in question ran generally parallel and were difficult of positive identification. So far as it is possible to re-

---

[22] This is hour given by 5th Marines *War Diary* hereinafter cited as 5th Mar *WD*.

[23] *Ibid.*

[24] A subsequent northward surge carried 2/5 nearly to the center of the airfield for the day's most substantial gain. See sub-chapter "The Japanese Strike Back".

[25] Exactly when this break occurred is not noted in the contemporary official reports. *Shofner* records that all three companies were tied-in during the early afternoon. The undisputable fact is that Co. L was no longer in contact with any elements of 3/5 at dusk.

[26] 5th Mar *WD* gives 1400 as the approximate hour this opposition was overcome. *Shofner* records that the strong point was encountered "about 1230". See also 3/7 *War Diary* and ltr Maj. C. A. Brooks to CMC, 8Feb50, hereinafter cited as *Brooks*.

[27] 3/5 *Record of Operations. Shofner. Brooks.*

[28] *Shofner.* There is an apparent discrepancy here, as TX 125–P lay entirely in 3/5 zone of action. Official reports make no specific mention of this message, but 5th Mar *WD* records: "At 1600 it was discovered that elements of the 3d Bn. had pushed some 300 to 400 yards ahead of the 7th Marines on our right and that the 7th was firing on our troops."

construct the situation from extant evidence, it would appear that when the first messages were exchanged the flanks of the two battalions were actually on the same trail, which curved sharply about 100 yards to the east within the zone of 3/7. Thus, while 3/5 pushed ahead to where 3/7 was believed to be, the latter battalion stood fast thinking the former would come abreast of it.

Immediate steps were taken to rectify the situation. In the 3/5 zone, Company K was ordered to bend its right flank back, and all available personnel from Headquarters Company were thrown in to extend the line in this direction in an effort to tie-in with 3/7 which was supposed to be moving its left forward simultaneously.[29] But no contact had been made by the time darkness fell.

It was evidently this effort which caused Company K to become separated from Company I, on its left, which in turn had lost contact with Company L sometime during the course of events.[30]

Then, as about 1700,[31] a well placed enemy mortar barrage struck the command post, wounding Colonel Shofner. By the time the commanding officer could be evacuated and the general disruption straightened out, control of the 3d Battalion as a unit had virtually ceased to exist.

Obviously, strong measures were called for. Lieutenant Colonel Lewis W. Walt, executive officer of the 5th Marines, assumed command of the scattered 3d Battalion following the evacuation of Colonel Shofner, but it was after dark before he was able to locate even one of his companies. Inasmuch as what Colonel Walt did to retrieve the situation was largely a one-man operation and is covered in no official report, the account which follows is drawn from his own narration of events,[32] except as otherwise cited.

The regimental command had made no radio contact with any elements of the 3d battalion, including the command post, since 1700. The first unit to be located was Company L, less one platoon,[33] at approximately 1830, on the right flank of the 2d Battalion. The 2d Platoon was tied-in with that battalion, the rest of the company in the jungle approximately 100 yards south of the airfield and 200 yards short of Peleliu's eastern shore where, out of contact with friendly troops, the men were digging-in an all around defense for the night. These were ordered back to the edge of the airfield, there to set up a lineal defense facing south, tied-in on the left with the 2d Platoon which, in turn, remained tied-in with 2/5, facing east along the shoreline. In this new deployment, Company L's front extended about 200 yards inland.

Walt next located the left flank of the 3d Battalion, 7th Marines. This had been extended by degrees all the way to the southern edge of the airfield at a point about 400 yards in from the western shore where its

---

[29] 3/7 had been held up for some time before a formidable enemy position and was unable to make any appreciable advance in this area, as described in sub-chapter following.

[30] "Company I had no contact with battalion headquarters. Radio batteries, which had been in use throughout the day were dead and replacements had been lost during the landing. . . . As darkness was setting in and adjoining units could not be located I gave orders for the company to dig in for the night. Even as we were digging in we were still attempting to locate companies, or at least friendly units on the left and right flanks. We were unable to do so." Ltr Maj J. A. Crown to CMC, 13Feb50, hereinafter cited as *Crown*.

[31] 5th Mar *WD*. There is some question as to the exact hour. 3/5 *RofO* gives it as "shortly before nightfall"; *Brooks* as "about 1830"; *Shofner* says merely that it occurred while the attempt was being made to close the gap on the right. Killed by the same barrage was the regimental communications officer, Capt. R. F. Kehoe, Jr., who had just arrived at the CP. Because his body was not readily recognizable, it was first identified as that of Col. Shofner, who was initially reported killed in action. *Brooks*.

[32] Contained in statement by LtCol Walt to Historical Div., USMC, 10Nov49, hereinafter cited as *Walt*.

[33] This platoon had been detached to serve as special security guard to the battalion CP whose position was open to the south because of the unclosed gap. *Brooks*.

left flank element was digging in on a defensive line facing east.[34]

Accompanied by his runner, Walt then moved out deeper into the dark jungle forward of the 3/7 line where, about 2100, he came upon Company I, some 200 yards south of the airfield and 300 yards short of the eastern shore. This unit, as noted, also had lost contact with friendly troops and was setting up a perimeter defense. It, too, was ordered to the airfield; to take up a position on the right of Company L, with the object of extending the south-facing line eastward to cover the 2d Battalion from attack from its rear.[35]

Company K was found 100 yards southwest of where Company I had been located and was ordered to the edge of the airfield to complete the new line: to tie-in with the left of 3/7 and the right of the new position of Company I. Then at last (about 2230) radio contact was made with the battalion command post, a short distance behind Company K, which also reached the new area by 2300.

But a gap still existed in the center of the new south-facing line, owing to the inability of Company I, groping in the darkness and jungle, to locate its designated position between Companies L and K.[36] This was not so serious as might appear, however, as the final deployment of the missing unit was immediately in front of this gap. In the words of its commanding officer: "Company I spent the night with its left flank on the edge of the airfield and its right flank in the air in the scrub woods. Our backs were to the field. No Japanese counterattack as such ever hit our lines, which was, of course, fortunate." [37]

The front of the 5th Marines, as it was finally set up for the night of D-Day, presents a rather odd appearance on the operational overlay: the three battalions facing in as many different directions (east, north and south), with 2d and 3d Battalions virtually back to back (see Map Number 6). Yet these lines were well enough integrated to stand firm throughout the hours of darkness.

THE SOUTHERN ZONE [38]

On the extreme right of the division front, the 7th Marines planned to land two battalions in column on Beach Orange 3, the remaining battalion (2/7) being kept afloat as division reserve. The scheme of maneuver called for the leading unit, the 3d Battalion, to drive across to the eastern shore in conjunction with the 5th Marines in order to split the island's defenders. The 1st Battalion, landing immediately behind, was to wheel to the right in line and commence the drive against the Japanese thus isolated in the southern pocket, 3/7 wheeling to move abreast once the island had been crossed.[39]

---

[34] This was Co. L, 7th Mar. How it came to be so deep in the 5th Marines zone of action and so far in the rear of the units of both regiments is explained in sub-chapter following.

[35] Pending the regrouping of 3/5, Major Gayle, at Colonel Walt's request, deployed the reserve company of the 2d Battalion (Co. F), facing southward, in the rear of the 2/5 line. As will be noted, at this time 2/5 was deployed across the near center of the airfield, facing northward.

[36] "I Company was to connect with L Company right flank and K Company left flank, but was unable to locate either company in the darkness and did not get into position." 3/5 *RofO*. This statement substantiated by *Brooks*.

[37] *Crown.*

[38] Basic documentary sources for this narrative of operations of 7th Marines are the following: *Regimental Narrative*, R-2 Journal, *1st Battalion Historical Report, 1st Battalion Bn-2, Bn-3 Journal, 2d Battalion War Diary, 2d Battalion Unit Journal, 3d Battalion War Diary, 3d Battalion Bn-2 Journal, 3d Battalion Operation Reports.* These are supplemented herein from other sources as specifically cited.

[39] A somewhat unusual command set-up prevailed in the 7th Marines at this time, described as follows by CO, 1/7: "During the landing and initial operations ashore, Company A was attached to 3/7; to revert to control of CO 1/7 upon his landing. Company A had the mission of advancing south in the left half of 1/7 zone of action. This maneuver was to provide initial flank protection for 3/7 as it was advancing eastward. The support company of 3/7 was attached to CO 1/7 for the landing and reverted to CO 3/7 upon landing." Ltr LtCol J. J. Gormley to CMC, 3Nov49, hereinafter cited as *Gormley.*

JAPANESE ANTITANK DITCH provides cover for 7th Marines Command Post on D-Day.

The 3d Battalion encountered serious difficulties from the outset. The reef in this area was so cluttered with both natural and man-made obstacles that the amtracks were often obliged to pick their way shoreward in column. This slowed down the whole approach and made the vehicles prime targets for the fire which now poured into them from the machine guns and antiboat guns on the southwestern promontory (sometimes called Ngarmoked Island) and the small unnamed island offshore beyond their right flank, as well as the ubiquitous artillery and mortars. Perhaps worse from a tactical point of view, the enfilading fire caused many of the LVT drivers to bear farther to the left, thus landing some elements on Orange 2 where they became intermixed with elements of 3/5, as previously noted.[40]

The inevitable delay attendant upon reorganizing in the designated zone of action was further compounded by a combination of mined beaches, barbed wire entanglements and stiff but spotty resistance from a system of mutually supporting trenches and re-

----

[40] This fire, combined with the obstacles mentioned, served to split the landing wave approximately in the center. Maj. Hurst, Bn CO, with about half the CP and half the troops landed on Orange 2. Maj. V. H. Streit, Bn ExO, landed with the other half on the southern extremity of Orange 3, where for a time this group constituted the right flank element of the division front, though out of physical contact with other elements. Oral statement LtCol Hunter Hurst, interviewed 9Mar50.

inforced pillboxes dug into, or blasted out of, the coral. Furthermore, naval gunfire, if it had accomplished little else in this sector, had blasted away enough of the jungle growth and inconspicuous terrain features to give the region a much different appearance from that shown in the advance intelligence, making orientation difficult.[41]

There was one man-made feature, however, which proved extremely useful in a way its makers certainly had not planned. This was a large Japanese antitank trench a short distance inland from Orange 3. Its existence had not been known prior to the assault, but one of the support aircraft spotted it in time to flash a report just in advance of the first wave. As the commanding officer of the 3d Battalion describes the situation:

Once officers were able to orient themselves it (the antitank ditch) proved an excellent artery for moving troops into the proper position for deployment and advance inland since it crossed the entire width of our zone of action approximately parallel to the beach. With respect to the battalion CP, I am convinced that it enabled us to join the two principal echelons of CP personnel and commence functioning as a complete unit at least an hour earlier than would otherwise have been possible. I landed with my half of the CP personnel, opposite the southwest turning circle of the airfield near the right flank of the CT–5 zone of action. Major Streit landed, with the other half of the CP personnel, equally as far from our intended position in the opposite direction to the southward. After announcing our early locations to each other, it was simply a question of jumping in the ditch, meeting in the middle, and jumping out again to displace farther inland.[42]

The advance was finally resumed with two companies in assault and made good progress for a while. By 1045 Company K, on the right, had advanced 500 yards, capturing an enemy radio direction finder in the process. But at about 1300 Company I, which had been experiencing increasing difficulties in retaining contact with 3/5 on

the left, was halted before a strong nest of Japanese defenses. This well organized position was "built around a large blockhouse, the concrete ruins of a barracks area, several pillboxes, concrete gun emplacements and mutually supporting gun positions."[43] This opposition had been expected, as the position showed clearly on the operational map. So, in order to minimize the casualties which would result from unsupported infantry assault, it was decided to await the arrival of the tank platoon which was an organic part of the landing team and had been briefed in advance for this particular mission.

Here a new and unexpected element appeared to contribute to the confusion: one of those small details which so often escape notice in advance. The flank battalion of each of the two regiments supposed to tie-in was the 3d Battalion (3/5 and 3/7 respectively), containing identically lettered companies (I, K and L). In this particular case, the tanks moving up in support of 3/7 were obliged to skirt the southern edge of the airfield in order to avoid the antitank ditch previously mentioned. Here they came upon a body of troops working forward and paused to inquire the location of "Company I." Informed that this unit was "Company I," they attached themselves and operated with it for some time before discovering that it was Company I, 5th Marines, instead of Company I, 7th Marines, which had been held up all this while awaiting them.

This delay completed the break in the already tenuous contact between the two regiments. Pausing to take stock, 3/7 was able to find no elements whatsoever on its left flank. Actually, Company K, 5th Marines, had pushed ahead, as has been seen. But there was no way of knowing that, for the jungle growth limited visibility in every direction. To protect the open flank in order that the attack might be continued, Company L was placed in position immediately behind Company I and echeloned to the left rear.

In an effort to reestablish contact, Company L worked patrols farther and farther

<hr>

[41] Oral statement by Major Victor H. Streit, interviewed 14Feb49.

[42] LtCol E. H. Hurst in written statement to Historical Div., USMC, dated 23Nov49, hereinafter cited as *Hurst.*

[43] 3/7 *War Diary*, 5; hereinafter cited as 3/7 *WD.*

to the left. Still groping, without success, the foremost patrol emerged at length on the southern edge of the airfield, entirely out of its regimental zone of action and several hundred yards directly in the rear of the unit with which it was attempting to tie-in.[44]

The command post of 3/7, had been in intermittent radio communication with that of 3/5 throughout the afternoon, with the resultant misunderstanding as to locations previously noted. It was not until Lieutenant Colonel Walt arrived on the scene that it proved possible to orient the units in relation to each other and eventually effect the redeployment described in previous subchapter.

In the meanwhile, the 1st Battalion, 7th Marines, had come in behind 3/7 as planned, landing on Orange 3 at 1030. By this time some of the early confusion on the beaches had been resolved, but the 1st Battalion encountered many of the difficulties that had plagued the 3d and a portion of its personnel likewise landed on Orange 2. Resistance was described as "light, except for heavy mortar fire"[45] until about 1200. But as the

---

[44] *Ibid.*, 6, states: "Patrols from 'L' Company had established visual contact with LT 3–5 on the airstrip and physical contact was established after dark." However, to judge by the relative positions of the units at this time, it was probably 2/5 with which visual contact was established, 3/5 being far ahead and not on the airfield. The physical contact established after dark was with K/5, as noted in previous sub-chapter, which Col. Walt had placed in position here.

[45] *1/7 Historical Report*, 1; hereinafter cited as *1/7 HistRpt. Gormley* states that the battalion "was subjected to antiboat, machine gun, and particularly heavy mortar fire from the southwest pro-

BLOCKHOUSE encountered by 3/7 late on D-Day was reduced following morning.

battalion began wheeling southward in accordance with its mission, enemy resistance stiffened notably and the terrain became increasingly difficult. It was discovered that a dense swamp, which did not appear on the operational map, blocked a large portion of the right half of the battalion's zone of action. The single trail skirting its west fringe, in Company C's area, was strongly defended by enemy pillboxes and bunkers.

Company A, groping around the swamp to the east, eventually extended itself some 250 yards into the 3d Battalion's zone. Company B was employed to tie-in the flanks of Companies C and A, but not until 1520 was Colonel Gormley able to announce the seizure of the intermediate phase line designated 0–A. During the night the Japanese staged a strong counterattack from the swamp, necessitating the alerting of shore party personnel to serve as a mobile reserve in case of necessity. Fifty of the enemy were killed in this action.[46]

When reports from shore indicated that the two battalions committed in the south would almost certainly fall short of the ambitious objective planned for the first day, General Rupertus, still aboard USS *Dupage*, became seriously concerned over this apparent loss of forward momentum. Shortly before noon he ordered the Division Reconnaissance Company [47] ashore as a reinforcement, and a little later, after some rather ambiguous communication with officers on the scene, attempted to commit the division reserve for the same purpose.[48]

The order to dig in for the night reached the front line units in the southern zone about 1700.[49]

Gains, in relation to the optimistic predictions, were disappointing. The 1st Battalion was on the 0–A line, as was the right of the 3d Battalion (Company K); but Company I, still held up before the strongpoint to its front because of the delay in the tanks coming up, was 400 yards short of the intermediate objective. And the still-open gap in the middle of 3/5 on the left constituted a potent threat to the entire southward-facing line.

However, the tactical situation was more propitious than it appeared to the minds of those in the division command post, still afloat, and little genuine concern was felt by the officers commanding ashore.[50] Local counterattacks, hampered by extensive illuminations by naval star shells and harassing fire by the 11th Marines, were beaten off during the night without undue difficulty, and the coming of daylight saw a quick rectification of the worst difficulties.

THE JAPANESE STRIKE BACK

As had been anticipated, the Japanese reacted violently as soon as they were able to recover their balance. The first and most vigorous manifestation began at approxi-

---

montory (Ngarmoked Island) and the small unnamed island off the west coast just prior to landing."

[46] *Gormley.* One platoon of ReconCo had been moved up earlier to fill a 40-yard gap in the line and sustained strong fire attacks during the night. Ltr Lt R. J. Powell, Jr. to CMC, March 1950, hereinafter cited as *Powell.*

[47] "This company was thrown in on the right with the 1st Battalion and suffered heavy casualties. This was an improper use of the Reconnaissance Company, as there later developed several opportunities for employment of this company in the manner for which it had been trained." O. P. Smith *PerNar.* See also *Fields.*

[48] This unit was 2d Battalion, 7th Marines, reinforced. For further detail regarding the circumstances of its being ordered ashore, and its failure to get there, see second sub-chapter following.

[49] 3/7 *WD.* 1/7 *HistRpt* gives the hour as 1715. O. P. Smith *op. cit.,* says that he issued the order to dig-in at 1600 after ". . . I was satisfied that the three regiments were in contact."

[50] "The enemy was groggy, disorganized, and devoid of communications, although bitterly defending every step of the way. At no time did we feel him capable of organizing a successful counterattack. . . . We at no time requested reinforcement, and, in fact, recommended against it since the beachhead was already overcrowded." *Hurst.*

mately 1650: a tank-infantry sortie in force across the northern portion of the airfield.[51]

This was not a *banzai* charge in the usual sense of that term, unless the peculiar conduct of some of the tank operators could be so construed, though the end result proved suicidal enough to satisfy the most discriminating devotee of *Bushido*. The attack was well planned and well organized; had it been better timed and better integrated, once under way, its chances of success might have been excellent. As it was, the Japanese waited too long, giving the invaders ample time to consolidate their positions. And the route of approach, while employing what was doubtless the terrain best suited to tank operations, led straight to the sector of the Marine front perhaps best prepared to cope with precisely such an assault.

There was nothing coincidental about the latter fact. The main point of contact lay within the zone of the 1st Battalion, 5th Marines, a short distance below where the flanks of the 1st and 5th Regiments tied-in. Little surprise was achieved: Japanese tank strength was well known, and every regimental and battalion commander had been looking for something of the kind for the past eight hours. Knowing that the 5th Marines in particular would be facing flat, open ground once the advance passed through the woods, the regimental commander had ordered both assault battalions to land their 37mm guns and heavy machine guns in the assault waves and emplace them in forward

positions as soon as the 0–1 line had been secured.[52] When further advance from there had proved impracticable, Lieutenant Colonel Robert W. Boyd, commanding officer of the 1st Battalion, had parked his three supporting tanks in partial defilade where they would enjoy a maximum of protection and at the same time be able to place fire to the front of the infantry.[53]

A marked increase in the intensity of enemy mortar and artillery fire brought the first intimation that the long expected was finally brewing. Soon thereafter a Japanese infantry formation of estimated company strength was observed advancing across the airfield. This was no tightly bunched knot of screaming, sword-waving fanatics. These men moved with the cool determination of the veterans they were: keeping well dispersed, taking advantage of the scanty cover of shell holes and ground folds, opening fire as they came within effective range.

In the meanwhile, an air observer spotted enemy tanks forming in defilade east of the ridges a short distance above the airfield, and presently the ground troops sighted these debouching on the open ground, more infantry clustered atop them wherever a handhold could be had. They passed through their advancing foot soldiers about 400 yards forward of the Marine positions, and for a moment the attack assumed aspects of genuine formidability.

But only for a moment. Instead of coordinating their movement to that of the infantry, the enemy tank drivers opened their throttles wide and lit out for the American lines like so many of the proverbial bats; too fast to support their assault troops or for those troops to support them.[54]

---

[51] After study extending over a period of months, the author is convinced that no satisfactory account of this Japanese attack will ever be written. Official contemporary reports are fragmentary and often conflicting. Consultation with scores of eyewitnesses five years after the event has served only to compound the confusion. It would appear that every Marine who participated, or even viewed the attack from a safe distance, has a personal and very positive version of exactly what happened, and it is virtually impossible to reconcile many of these on any particular points. The following narrative is frankly conjectural. The only undisputed fact, and the one most important historically, is that Japanese tank strength on Peleliu had ceased to exist, to all practical purposes, by the end of D-Day.

[52] *Walt.* Script notes and related interviews with Col. H. D. Harris by Historical Division, USMC, 28–31Oct49, hereinafter cited as *Harris*.

[53] Monograph by LtCol R. W. Boyd, Marine Corps Schools, March 1949, hereinafter cited as *Boyd Mono*.

[54] "Had they advanced at the rate of their infantry, the tankettes (actually only light reconnaissance vehicles) would . . . never have even gotten to the middle of the airfield." *Stuart.*

At this point the attack assumed more the aspects of an old fashioned cavalry charge than anything in modern scientific warfare: very dashing and gallant according to the standards of the 19th Century. Only this happened to be the 20th Century. And these flimsy Japanese obsolete model "tankettes" (not comparable even to U. S. light tanks) were little less vulnerable to modern armor-piercing weapons than horse cavalry had been to the magazine rifles, Gatling guns and shrapnel which made that branch obsolete.[55]

Most contemporary accounts agree that 13 tanks were involved in this attack.[56] Beyond this point, however, there are nearly as many versions of what happened next as there were witnesses.

The tank drivers apparently made some effort to take advantage of such scanty cover as there was, keeping as close as possible to the edge of the jungle north of the airfield as long as they could. Thus, when they cut southwestward over the open ground, their course took them diagonally across the front of the 2d Battalion, 1st Marines, where they were subjected to devastating fire into their flank.[57] Two of the tanks veered into the lines of this battalion, hurtled over a coral embankment and crashed into a swamp

just behind the front where their crews, attempting to escape, were disposed of by the infantry.[58]

Meanwhile the men of 1/5 had opened with everything they had: 37mm guns, bazookas, AT grenades; all organic infantry weapons plus the 75's of the tanks which Colonel Boyd had posted in support. A Navy dive bomber, happening upon the scene, came in low and dropped a large bomb into what appeared to be the midst of the on-swarming enemy. In the face of all this fire, the tank-riding infantry, so many sitting ducks, simply seemed to disintegrate into thin air. Tanks began exploding and burning, but the survivors kept coming. They struck the 1st Battalion lines in the narrow sector held by the left platoon of Company B.[59] And overran them.

The remarkable aspect here was that, while the enemy tanks overran the lines and penetrated 150 yards beyond—one of them nearly reached the beach before being liquidated—nowhere did they cause a break in the front. If any Marines felt an urge to quit their positions, they scarcely had time, so rapidly did these events take place. Two men were caught in the path of one of these onrushing machines and crushed to death. A few others were burned or wounded by flying fragments as tanks were destroyed in their midst. The rest dodged by one means or another and kept on fighting, for the Japanese assault infantry was still coming—or so they thought.

What happened to these enemy troops is one of the several features of this action which will never be known with any certainty—except that they did not close with the Marines. Perhaps they were annihilated by the fire poured into them before they were able to close.[60] Or perhaps they were

---

[55] "These vehicles . . . with only ¼" to ⅜" armor . . . were never intended for frontal action against heavy weapons of major units and . . . their easy destruction is no grounds for smugness in regard to our antitank prowess. Had the Japanese possessed modern tanks . . . and attacked in greater numbers the situation would have been critical." *Stuart.*

[56] Even on this point there was some subsequent disagreement. A later check-up when it was possible to study the ground carefully indicated that there may have been as many as 19 tanks. *Walt.* The possible discrepancy stemmed from the highly confused nature of the action itself which made any count unreliable, and the fact that when it was over many of the tanks had been so thoroughly demolished that it was impossible to tell which parts had belonged originally to which tanks.

[57] Written statement by LtCol R. E. Honsowetz to Historical Division, USMC, 15Nov49, hereinafter cited as *Honsowetz.* Most other individuals consulted on this point were under the impression that the Japanese tanks made a beeline across the airfield from the ridge nose to the point of contact.

[58] *Ibid.*

[59] *Boyd Mono* gives six as the number of tanks getting through to the lines. No other report states any specific number, but all agree that several did.

[60] It should be noted that one battery (Battery E) of 2d Bn., 11th Marines, had brought its 75mm pack howitzers to bear on both enemy tanks and infantry. 2/11 *Action Report.* See also *Walt* description of U. S. tank sortie, quoted below.

JAPANESE TANK-INFANTRY counterattack, afternoon of D-Day, disintegrated in face of Marine fire-power.

so disgusted by the spectacle of their supposed armored support intent on encompassing its own destruction that they simply went away from there. In any event, when the smoke and dust dissipated, a few dead on the scene were all that remained. The fight was over.

Exactly who knocked out what—and where and when—is another matter shrouded in mystery. If two of the enemy tanks escaped, as reported,[61] that would mean that only 11 (or 17, depending on conflicting reports) were destroyed. Yet one officer with a flair for figures calculated later that if every individual claim of a tank knocked out were to be accepted at face value, there would have had to be 179½ of them. The fact appears to be that every tank was hit so many times by so many different weapons that in all probability no single hit could be held responsible for its destruction.[62]

The exact part played by U. S. tanks in the repulse of this attack is another point upon which there has been some disagreement, another example of the platitude that no single man on the ground can see more than a very small segment of any battle, even such a spectacular one fought almost

---

[61] 5th Mar *WD*. 1/5 *Bn–3 Journal*. *Walt*. Other pertinent reports simply list all 13 as being destroyed on the scene.

[62] An immobilized tank presents an especially tempting target which few troops can resist taking a crack at. Notably, on the occasion of the big enemy tank attack on Saipan on the night of 16Jun44, U. S. tanks and half-tracks, arriving at dawn, began firing into, and claiming destruction of, tanks which the infantry on the scene declared they had knocked out several hours before. *Saipan: The Beginning of the End*, monograph by Maj. C. W. Hoffman, published by Historical Division, USMC.

entirely on flat, open terrain. The three tanks attached to 1/5, as has been noted, were immobilized and played only a static defensive role. And as luck would have it, all but one of the Shermans supporting 2/1 had returned to the beach to rearm at this particular time.[63]

However, the 2d Battalion, 5th Marines, was operating in the woods across the southern end of the airfield, with its leading element (Company E) and the advance command post near the eastern shore: about 1200 yards away, diagonally across the open ground. The advance of the enemy was plainly visible from there, and Major Gayle immediately dispatched the tanks acting in support of his unit to the secene of the attack. What followed is described by the executive officer of that regiment, who witnessed the action from a vantage point on the right of 1/5:

At the time the enemy tanks were approximately half way across the airfield, four Sherman tanks came onto the field in the 2/5 zone of action on the south end of the airfield and opened fire immediately on the enemy tanks. These four tanks played an important role in stopping the enemy tanks and also stopping the supporting infantry, the majority of which started beating a hasty retreat when these Shermans came charging down from the south. They fought a running battle and ended up in the midst of the enemy tanks.[64]

But regardless of exactly who did what, the important thing is that the attack was completely frustrated, a fact which was to have a significant effect on the enemy's subsequent conduct of the campaign.

Not that there was no more counteraction on the part of the Japanese. Actually they attacked again and again throughout the rest of the afternoon, short, sharp thrusts against various sectors of the Marine line, and infiltration attempts continued throughout the night. But none achieved the proportions and determination of that first thrust which, in the tactical conception of Peleliu's defenders, was evidently intended to be climactic.

The most notable began about 1730: infantry supported by two tanks (perhaps the two reported to have escaped destruction previously) moving west across the airfield's northern taxiway. This thrust was aimed at the junction of the 1st and 5th Marines, the brunt being borne this time by the former unit. Both tanks were destroyed, and the enemy foot soldiers failed to reach the lines. There was another flurry a half hour later near the center of the 5th Marines where the 1st and 2d Battalions tied in on the 0–1 line, but this was quickly over. And before daylight the following morning, 1/5 was hit again by still another two tanks and infantry, without notable results.

The precariously positioned left of the 1st Marines was subjected to unremitting pressure, and Captain Hunt's men passed a nerve-racked night isolated on the point they had captured. But the attack in force along the shore line which might have rolled up the division left flank failed to materialize until the situation there had been rectified (see Chapter IV), evidently because the careful preinvasion plans of the Japanese had not envisaged a major effort from this direction and they were not prepared to regroup in time to make one which had any chance of success.

On the south, too, the situation was one to cause some concern, but not nearly so much. There were many infiltration attempts in this area. The 3d Battalion, 7th Marines, withstood one counterattack of no very formidable proportions shortly after dark,

---

[63] *Honsowetz.* "Tanks were in the process of rearming but were able to engage the Japanese tanks by moving only a few yards out of the brush; a distance of approximately 50 yards from our rearming area. At least eight (8) of the tanks . . . engaged the Japanese tanks." Ltr Capt R. E. Brant to CMC, 9Feb50, hereinafter cited as *Brant.*

[64] *Walt.* "It is not believed that any of our tanks engaged in what is stated as a 'running battle.' " *Brant.* "The comment of LtCol Walt appears to be most accurate." *Jerue.* "Enemy tanks were taken under fire by . . . our three tanks in defilade." *Boyd Mono.* "Tanks of the 2d platoon moved out on the airstrip . . . as soon as the first Jap tank touched the other side of the airport." Ltr Maj J. R. Mundy to CMC, 13Mar50.

and 3/5 beat off two others during the early morning hours. In all zones, harassing artillery fire discouraged the enemy, and illumination shells were used liberally to forestall surprise throughout the night.

The order to prepare positions for the night found the units of the division, with one exception, pretty well immobilized: more intent on rectifying their own situations than in making further advances. On the 0–1 line, 2/1 and 1/5 were firmly tied-in and well sited along the edge of the woods, facing the airfield, but unable to move owing to the precariousness of the extreme left. In the south, the two battalions of the 7th Marines were well enough off, but too occupied with trying to tie-in with the as yet unlocated elements of 3/5 to be much interested in anything else.

The one exception was the 2d Battalion, 5th Marines. This unit had fought its way across the southern edge of the airfield nearly to the eastern shore, where it was in contact with the lone platoon of Company L which faced eastward along the shore line. Quick to take advantage of the enemy being off balance, the battalion drove northward close in the wake of the repulse of the main tank counterattack and succeeded in reaching nearly the center of the airfield against minor resistance before halting for the night. This was the most substantial advance scored all day, and significant in that it greatly increased the area of depth necessary for the emplacing of artillery.

THE COMMAND SITUATION

The division command post did not land on D-Day, but at about 1130 the assistant division commander, Brigadier General O. P. Smith, came ashore with a skeleton staff and set up an advance command post in an overrun antitank ditch a short distance inland from Beach Orange 2. His communications men were able to cut in on the Shore Party telephone line, putting him in touch with the command posts of the 5th and 7th Marines. Radio contact was soon established with

General Rupertus still afloat,[65] but the line to the 1st Marines zone had been broken, and radio efforts elicited no response from that quarter. As noted earlier in this chapter, five LVT's [66] carrying the regiment's headquarters personnel and communications equipment had been hit crossing the reef, a serious loss further compounded later when a Japanese shell struck the regimental CP just after Colonel Lewis D. Puller had moved out to set up farther forward.[67]

For whatever combination of reasons, the division command had no very clear picture of the 1st Marines' situation during most of the day. A liaison officer was sent in from the regiment about noon, but at that hour there was still no definite indication of how matters might develop. A runner got through during the afternoon, but en route he became involved in the Japanese tank attack and arrived too scared to be very coherent. Toward evening a fragmentary radio message conveyed a disquieting hint with a urgent request for corpsmen and communicators. But when the field telephone line was finally spliced and General Smith put in direct touch, Colonel Puller made no mention of heavy losses, of gaps in his front, nor of needing any help, but reported that the regiment was firmly established on the beach

---

[65] For maintaining communications on D-Day, the advance CP relied largely on a curious experimental LVT(A) especially equipped to serve as a mobile radio station (facetiously dubbed "USS *Fubar*"). This performed valuable service in this emergency but developed too many weaknesses to be considered wholly successful. Establishment of the initial wire network presented almost insurmountable difficulties owing to heavy fire, lack of natural growth for raising it aboveground, and the congestion of the beachhead area which caused the wires to be chewed up by vehicles when laid on the ground. *Ramsey*. See also 1st MarDiv *SAR*, II, Annex E.

[66] 2/1 Bn. executive officer states that these were DUKS's rather than LVT's, traveling in sixth wave. Ltr Maj. C. H. Brush to CMC, undated, hereinafter cited as *Brush*.

[67] O. P. Smith *PerNar*. 1st *MarNar*, 3. *Hist 1st Mar*, 5.

"SOMETIMES WE GOES where the roads are, but mostly we goes where they ain't."   Kipling's verse applied aptly to the tanks on Peleliu.

and held approximately the objective line 0–1.[68]

General Rupertus had planned to seize the 0–2 phase line by nightfall, this embracing all of the island below the foot of the northern ridges which commenced a short distance above the airfield. As the day wore on with forward movement halted along most of the front, he became increasingly concerned over what seemed to him the loss of initial momentum by the assault elements.[69] But his eye turned not to the north, where the precarious flank situation was holding up the

---

[68] O. P. Smith *PerNar.* Same source adds: "He (Puller) had as yet no very definite idea as to the number of casualties he had suffered." *Hist 1stMar* covering this period states: "Casualties from the day's fighting were estimated at 500."

[69] Personal interviews with Generals O. P. Smith and John T. Selden, February, 1949. As had been seen, Smith was commanding on shore at this time, while Selden, as chief of staff, was still at General Rupertus' side aboard the command ship. Because of their wide separation, the opinions of these officers do not agree fully on all points, but they are unanimous in the belief that it was worry over losing momentum which was mainly responsible for the CG's subsequent actions. General Selden adds that an early dispatch which exaggerated losses sustained by 1/7 in crossing the reef contributed greatly to general mounting anxiety. Substantiated by *Fields.*

advance of the left and most of the center, but toward the south, where the 0–1 line included the entire zone of action of the 7th Marines.

Accordingly, the commanding general ordered the Division Reconnaissance Company in to Orange 3 to reinforce the 7th Marines,[70] and shortly thereafter commenced querying the commander on shore in regard to committing the entire division reserve: 2d Battalion, 7th Marines.[71] His persistence rather puzzled General Smith, whose knowledge of conditions in the area led him to believe that additional troops, far from sustaining momentum, would only further crowd the constricted beachhead then existing. A call to Colonel Herman J. Hanneken confirmed this belief, but the colonel added that, should the commanding general insist on sending the unit ashore, he (Hanneken) would find an assembly area for it where it would not be in anybody's way. This somewhat ambiguous word was relayed to the command ship, and the last reserve under division control was ordered to land.[72]

General Rupertus was also becoming concerned over remaining on the command ship while obscure but obviously heavy fighting was developing on shore, and began importuning General Smith to inform him when it would be feasible for him to bring in the command post. Smith, who had been less sanguine from the first over the possibilities of a quick conquest, saw little in current developments to inspire optimism. He returned negative replies until, aware of the Commanding General's mounting anxiety, ". . . late in the afternoon, against my better judgment, I radioed him that the situation appeared favorable enough for the CP to move ashore." [73]

Aboard the command ship, however, Colonel Selden was unalterably opposed to this idea. The chief of staff pointed out that one command group was already ashore and doing all that reasonably could be expected in a situation which he could visualize only too clearly; that to bring the entire staff into a shallow beachhead across a reef which was still under heavy shellfire would be to risk the annihilation of the division's whole top echelon to no useful purpose. In the ensuing debate a compromise was reached. Colonel Selden agreed to take in the bulk of the staff while the commanding general would forego his determination to land until the following morning.

Accordingly the chief of staff ordered his people, who had been standing by all day for such a move, into two LCVP's and set out for shore. Arriving at the transfer control line, he discovered elements of the division reserve standing by in their landing craft for lack of amtracks to ferry them in across the reef. The colonel thereupon

---

[70] "When he committed the Reconnaissance Company it was not, in the CG's mind (in my opinion) that it was a unit but that it was a group of individual infantry replacements." *Fields.* 1st MarDiv *SAR*, II, 2, lists 1227 as hour orders were issued. 2/7 *Unit Journal* says orders were received at 1100, debarkation commenced at 1145 and all Recon Co. personnel off the ship at 1300.

[71] This unit, as in the case of all units similarly designated herein, was a battalion landing team (BLT): an infantry battalion reinforced with attached elements of engineers, JASCO, artillery liaison, special weapons, etc., commanded by LtCol Spencer S. Berger. The ReconCo was also one of the original components but was detached at the time it was ordered to land. 2/7 *WD*.

[72] "At 1505 LT 2/7 received orders to be prepared to land in any boats available." *Ibid.* 1st MarDiv *SAR*, II, 2, gives 1600 as hour actual landing order was issued. Foregoing version of events leading up to this order derives from interviews with General Smith previously cited, in part elaborated by O. P. Smith *PerNar*. General Selden, on the command ship, received the impression that the CG committed the reserve with great reluctance, only after the command ashore had specifically re-

quested it. This opinion is corroborated by *Fields*, but hurriedly compiled 1st MarDiv *D–3 Journal* logs no such request prior to issuance of landing order. While 2/7 was last reserve under division control, the entire 81st Infantry Division was still available in corps reserve in case of emergency (See Chap. VI.)

[73] O. P. Smith, *PerNar.*

boarded the nearest control craft to use its superior communications equipment in an effort to clarify the situation.

Everything he could learn strengthened his own conviction that the need ashore was for combat troops rather than additional staff personnel, and that there appeared small likelihood of sufficient amphibian tractors arriving to accommodate both. Finally, with darkness closing in and enemy high velocity guns beginning to range in on the control craft, he radioed General Rupertus to this effect and announced that he was bringing his group back to the command ship in order to give landing priority to the reserve battalion.[74]

As events decided, sufficient amtracks never did appear that night. Therefore, shortly after the return of the staff the reserve battalion was likewise ordered back to its transports,[75] a development which was to prove a piece of good fortune in disguise (see Chap. IV).

So General Smith remained in command on shore throughout that critical night. His troops held a beachhead 3,000 yards in length and averaging 500 yards in depth, with one maximum penetration of about 1,500 yards.[76] The artillery had one and one-half battalions of 75mm pack howitzers and one and one-third battalions of 105mm howitzers in position and registered. These gains, so disappointing when viewed beside preliminary predictions, had cost the division 210 dead (killed in action, died of wounds, missing presumed dead), and 901 wounded in action: total casualties of 1,111, not including combat fatigue and heat prostration cases.[77]

The enemy's impression of what goes on in battle is always interesting, even though, particularly in the case of the Japanese, their reports are sometimes a bit difficult to reconcile with reality. For instance, the several thousand Marines engaged on shore at the time would no doubt be mystified to learn that, according to Colonel Nakagawa's report, their "daring" attempt to land had been completely frustrated: "By 1000 hours our forces successfully put the enemy to route." Then: "At 1420 hours, the enemy again attempted to make the perilous landing on the southwestern part of our coastline. The unit in that sector repulsed the daring counterattack and put the enemy to route once more. However, in another sector of the coastline near *Ayame* (Orange 3)

---

[74] "He (the CG) didn't like what I had done at the time and while he did not come out flat-footedly and say so, it was quite evident to all of his staff who were present when we returned aboard." Ltr BrigGen J. T. Selden to author, 26Oct49. The foregoing description of this rather curious incident derives from a series of interviews with Gen. Selden during winter and spring, 1949. Details are corroborated by various staff members present at the time, including this writer.

[75] "This (return to ships) was never fully accomplished. Portions of the Battalion landed on Peleliu that evening and night." Ltr LtCol E. D. Graves, to CMC, 14Mar50, hereinafter cited as *Graves*. "Due to the darkness and fact that transports upped anchor and moved out, it was daylight the next morning before the Battalion was gathered together again." *Berger*.

[76] 1st MarDiv *SAR*, II, 2. While essentially accurate, the yardage figures convey no true picture of the situation, since military values cannot be assessed in averages. No allowance is made for the critical condition on the extreme left, where the most advanced troops were still far short of the 0–1 line, with one element entirely cut off. A synthesis of the several unit situation maps shows the penetration nowhere deeper than about 300 yards north of Orange 2, while south of Orange 3 more than two days of hard fighting remained to complete the occupation of 0–1.

[77] Figures certified and released by USMC Personnel Accounting System, 18Apr50. 1st MarDiv *SAR*, II, 2, citing reports turned in at the time, lists 92 killed, 1,148 wounded, and 58 missing in action, for a total of 1,298. Such discrepancies are characteristic of statistics compiled under the chaotic conditions of battle, when medical personnel are less interested in working out meticulous records than in getting the wounded treated and evacuated. Figures on cases initially reported as missing in action are especially deceptive. See discussion of medical activities, Chapter V.

the enemy with the aid of several tanks were successful in landing, although they were encountering heavy losses inflicted by our forces."[78]

All of which indicates that optimism was not confined exclusively to the Marines at this stage.

---

[78] *Central Pacific Area Operational Record*, Vol II, compiled under the auspices of 1st Demobolization Bureau, Sep46. The Peleliu Garrison command was in communication with Hq Palaus Sector Group throughout the operation. This record of messages received was drawn up by Col Tokechi Tada, IJA, former chief of staff of the higher echelon, assisted by Col Kiyoshi Nakagawa, IJA (not to be confused with Kunio Nakagawa, commanding on Peleliu), a former member of the same staff. Except as otherwise noted, all Japanese material referred to herein derives from this work, hereinafter cited as *Tada Record*. See also Appendix F.

CHAPTER IV

Second Operational Phase: D-plus 1-D-plus 7 (16–22 September)

The events of D-Day revealed to a great extent the pattern of the Japanese defense of Peleliu, which subsequent developments would substantiate. In the main, this conformed to that of previous island defenses, with certain variations and refinements which showed that not all of the lessons of previous disasters had been lost upon the enemy.[1]

They still displayed that fundamental inability, stemming from lack of coordination among their scattered observation posts, to mass the fires of their heavy weapons. On Peleliu, terror of U. S. air observers provided a further inhibition. Discovering early that spotting of their positions invariably brought down a deluge of heavy gunfire and bombing, they resorted to the practice of keeping their artillery and mortars concealed in caves and other emplacements, running them out to let off a few rounds, then pulling them back to cover in all haste. This weakness was not readily discernable to the amtracks crossing the reef nor to the infantry operating on the open airfield; only after the division discovered how much heavy ordnance the Japanese actually had available did it come apparent how infinitely worse the destruction might have been.[2]

As always, they displayed their childlike faith in the tactic of infiltration, though their aptness here exceeded anything they had shown previously. Enemy soldiers knew their own sectors thoroughly, and individuals and small groups moved with certainty toward definite objectives over familiar terrain. Their main purpose was to reoccupy emplacements already overrun from which to harass the Marines' rear areas from concealment. That three of them penetrated into the heart of General Smith's command post on the night of D-Day indicates some measure of their success.[3] Similar instances occurred throughout the operation, always with disquieting effect; but infiltration it still remained, with negligible influence on the ultimate outcome.

There had been no *banzai* charges on D-Day, and there were to be none during the entire operation. The counterattacks had been well planned, if poorly timed, and so they continued to the end: usually short, sharp thrusts with limited objectives. Both

---

[1] For further detail on the military thinking underlying the Japanese defensive concept on Peleliu, see Appendix C.

[2] IIIAC *OpnRpt*, 2–4. This report gives a particularly cogent and lucid analysis on Japanese tactics on Peleliu.

[3] O. P. Smith *PerNar*.

RUINED JAPANESE INSTALLATIONS in vicinity of Administration Building. Above ground targets such as these were pulverized by naval gunfire which left many hidden positions untouched.

the Iwo Jima and Okinawa operations would follow this pattern, but because Peleliu set the precedent the seeming phenomenon puzzled many people at the time. Throughout the campaign Marines continued to watch hopefully for some crack in morale to produce that peculiarly Japanese manifestation which had so greatly simplified the mop-up of other islands. But the troops here included some of the finest Japan ever put in the field, under officers who had learned the futility of pitting *Bushido* against fire power and steadfastly refused to play into their enemy's hands.

The Japanese plan consisted basically of an organized and carefully integrated defense in depth, but it possessed far greater strength and flexibility than anything yet encountered in the Pacific.

This increased strength resulted from skillful utilization of naturally difficult terrain, combined with time and materials for developing defensive positions of maximum effectiveness. As noted in Chapter I, the fall of the Gilberts and Marshalls had confronted the Japanese with the problem of strengthening hurriedly their second line of defense. Miscalculating our initial objective, they had given first priority to the Palaus at the expense of the Marianas. Thus, Marines attacking Saipan, Tinian and Guam had found the defenses incompletely developed, with quantities of heavy weapons and fortification materials lying around for lack of time to put them to use.[4] The Japanese on Peleliu not only received the wherewithal first, but an added three months grace in which to make the most of it. They did.

The flexibility stemmed from a system of zone defense which combined features of the mobility necessary on a land mass the size of Saipan, and the dug-in defense-to-the-death characteristic of the much smaller islands of Tarawa and the Marshalls. Uncertain exactly where our landing would be attempted, Colonel Nakagawa set up his defenses in four zones (see Map 5), each assigned to one reinforced battalion, with the remaining battalion held in general reserve in the ridges of the northwestern peninsula. Operating on interior lines, troops occupying the unaffected zones were in a position to move swiftly to the reinforcement of whichever zone was attacked once our intentions became known.[5]

However, the successful drive across the island on the afternoon of D-Day effectively isolated the battalion defending the southern zone, members of which were thenceforth fated to fight to the death in their holes in the conventional Japanese manner, unable to furnish direct support to their compatriots elsewhere. This circumstance, combined with the failure of the major D-Day counterattacks, determined Colonel Nakagawa to shift his strategy to a last ditch stand in the most formidable terrain available. As events soon proved, troops originally posted to defend the eastern zone abandoned some of the most formidable installations on the island (Beach Purple) and retired to the ridges, where they redeployed in conjunction with the troops already in that area. Into these same ridges came other Japanese, falling back before Marine pressure, there to make the conquest of the island as costly as possible.

In this, no doubt, they were influenced to some extent by their advance intelligence. This was somewhat better than in many instances: the garrison was alerted as to the probable time and place of the coming attack as early as 3 September, and just prior to D-Day General Julian Smith was identified in command, though placed in the wrong area (Morotai). Within five days the landing force had been correctly estimated as "probably a division." However, the same entry (20 September) reveals a serious misapprehension regarding the invaders' intentions which colored Japanese tactical and strategic conceptions for some time to come:

It seems as if they (U. S. forces) had been planning on taking up their positions in Koror and Palau Island (Babelthuap) following the main forces' occupation of Peleliu. However, the enemy was unable to withdraw its main forces from Peleliu, because they had received heavy losses there. Also, they were constantly harassed by the danger of being attacked by our aggressive artillery from Angaur, and by counterlanding on Peleliu which may be staged by our Angaur forces. Because of these facts the enemy were compelled to change their plan and land their reserve forces on Angaur.[6]

These developments in enemy thinking could not be known to the invaders on D-Day, nor for some days to come. Hence, throughout the second operational phase the attack continued in accordance with the original plan, even while gains actually achieved fell further and further behind that optimistic schedule.

The commanding general and his staff landed at about 0950 on D-plus 1 and took over direction of the operation, occupying the advance command post which General Smith had set up the previous day. As described in Chapter III, this was located in an overrun Japanese antitank trench a short

---

[4] Hoffman *op.cit.*, incompleteness of Japanese defense installations in the Marianas is noted in action reports of most U. S. units participating.

[5] It is believed that many of the troops used in the Japanese counterattacks against the 5th Marines on D-plus 1 were drawn from the Beach Purple Area. *Harris.*

[6] *Tada Record.* This persistent belief that the action on Peleliu served to thwart a planned attack on islands to the northward may have been wishful thinking, but it appears to have had a real effect on attempts to reinforce and supply the beleaguered garrison. See Appendix F.

SOUTHERN PELELIU, thoroughly fortified and defended by a reinforced battalion, fell to the 7th Marines by the afternoon of D-plus 3.

distance inland of Beach Orange 2. By digging into the reverse bank of this sharp declivity, the division's nerve center achieved excellent protection from the ubiquitous enemy shells which continued to come snarling and screeching into the area in slowly diminishing numbers for the next week. These blew up a couple of small ammunition dumps nearby and knocked out a 105mm howitzer, but only a single shell scored on the command post proper, landing in the message center and killing one man.[7]

---

[7] There were repeated hits and casualties in adjoining areas, however, one of these within 50 yards of the CP proper. *Ramsey.* The Japanese appeared to have certain weapons registered on primary beaten zones in the vicinity of the beach, for "The Division CP and 2–11 CP operated with relative impunity for several days immediately adjacent to an area approximately 50 x 150 yards in size that received, by actual count, over 200 major caliber shells in a two hour period." Ltr LtCol N. P. Wood to CMC, 14Mar50, hereinafter cited as *Wood.*

Orders called for the assault to jump off at 0800 on D-plus 1 on all fronts, following an intensive preparation by naval gunfire, air strikes, and the massed fires of the artillery emplaced on shore. On this day, and increasingly throughout the phase under discussion, the operation broke down into three distinct patterns in accordance with the missions of the respective combat teams, which will be dealt with in turn as they fitted into the picture as a whole.

CLEAN-UP IN THE SOUTH [8]

Final dispositions on the night of D-Day had seen two battalions of the 7th Marines in line, facing generally eastward and southeastward. On the right, the flank of the 1st Battalion was anchored firmly on the western

---

[8] This account synthesized from basic reports of 7th Marines previously cited, except as otherwise noted.

shore well below the extremity of Beach Orange 3, and extending inland along the 0–A line. But the 3d Battalion was still well short of the eastern shore where Company I remained held up by that blockhouse strong point which it had been unable to reduce before dark, and where Company L had been echeloned to the left rear in order to tie in with 3/5.

Early on the morning of 16 September (D-plus 1), tank support and heavy preparatory fire enabled Company I, attacking eastward, to seize the supporting positions to its front—three concrete dual-purpose gun positions and a barracks area—with no great difficulty, but the blockhouse itself proved to be a very tough nut indeed. Upon its eventual capture, its walls were found to be of reinforced concrete more than five feet thick on all sides. This withstood direct hits by all infantry weapons, and 75mm tank guns merely bounced off it. Flame-throwers, unaided, could make no impression, as the two entrances were below ground level and, like the fire ports, protected by one-inch armor plate.[9]

This fortification was finally reduced by demolition teams working under the concealment of smoke placed to blanket all of its apertures, and Company I reached the eastern shore just beyond at 0925.[10] While this unit consolidated the beach positions against enemy counterlandings or attacks through the mangrove swamp a short distance above, Company K attacked southward in line on the left of the 1st Battalion, with Company L in support.

The terrain over which this drive moved might possibly answer the loose description of "low and flat", which persistent intelligence reports had applied to the entire island, but only in comparison with some vastly worse terrain which the invaders would encounter a little later. Scrub jungle overgrew most of it, hampering even infantry maneuver and greatly complicating the bringing up of support weapons.

And the Japanese had improved on nature. They had reason to believe that U. S. troops might attempt an initial landing in this area, as indeed the planners had seriously considered, and from shore to shore the region was honeycombed with strongly reinforced and cleverly camouflaged defensive installations with cleared interlocking fields of fire: pillboxes, casemates, bunkers, rifle pits, and trenches. These had been blasted out of coral bedrock so adamant as to make digging-in virtually impossible for troops in assault; once off the sand beaches, the men could take cover only behind natural features or by piling up improvised breastworks of such loose rocks and blasted tree trunks as came to hand.[11] This characteristic would operate to the attackers' disadvantage throughout all phases of the campaign. To an extent not equalled in any other Pacific operation, natural features pitted the unprotected Marine in the open against the hidden Japanese in a thoroughly fortified position.

The fighting in the south continued grim and deadly, but unspectacular. It boiled down to overpowering, in turn, individual positions more often than not mutually supporting. There was a redeeming feature in this connection, however. Because they had been prepared in anticipation of an amphibious landing, these installations presented their strongest faces seaward, so that the Marines advancing from the north caught them, to a greater or lesser degree, in the flank and rear. But, from whatever direction approached, their occupants had no intention of surrendering. Assigned to the defense of this area was the 3d Battalion,

---

[9] 3/7 WD, 6. This source contains a detailed description of this formidable structure.

[10] Ibid. This maneuver had the effect of pinching out most of the elements of 3/5. For their subsequent disposition, see sub-chapter following.

[11] A minor classic of descriptive understatement was contributed by a young lieutenant of the 5th Marines. Surveying the terrain with increasing disapproval, he turned to his battalion commander and observed, in a voice out of deepest Texas: "Majah, this sho' is po' land."

15th Infantry,[12] reinforced, one of the elite units of the Imperial Japanese Army, and its members fought to the death with all the skill which their situation permitted.

After reduction of that massive blockhouse, the 3d Battalion had the easier going during the drive southward. Company K, advancing in line on the left of the 1st Battalion, blasted and burned out successive enemy installations in its path to such good effect that by 1025 the leading elements came within sight of their final objective, the southeastern promontory, its approaches now defended on the landward side by only two pillboxes. By 1200, both of these had been reduced.

However, the combined strain of protracted fighting and debilitating heat (to be described subsequently) were now exacting their toll. The men were desperately in need of water [13] before they would be in shape to assault again, so here the advance was halted. When it became clear that the supplies could not be delivered until late afternoon, the company was ordered to "dig-in" behind piled up coral rocks for the night. The remaining hours of the day were turned to good advantage by bringing up tanks to fire directly into enemy defense installations on the promontory and at the same time cover details of engineers clearing out the mines found to be liberally sown across the open sand spit which provided the only approach by land.

In its somewhat wider zone of action, the 1st Battalion advanced with Companies C and A in line (right to left), Company B in reserve. Progress was facilitated, as was that of the 3d Battalion, by strong support by heavy weapons: not only landbased artillery, but naval gunfire, called air strikes, and LCI rocket concentrations. But the area was defended in exceptional strength. In addition to the conventional pillboxes, bunkers and casemates, the battalion had to knock out four 5-inch guns and three lighter dual-purpose antiaircraft weapons before the morning was over. Nevertheless, 1/7 gained the southern end of the island proper only a short time after Company K. And there, for the same reason, a halt was called until the men could be in some measure rehabilitated; a halt which was to last through the night, while similar preparations were made for the following day's assault on the southwestern promonotory, or Ngarmoked Island.

Throughout D-Day the 1st Battalion had been harassed by fire from the small unnamed island lying just north of Ngarmoked which naval gunfire and air strikes had been unable to silence. The main gun position there was subsequently spotted from the beach and knocked out by tank fire, with such good effect that a patrol sent across the reef at low tide found no more live Japanese there. However, during the night of D-plus 1 the enemy made several attempts to reoccupy it, evidently with the object of getting once more on the flank and rear of the attackers. Illuminating shells revealed large numbers in the act of wading across from the southwest promontory, making them excellent targets for machine gun and rifle fire. No further trouble was experienced from that direction.[14]

The 2d Battalion, 7th Marines, unable to come ashore on the evening of D-Day for lack of transportation, landed on Orange 3 during the morning of D-plus 1, still in division reserve. The tentative intention of the division command had been to commit it in support of the southward drive of its parent regiment, and Company G and 81mm mortar platoon actually moved forward for that purpose. However, the precarious situation in the 1st Marines zone on the division's left was at last becoming apparent, in contrast to the comparatively satisfactory progress in the south, and shortly after noon the reassembled battalion displaced to Beach

---

[12] The defending unit was identified definitely as early as 1222 on D-plus 1. 7th Mar *R-2 Journal*, Sheet #21.

[13] Some indication of the men's conditions is provided by a terse dispatch, CO 3/7 to CO-7, logged at 1324: "Out of water. Troops having dry heaves." *Ibid.*, Sheet #22.

[14] *Gormley.*

White 2.[15] There it was attached operationally to the 1st Marines, in which capacity it served throughout the remainder of this phase of the fighting.[16]

In the 3d Battalion zone, the plan for D-plus 2 called for Company L, in reserve the previous day and hence comparatively fresh, to pass through Company K and assault the southeastern promontory. The attack was originally scheduled to jump off at 0800, and a preparatory air strike was delivered accordingly. However, the engineers, working farther forward, discovered another enemy minefield laid across the sand spit. The jump-off was postponed until 1000 in order to give them an opportunity to clear this out, which dangerous work the engineers accomplished without casualties under heavy covering fire delivered by the tanks and infantry.

This precaution paid off. Assaulting in the wake of a mortar and artillery barrage, one platoon of Company L, supported by three tanks, gained a foothold on the promontory at 1026 and occupied enemy installations knocked out by tank fire the previous afternoon. With the approach thus cleared, the remainder of the company was rushed across the spit in amtracks against only scattered rifle fire. The southern portion of the promontory was seized first in order to obtain positions from which fire could be placed across the lagoon on the opposite (Ngarmoked) promontory to support the attack of the 1st Battalion. The drive then turned northward across not too difficult terrain, overrunning a series of enemy positions. The entire promontory was declared secure at 1320, although, as is always the case in areas prepared for defense by the

PRIVATE FIRST CLASS ARTHUR J. JACKSON, 3d Battalion, 7th Marines, won the Medal of Honor and subsequent promotion to 2d Lieutenant for his courageous and effective assault on several Japanese pillboxes during the fighting on southern Peleliu.

Japanese, mopping-up proved difficult and arduous. The last twenty-odd enemy survivors were driven into the water, where they were picked off by riflemen while attempting to escape northward across the reef.

No such quick victory awaited the 1st Battalion. The southwestern (Ngarmoked) promontory was much the larger of the two, its terrain higher and more rugged, its defenses more numerous and formidable.[17]

---

[15] 2/7 *War Diary*, 3, gives 1010 as the hour Co G returned to battalion control, 1245 when Bn CO reported to 1st Marines. The 81mm mortar platoon was not released by 7th Marines at this time and did not rejoin the battalion until 1730 the following day, 2/7 *Unit Journal*.

[16] 7th Mar *R–2 Journal*, Sheet #20. 1st MarDiv *SAR*, II, 4. Subsequent activities of 2/7 are treated herein in sub-chapter dealing with operations of 1st Marines.

[17] As in the case of the southeastern promontory, a narrow sand spit provided the only dry approach. Under cover of darkness on D-plus 1 a demolition crew disarmed the numerous mines sown across it, making possible the use of tanks and half-tracks in the subsequent attack. *Gormley.*

Here the attack moved out according to the original schedule. Again, the comparatively fresh company which had been in reserve the previous day was committed to the assault, and initial momentum carried one platoon of Company B with one tank across the spit. At 0835 these encountered the enemy main line of resistance and were stopped cold without being able to gain a foothold. The company requested permission to withdraw these elements in order to give heavy supporting weapons an opportunity to work over the ground further. Permission was not granted until 0935, when the withdrawal was effected with some difficulty under galling crossfire from the not yet secured southeastern promontory.[18] By this time, Company B had been roughly treated and was passed once more into battalion reserve.

While artillery and mortars poured concentrations into the target, the 1st Battalion pulled itself together for another try. All available tanks and LVT(A)'s were moved into the area, and half-tracks and 37mm guns from the Weapons Company were brought laboriously forward. The early success of the 3d Battalion on the opposite promontory released many of the supporting weapons attached to that unit, as well as substituting friendly supporting fire for the enemy's flanking fire.

Company A attacked at 1430, preceded by a 10-minute air strike and supported by three tanks. This time the Japanese first line of defense was carried. The company gained the high ground and commenced the grim business of slugging its way southward, while artillery and mortar concentrations blasted enemy positions to its front. At 1530, Company I was moved over from the 3d Battalion as a special reserve, and four minutes later Company C, thus released, was committed on the promontory to develop the right flank, here greatly lengthened by the bulge of the western shore. An hour

later, Company B was ordered across the spit to positions immediately behind the two assault companies, and thus the entire 1st Battalion was in the fight.

Resistance was stubborn all along the line. Company C progressed to the western shore, in the process reducing the heavy enfilading weapons which had been playing such havoc with the Orange Beaches. But when the company attempted to advance southward, it soon came upon a sizeable swamp which threatened to break off its contact with Company A on the left. The defensive line as set up for the night was in the shape of an inverted U, with a shallow penetration in the middle where the swamp intervened, but a substantial hold on the shore on either flank. Four tanks, four armored amphibians, and two half-tracks were on the scene; Company B was in close support, ready to be committed wherever needed, and Company I in reserve just across the spit.

With the end plainly in sight, the 1st Battalion was in no hurry to resume the attack the following morning (D-plus 3 18 September). While preparatory fires pounded the terrain to the front, dispositions were made with the utmost care. When, at 1000, the advance finally began, all of the armor which had been brought up during the previous afternoon and night was in position to move forward in support.

The plan for this day's fighting called for Companies C and A to circle the impeding swamp, on the right and left respectively, tie in their flanks to the south of it, and drive in line to the end of the promontory. Company B was committed on the extreme left to pinch out the eastward bulge of land which widened the front a short distance ahead of the jump-off line.

Experience of both battalions on the preceding day had indicated that some Japanese were bound to be overrun in the course of such a drive, hiding out either in their dug-in positions or in the numerous caves in this region of jumbled coral high ground. All units in assault were directed to ignore these and press on toward their objectives,

---

18 "The heroic action of stretcher teams, evacuating wounded across the narrow sand spit under intense enemy fire, merited particular praise."—*Ibid.*

leaving mopping-up to demolition teams supported by reserve elements specially detailed for the purpose.

This soon proved to be far more of a problem than anyone had expected up until now. Company C detached 15 men to cover suspected openings of caves and pillboxes in its rear, only to have these pinned down in short order by Japanese swarming out from the underground in numbers which, at this early stage of the operation, seemed astonishing.[19] Eventually it became necessary to commit most of the special battalion reserve (Company I) and the Division Reconnaissance Company, which had been attached to the 1st Battalion since D-Day afternoon, to bring the situation in the rear under control.

The attack developed according to plan, but slowly in the face of last-ditch resistance in every sector. By 1048 Company B, now deployed on a line running north and south, had pinched out the eastern bulge of the promontory. With its flank thus covered, Company A, reached the southern shore in its zone of action at 1224, Company C completing its mission on the right at 1344.

It was now becoming apparent that Company B had drawn the most difficult assignment. The defense system in its area had been strategically designed to cover the entrance to the nearly circular lagoon, or cove, lying between the promontories against an anticipated U. S. landing. The shore approaches were heavily mined, and enemy prepared positions crowded thickly in upon one another. At 1354 the company estimated that it had killed 350 Japanese, and resistance had been constricted to a single hard core only about 50 square yards in area. However, by this time the tanks supporting the infantry had withdrawn to rearm, and the half-tracks had bogged down. Thus, the

attack had to wait until a bulldozer could be brought forward to extricate the latter.

As the company waited, significant sounds to its front indicated that at last the Japanese had decided to cooperate—by blowing out their own brains.[20] Many others leaped into the sea. When the final position was taken shortly afterward, 15 or 16 of these last die-hards were found to have been officers.

So far as the southern part of the island was concerned, the fighting was over, save for the inevitable mopping-up. A fine Japanese reinforced infantry battalion, in strongly fortified positions, had been sent to join its ancestors. As the two Marine assault battalions straightened themselves out and squared away for a little well earned rest, the regimental command notified Division Headquarters optimistically: "At 1520, 0–1 was taken. The Seventh Marines Mission on Peleliu is completed."[21]

ADVANCE OF THE 5th MARINES [22]

By far the most substantial gain in the actual ground secured during the Second Operational Phase was to be achieved by the 5th Marines. But there was small indication that this would be the case on the morning of D-plus 1.

The regiment began this day with a near-catastrophe when one Japanese shell struck the field telephone switchboard, wiping out a good portion of the wire section, while a second shell scored a direct hit on the regimental command post. This was located in a section of captured enemy trench [23] near the edge of the airfield, and the shell struck

---

[19] Although they did not comprehend its full significance at the time, the Marines were encountering the Japanese tactic of "passive infiltration," which was to assume the proportions of a major problem during later phases of the Peleliu operation. See Chapters VII and VIII.

[20] 7th Mar *R–2 Journal*, Sheet #43.

[21] *Ibid.*, Sheet #44.

[22] Derived from basic reports of 5th Marines previously cited. Supplementary sources specially noted.

[23] A zig-zag communication trench, without revetments. A map captured later indicated that it served as a registration area for a Japanese battery. This was the third time since its establishment that it had come under heavy fire. On this particular occasion, 15 to 20 rounds were received, the two noted doing the most damage. Ltr Capt L. T. Burcham to CMC, 7Mar50.

OPEN AIRFIELD area favored tank operations, but dominating ridges to the north demanded fast action.

the parapet, knocking out the R-1, R-3, and a newly arrived replacement major, as well as the naval gunfire liaison officer. The commanding officer, Colonel Harold D. Harris, was almost completely buried by the explosion; miraculously, he escaped being wounded but sustained a severely wrenched knee which kept him partially incapacitated and in great pain for several days.

How seriously this blow impaired the command situation can be understood more clearly when it is remembered that the executive officer, Lieutenant Colonel Lewis W. Walt, had been detached from the staff the previous evening in order to take over the disorganized 3d Battalion. Replacements were brought up hurriedly from the division command post,[24] with the result that the attack jumped off on time. Later in the day Colonel Walt returned to his regu-

lar post which had become of added importance because of Colonel Harris' injury.

The 5th Marines, it will be remembered, had for its initial mission capture of the airfield. The 1st Battalion, on the left, had spent the night in the woods at the edge of the open ground, along the 0-1 phase line, where it had halted of necessity in order to maintain contact with the stalled 1st Marines. On the extreme right 3/5, on the eastern shore and along the southern edge of the airfield, also enjoyed some cover. But the 2d Battalion, which had advanced rapidly in the wake of the repulsed tank attack late the previous afternoon, now lay in line nearly midway across the open airfield. All three units beat off short, sharp counterattacks during the night, and with the coming of dawn became subjected to intensive and effective shell fire.

The terrain here, even more than to the south, might be compared to that of the atoll

---

[24] The R-1 replacement was Captain Paul H. Douglas, division adjutant, who thereupon entered a colorful and distinguished phase of his military career which has gone down in the traditions of the 1st Marine Division. He was wounded in turn during a later stage of the operation and again, more

seriously, on Okinawa. A former Professor of Economics at the University of Chicago, LtCol Douglas at this writing (April 1950) is serving as U. S. Senator from Illinois.

FIRESWEPT AIRFIELD, here being crossed by 5th Marines, was naked of cover.

islands of the Gilberts and Marshalls. But with a difference: the airfields on Betio, Roi and Engebi were not dominated by concentrations of heavy weapons posted on high ground and directed from observation posts at elevations as high as 300 feet from which the enemy could "look down the throats" of the attackers. There was little actual ground resistance on the airfield itself, but deadly fire poured from the ridges and from installations in the woods, or scrub jungle, on the north and east which made a terrain compartment of the entire area. While these woods might provide covered approaches to the heights, there were no covered approaches to the woods; they had to be taken by determined tank-infantry attack, supported by naval gunfire, air strikes, and all the artillery and mortars which could be spared from other sectors.

The advance on this day took the form of a wide turning movement toward the northeast, pivoting on the extreme left of the 1st Marines. In the 5th Marines zone of action, the most substantial gains were achieved by the 1st Battalion. Lieutenant Colonel Boyd had Companies A and B in line (left to right), with Company C echeloned 200 yards rearward behind Company A. In this formation, the battalion swept the entire northern portion of the airfield. In a little more than an hour, advance elements reached the main service apron and hangar area. Here they found the Japanese installed in strength in a large antitank trench and several stone revetments and ousted them only by dint of some heavy fighting. This position was consolidated, and during the afternoon the battalion pushed forward to the 0–2 line. There was no possibility of digging-in here, however, so a withdrawal was made to the anti-tank trench for the night.

Throughout the day the 1st Battalion experienced contact difficulties on both flanks. On the left, the 2d Battalion, 1st Marines, was meeting a somewhat different tactical situation (see sub-chapter following) and had troubles of its own. Colonel Boyd succeeded in tying-in firmly with Company F of that regiment, only to discover a little later that this unit was out of touch with the rest of the 1st Marines. The gap there, estimated as 200–250 yards, was covered by bringing up Company I from 3/5 (see below), but F/1 remained attached to 1/5 throughout most of the day. However, because of the excellent visual contact and the open nature of the ground, physical tie-in was not considered essential.

The 2d Battalion made slower progress. Major Gayle's unit had to cope not only with the shell fire that lashed the open ground, but with the woods that bounded the airfield on the east, giving way along an ill-defined shore line to dense mangrove swamp. These woods were in actuality a nearly impenetrable tangle of scrub jungle, difficult to travel in itself and infested with Japanese who had to be eliminated by the costly hand-to-hand process, supported where possible by tanks operating on the open ground. By nightfall the 2d Battalion had closed up on the flank of the 1st and enjoyed some surcease from the galling fire from the ridges under cover of the captured woods. But with the coming of darkness, the battalion found it expedient to fall back a short distance on the open airfield in order to obtain clear fields of fire to its front.

The 3d Battalion, 5th Marines, played a comparatively minor role in this day's fighting. The simultaneous pushes of its own regiment northward and the 7th Marines first to the east [25] and then to the south, each with a flank on the eastern shore, had the effect of pinching out 3/5 for practical purposes. During the morning, the battalion expanded its hold along the shore line behind the advance of the assault units, elements of Company L assisting the flank of the 2d Battalion, Company K cooperating with 3/7. But with the two drives proceeding in opposite directions with all possible speed, both companies were soon over-extended. Company I was ordered to fill the gap which was developing between them, but before this move could be effected, about 1200, new orders arrived sending Company I to the north of the airfield to reinforce the battered 1st Battalion.

Because of the urgent need for Lieutenant Colonel Walt in his regular post as regimental executive officer, he was relieved in his temporary command of 3/5 at 1500 that afternoon. Major John H. Gustafson was designated to command the battalion, with Major Hierome L. Opie moving in to take over as Executive Officer. These officers received word of this new assignment only at dusk and had little time to learn the true condition of the unit and its equipment before the battalion was moved up to relieve 1/5 in its forward positions the following morning.[26]

D-plus 2 (17 September) was a significant date in the story of the operation, as this day brought the invaders squarely up against what was to prove the major terrain feature of the island's defense: the ridge system which began just above the Japanese barracks area and followed the axis of Peleliu's northwestern peninsula, harboring the hard core of enemy resistance. As this lay entirely within the zone of action of the 1st Marines, the fighting there will be discussed in detail in connection with the operations of that regiment (see following sub-chapter).

The line of advance of the 5th Marines lay across the low ground to the east of the

---

[25] 3/7 did not start sweeping southward until completely across the island in its zone of action; hence, its initial attack crossed the front of the position organized by 3/5 on D-Day night. *Walt.*

[26] Ltr Maj J. H. Gustafson to LtCol G. D. Gayle, 8Nov49, hereinafter cited as *Gustafson.* Up to this time, Major Gustafson had been Executive Officer of the 2d Battalion, Major Opie Bn-3 of the 1st Battalion.

ridges. Thus, every forward movement brought the elements of that regiment under increasingly heavy flanking fire from the enemy's commanding positions on the left. This, combined with the necessarily slow progress of the 1st Marines, was to be a controlling factor in this area as long as the regiment operated there—and for some time after that.

The situation was especially acute in the zone most adjacent to the high ground where open terrain provided virtually no concealment and little cover. Attacking early on the 17th behind adequate fire preparation, the 1st Battalion reached the 0–2 phase line once more by mid-morning against light ground resistance but heavy mortar and artillery fire from elevated emplacements on the left. This time the position was secured, and there 1/5 was relieved by the 3d Battalion which had been alerted for this mission the previous evening.[27] But when the latter unit attempted to move forward again in the afternoon, it was pinned down so effectively by that flanking fire that gains on the left were negligible.

On the right, the 2d Battalion had the advantage of excellent concealment in the woods; and its concomitant disadvantage: so excellent was the concealment that the jungle was all but impenetrable. Thus, the men were relatively free from that galling fire from the left, though Japanese observers in the hills promptly called down concentrations whenever any personnel showed themselves in the open. This was particularly the case during the morning when a tank attempted to cooperate along the jungle's edge; it drew such volume of fire as to cause more harm than it could do good and had to be withdrawn.

Resistance on the ground was limited to the sporadic fire of a few scattered snipers. However, after the experience of the previous day in similar territory, this could not be foreseen, and the troops combed through the area in a skirmish line, hacking their individual ways as best they could. The brutal heat which now gripped the island was beginning to exact its toll. Heat prostration cases mounted, and it was necessary to call frequent halts to rest the men. Supply difficulties, especially getting water forward, did nothing to help.

Nevertheless, the 2d Battalion's advance passed well beyond the 0–2 line for a gain of 600–700 yards. Company E, on the left, dug in in contact with the 3d Battalion where Company K, having found some woods in its own area, had pushed forward to the edge of a coconut grove near the point designated "Omaok" on the map: a native village at one time but now an area of demolished Japanese barracks and utility buildings. Company F anchored the battalion's right flank on the edge of the mangrove swamp with Company G, in reserve, extending southward along the shore from there, facing that dismal morass from which nobody knew what to expect.

Progress continued slow on the left of the 5th Marines throughout 18 September (D-plus 3). The regimental zone of action in this area was bounded by a tactically important thoroughfare which became known as the East Road, which here began skirting the base of that hill system identified on the maps as Umurbrogol Mountain.[28] The 1st Marines had gained a foothold on the most adjacent ridge late the previous afternoon (see sub-chapter following), but fire from innumerable other elevations farther to the west and north continued to hamper the advance of troops traversing the open ground. This, combined with the necessity for keeping tied-in with the adjoining regiment, now heavily engaged with both the

---

27 This relief was commenced in mid-morning and effected with great difficulty as 1/5 was receiving heavy fire from the left flank and suffering many cases of heat prostration. Relief was completed about 1230. *Gustafson.* 5th Mar *WD.* 1/5 *Bn–3 Journal* gives hour of completion as 1410. The 1st Bn. passed into regimental reserve where it remained throughout this phase of the operation.

28 For further description of the tactical parts played by both the East Road and the Umurbrogol, see Chapters VI and VII.

enemy and the terrain, halted the forward movement of the 3d Battalion around midday.

Conditions on the right, however, were very different, and soon changed the entire nature of the 5th Marines' mission.

Jumping off at 0700, the 2d Battalion continued to hack its way through the concealing jungle, relatively immune to enemy shellfire and encountering only scattered ground resistance. This advance was aided greatly by a half hour's concentration of artillery time shell (air burst) fire on the woods and mangrove swamp to the front and flank by 2/11. Within two hours advance elements of Company F reached an improved road leading eastward to the Ngardololok area,[29] beyond which lay Purple Beach and the ill-defined shore contours and semi-islands which constituted the northeastern peninsula, or shorter prong of the Peleliu "lobster claw", seizure of which constituted an important part of the regiment's mission.

A short distance to the east of where the Marines first reached it, the Ngardololok Road was so closely bordered by swamps as to become in effect an open causeway: a perilous bottleneck which threatened to check any advance in force beyond this point. Aerial observation had revealed major Japanese installations both in the RDF area and the vicinity of Purple Beach, but the nature of the resistance encountered during the past two days indicated that the enemy might have withdrawn. To test this possibility, at 1040 the commanding officer of Company F was ordered to take a patrol across the causeway and see what happened. The patrol accomplished its mission by 1120 without drawing any fire whatever, whereupon an air strike on Ngardololok was called for to prepare the way for a crossing in force to set up a bridgehead.

Now began a series of misadventures which, alone, hampered the progress of the 2d Battalion on this day. The air strike, staged at 1245, missed the target altogether. To make up for this, an artillery barrage was placed on the area, and at 1335 Company F, reinforced by elements of Company G, commenced the perilous crossing of the causeway. Before this could be accomplished, a second and wholly unexpected air strike [30] came diving down to strafe the advancing troops. The bridgehead was set up, nevertheless, but Company E and the battalion command post, moving forward in support, were caught in the open approaches to the causeway by a misplaced artillery concentration, and a little later on the causeway itself by friendly mortar fire.

Even before the crossing of the causeway, a new tactical factor had arisen to change the nature of the 5th Marines' mission. The long, shallow arm of the sea which separated the island's northwestern and northeastern peninsulas had been reached which, in effect, split the regimental zone of action well over toward the left. All that remained on the west was the strip of ground between the East Road and the deep swamp that fringed the inlet, a front which could be maintained adequately by a single company rather than requiring an entire battalion. Company L, therefore, was left here to tie-in with, and protect the flank of, the 1st Marines, while the rest of 3/5 was hurried eastward across the causeway to aid in exploiting the gains of the 2d Battalion. At 1700 that evening Companies I and K dug in on the right (south) of 2/5, which had expanded its initial bridgehead to the north and east: holding all of the shore line in its area and facing the main Ngardololok installations across open ground.

---

[29] A Japanese radio direction finder was located here, leading the region to be labeled on the maps, and frequently referred to in reports, as the "RDF Area".

[30] The second air strike was ordered by regimental command, but word failed to reach the Battalion CP which was then in the process of displacing forward. *Harris.* Nearly all of the 34 casualties sustained by the 2d Battalion during this day resulted from friendly fire.

It will be remembered that this was the day (D-plus 3) when the 7th Marines secured all of the remainder of southern Peleliu. This accomplishment released additional personnel of that regiment, with the result that 3/7 took over most of the swamp line still held by the reserve battalion of the 5th Marines, enabling 1/5 to move up in closer supoprt of its parent regiment in preparation for the drive to come.

In the positions they occupied that night, the 2d and 3d Battalions were poised for the completion of the regimental mission, which proceeded systematically and uneventfully from this point on. An air strike paved the way for the 2d Battalion to secure the remainder of the RDF area during the morning of 19 September. Opposition was limited to a scattering of Japanese, evidently stragglers, who lurked among the demolished installations. They inflicted a few casualties but for the most part showed a greater disposition to hide than to fight, lending weight to the earlier supposition that the first class enemy troops originally assigned to this area had been withdrawn.

Subsequent operations of this day substantiated the supposition beyond further doubt. The 3d Battalion, pushing southward through tangled jungle following artillery and mortar concentrations, killed a handful of Japanese with virtually no resistance. Company I reached the ill-defined shore line across the mangrove swamp from the airfield area where the 2d Battalion had encountered so much trouble two days earlier, and Company K pushed a strong patrol to the east coast just below Purple Beach. Later that afternoon, Company G occupied the southern end of the beach, and commenced vigorous patrolling to the northeast.

The abandoned defenses of Purple Beach proved to be very formidable indeed as they faced seaward, confirming further the wisdom of the planners in deciding early against attempting a landing there. The beach itself was heavily mined and obstructed with tank traps and barricades which slowed progress much more than mopping up the few scat-

tered enemy remnants. Nevertheless, by late afternoon of the following day (20 September) Company G had secured the northern tip of the northeastern peninsula proper and sent a patrol to the off-lying island (designated "Island A" in current reports) which was found to be unoccupied.[31]

Simultaneously, a patrol from Company I moved southwestward along the narrow projection below the beach. Like the 2d Battalion elements, this patrol employed war dogs, one of which was credited with alerting the troops to an enemy ambush[32] during the late afternoon. A sustained fire fight failed to prove decisive by nightfall, and the men of Company I dug in short of their goal. Night infiltration attempts weakened the Japanese defenders, however, and the objective was secured the next morning with no great difficulty.

The remainder of the 5th Marines story for this phase is quickly told. The 2d Battalion continued its northward push, hampered only by natural obstacles. On the morning of 21 September, Company B seized Island A which the previous day's patrol had found unoccupied. Company F then passed forward and secured the larger adjacent island of Ngabad, again without opposition. The battalion command post kept pace with the advance, and Company E, in reserve, moved up in the rear to help in organizing the newly occupied territory. On 23 September, Company G's seizure of the small unnamed—and undefended—island due north of Ngabad and midway across the opening of the Peleliu "lobster claw" completed the regiment's mission in this zone of action, iso-

---

[31] 5th Mar *R-2 Reports* states that this patrol "encountered no resistance," but adds that it "killed three enemy." The patrol returned to the main island for the night at 1730. 5th Mar *WD*. (2/5 *Journal* gives hour of return as 1615).

[32] 5th Mar *WD*, confirmed in detail by *Walt*. The extensive jungle and swamp patrolling during this phase of the operation provided the dogs with almost their only chance to prove their usefulness on Peleliu. Mistaken attempts to employ them elsewhere led to their virtual annihilation. The *Action Reports* of the 4th and 5th War Dog Platoons make pitiful reading.

lating all enemy resistance on the north-western peninsula.

Behind the rapid advance, the 3d Battalion (less Company L) completed mopping-up and set about organizing Purple Beach for defense against anticipated counterlandings by Japanese troops from the central Palaus. On 21 September the 1st Battalion, which had been in regimental reserve farther south, moved up to Ngardololok and undertook similar work thereabouts. From then until the end of the Peleliu operation, the entire region was designated a defense area and was occupied in turn by various assault units relieved from the lines for a brief rest.

During this far-reaching expansion, Company L had remained tied-in with the 1st Marines to the west of the inlet which divided the 5th Marines' zone of action, and its movements during this period were governed by those of that regiment. The position held by Company L on 18 September, the day that the rest of the 3d Battalion crossed the causeway, described a rough arc from the East Road across to the southern end of the swamp which fringed the inlet, facing northward. On 19 September, a forward surge by the right of the 1st Marines carried to the summit of the dominating elevation in that area,[33] and Company L tied-in with the advance by pivoting on its right flank to form a north-south line along the edge of the swamp.

The 1st Marines, however, failed to hold the ground thus gained, and with the retirement of the survivors the following morning, Company L fell back to the position previously occupied. There it remained without participating in any further movements of importance until, with commitment of the 5th Marines in the Third Operational Phase of the campaign, it rejoined its parent regiment and played its part in the operations to the northward, as narrated in Chapter VI.

DIFFICULTIES OF 1st MARINES [34]

The over-all scheme of maneuver had anticipated that the 1st Marines would encounter the most difficult opposition. This forecast had been more than substantiated on D-Day, and the appalling extent to which it was true became increasingly evident.

As previously recounted, the regiment's situation on the evening of D-Day left a good deal to be desired: with most of the left flank company isolated and a gap in what should have been the beachhead line where the Japanese still held the northern half of that formidable coral ridge which barred progress inland. Jumping off to the attack on the morning of D-plus 1, Lieutenant Colonel Honsowetz's 2d Battalion, on the right, made excellent progress, crossing the west turning circle of the airfield within half an hour. But on the left of the 3d Battalion zone the line was unable to advance at all.[35]

Tactically, this immobility was not serious in itself, for the over-all plan called for the northward drive to pivot on the left flank. But the fact that the immobility was enforced, with, in effect, an enemy salient driven into the line, called for cogent measures. The regimental reserve (1st Battalion) attacked strongly in the early afternoon with Company C, the last fresh element, in assault and one platoon of Company B in reserve. Two tanks had been brought up, and with their support the infantry succeeded in capturing a 500-yard segment of the ridge.[36] With this high ground as a lever to pry the left of the line, the remainder of Company B was able to advance and gain contact with Captain

---

[33] Subsequently designated Walt Ridge (see Chapter VII). The attack which reached its summit on 19 September was that by Captain Everett P. Pope's Co C, 1st Marines, described in sub-chapter following.

[34] Synthesized from basic 1st Marines sources previously cited except as otherwise noted.

[35] 1st Mar *Nar.*

[36] *Davis.*

CLOSE INFANTRY ACTION through the rubble of building area north of airfield.

Hunt's command on the point which by then had been cut off for thirty hours.

A brief digression here to complete the saga of Company K. With the sea at their backs and Japanese in every other direction, the survivors of the two platoons had withstood sharp counterattacks throughout the night of D-Day. An amtrack operating across the reef carried out their wounded and brought in supplies and ammunition, and eventually the platoon which had been pinned down in the tank trap. The enemy were determined to recapture that bitterly contested point, but they were unable to muster forces for a major attack until about 2200 on the night of D-plus 1.

This took the form of a frontal assault against the high ground by an estimated 350 Japanese, together with a secondary, or diversionary, attack along the narrow flat at the shore line. At one stage during the previous night, Captain Hunt had been down to 18 men and must surely have been over-whelmed. Now most of Company B [37] was in position, as well as what remained of his own command; he was tied-in with the battalion line, and had telephone communication with the mortar platoons of both companies, which were already registered on the ground to his front.

Thus, the Japanese faced all the disadvantages attendant upon assaulting adequately manned prepared positions, covered by well placed defensive fire. What developed was a shambles, and by 0200 on 17 September a great tranquillity lay upon the area.

When the advance jumped off on the morning of D-plus 2, Company I passed through

---

[37] "At this point the 1st Battalion was tied-in in the middle of the 3d Battalion with Company K on our left and Company I on our right. . . . I had just finished a final check of our tie-in when the counterattack came. Hunt bore the brunt of the attack, but flanking fire from Companies B and C plus all our mortars no doubt aided him in beating it off." *Ibid.*

"A JOB FOR THE INFANTRY." Typical terrain in Peleliu's coral limestone ridges.

the position and Company K was ordered into reserve. Of Captain Hunt's complement of 235 men who had landed two days previously, 78 were left.[38]

Elsewhere in the 1st Marines zone, progress during the second day was the most satisfactory the regiment was destined to experience during its operations on Peleliu. The arbitrary line demarking this zone from that of the 5th Marines was so drawn that the two regiments, closely tied-in as they were, encountered essentially different terrain problems. Whereas the 5th Marines advanced almost entirely across open ground, the 1st, after cutting across one corner of the airfield, entered the building area to the

north. Many of the structures here had been made of reinforced concrete, now blasted to rubble by the heavy naval gunfire. These ruins provided at least some cover from the brutal shelling pouring from the high ground. Of course, they also provided cover for the defending Japanese infantry, with the result that the area became the scene for some savage close-in fighting.

The center of the regimental front, comprising the right company of the 3d Battalion and the left elements of the 2d, broke through and pushed on to gain control of a valuable stretch of road running east-west. On the right, however, the Japanese stubbornly defended the junction of the main road which circled the base of the ridge be-

---

[38] Hunt, *op.cit.*, 139.

yond the airfield headquarters, then angled off to run the whole length of the northwestern peninsula.

This road, marking the 0–2 phase line, was still 200–300 yards beyond reach when the time came to set up positions for the night. The extreme left, not having moved beyond the point where Hunt's men had been fighting for two days, was still more than 100 yards short of the 0–1 line.

All the trials which the 1st Marines had suffered up to this point were compounded by the protracted hell which commenced for the regiment on D-plus 2. For this was the day its personnel made the acquaintance of the Peleliu ridges at first hand. Preliminary aerial photography had done scant justice to this outlandish formation. At that time scrub jungle cloaked the high ground, blurring the outlines and softening contours, so that it might have passed for pleasantly undulating country of hills and dales. Now naval gunfire, if it had accomplished little else of great importance, had sheared away vegetation like a giant scythe, and the true features of the ridges stood revealed in all their stark horror—or so they appeared to the eyes of military men ordered to attack them.

First Marines *Regimental Narrative* (pp. 7, 8) describes the terrain thus:

The ground of Peleliu's western peninsula was the worst ever encountered by the regiment in three Pacific campaigns. Along its center, the rocky spine was heaved up in a contorted mass of decayed coral, strewn with rubble, crags, ridges and gulches thrown together in a confusing maze. There were no roads, scarcely any trails. The pock-marked surface offered no secure footing even in the few level places. It was impossible to dig in: the best the men could do was pile a little coral or wood debris around their positions. The jagged rock slashed their shoes and clothes, and tore their bodies every time they hit the deck for safety. Casualties were higher for the simple reason it was impossible to get under the ground away from the Japanese mortar barrages. Each blast hurled chunks of coral in all directions, multiplying many times the fragmentation effect of every shell. Into this the enemy dug and tunnelled like moles; and there they stayed to fight to the death.

General O. P. Smith (*Personal Narrative*) adds:

Ravines, which on the map and photographs appeared to be steep-sided, actually had sheer cliffs for sides, some of them 50 to 100 feet high. With nothing else on your mind but to cover the distance between two points, walking was difficult. . . . There were dozens of caves and pillboxes worked into the noses of the ridges and up the ravines. It was very difficult to find blind spots as the caves and pillboxes were mutually supporting. . . . These caves and pillboxes housed riflemen, machine gunners, mortars, rockets, and field-pieces. The Japanese technique was to run the piece out of the cave, fire, then run the piece back in the cave before we could react.[39]

Even before encountering the ridges, the 1st Marines received reinforcements. The inability of the division reserve (2d Battalion, 7th Marines) to land late on D-Day for commitment in the southern area made it available for the more critical northern zone, and this unit was moved to the White Beaches on the morning of D-plus 1 and attached operationally to the 1st Marines, as described in previous sub-chapter. Initially the battalion was held in special reserve,[40] but it was destined to play its active part all too soon.

Before the attack could jump off on the morning of D-plus 2, some reorganization was necessary. The regiment's casualties now exceeded 1,000, and the units were so depleted that it was necessary to use all three battalions in line. Owing to the difficulties on the left, the 1st Battalion had been committed in the middle of what had been originally designated the 3d Battalion zone. Now 1/1 was ordered to move into the center of the regimental line at dawn, while 3/1 tied-in in its own sector. The 2d

---

39 For a more particularized description, see Chapter VII of this monograph; also Appendix D.

40 At this stage 2/7 was earmarked for the shore-to-shore operation to seize the off-lying island of Ngesebus, to the North. According to the Commanding General's optimistic time schedule, the ground should have been prepared for this move within two or three days; hence, it was desired to keep the battalion intact. The fight in the ridges, however, necessitated a hurried revision of the entire Ngesebus plan.

Battalion retained its position on the right, in contact with the 5th Marines, and one company of the newly arrived reserve battalion (Company E, 7th Marines) was moved up in close support.

The 2d Battalion was the first to meet the ridges. Pushing forward in the wake of the artillery and naval gunfire preparation, the assault companies quickly overran the important road that marked the 0–2 phase line and captured the enemy position at the vital road junction which had held up the advance on the previous afternoon. This placed the battalion astride the island's second main traffic artery: the East Road, which ran from the administrative area through the village of Asias and along the narrow flat between the swamps and the eastern base of the high ground, then angled across the peninsula to join the West Road near the northern radio station (Road Junction 15—see Map 3).

The foremost units had progressed along the road for about 150 yards when they were stopped abruptly by a combination of brief loss of contact with the 5th Marines on their right, and the intensity of fire from the rugged coral ridge which now loomed menacingly on their left.

This ridge attained an elevation of 200 feet (henceforth known as Hill 200) and paralleled the East Road, thus thrusting a formidable salient ever deeper into the zone of action of the 2d Battalion as that unit advanced. Its flanks were steep, precipitous in places (much worse would be encountered) and honeycombed with caves which held observation posts, from which fire on the airfield area was directed, and many of the weapons which delivered this fire.

The battalion wheeled left and took the ridge under attack, scaling the steep slopes in the face of withering small arms fire and point-blank salvos from mountain guns and dual-purpose pieces which were run in and out of cover. At such close range this fire was extraordinarily accurate. Casualties among the assault troops mounted, and tanks and LVT(A)'s moving up in support were knocked out right and left. By nightfall virtually all of the crest had been taken. The men dug in [41] as best they could against the fire that now poured on them from elevations farther forward and from a second, slightly higher ridge (Hill 210) which paralleled Hill 200 on the west. The narrow, steepsided ravine separating the two teemed with Japanese who effectively prevented further assault in that direction.

According to the Japanese version, as set forth in *Tada Record*, 18 September: "At 1300, under protection of heavy naval gunfire, an enemy unit composed of two tanks and approximately two companies of infantry successfully advanced up to a high spot on the east side of *Nakayama*" (Japanese designation of Hill 200). Such apparent discrepancies in date appear frequently and might be accounted for either by faulty communications or the commander's natural reluctance to report a reverse until convinced that it was irremediable. At this time Nakagawa's CP was farther north in the same ridge, and the success of the Marines in gaining a foothold on the crest may have been the determining factor in causing him to displace later that day to the cave in the heart of the enemy final pocket of resistance which he occupied henceforth.

The capture of this strategic height had two immediately important effects. First, it greatly reduced the flanking fire which had been so hampering the 5th Marines, enabling that regiment to proceed with its main mission. Second, it exactly reversed the previous situation: instead of confronting a deep salient thrust into its own lines, the battalion now held an equally formidable salient driven into the Japanese defensive stronghold.

In the meanwhile, the other elements of the 1st Marines had commenced the day with an equally swift advance, a pace they

---

[41] The impossibility of "digging in" in any accepted sense of that term cannot be over-emphasized if a true picture of the fighting on Peleliu is to be given. Repeatedly it was the controlling factor in nullifying costly gains.

SCENE OF SOME OF 1st MARINES HEAVIEST ACTION on D-plus 2, 3. Troops on Hill 200 (left) exchanged fires across gulch with Japanese still holding Hill 210 (right).

were able to sustain considerably longer. In the center, 1/1 had to cope with an obstacle which, according to its officers' not unreasonable reckoning, should not have been there. This was a formidable blockhouse, with reinforced concrete walls four feet thick and protected by twelve pillboxes, all connected by a maze of tunnels. Unlike the hidden installations in the hills and jungles, this building showed clearly on the pre-landing aerial photographs and was pinpointed on the map issued to all ground troops; yet although Admiral Oldendorf had reported before D-Day that the fire support ships had run out of profitable targets, the

blockhouse had not been so much as nicked, much less reduced.[42]

This omission was quickly rectified, however. The old battleship USS *Mississippi* had been assigned in direct suport of the

---

[42] This blockhouse was not identified as such on the map, showing merely as a large building. The difficulties under which the admiral labored at this time go far toward explaining what appeared a serious oversight: "At the time, in spite of all my previous recommendations. . . . I had only a cruiser division operating staff, consisting of four officers. . . . During the preliminary bombardment and until several days after the landing, my entire staff were on the sick list, only my flag lieutenant remaining on his feet." *Oldendorf.*

SOUTHERN RIDGES; air view from southeast. Long razorback at left is Hill 200, with Hill 210 just behind it. Five Sisters in center, Walt Ridge right foreground.

battalion, and very shortly after the shore fire control party was able to adjust her 14-inch guns, the blockhouse began disintegrating. The big armor piercing and high capacity shells crumbled the walls, and their terrific concussion killed those Japanese missed by fragmentation. Smaller naval guns, tanks and infantry support weapons concentrated on the protecting pillboxes, and presently the advance overran the position and rolled on into dense jungle to the 0–1 line.[43]

During this action the front had become over-expanded, necessitating the forward movement of two platoons of the reserve in order to protect the flanks, and here the battalion paused to regroup.

By now the 1st Battalion, too, was face to face with the ridges. The arbitrary phase line 0–2 had been laid along the main road, here running northwest-southeast parallel to the battalion's front. Just across the road began that irregular, unpredictable rising of the land which was such a familiar fea-

ture of the landscape of Peleliu's northwestern peninsula. No sooner had 1/1 halted to reorganize than the line was assailed by a fury of fire from the high ground, and casualties began to mount alarmingly.

As quickly as it could be managed, reorganization was completed and the men surged forward again, slugging their way upward much in the manner the 2d Battalion was storming Hill 200. There was no other way: clawing up and over razorback crests, shinnying coral pinnacles, plunging down into sheer-sided gullies and ravines, dodging behind boulders. By evening they had gained the forward slope of the first series of hills and were firmly, if uncomfortably, established.[44] One significant feature of this advance was that in the course of it the infantrymen were obliged to knock out 35 separate Japanese-manned caves, existence of which had not been noted in their advance intelligence.[45]

---

[43] Activity in this blockhouse had been reported late the previous day, and the naval gunfire mission was delivered prior to the jump-off on D-plus 2. Major Davis had his CP in what was left of the blockhouse by 0930, "mingled with about 20 freshly dead Japanese." *Davis.*

[44] *Hist 1st Mar*, 10. The Japanese, however, appeared to disagree: "The enemy began to attack our lines along the hills of *Tenzan* (southwestern ridges) . . . but were repulsed by our timely firing." *Tada Record*, 18Sept44.

[45] Experience in the Marianas campaign had convinced intelligence officers that there were doubtless many caves in the Peleliu ridges, so the division

Writing of this mission long after the event, Lieutenant Colonel Davis, in his letter previously cited, described it as "the most difficult assignment I have ever seen. . . . Company A depleted itself on the bare ridge on the right as Company C became seriously over-extended on the left and was faltering. Everything was thrown in to exploit Company C's success. Remnants of Companies A and B, Engineer and Pioneer units were committed to fill the gaps as darkness came. Headquarters personnel were formed into a meager reserve. . . . Company C had moved 800 yards during the day, and we had been able to hold on although the cost was extremely heavy."

On the 1st Marines' left the story was somewhat happier. Lieutenant Colonel Stephen V. Sabol's 3d Battalion, which had had the most difficult going up to now, was destined to have the easiest henceforth. For its course lay along the coastal flat (or comparative flat), with the high ground to its right. Slow to get started, the battalion rolled on against minor resistance for an average advance for the day of 700 yards, and all that stopped it then was the danger of over-extending its front through the necessity of keeping tied-in on the right. As with the fighting in the ridges, this condition was to set the pattern of the regiment's advance for several days to come.

The varying fortunes of the different units resulted in an odd-appearing and far from reassuring contour to the front line on the evening of 17 September. Because of the inability of the 2d Battalion to secure Hill 210, the right of the 1st Marines' zone somewhat resembled a constricted letter "W". And there were two ominous features. While the Marines held a deep salient in enemy territory along the crest of Hill 200, this

was precarious in the extreme. For in Japanese hands, the parallel ridge to the west formed an equally deep salient in U. S. territory.

Furthermore, in adjusting the lines in this area after dusk, a gap was created between the flanks of the 2d and 1st Battalions. This the night-prowling enemy soon discovered and commenced to infiltrate in force. To cope with this situation, it was necessary to commit Company F, 7th Marines, and that unit was obliged to fight its way into position before the gap could be closed. Pressure on Hill 200 was so sustained and heavy throughout the night that at 0200 on the morning of 18 September, the 2d Battalion was obliged to bring up Company G, 7th Marines,[46] to bolster the position there. However, any overwhelming counterattack which might have made the situation something worse than precarious was effectively interdicted by concentrations of well placed artillery and naval gunfire on the approaches.

This brings the narrative of the 1st Marines to the morning of D-plus 3 (18 September). That day, as has been noted, was when the 7th Marines completed the securing of southern Peleliu, and the 5th Marines, leaving only Company L to maintain contact, set off on its quick overrunning of the eastern and northeastern portions of the island. But no such decisive results were in store for the hard-fighting 1st Marines, that day or ever during this campaign.

Casualties had been heavy, especially among the front line units, as was to be expected. For example: of 473 total effectives remaining in the 3d Battalion, 200 were headquarters personnel. Total losses for the regiment ran 1,236. Yet there appeared to be grounds for satisfaction with the progress made. A good foothold had been gained in the high ground, and the stiffest resistance the Japanese had been able to offer (so far) had been overcome. In any case, Colonel Puller reported to the

---

was not wholly unprepared. But nothing in this or any other war gave any hint of the magnitude of the problem which developed here. These caves and the methods developed for reducing them are dealt with in detail in later chapters and in Appendix D. For the time being suffice it to quote *Time*, 16Oct44, which characterized them, without being accused of overstatement, as "the incarnate evil of this war."

---

[46] *2/7 Unit Journal*. 1st Mar *Nar* erroneously identifies this as Co E. One platoon was virtually wiped out while fighting with 2/1. *Berger*.

PERILOUS APPROACH. Japanese emplaced in precipitous Hill 200 (background) poured flanking fire into troops attempting to assault the Five Sisters (right, partially hidden by tree).

division command post with an optimism which was contagious. The general feeling seemed to be that a break-through was imminent, whereat enemy resistance would collapse, or at worst disintegrate, as had happened on Saipan, Tinian and Guam after a certain point had been passed.

The trouble with this reasoning was that on the other islands the collapse had occurred upon U. S. troops reaching favorable terrain and had been heralded by at least one suicidal *banzai* charge. But there had been no *banzais* on Peleliu, and the terrain was becoming worse instead of better.

Optimistically, necessary regroupings were ordered, preparatory to resuming the at-

tack on the morning of 18 September. Unit commanders put every available man in the lines, including headquarters personnel not absolutely indispensible elsewhere. Company D, 1st Pioneer Battalion, sent up 115 replacements who were divided among the assault units. At 0600 the reserve battalion (2/7) took over the center from 1/1 which was relieved for a brief spell in regimental reserve (very brief indeed in the case of Company B), and the assault jumped off at 0700 behind a 30-minute preparation by planes, artillery and naval gunfire.

D-plus 3 combined the worst features of D-plus 2 with a lot of new ones, and the best that can be said for the day's progress was that in general the alignment of the front was rectified. The enemy salient on Hill 210 was finally pinched out by dint of savage and costly fighting on the part of 2/1 and 2/7. The Japanese, in turn, concentrated a murderous fire on 2d Battalion elements on the forward nose of Hill 200. Following up with powerful counterattacks, they made the position untenable and forced a short withdrawal from the ground so painfully won the previous afternoon.

At 1400 Lieutenant Colonel Honsowetz reported the 2d Battalion situation as desperate and requested immediately reinforcements and smoke barrage to screen the position. Company B was ordered up from the 1st Battalion's reserve area, attached to the 2d Battalion, and thrown in assault against Hill 205, slightly forward and to the right of the ridge to which it was hoped to gain direct access by this means. Somewhat to the surprise of all hands, they secured the hill with comparatively light casualties by 1630. However, it proved to be isolated from the main ridge system, hence of value only as an observation point and for relieving some of the pressure. Pushing on from there, Company B was decisively thrown back before the most formidable terrain obstacle yet encountered: an incredible complex of up-ended peaks and palisades which was to gain evil fame under the name of the Five Sisters.[47]

Progress was somewhat better on both flanks. In the 3d Battalion's zone on the left, the advance, as on the previous day, met only minor opposition, but the assault elements were obliged to halt after moving only a few hundred yards in order to maintain contact with 2/7, which was operating with great difficulty in the high ground. Those elements of 2/1 on the extreme right, moved across the comparatively level flat below Hill 200 to what had been the village of Asias, tying in there with the left company of the 5th Marines,[48] the rest of whose zone would now be separated from that of the 1st Marines by swamps and a long indenting arm of the sea. Thus at dusk the regimental front as a whole formed a shallow "U", a situation sounder tactically than the constricted "W" of the previous evening. But in the center the day's gains looked something less than imposing on the map, and on Hill 200 there was actual retrogression.

It should be borne in mind that position lines shown on the operations maps during this phase of the fighting are intended only as approximations. Owing to the inadequacy of the maps in this particular region and the incredibly broken nature of the terrain, exact orientation was all but impossible, and many misunderstandings resulted. As a participating battalion commander puts it:

There was no such thing as a continuous attacking line. Elements of the same company, even platoon, were attacking in every direction of the compass, with large gaps in between. When companies were asked for front lines they were apt to give points where the Company Commander knew or thought he knew he had some men. . . . There were countless little salients and countersalients existing.[49]

IRRESISTABLE FORCE VERSUS IMMOVABLE OBJECT

After surviving a night of constant harassing artillery and mortar fire, what was

---

[47] This was the original "Bloody Nose" ridge, so christened by the troops who first came up against it. The designation immediately became popular, however, and from reports which have come in it would appear that virtually every battalion in the division had a different conception of exactly what terrain feature "Bloody Nose" applied to. Communiques and news dispatches of this period usually referred to "Umurbrogol Mountain", a name appearing on the early maps but applying generally to the peninsula's entire southern ridge system. See subsequent notes on Peleliu place names.

[48] This was Company L. As described in the previous sub-chapter, D-plus 3 was the day when the main strength of the 5th Marines began the long stride which resulted in securing all of eastern and northeastern Peleliu.

[49] *Berger.* In this connection it may be significant that a study of 2/7 *War Diary* indicates that some of the target areas on which preparatory fires were ordered on the morning of 19Sept lay behind or squarely upon positions shown on some unit overlays as having been occupied the previous day.

left of the 1st Marines (plus 2/7) resumed the attack on 19 September (D-plus 4). Artillery and mortars opened preparatory fires at 0620, naval gunfire at 0645, and the assault jumped off at 0700. Again, the 3d Battalion found comparatively easy going across the coastal flat on the left and advanced about 400 yards before being obliged to halt in order to maintain contact.

But in the 2/7 zone of action in the center: "Progress was extremely slow and costly. The terrain was rugged, visibility extremely poor, there were only poor fields of fire and it was extremely difficult for the companies to use their mortars and automatic weapons to full advantage." [50] Here the advance moved in a direction varying from northeast to almost due east as the Japanese core of resistance hardened in the higher ridges.

On the right 2/1 slugged its way forward under generally similar conditions until about noon, when it was brought up short by the same obstacle which had repulsed Company B's abortive effort the previous afternoon: the Five Sisters. Although there was no way of knowing it then, these elements had reached the southern face of what was to prove the final pocket of Japanese resistance on Peleliu.

This curious formation, in contrast to most of the ridge topography, was oriented generally transverse of the island. Thus, in effect, it formed a wall barring passage northward, its southern face almost sheer. Even if the summit could be reached, working along it from peak to peak would be next to impossible owing to the precipitous drops between them. The Sisters were not destined to be permanently secured until November, after most of their supporting positions had been knocked out. However, at this period the Tables of Organization did not provide for any crystal-gazers at regimental level; so, once the advance positions had been consolidated, the battalion optimistically set about mounting another assault.

---

[50] 2/7 WD.

All ground weapons were brought into play where possible including tanks, bazookas and flame-throwers, both portable and self-propelled, and mortars and machine guns blanketed the targets. Losses were terrible, and the attack against the main objective got nowhere. However, on the open low ground on the extreme right, 2/1, with Company C and the Division Reconnaissance Company attached, succeeded in pushing some distance forward past the eastern flank of the ridges, though at such cost that Companies F and G had to be combined with a squad from the 4th War Dog Platoon to make up a single skeleton company. But the day's operations resulted in the deepest penetaration to be achieved by the 1st Marines in this zone, seizing ground which, following a subsequent withdrawal, was not destined to be regained for nearly two weeks.

Company C began this action with 90 men. About noon, Captain Everett P. Pope, its commanding officer, was ordered to seize Hill 100,[51] a steep, seemingly isolated elevation which dominated the East Road and the swampy low ground to the battalion's right front. Company C approached through the swamp and reached the road at the base of the hill, where two strong pillboxes were discovered. The men were in the process of assaulting these when they were suddenly pinned down by machine-gun fire at a range of about 50 yards from across a small pool on their right. Unable to get at these assailants, the captain obtained permission to withdraw the way he had come, pass to the left of the main lagoon and attack up the road with the support of tanks.

---

[51] To differentiate this tactically important elevation from several others also known as Hill 100, it will be referred to hereinafter as Walt Ridge, the name by which it came to be designated on a subsequent map. Lack of indigenous place names on Peleliu necessitated some hurried improvisations in order to orient terrain features, and some titles selected gave rise to much disgruntlement. In the interests of simplicity, this monograph will use the names, however unjustly applied, by which they came to be known most generally. See Chapter VII.

HORSESHOE CAUSEWAY, where two tanks came to grief supporting Company C, 1st Marines, on D-plus 4.

The road at this point angled sharply to the east, traversing the main lagoon, or sink hole, on a causeway across the mouth of a wide draw which was to gain an evil reputation under the name of Horseshoe Valley, or just "the Horseshoe." Beyond that, it skirted the base of the objective hill past the positions where the company had previously been pinned down, then angled to the northeastward.

The withdrawal was effected successfully, but it was late afternoon before the new advance began. The first tank to attempt the causeway slipped over one side and became immobilized. A second tank, in an effort to extricate it, slipped off the other side,[52] thus blocking the narrow approach to further supporting arms. Nevertheless, Company C crossed it in squad rushes, paused momentarily at the foot of the hill, then assaulted with only mortar and machine-gun support. The men's rush carried to the summit, where they were disconcerted to discover that, instead of having seized the crest of an isolated hill, they had merely gained the nose of a long ridge where their own position was dominated by a higher knoll only some 50 yards to the front.[53]

The Japanese reacted with promptitude and vigor. On that open ridge crest, the men of Company C were exposed not only to fire from the commanding ground to their front, but crossfire from the parallel ridge that rimmed the Horseshoe on the west: the Five Brothers (see Chapter VII). Counterattacks were incessant throughout the night

---

[52] The Japanese apparently believed that they had knocked out these tanks, for they wasted no more fire on them. Both were subsequently retrieved undamaged.

[53] Unit reports deal with this action only in general terms. Detail herein derives from Ltr Maj E. P. Pope to CMC, 8Mar50, hereinafter cited as *Pope.*

CAPTAIN EVERETT P. POPE, who was given the Medal of Honor in recognition of his valorous conduct in the abortive seizure of Walt Ridge on D-plus 4.

and produced some savage close-in fighting that degenerated into a matter of fists and rocks and throwing the enemy bodily over the cliffs. But at dawn, with only 15 men and one officer left, Captain Pope was ordered to withdraw to the main line, a movement again effected successfully through the swamp.[54]

It had not been Colonel Honsowetz's intention to send Company C on this mission alone, and the Reconnaissance Company had been ordered to support it on the right. However, Captain Pope had already carried the summit before the 2d Platoon of the latter unit, supposed to tie in here, could get into position to assault, and "There is some doubt as to whether Captain Pope realized this platoon was supporting him during the entire night to follow."[55] With no flank contact with the troops atop the ridge, the platoon also received some rough treatment throughout the night, and at dawn fell back to the cover of the swamp's edge before an attack in force. For some reason, the Reconnaissance Company did not receive the withdrawal order until half an hour after the retirement of Company C and came under additional fire from the reoccupied positions on the ridge crest. Falling back at last via the swamp route, the survivors reached the main line safely, where soon afterward the depleted unit was relieved.

Concurrently with the action in the eastern zone, 2/7, tying in on the left of 2/1, slugged its way through the jumbled high ground in an effort to draw abreast of the western flank of the Five Sisters. Some progress was made, but as a flanking movement the attempt was fruitless in that Japanese resistance kept the assailants from reaching any commanding ground from which to bring supporting fires to the assistance of 2/1's attack. Company A, 1st Marines, passed through elements of 2/7 in a turning movement from the west with 56 men in assault. These gained a little ground along a ridgetop which was swept by machine-gun fire, only to find themselves suddenly stopped by a sheer drop of 150 feet. Only six of the Marines who participated in this fight were still unwounded when they finally got back to 2/7 lines.

The attack on the morning of D-plus 5 (20 September) had for its main objective the recapture of Walt Ridge. Once more 2/1 assaulted with the 1st Battalion (less Company A) and the Division Reconnaissance

---

[54] "Only seconds after we had abandoned the summit, the enemy had moved in, putting in action a LMG." *Pope.* Capt Pope was the only company commander in the 1st Battalion to retain his post through the operation. He was awarded the Medal of Honor for this desperate fight, and four of his officers and men received the Navy Cross.

[55] Ltr 1stLt R. J. Powell, Jr., to CMC (undated) received 21Mar50. As no reports of the Recon Co are extant, this document provides the only source for details of the action described.

FORWARD POSITION of 1st Marines in lee of Horseshoe causeway.   Southern nose of Walt Ridge in background.

Company attached. Every resource under the regiment's control was employed. Every officer and man who could be spared from regimental and battalion headquarters was attached to the companies.[56] Additional tanks, LVT(A)'s, half-tracks, 37mm guns, and mortars were brought forward as far as possible. Deadly Japanese crossfire knocked out many, and those remaining proved inadequate to support the infantry successfully against the combination of cruel terrain and devilishly prepared positions.

This was an all-out effort; there was nothing in reserve. Its result is described as well by the Japanese as in any Marine reports, and a great deal more succinctly:

Since dawn the enemy has been concentrating their forces, vainly trying to approach *Higashiyama* (Walt Ridge) and *Kansokuyama* (Hill 300, at this time considered by Marines as part of the Five Sisters formation) with 14 tanks and one infantry battalion under powerful aid of air and artillery fire. However, they were again put to rout, receiving heavy losses.[57]

Although some advance was made, the low ground proved untenable, and the exhausted survivors fell back to a position where they could cover, at a respectful dis-

---

[56] Indicative of conditions in the assault units is the following entry for this day in 1/1 *Unit History* (p. 28): "The Battalion 2 Section, cooks, jeep drivers and men from general duty of Hq. Company were organized into machine gun platoons under Lt. Stanfield, the Battalion Adjutant."

[57] *Tada Record*, 20Sept44.

tance, the mouth of the Horseshoe. After six terrible days, it had to be admitted that the 1st Marines had been definitely stopped. More days were to elapse before graves registration men could get to the dead at the points of fartherest penetration.[58]

In the center 2/7 advanced slowly almost due east, battling sheer cliffs as well as heavy fire, and by mid-afternoon Company F, on the right, succeeded in gaining the crest of a ridge (then designated Hill 260) facing the Five Sisters from the west across the mouth of narrow, steep-sided declivity.[59] The battalion front had been narrowed and shifted farther to the right by having 3/1, on the western coastal flat, extend its front across the road to the foot of the rising ground, which movement once more held up the advance of the latter battalion.

First Marines casualties reported on 21 September totalled 1749. That the preponderance of these were among the front line units further served to lower combat efficiency far beyond the danger point.[60] Although the 3d Battalion continued in its zone under regimental control for two days longer, pushing patrols as far forward as the coastal village of Garekoru, the 1st Marines, as an assault unit on the regimental level, had ceased temporarily to exist. In accomplishing its mission to this point, it had killed an estimated 3,942 Japanese and had reduced the following major enemy positions and installations: 10 defended coral ridges, 3 large blockhouses, 22 pillboxes, 13 antitank guns, and 144 defended caves.

Defensive positions on southern Peleliu were taken over by artillery elements, and the 7th Marines (less 2d Battalion), after due reconnaissance of its new positions, completed the relief of 2/1, 1/1 and 2/7 [61] at 1820 on the afternoon of 20 September. The battered remnants of the regiment came down out of the ridges at last, to recuperate as well as conditions permitted in the more or less static eastern defense zone (RDF area, Purple Beach, and the northeastern islands) which had been set up by the 5th Marines, whom they relieved.

But the arrival of comparatively fresh troops at the main scene of action had no immediate effect on either the tactical plan [62] or the results achieved.

The 1st Battalion, 7th Marines, took over the zone on the right from 1/1 and 2/1, and the 3d Battalion relieved 2/7 in the center, with 3/1 and the 1st Marines command post remaining in position on the left for the time being. The 1st Battalion resumed the attack promptly in the morning of 21 September, in the same direction as the final assault the previous day, and with the same objective: recapture of Walt Ridge. The jump-off was postponed until 0800 owing to delay in the arrival of the supporting tanks, giving artillery concentrations and an air strike plenty of time to work over the target.

The plan called for an advance up the East Road. Because of the narrowness of this approach, only one company was placed in assault: Company C, with Company A following close to provide infantry support for the tanks and be in ready position to pass through should the situation demand.[63]

Smoke shell concentrations from the battalion's 81mm mortars helped to screen the approach, and initial opposition was described as light. The tanks were unable to

---

[58] The bodies of Captain Pope's dead atop Walt Ridge were not recovered until the final securing of that elevation on 3 October.

[59] "Death Valley" (see below).

[60] Over-all regimental casualties after the last elements had been relieved came to 56%: 71% in 1st Bn., 56% in 2d Bn., 55% in 3d Bn., 32% in Regimental Headquarters and Weapons Company. Of the nine rifle platoons in the three companies of the 1st Battalion, 74 men—and no original platoon leaders—remained. 1st Mar *Nar*, 12.

[61] In three days and nights of steady fighting with the 1st Marines, 2/7 had sustained more than 300 casualties while achieving a maximum gain of 800 yards. *Berger*. The battalion reverted to control of its parent regiment upon relief.

[62] For discussion of the tactical decision confronting the Comamnding General at this time, see Chapter VI.

[63] 1/7 *Historical Report*, supplemented by 7th Mar *R–2 Journal*. These two documents provide the only official sources currently available on this particular action.

negotiate the still blocked causeway across the mouth of the Horseshoe, but they succeeded in circling the swamp, or sink hole, to the northward, thus entering that ill-famed valley itself, and rejoined Company C on the road beyond, where it skirted the base of Walt Ridge.

The flat here was narrow, hemmed in on the east by that fringing swamp which comprised a major terrain feature along most of this flank of the northwestern peninsula. No enemy resistance was encountered from there, but fire from the ridge intensified as the troops moved abreast of it. And as the advance elements wheeled to the left and commenced the steep ascent, they were caught in a vicious mortar barrage that blanketed the entire eastern face, supplemented by grenades and small arms fire from caves higher up the slope itself.

WHERE THE NORTHWARD DRIVE WAS HALTED. East Road skirts base of Walt Ridge, which faces Five Brothers across floor of the Horseshoe. Five Sisters and Hill 300 on left, with weird contours of China Wall barely discernable at upper left. Swamp in foreground channeled assault approaches.

Mounting losses made further advance impossible, and the ground gained quickly became untenable. To commit Company A at this juncture would have been fruitless, and by mid-morning both companies had rejoined Company B which had remained on the defensive line from which the attack had originated. There the 1st Battalion was relieved in position by the Regimental Weapons Company at 1800.[64]

On this same morning (D-plus 6) the 3d Battalion attacked from its new positions deeper in the ridges on the left of 1/7 behind naval gunfire, air, artillery and mortar preparations. Three medium tanks and an LVT flame-thrower were in support but could be of little use because of the broken nature of the ground. Companies I and K in assault (left to right) reported a gain of about 100 yards at 0918, but "the advance for the rest of the day was slow and tedious and measured in yards."[65] The battalion's left tied in with the flank of 3/1, the last element of the 1st Marines remaining committed, on the western slope of the ridge system, but a gap began to develop between 3/7 and 1/7 on the right. It was now apparent that the only substantial gains were likely to be achieved on the western coastal flat, and the 3d Battalion's front was accordingly narrowed in order to make some of its elements available for support in that zone.[66] This was accomplished by ordering the 2d Battalion, which had reverted to parent control at the time of its relief the previous day, back into the center of the line to maintain contact.

The 7th Marines attacked again on 22 September. On its narrowed front, the 3d Battalion moved out in column of companies, Company L passing through Company I to take the lead (Company K had been pinched out the previous evening and gone into battalion reserve). The terrain became rapidly worse; mortar and machine-gun fire pinned the troops down repeatedly. The maximum gain for the day was recorded as only 80 yards, with even less on both flanks.[67]

This retarded advance limited, in turn, the progress of the 3d Battalion, 1st Marines, on the extreme left. The right flank of this unit was now also operating in the high ground, where it was having troubles of its own. Not until late afternoon did Company L, by dint of hard fighting all day, succeed in seizing a crucial elevation as an anchor for a tenable defensive line for the night. By that time 3/1 was so depleted and exhausted that it was necessary to bolster the line with elements of the 1st Battalion, 1st Marines, which, reorganized into two abbreviated companies, had been moved up in reserve.[68]

In the afternoon still another head-on assault was launched against the southern face of what it was becoming apparent was the enemy main line of resistance. At 1530 the 1st Battalion, 7th Marines, which had spent the night in bivouac north of the airfield, moved forward to the left of the defensive line sector held by the Weapons Company in an effort to seize the Five Sisters. Company B, in reserve throughout the battalion's fruitless attempt on Walt Ridge the previous day, was now in assault, to be supported as necessary by Companies A and C. Company E, tying in the right of the 2d Battalion's defensive line with the flank of the Weapons Company was also made available in case of need.

Artillery concentrations by 75's and 105's prepared the way, and a platoon of tanks

---

[64] With a few offensive sorties to lend variety, the Weapons Company was destined to occupy this containing position for the next two weeks, until the jutting jaw of Major Joseph E. Buckley, its CO, became as familiar a terrain feature as Walt Ridge.

[65] 3/7 *WD*, 10.

[66] At this time it was contemplated that the 5th Marines would be employed to exploit the soft spot on the left, and FO #2–44 dated 21Sep44 was issued accordingly. This plan was revised the following day in FO #3–44. 1st MarDiv *SAR*, II, 5.

[67] 3/7 *WD*, 10.

[68] 1st Mar *Nar*, 12. 3/1 patrols operating forward of the battalion position worked more than 1000 yards up the coast to the village of Garekoru on this day or the one following. *Ibid.*, and 7th Mar *R–2 Journal* disagree on the date, and 3/1 *Record of Events* makes no mention of the movement.

DEATH VALLEY was first entered by 7th Marines on D-plus 7, in an attempt to seize Five Sisters (right) from southwest.

from Company B, 1st Tank Battalion, advanced with the infantry. The Weapons Company contributed a fire feint against the objective of the day before: Walt Ridge and the lower end of the Horseshoe. Mortars placed so effective a smoke screen that the assault company advanced 250 yards over ground so rocky that it slowed the tanks to a crawl without encountering anything worse than "moderate" sniper fire.

In short, what should have been adequate conventional fire support for such an attack had been provided; yet at this point Company B began to receive machine-gun fire from its front and the ridge on the left,[69] which became progressively worse as the advance continued. A few minutes later, *1/7 Historical Report* records the time as 1630, the troops reached the mouth of a narrow draw, on the left lip of which elements of the 2d Battalion were in position.

---

[69] This was the northerly extension of Hill 200, called *"Nakayama"* by the Japanese. Although friendly troops occupied the crest, they were unable to get at the enemy still emplaced in strength in caves along the precipitous slope. The relative positions as of 24 Sept are clearly indicated on a Japanese sketch map captured subsequently. This route of attack remained in peril from the flank until the final wiping out of the holed-in enemy on 3 Oct.

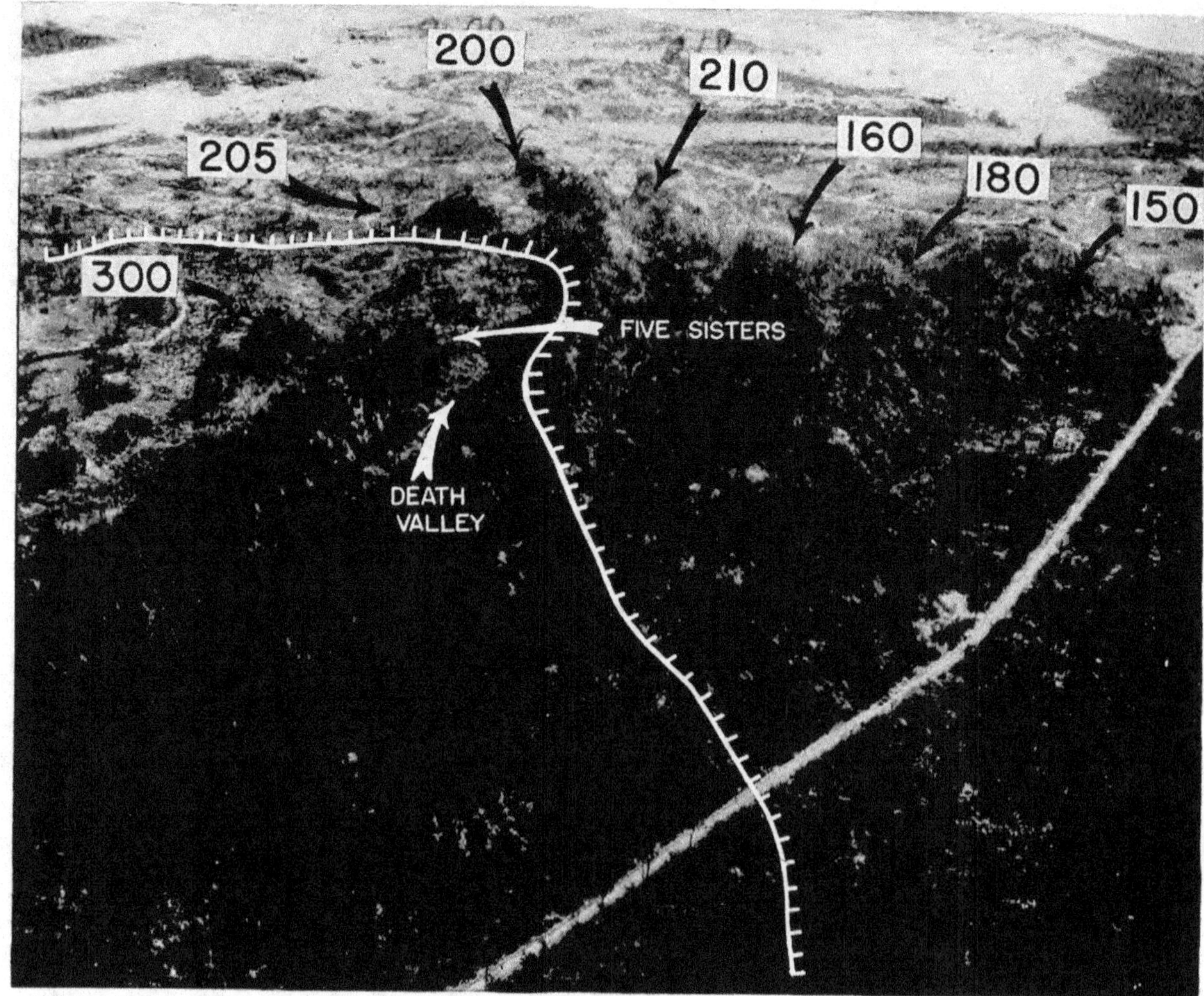

RIDGES WHERE 1st AND 7th MARINES FOUGHT D-plus 2—D-plus 7.   Approximate front held at end of phase sketched in.

The tanks fired pointblank into the cave openings which pocked the steep walls. A platoon of Company A moved up to reinforce Company B, now suffering severe casualties. But the assault had not moved far before discovering that the draw was walled in on the north by a high, steep coral formation. The depleted units found themselves in a topographical funnel, with sheer sides from which mutually supporting dug-in enemy positions covered the low ground with fire from every angle,[70] and which were impervious themselves to infantry assault.

Once more, an untenable position had nullified a day's substantial gains. At 1749 Company B commenced its tortuous withdrawal. The canyon was again blanketed with smoke, and the tanks and Company A closed up to help in covering the extrication. By 1830 what was left of the 1st Battalion, which had begun this action with only 60% effective strength, was safely back in its bivouac area behind the lines. Only there was not much left.

Again, the Japanese version of the action is terse and to the point: "This afternoon

---

[70] This declivity was christened "Death Valley", at that time (D-plus 7) and continued to be so designated throughout the operation. They could not know it then, of course, but the Marines had

penetrated within 100 yards of Colonel Nakagawa's CP, the nerve center of Japanese resistance and the last strong point on the entire island to be secured. See Chapters VII and VIII.

the enemy attempted to demolish our positions around *Kansokuyama* and *Higashiyama*. Attempt unsuccessful, and only a part of the enemy advanced to a hill west of *Kansokuyama*." [71] The last allusion is not wholly clear, as the Marines claimed no advance. It may possibly refer to the seizure the previous day of the northern extension of Hill 200 where it bounds the western mouth of Death Valley, news of which might have been delayed in reaching the Japanese command post.

The Japanese estimates of their own accomplishments up to this point contain a few interesting items, but perhaps are not much more out of line, at that, than Marine estimates of 6,880 Japanese killed. [72]

Enemy's total losses (except for those during landing operations):

    Casualties to personnel............at least over 5,000
    Tanks including alligators.................over 120
    Artillery guns ....approx. 15 [73]

Marine reports of the same date listed personnel casualties of 3,946 (including landing operations) and one 105mm howitzer lost to enemy action (three others lost when DUKW's carrying them sank en route back to ship); 19 out of 30 tanks were operative, only six being total losses during the entire period of 1st Tank Battalion's participation in the operation. [74]

Repeated Japanese use of the term "alligator" evidently stems from one of their early intelligence bulletins which identified and described the LVT(1) (now obsolete) which was designated by that title. It is not clear whether Nakagawa was lumping all tracked vehicles with the tanks, or including only LVT(A)'s where the comparison is reasonably apt, but his figure is rather startling in any case. No accurate reports are available regarding total amtrack losses up to this date, but only 22 LVT(A)'s were permanently knocked out during the entire operation. [75]

With this day's action, a definite phase of the Peleliu operation came to an end. The immovable object had stopped the irresistable force—for the time being. But there was another day coming up; many other days, in fact.

---

[71] *Tada Record*, 22Sept44.

[72] 1st MarDiv *SAR*, II, 7.

[73] *Tada Record*, 22Sept44.

[74] All figures from 1st MarDiv *SAR*, II, 7; Anx H; Anx J.

[75] *Boyer Monograph*.

CHAPTER V

"A Horrible Place"

Among the few civilian news correspondents who chose to share the fate of the Marines on shore was Robert ("Pepper") Martin, of *Time*, who furnished the following description of what it was like there:

> Peleliu is a horrible place. The heat is stifling and rain falls intermittently—the muggy rain that brings no relief, only greater misery. The coral rocks soak up the heat during the day and it is only slightly cooler at night. Marines are in the finest possible physical condition, but they wilted on Peleliu. By the fourth day there were as many casualties from heat prostration as from wounds.
>
> . . .
>
> Peleliu is incomparably worse than Guam in its bloodiness, terror, climate and the incomprehensible tenacity of the Japs. For sheer brutality and fatigue, I think it surpasses anything yet seen in the Pacific, certainly from the standpoint of numbers of troops involved and the time taken to make the island secure.[1]

On the second day, the temperature reached 105° in the shade—and there was very little shade in most places where the fighting was going on, and no breeze at all anywhere. It lingered around that level as the days dragged by (temperatures as high as 115° were noted). Water supply presented a serious problem from the outset. This had been anticipated (see Chapter II), and in actual fact the solution proved less difficult than expected; the engineers soon discovered that productive wells could be drilled almost anywhere on the compara-

tively low ground, and personnel semi-permanently stationed near the beach found that even shallow holes dug in the sand would yield an only mildly repulsive liquid which could be purified for drinking with halizone tablets. But it continued necessary to supply the assault troops by means of the scoured-out oil drums and 5-gallon field cans previously mentioned.

This presented a problem even in the case of troops operating on comparatively level and open ground. Once the fighting entered the ridges, terrain difficult merely to traverse without having to fight, the debility rate shot upward so alarmingly that an emergency call was sent to all the ships offshore to requisition every available salt tablet for issue to the 1st Marines.

The statement that heat prostrations equalled wound casualties is apt to be misleading.[2] Most of those evacuated were returned to duty after a day or two of rest and rehabilitation; hence, did not permanently impair the combat efficiency of their units. But such cases did occur in sufficient profusion as to add a severe strain on the already overburdened Medical Corps elements.

---

[1] *Time*, 16Oct44, 38.

[2] The literal truth of this statement is impossible of proof, as no adequate records are available. Many prostration cases were never evacuated beyond the bivouac areas of their own units, hence were not recorded at all.

BUNKER, OR PILLBOX, of the type that infested Peleliu's low ground.   After assault troops had overrun such positions, Japanese often sought to reoccupy these by infiltration.

A high initial casualty rate had been anticipated and provided for. Wounded were to be evacuated from the island with all facility to the first available transports which indicated, by flying signal flags, that they still had capacity for handling them. So efficiently did this system work on D-Day that the nearer ships had begun receiving casualties within an hour of the time the assault waves hit the beach.[3]

What had not been fully anticipated was the continuing high casualty rate and the slow inland progress of the attack. The original plan called for the attachment of Companies A, B and C of the 1st Medical Battalion to the 1st, 5th and 7th Marines respectively. But such were conditions ashore during the early stages that none of these units was able to set up adequate hospital facilities until D-plus 5.[4] In the meantime, their personnel was used to aid in collecting the wounded and as replacements

---

[3] As mentioned in Chap II, diversion of many LVT's to this humane work had much to do with the delay of later waves in getting across the reef.

[4] Company A ("A-Med") was the first Medical Battalion unit to set up, as such, near the White Beaches. Even after they were all established, the hospitals in the more forward positions were repeatedly harassed by infiltrating Japanese, and on several occasions special defensive and mopping-up details had to be provided for their protection. 1st Mar Div *SAR*, II, Anex D, 4.

CAMP RISES amid ruins at base of Umurbrogal. Administration Building, center, served as 1st Division CP, within easy rifle range of Japanese still in the ridges.

for Medical personnel organic to the regiments and battalions, who were themselves becoming casualties at an alarming rate; also the Shore Party Casualty Evacuation Sections which continued to handle evacuation and emergency treatment on the beaches under sustained heavy shell fire. As the limited capacities of the transports became filled, the problem became increasingly acute.

The number of Hospital Corpsmen assigned each infantry battalion had been increased from 32 to 40. Ninety-six stretcher bearers were assigned to each combat team, likewise an increase over the allowance used in the Cape Gloucester operation. These men were given instruction in first aid and actual practice in the handling of litter cases at the staging area. They provided a sizeable nucleus of trained personnel, but before the campaign had progressed far their numbers proved inadequate to their task.

To supplement them, Negro Marines from the 16th Field Depot were assigned as stretcher bearers and "were most proficient in this type of activity." [5]

Another element which contributed to making Peleliu a "horrible place" was the insect life, combating of which also came under the auspices of medical personnel.

As in all campaigns fought in the tropics, flies abounded; especially that odious creature known as the blowfly, which thrived and multiplied on dead bodies, waste food and rotting enemy supply dumps. Mosquitoes bred lustily in the extensive swamps which fringed much of the shore line and

---

[5] *Ibid*, 3. This report adds: "All unit commanders praised their efficiency, zeal and cheerfulness in performing their duties. They are considered ideal for this type of duty." During later phases of the operation when non-assault troops were used to contain the enemy (see Chap VI), many of these men served in the lines as volunteers.

GETTING THE WOUNDED OUT of the high ground was difficult, dangerous and painful.

were dotted liberally across the island's surface, areas far too extensive and too tangled to make effective control possible.

In this respect, Peleliu was at once worse and better than most similar combat areas. The mosquitoes proved a source of major discomfort to already miserable men, but they were entirely of the pest variety and included none of the sinister species which carry malaria and yellow fever. At its height, the fly population probably exceeded any encountered by U. S. troops until Okinawa, its growth not in the least retarded by inadequate troop sanitation, all but impossible of enforcement in terrain of this nature during a campaign so violent and so bloody. Yet the Peleliu operation was unique in that:

"For the first time in the history of military operations, there has been practically no illness that could be attributed to flies or mosquitoes." [6]

Elaborate steps were taken to exploit thoroughly the virtues of that newly developed insecticide, DDT, then still in the experimental stage. At Peleliu it received what must stand as its most extensive single testing as an implement of war. Mixed with Diesel oil, DDT was sprayed liberally on all insect breeding and feeding places. Combined with lighter kerosene, it was similarly

[6] *Ibid*, 4. This literal quotation has been widely challenged on the basis of the frequent incidence of dysentery, references to which occur in several unit reports.

applied to nets, jungle hammocks and, when such became available, both exteriors and interiors of tents and other personnel shelters.

The methods devised for handling it were varied. Perhaps the most novel, and ingenious, was the equipping of three 15-man sanitary squads with knapsack sprayers. These squads landed on D-Day, each attached to one combat team, and followed close in the wake of the assault units, spraying dead bodies, scattered food, straddle trenches, latrines and pools. A large power sprayer was mounted on a truck for more wholesale operations, and a special device was improvised which would enable planes to spread DDT in clouds across the whole area. Owing to combat conditions, however, the two last named appliances were unable to operate until D-plus 12.

That this work was successful on the most essential score is witnessed by the somewhat broad statement, quoted above, regarding insect-borne disease. But the technique had yet to be perfected in all details; for it was found that, while DDT was deadly to adult flies, it was almost wholly ineffective on their larvae. Consequently, during the earlier stages the flies bred more rapidly than they could be destroyed, reaching peak numbers about the second week in October. By then, the strenuous methods employed by truck, plane and ground crews began to bear fruit, and a gradual decline set in. The problem, obviously, was still far short of complete solution, but a far-reaching advance had been achieved.

SUPPORTING ARMS AND AUXILIARY ELEMENTS

During the early phases of the operation, the basic tactical unit on Peleliu was the regimental combat team. Thus, the story of most of the auxiliary elements is the story of the particular infantry regiment with which each was designated to operate.[7]

Subsequent alterations in the tactical situation led to some plain and fancy improvisation on the part of many elements, but this could not be foreseen during the first two weeks.

The Artillery Group, commanded by Colonel William H. Harrison, comprised the 11th Marines, the 1st Marine Division's organic regiment, plus two battalions of III Amphibious Corps artillery: the 3d 155mm Howitzer Battalion, and the 8th 155mm Gun Battalion. The original operation plan assigned the 1st Battalion, 11th Marines (75mm pack howitzers) to suport of the 1st Marines,[8] and the 2d Battalion (also 75's) to the 5th Marines, with the 3d and 4th Battalions (105mm howitzers), together with the Corps Artillery, in general support. Development of the situation soon caused assignment of 3/11 to support of the 7th Marines. Although all battalions reverted to regimental command shortly after landing, the three mentioned continued to operate primarily in immediate support of their designated combat teams throughout the crucial phases of the campaign.

Despite the difficult landing conditions, most of the division artillery was ashore and registered by dark on D-Day. Only 2/11, however, came in on schedule and took position according to plan. Because of the shallow penetration inland of the White Beaches, 1/11, after some delay, finally came in on Orange 1. The two 105mm howitzer battalions landed to discover that their designated firing positions were still in the hands of the Japanese. The 4th Battalion went into makeshift positions near the southern end of Orange 3, and the 3d Battalion finally managed to get one battery set up on Orange 1 to fire to the south.[9]

---

[7] The term "regimental combat team" (RCT) was official in the Marine Corps as well as the Army, but the common practice of referring to them by regimental designation still persisted at this period. For detail of task organization, see Appendix H.

[8] Owing to the tactical situation ashore on D-Day, 1/11 actually landed attached to the 7th Marines. This did not affect its basic mission, however: from the outset it acted in support of the 1st Marines and subsequently (see Chap VI) the 321st Infantry.

[9] Because of heavy enemy fire and their inability to find suitable operating positions, the two remaining batteries of the 3d Bn were ordered to reembark on LST's for the night. Three of the DUKW's

There was no room ashore for the Corps Artillery during the first day and night, but the 3d 155mm Howitzer Battalion began landing on D-plus 1 and had all batteries in position and firing the following day. This unit's initial assignment was a dual one: deep support missions to the north, and what often amounted to point-blank fire (starting at ranges of 200 yards) against enemy installations to the southward in support of the 7th Marines. With completion of that regiment's mission in this area (on D-plus 3), all batteries were faced northward and continued to supply fires in that direction as long as it was practicable to do so.

The 8th 155mm Gun Battalion landed on D-plus 2 and went into position near the 3d Battalion on the newly secured southern zone of Peleliu. This unit's initial mission was an unusual one: support of the assault on Angaur by the 81st Infantry Division (see Chapter VI). Its fire was not called for in this connection, however, and the battalion reverted to 1st Marine Division control on D-plus 4. In turn, it faced about to the northward and assumed its part in support of operations on Peleliu.

During the entire first two weeks, artillery was employed in the conventional manner prescribed by "The Book," and with such businesslike efficiency as to make its work appear unspectacular.[10] Preparatory, harassing and interdicting fires were furnished as the occasion demanded. Three aerial observers were maintained on station during daylight hours, and each battalion had its own forward observers with the combat team it had been assigned to suport. These called down special fire missions on designated targets as desired, and since all the artillery on the island remained under 11th Marines control following the initial landing, there was little difficulty in supplementing such missions with additional fire from the elements in general suport.

Perhaps the best example of this flexible system at work was provided on the morning of 28 September (D-plus 13) when all battalions, with the exception of 1/11, concentrated intensive fires on Ngesebus (see Chapter VI) in preparation for the shore-to-shore assault on that island, and continued throughout the day to furnish what amounted to a rolling barrage to the front after the infantry had landed.

However, with the capture of Ngesebus and the securing of all of northern Peleliu on the following day, Japanese resistance was constricted within a pocket too small to permit further employment of massed fires without danger to friendly troops, and the function of the artillery in any conventional sense came to an abrupt end. The two 75mm pack howitzer battalions (1/11 and 2/11) were ordered evacuated [11] with the first echelon of the division to leave Peleliu. A few of the 105's and 155's of the battalions remaining were adapted to some unique direct fire missions improvised for special occasions, and personnel not thus employed, reverting to the Marine's basic function as infantryman, manned a 1,000 yard sector of the containing lines west of the enemy pocket for more than two weeks until relieved by elements of the 81st Infantry Division on 16 October.

Participating elements of the 1st Tank Battalion were likewise attached initially to the combat teams: Company A (15 tanks) to the 1st Marines; Company B (9 tanks) to 5th Marines; Company C (6 tanks) to 7th Marines. Although all companies reverted

---

had been so seriously damaged during this double reef crossing that they sank upon reaching deep water, taking the guns and other gear with them. What remained of the two batteries came in again the following day, but another of the 105's was knocked out by enemy fire that evening. The eight guns remaining performed their mission satisfactorily from that point on. Wood, *MCS Monograph.*

[10] "The 11th Marines were employed in supporting the attack in accordance with the accepted doctrines and principles for the employment of field artillery; it was well handled and rendered timely and effective support throughout the normal attack phase of the operation." Wood, *op.cit.*

---

[11] By what proved great good fortune, a heavy storm prevented loading of these units' howitzers, several of which subsequently performed valuable service in a new role. See Chap VII.

"INFANTRYMAN'S ARTILLERY," the bazooka was the heaviest weapon portable to much of the high ground. Every opening and crevice might harbor stubborn Japanese.

to concentrate maximum tank strength where it was most urgently needed.

The shortage of tanks traced back to that perennial problem which had so complicated the final aspects of the planning phase for the operation: shortage of shipping. Only two LSD's were made available for lifting 1st Marine Division tanks to Peleliu. These provided space for only 30 machines, necessitating leaving 16 behind with the rear echelon.[13] This situation gave rise to some pointed criticism of the over-all planning which provided the same number of LSD's for the assault on Angaur, where much of the terrain made tank operations impossible and which was defended by approximately one-tenth the garrison strength of Peleliu.[14]

In no operation anywhere did tanks and infantry work in closer mutual support, more as a team. This happy cooperation had its genesis as far back as when the division was training in Australia following the Guadalcanal campaign, and tank elements began working on a semi-permanent basis with the assault units they would suport in combat, each becoming acquainted with the other's personnel and problems. This policy had paid dividends at Cape Gloucester and reached full fruition at Peleliu—and again, later, at Okinawa.

Peleliu was essentially an infantryman's battle, and the tanks went in with the infantrymen wherever it was physically possible to do so—and a great many places where few would have believed it possible. Their guns and armored protection staved off innumerable casualties, and the men on foot were grateful. Says the 1st Tank Battalion's report: "Throughout the operation our infantry rendered most faithful close-in protection to tanks regardless of frequently heavy casualties. This saved many badly needed tanks from destruction. Tank crews

to battalion control on D-plus 1, in general they continued to operate in close-up support of their designated units for the duration of their stay on Peleliu.

However, a greater flexibility was displayed in the employment of the tanks than was the case with perhaps any other reinforcing arm. This was necessitated by the fact that there were too few tanks to begin with, and during the early stages when the terrain was excellently adapted to tank operations, their services were at a premium. Furthermore, heavy enemy fire and the liberal distribution of mine fields called for some heroic maintenance measures to keep even those there in action.[12] Units and parts of units were constantly shifted from one regiment or battalion to another in order

---

[12] Forty major tank casualties were sustained by the battalion, of which only nine proved total losses. Of the 30 tanks landed, never were there less than 18 operational at one time, and the average was 20. 1st MarDiv *SAR*, Annex J, 10.

[13] The personnel to man these tanks were brought along, however, and proved valuable as replacements, battalion casualties running high during the opening phases of the operation. *Ibid*, 12.

[14] *Ibid*, 7, 8. See also Chapter VI, this monograph.

reciprocated by fighting tanks unbuttoned when necessitated by rain or other causes in an effort to match the indomitable spirit and sacrifice of the infantry." [15]

At the end of 16 days of heavy fighting, both men and machines of the 1st Tank Battalion were badly depleted and debilitated. Furthermore, the fighting had become localized in regions which did not appear practicable for armored operations on any extensive scale (see Chapter VII). For these reasons, the battalion was relieved as a unit by the 710th Tank Battalion, U. S. Army,[16] and departed the Peleliu scene with the first echelon on 1 October, a move which some believed at the time, and many more subsequently, to be premature.

Amphibian tractor personnel, like the artillerymen, became gradually pinched out as their primary missions were progressively accomplished. Their function as troop carriers on any major scale came to an end with the Ngesebus landing (see Chapter VI). With the construction of a pontoon causeway across the reef on the western shore [17] and the development of an LST beaching area on eastern Purple Beach, their usefulness as water-borne and reef-borne cargo carriers diminished. And on shore, once a satisfactory road network had been constructed, they were displaced by the more efficient DUKW's and conventional wheeled transport.[18] A few machines and their crews

---

[15] *Ibid*, 7.

[16] Company A, 710th Tank Battalion, arrived on Peleliu with RCT 321 (see Chap. VI) and was attached operationally to the 1st Tank Battalion. Following relief of the latter unit, Col Stuart and several of his staff remained on the island to assist and advise the 710th, whose previous training in tank-infantry tactics was considered rather sketchy.

[17] This causeway ran seaward from the lower end of Orange 3, and was in full operation by 21 Sept. 1st MarDiv *SAR*, II, 6.

[18] Although the 1st Motor Transport Bn brought in the trucks of only one company, many other units were permitted to land some of their organic vehicles. All these were supposed to be pooled under control of 1st MT Bn, but owing to the diverse interests involved, such control was difficult to exercise and the system proved less than satisfactory. *De Bell*.

PRIVATE FIRST CLASS JOHN D. NEW, Medal of Honor winner, unhesitatingly flung himself upon an enemy grenade to save the lives of two forward observers.

continued to be used for specialized missions, but the rest of the personnel reverted to the Marine's basic function of combat infantryman. Like the de-gunned artillerymen, they were used to man the containing lines during the closing phases of the operation.

So were most of the personnel from the Armored Amphibian Tractor Battalion. On land the LVT(A) was too vulnerable to substitute satisfactorily for the Sherman tank, though a number of them did pinch-hit in this capacity in emergencies. After their excellent performance during the first assault phase, they were employed mainly for reef patrol to the northward against Japanese counter-landings and for special direct fire missions against targets which could be reached only from offshore. The number and importance of these missions, too, gradually decreased.

The several assault elements of the 1st Engineer Battalion remained attached to their respective combat teams much longer:

Company A and H&S Company (less Heavy Equipment Section) to 1st Marines, Company B to 5th Marines, and Company C to 7th Marines. These units did not revert to parent control until D-plus 10, and even after that were held in close contact with the combat teams to be available for special missions on call.

Their functions were, to a greater or lesser degree, the conventional ones of combat engineers. Especially in the case of demolitions work, a major factor throughout the Peleliu campaign, they operated directly with, or even in advance of, the assault infantry, and heavy casualties were suffered among highly trained specialists. Infantry officers were unanimous in praising the work of the engineers in the highest terms, but the engineer command echelon took a somewhat more restrained view of the infantry's methods of employing them.[19]

Road building, airfield repair and maintenance, beach development, water supply, etc., were handled by the Engineer Group, consisting of Heavy Equipment Section of H&S Company, 1st Engineer Battalion, and the 33d and 73d Naval Construction Battalions.[20] All of these operations were carried through promptly and efficiently. Enemy shelling and delay in getting heavy equipment ashore slowed somewhat the repair of the airfield, but the target date was met. On the other hand, water supply proved a less serious problem than anticipated, and because of the short duration of the operation building construction was never more than a minor factor.

Existing roads built by the Japanese proved capable of handling the increased load temporarily following the landing, so priority was given to the construction of new roads to the additional unloading points so urgently needed. The first such artery ran to Scarlet Beach, following the securing of southern Peleliu. Then engineers worked closely behind the 5th Marines on that regiment's drive to Purple Beach on the eastern shore. The natural advantages existing at this spot were developed by the construction of LST landing ramps and pontoon causeways, and with completion of the vehiclular highway, Purple Beach became the most important unloading point on the island.

Other construction projects included an airfield perimeter road and the improvement and maintenance of trails to facilitate supply of advancing infantry units. A main road along the west coast, in southward extension of the existing West Road, was begun but, owing to higher priorities elsewhere, had not been completed at the time engineering functions passed to the Island Command.

The primary function of the 1st Pioneer Battalion was to provide the nucelus for the Division Shore Party. The comanding officer of the Pioneers became the Division Shore Party commander and was responsible for the organization and training of the Shore Party, and for effectively carrying out the functions of organizing the beaches, unloading supplies and equipment of the division, evacuating casualties from the beach, and defending his assigned beach area. The percentage of Shore Party casualties on Peleliu was nearly double that of any previous operation, and there were many other factors to retard unloading, including mined beaches. Yet "no noticeable decrease in the unloading rate occurred." [21]

The 1st Marine Division early recognized that Shore Party operations were a Division affair. Consequently regimental shore parties were attached to regiments for transportation to target only and passed to divi-

---

[19] "Infantry demolitionists were not employed as such, and engineer troops were called on for *all* (sic) major and minor demolition tasks." 1st MarDiv *SAR*, Annex I, 4.

[20] Approximately 550 men from the attached naval construction battalions ("Seabees") operated with the Shore Party during the first ten days on the beaches, after which time responsibility for unloading passed to garrison elements.

[21] 1st MarDiv *SAR*, II, Annex C, 3. One favorable factor was the short haul once ashore to effect distribution: "Amtracks and DUKW's could move directly from the water to the Regimental dumps in most cases." Ltr Col John Kaluf to CMC, 7Mar50, hereinafter cited as *Kaluf*.

sion control upon establishment of the Division Shore Party Commander ashore, though still in support of the regiment they had accompanied. Some 500 replacements for the division had been turned over to the shore party, and these were organized, for administrative purposes, into Companies D and E of the 1st Pioneer Battalion. These companies were relinquished to division commencing about D-plus 3, and the entire Pioneer Battalion was relieved on D-plus 10 by garrison unloading elements which had been functioning from the beginning as part of the Division Shore Party.

Upon being relieved, most of the battalion's heavy equipment was shipped back to the division's base camp in the Russell Islands. So was Company A, which had seen rigorous service in support of the battered 1st Marines and had been reattached to that unit upon its evacuation (see Chapter VI). Companies B and C were ordered up to front line defensive positions in the western ridge zone on 27 and 28 September, where they relieved units of the 7th Marines for further offensive operations. Here they remained in occupancy throughout the remainder of Marine participation in the Peleliu campaign until relieved by elements of the 321st Infantry on 17 October [22] (see Chapter VII).

---

[22] 1st MarDiv *SAR*, Annex C, 5.

SUMMARY

A solid week of hard fighting had achieved tactical results of great importance. As sumed up by General O. P. Smith:

Seven days after landing, all of the southern end of Peleliu was in our possession, as well as the high ground immediately dominating the airfield. All the beaches that were ever used were in use. There was room for the proper deploymnt of all the artillery, including the Corps Artillery. Unloading was unhampered except by the weather and hydrographic conditions. The airfield was available and essential base development work was underway.[23]

Furthermore, the Japanese potential for effective counteraction on a major scale had been destroyed with the elimination of an estimated two-thirds of effective enemy strength. This achievement had cost a total of 3,946 Marine casualties: [24] the virtual elimination of one infantry regiment, as such, and the serious depletion of two others.

In that all of Peleliu that possessed any strategic value had been secured, the commanding general's early prediction of quick conquest had not fallen so far short of literal realization.

Organized resistance, clearly, was far from at an end. But even at this stage, no one not gifted with clairvoyance would have predicted that two more months were destined to elapse before it would be.

---

[23] Smith, *op. cit.*
[24] 1st MarDiv *SAR*, II, 7.

CHAPTER VI

Third Operational Phase: D-plus 8-D-plus 15 (23–30 September)

The drive to seize northern Peleliu was motivated by two main tactical considerations. (1) It was desired to by-pass and isloate the pocket of resistance which had stopped both the 1st and 7th Marines, and thus gain less formidable approaches from which to assault it. (2) All of northern Peleliu should be seized in order that suitable ground be obtained from which to stage a shore-to-shore attack on the off-lying island of Ngesebus, whose unfinished fighter strip constituted one of the original objectives of the entire campaign.

And a third consideration had arisen suddenly to give point and urgency to the other two. At dawn on 23 September, the disconcerting discovery was made that, despite all vigilance by naval patrols, the Japanese were reinforcing their Peleliu garrison from the strongly held islands to the north.

Owing to darkness and distance, what actually happened is difficult to reconstruct. According to U. S. reports, several barges were detected approaching some distance north of Akarakoro point and promptly brought under fire by naval vessels and land based artillery, which claimed destruction of seven. At 0245 on the 24th another group was taken under fire; 8 were observed to explode, and 10 wrecks were observed on the reefs after daybreak. According to a captured survivor, the convoy included 13 barges and a motor sampan, all of which were believed destroyed. It was conceded that a few stragglers might have reached shore across the reef, though probably without equipment and certainly without supplies.[1]

The Japanese version, however, differs substantially. No mention is made of any losses during the first landing: "The advance detachment, part of the 2d Battalion, 15th Infantry Regiment, made a succesful landing at 0520, under command of 1st Lieutenant Murahori." As for early morning, 24 September: "The main body of the garrison reinforcement left Palau proper [Babelthuap] on the night of the 23d. Nine barges arrived safely, but six were shelled and burned while taking the wrong landing route. Most of the personnel of these were able to land by walking through the shallows."[2] So far as Colonel Nakagawa was concerned, the 2d Battalion, 15th Infantry, had arrived, accepting losses inevitable to

---

[1] CTF 32 *OpnRpt*, 57, 61. There were as many different versions of these incidents as there were echelons reporting. Because the action was essentially naval in nature, Adm Fort's version is accepted here.

[2] *Tada Record*, 23Sept, 24Sept44.

SOME DID NOT MAKE IT: LVT(A) patrol investigating Japanese landing craft.

such an operation; a fact partially borne out by subsequent intelligence which indicated that 300 to 600 men of that unit were fighting on Peleliu.[3]

To prevent any further recurrence of such incidents, LVT(A)'s were detailed to patrol the northern reefs, inaccessible to naval vessels, and air searches were instituted to find and destroy all possible barges and other craft in the Central Palaus. But the surest preventative, obviously, was to seize all of northern Peleliu itself and thus deny the enemy a practicable landing place, which would be one of the many benefits resulting from successful execution of the tactical plan activated by Field Order No. 3–44.

Ever since D-plus 2 the division commander had been facing a difficult tactical decision. From the time the Marines first came up against the ridges on the northwestern peninsula, it had been increasingly clear that the enemy's weakness lay to the west where 3/1, advancing against light resistance along the comparative flat ground, was obliged repeatedly to halt in order to maintain contact with the slow-moving elements in the ridges on its right. The question, then, was whether to exploit this soft spot and greatly extend the front in what might prove a highly complicated maneuver, or to keep hammering at the rugged high ground in the expectation that a decisive breakthrough here would end organized resistaance at a stroke. By the time it became unmistakably evident that no quick breakthrough was possible here, the combat efficiency of the 1st Marines had been so reduced by casualties and exhaustion that that regiment was in no condition to exploit anything.

---

[3] It is quite possible, of course, that Nakagawa deliberately concealed his losses when reporting in order to encourage General Inoue to send him further reinforcements by this means. See Appendix F.

Clearly, reinforcements were needed. The most readily available unit of appropriate strength was the Army's 321st Regimental Combat Team, a component of the 81st Infantry Division, which had completed its mission on nearby Angaur on 20 September. General Rupertus' reluctance to employ Army troops had become increasingly apparent from the outset,[4] and sentiment throughout the division would have preferred a Marine unit had any such been available. However, it happened that RCT 321 was especially well conditioned for that particular mission at this moment, for reasons which will require a brief digression.

THE 81st DIVISION ON ANGAUR[5]

The 81st Infantry Division, commanded at this time by Major General Paul J. Mueller, USA, had received exceptionally thorough training. Nicknamed the Wildcat Division and wearing a reproduction of this febrile feline as a shoulder patch, it had been in existence for two years and three months at the time it was committed in Operation STALEMATE II. During this period the Wildcats had participated in extensive maneuvers in Alabama and Tennessee, and in the California and Arizona deserts. Upon being designated for island operations in the Pacific, they had been taken in hand by the Amphibious Training Command, Pacific Fleet, the resultant specialized training being topped off by landing rehearsals in the Hawaiians and on Guadalcanal in preparation for the first specific combat mission assigned them.[6]

The STALEMATE II operations plan called for the entire 81st Division to remain afloat, prepared to act as corps reserve as might prove necessary, then to assault Angaur with two regimental combat teams (RCT's)[7] on F-Day, the date of which was to be determined by developments on Peleliu. Accordingly, the convoy carrying the Wildcats steamed northward on D-Day and staged a feint landing off the big central island of Babelthuap. When, on the afternoon of 16 September, it became apparent that the Marines had the current situation adequately in hand on Peleliu, F-Day was set for the following morning, and the ships moved to their assigned transport areas.

Angaur is a smaller and more compact island than Peleliu: roughly 5,000 yards long and nearly 4,000 yards maximum width, an estimated area of 2,000 acres. The terrain is generally more flat, hence not so naturally defensible. At the time of the attack the garrison had been reduced to one battalion (1st Battalion, 59th Infantry), plus

---

[4] "General Geiger and I proceeded to the Division CP. . . . During the course of the discussion General Geiger stated that he thought that the 1st Marines should be relieved and that he was considering moving an Army RCT over to replace them. At this, General Rupertus became greatly alarmed and requested that no such action be taken, stating that he was sure he could secure the island in another day or two. . . . The upshot of it was that General Geiger directed the Division Commander to prepare plans for embarkation of the 1st Marines for evacuation and . . . further stated that he would immediately take steps to attach an RCT of the 81st Division to the 1st Marine Division." Ltr Col W. F. Coleman to CMC, undated, hereinafter cited as *Coleman.*

[5] On many earlier maps the name of this island is spelled with the last two vowels transposed: "Anguar." Spelling of Pacific native place names is necessarily phonetic, and not necessarily uniform. That used herein appears in all reports of the 81st Infantry Division which, having taken the place by force of arms, certainly earned the right to designate what it should be called. It has come to the writer's attention that what some of the doughboys called it was not always printable.

[6] See Chapter II, this monograph. Except as otherwise cited, material used herein on this division derives from its own basic sources: the official 81st Infantry Division *Operation Report,* hereinafter cited as 81st *OpnRpt* (Phase I, Angaur; Phase II, Peleliu); and the unit history, *The 81st Wildcat Division in World War II* (Infantry Journal Press, 1948), hereinafter cited as 81st *Unit Hist.*

[7] In an effort to adhere to the terminology most common to its basic sources, this monograph will use the designation RCT in connection with the reinforced infantry regiments of the 81st Division, as it appeared generally in the reports of that unit. Most Marine reports, on the other hand, clung to the old regimental designations, as did references to such Marine units in 81st Division reports.

some miscellaneous reinforcing elements, with a total strength of approximately 1400.[8] To make things even more difficult for the Japanese commander, Major Goto, this small force had to be widely dispersed in order to man the prepared defenses covering Angaur's several excellent landing beaches: on the western, southern and southeastern shores.

None of these was chosen for the landing, however. Instead, RTC 321 came in on Blue Beach, about midway along the eastern shore, and RCT 322 on Red Beach, on the northeastern shore. That they encountered no organized beach defenses and only light, scattered small arms fire plus a few mortar shells testifies to the degree of tactical surprise achieved.

The landings received the full preparatory treatment: naval gunfire, LCI rocket barrages, and strafing and bombing from the air. To furnish additional support, the 8th 155mm gun Battalion was placed in position on southern Peleliu and registered on Angaur.[9] No fringing reef impeded the approach to either beach, so that the landing craft carrying the support waves were able to come all the way in right behind the amtracks—and even the bulky LST's not far behind them. But the Wildcats were not long in discovering why Major Goto had seen fit to concentrate his strongest beach defenses elsewhere. Driving inland from the beach, the advance elements of both RCT's found themselves snarled up in rain forest jungle so dense and tangled as to constitute a far more impenetrable barrier than anything the Japanese could have devised.

And there were Japanese posted in it; not in any great force, but sufficient to constitute an added nuisance and genuine menace. Snipers fought with their customary stubborness, concealed in the foliage of tropical trees and the luxuriant jungle beneath them. Machine guns stuttered from improvised bunkers which the enemy had always proved so skillful in constructing and camouflaging quickly in country like this. Between the jungle and the Japanese, the first hundred yards advance cost the Wildcats an hour of backbreaking labor and their first battle casualties of the war.

RCT 322 had the easier going that day, and the next, and by nightfall succeeded in occupying the northern half of the 0–2 phase line in its sector. The 321st dug in beyond the 0–1 line at several points, but a pocket of enemy riflemen still occupied the intervening space so that the two units, approximately 1,500 yards apart when they landed, were unable to tie in their flanks. Accordingly, each formed its own perimeter defense, anchored on the beach.

That night was a nerve-racking experience for all hands, as first nights in enemy territory invariably are. Like all troops green to combat, the men were "trigger happy": firing at moving shadows, unfamiliar sounds [10]—and rain forest jungle is always alive with movement and sound. Both RCT's withstood counterattacks during the hours of darkness, the most severe striking the southern flank of the 321st shortly before dawn: at about 0510 on 18 September. This sector was held by the 1st Battalion the brunt being borne by Company B which was eventually obliged to withdraw approximately 50 yards.

With the coming of daylight, rocket attacks and strafing interdicted further enemy effort in this area, and the Japanese withdrew. Because of casualties sustained, Company B was withdrawn to regimental reserve, replaced in position by Company G. But new counterattacks struck this zone at 0905 and 0935, necessitating a withdrawal of the extreme left to the southern edge of the landing beach in order to allow direct support planes on station to saturate the area with bombs, rockets and machine-gun fire. An LCI gunboat closed in to help, and

---

[8] The Japanese suffered total casualties: estimated 1,338 killed and 59 taken prisoner. 81st *OpnRpt*, I, 69.

[9] 1st MarDiv *SAR*, II, Annex H. However, 81st Division did not call on this fire support, and the battalion reverted to 1st MarDiv control on D-plus 4. *Harrison*.

[10] 81st *Unit Hist*, 78.

mortar concentrations contributed their share. No further Japanese offensive thrusts developed here.[11]

Division artillery emplaced on shore contributed to the three hour fire preparation for the second day's attack. RCT 322, advancing westward across the island's greatest breadth, soon reached the outer edge of the jumbled high ground which was to prove the most formidable terrain on the island. Stiffening resistance slowed down forward movement of the center and right, but the left of the regiment succeeded in driving a deep salient which included the large phosphate plant within easy striking distance of the western shore.

On the right of the 321st zone that regiment's 2d Battalion established physical contact with the 322d on the 0–2 line, isolating the enemy elements which had prevented this junction the previous day and leaving them to the mopping-up attentions of the Reconnaissance Troop. The center also made good progress westward and began a turning movement toward the south. The 1st Battalion, however, driving in a southwesterly direction on the heels of new counterattacks, soon came up against the first organized prepared positions yet encountered on Angaur.

A complicated system of mutually supporting pillboxes,[12] rifle pits and intercommunicating trenches, this strong point had been constructed for the principal purpose of preventing a landing on Green Beaches 1 and 2. Hence, its greatest strength faced seaward. But such advantages as accrued to the Wildcats from taking the position on the flank and rear were mitigated to a great extent by the fact that approaches from the north lay through the dense jungle, and from inland through a swamp as well. The task of bringing up tanks and other supporting weapons through this tangle was time-consuming and backbreaking.

The fighting on the third day (19 September) saw the island cut in two on a wide front, the enemy remnants isolated in three scattered pockets of resistance: the Green Beach positions and the southern tip, both in RCT 321's zone, and the much larger pocket embracing all the rugged high ground in the northwestern corner. With the liquidation of the two former the following morning, Angaur was declared secure at 1034 on 20 September.

This did not imply that all fighting was over on the island;[13] simply, that the enemy were now considered incapable of further offensive operations of a nature calculated to jeopardize the U. S. grip. A sizeable pocket of resistance remained, isolated in the northwest corner. The terrain here was generally reminiscent of Peleliu's ridges, but fortunately neither so extensive nor so formidable. This lay within the zone of action of RCT 322, which was destined to continue mopping up here until mid-October. But the area was too constricted for the employment of more than one regimental combat team, freeing the rest of the division for new missions.

RCT 323, which had been kept afloat as corps reserve, was now committed for the seizure of Ulithi, the mission for which it had been designated at the time of the final revision of the STALEMATE II plan. The regiment departed early the following day (21 September) and secured the target with-

---

[11] 81st *OpnRpt*, 33, 35.

[12] "Pillbox" has come to be a loosely used term. It is applied to the Green Beach installations by 81st *OpnRpt* and *Unit Hist*, but photographs and detailed descriptions in the latter would appear to indicate that most of these works were what strict definition would call "bunkers": i.e., field fortifications contrived from the natural materials at hand (coconut logs, sand, coral, etc.), without benefit of such man-made reinforcing as steel and/or concrete.

[13] Following the break of communications between Angaur and Peleliu, Col Nakagawa continued to report the heroic deeds of his compatriots on the former island long after the men of RCT 322 had been able to forego fighting in favor of baseball and the movies, and were speculating hopefully on the possibility of an imminent visit by the USO. By mid-November, however, he had the grace to concede that this was just "my guess." *Tada Record, passim.*

out opposition, but was wholly absent from the Palaus area for a month. (See Chapter VIII.)

That same afternoon the corps commander, taking matters into his own hands,[14] queried the commanding general, 81st Division, regarding the possibility of obtaining a regimental combat team for immediate employment on Peleliu. General Mueller replied promptly that the 321st would be available as soon as it could be reorganized, whereupon Generals Geiger and Julian Smith and Admiral Fort proceeded at once to his headquarters to expedite arrangements for the unit's transfer to the other island and operational attachment to the 1st Marine Division.

The three-day fight on Angaur had provided just what was necessary to convert a well trained, fundamentally sound regimental combat team into a genuine combat unit. The Wildcats of the 321st had met the enemy and overcome him. They had seen their own dead and wounded, and now that they knew what Japanese fire sounded like, their original trigger-happiness had notably diminished.

The strain had not been so long, nor the casualties so severe, as to impair the unit's strength, while morale grew through the regiment's newly confirmed confidence in itself and in its leaders. In short, officers and men were ready, willing and able.[15]

RCT 321 was commanded by Colonel Robert F. Dark, USA. At the time it was attached operationally to the 1st Marine Division on Peleliu it was composed of the following elements: [16]

---

[14] "The Corps Commander was disinclined to impose any particular line of action upon the [1st] Division Commander although more than once he had felt the urge to do so. Just what induced this reluctance on the part of General Rupertus was never understood by Corps." *Wachtler.*

[15] "These were now battle tested veterans, sure of their abilities and anxious to demonstrate the prowess of combat infantrymen to the Marines." 81st *Unit Hist*, 138.

[16] 81st *OpnRpt*, II, 13.

321st Infantry Regiment
Company A, 306th Engineer Combat Battalion plus Detachment, Headquarters and Service Company
Company A (plus Company D less two platoons) and Detachment of Headquarters, 306th Medical Battalion
Detachment, 781st Ordnance Light Maintenance Company
154th Engineer Combat Battalion (less one company) plus Detachment, Headquarters and Service Company, 1138th Engineer Combat Group
Detachment, 592d Joint Assault Signal Company
Detachment, 481st Amphibian Truck Company
Company B, 726th Amphibian Tractor Battalion, plus Detachment, Headquarters and Service Company
Company A, plus Provisional Mortar Platoon, 710th Tank Battalion
Detachment, Provisional Graves Registration Company
Detachment, Translator-Interpreter Team "A", Headquarters Company, Central Pacific Area.

Brigadier General Marcus B. Bell, USA, assistant division commander of the 81st, was designated liaison representative to Headquarters IIIAC to coordinate details of the movement from Angaur to Peleliu, supply, and attachment of RCT 321 to the 1st Marine Division, and took over in this capacity on 22 September (D-plus 7). On the same day Colonel Dark reported for instructions, first to commanding general, IIIAC, then to commanding general, 1st Marine Division. An advance echelon of the 321st was dispatched to Peleliu to complete arrangements, and the remainder of the unit began debarking on Orange Beach at 1200 the following day.

ISOLATION OF THE UMURBROGOL

Of the two tactical objectives previously listed, that of isolating the pocket of enemy resistance in the region labeled on the map "Umurbrogol Mountain" was assigned to RCT 321, with cooperation of the 7th Marines.

The latter regiment, it will be recalled, had relieved two battalions of the 1st Marines and held the line directly below the formidable terrain which had halted the northward drive through the ridges. It now became the task of the 1st and 2d Battalions

WILDCATS ARRIVE. Men of RCT 321 land on Peleliu via pontoon causeway built across the reef.

to contain the Japanese under pressure on the south (swamps contained them effectively on the east). The 3d Battalion was to extend the containing line northward along the ridges following behind and in contact with the Army regiment, whose advance lay through a zone of action extending from the western shore to the crest of the nearest high ground. That unit's mission was to by-pass the pocket for as far as might prove necessary, probing meanwhile for a soft spot in the enemy defenses which might be exploited successfully for a drive across the high ground to the eastern shore of the peninsula.

Immediately upon landing (on 23 September), the 2d Battalion, 321st Infantry, moved up the west shore and relieved the 1st Marines [17] in position at 1500. The 3d Battalion followed, prepared to act in immediate

support, while the 1st Battalion was designated as regimental reserve and bivouacked around the newly established command post.

Although patrols from 3/1 had already penetrated as far as the village of Garekoru, some 1,200 yards forward, Colonel Dark, quite understandably, wished a first-hand reconnaissance and immediately sent out a patrol from his own unit over the same ground. Like the previous patrols, this one encountered negligible resistance and sighted only a few indifferent defense works. This led to the belief that the enemy had withdrawn; so upon receipt of Colonel Dark's report, the division command ordered a general advance in an effort to reach the 0–4 line, a short distance beyond Garekoru, before nightfall.

Now the inadequacy of this and previous reports became quickly apparent. The pa-

---

[17] 81st *OpnRpt*, II, 15, reports erroneously that 2/321 took over positions occupied by the "entire First Marine Regiment." It is true that this was known as the 1st Marines sector, but at this time

it was held by only the remains of the battered 3d Battalion, the rest of the regiment having been relieved three days earlier. 1st MarDiv *SAR*, II, 7.

trols had all operated close to the shore, west of a low coral ridge which partially masked their movements from observation by the enemy in the main ridge system. The company moving over the same ground now advanced a hundred yards with no more difficulty than had the patrols. But the elements on the open flat to the right of the road were in plain view of the Japanese observation posts and were promptly pinned down by heavy plunging fire from the high ground. By then the hour was past 1730, so the left was withdrawn to rectify the line and defenses for the night were prepared.

The following morning (24 September) 2/321 moved out again in the wake of an hour of naval and air preparation and 15 minutes of intensive artillery fire. This time the battalion formed with its main strength in partial defilade to the west of the road where excellent progress was possible. However, elements on top of the ridge encountered such heavy fire that the 3d Battalion, 7th Marines, was unable to detect any appreciable advance as late as 0950,[18] hence could not advance itself.

The tactical situation at this stage and the developments which followed are described in the words of the then commanding officer, 3d Battalion, 7th Marines:

The ridge in question parallels the West Road and completely dominates the road at that point, being only approximately 50 yards away. For this reason, the ridge was made inclusive to the 321st's zone of action as further evidence of the recognition that it had to be controlled to insure the safety of the movement northward along the road. It was perfectly obvious to anyone who stood on that ridge that its control by the Japs would have been disastrous to the whole effort. We had been ordered to maintain contact with them (RCT 321) by trailing their right flank in column along the crest of the ridge from the point where we had earlier tied in with 3/1. They moved forward along the ridge for a few yards until they encountered the first enemy positions, then gave it up as a bad idea, and bore sharply to their left front to the coastal road below.[19]

This withdrawal from the high ground created a gap on the right of RCT 321, and complaint by that unit caused one platoon of Company K to be committed down the slope on the left of 3/7. A second platoon was similarly committed at 1007 upon receipt of an order from commanding officer, 7th Marines, for the 3d Battalion to "extend their left flank to relieve and assist 321st."[20]

Meanwhile, Company G, leading the advance of 2/321, moved rapidly along the shore. The coastal flat widened gradually as the troops moved northward, scrub jungle giving way to coconut groves and the high ground receding to the eastward. At about 1200 the forward elements came to a point, some 300 yards short of Garekoru village, where a well defined trail angled eastward from the main road across a patch of swamp into the ridges. The tactical potentialities of this were quickly recognized and steps taken to seize it.

The junction was defended by a few prepared positions, but these proved to be held in no great strength. In overcoming them, the Wildcats captured one antitank gun, three machine guns, and a partially emplaced naval gun. Leaving more rearward elements to exploit this acquisition, Company G rolled on through Garekoru and reached the 0–4 line at 1535.[21] This being the objective ordered for that day, the advance halted here and commenced preparing positions to secure what would be the regiment's left flank when the planned movement had been completed.

This rapid pace had placed the 2d Battalion well ahead of 3/7. The 3d Battalion, 321st, followed in column, and it was this unit with which Company K, 7th Marines, tied-in by sending two platoons down from the high ground to the open area on the right

---

the 321st Infantry later pulled its right flank off the ridge to the coastal road where the going was easier."

[20] 7th Mar, *R–2 Journal*, Sheet #80. The order quoted originated with division operations officer (D–3) and was transmitted to the battalion by regimental executive officer.

[21] 81st *OpnRpt*, II, 17.

---

[18] 7th Mar *R–2 Journal*, Sheet #80.

[19] *Hurst*, 4, 5. 3/7 *WD*, 11, describes this incident as follows: "In order to speed up the advance

of the road,[22] sustaining several casualties in the process. What happened next, in accordance with the original tactical plan, is described in 81stDiv *OpnRep.*:

> The 3d Bn 321 Inf advanced along the left of the road. The movement was partially defiladed by the low-lying ridge which paralleled West Road. Its leading elements soon outdistanced those of the Marine battalion on the right and began probing the ridge[23] to the east to find a weakly defended route over which an advance could be made to outflank from the north enemy forces in the Umurbrogol Mt. area. This effort brought troops out into the open ground where they too suffered the well aimed fire from the enemy held ridge.[24]

Failure of the Wildcats to regain, the vacated positions on the ridge crest, along which it was 3/7's mission to follow them, was causing Major Hurst increasing concern for the success of the northward movement, since this high ground dominated the narrow line of communication.[25] Accordingly, he committed Company I on the left of Company K, and in a dispatch logged at 1310 informed his regimental commander: "... 3 Bn. 321 has withdrawn from the hills toward the road leaving a gap on the left flank of 3/7 undefended. The Japs reoccupied the hills and 3/7 is fighting to retake them." [26]

The commanding officer of Company I was killed in the ensuing action, which led to a certain amount of bitterness among the officers and men of the 3d Battalion, who, not fully understanding the 321st's mission, expected that unit to hold the ground, making this particular fight unnecessary.

Contact was reported reestablished at 1450, with the left of Company I echeloned down from the high ground to within 30 yards of the West Road. This position was reported as unchanged at 1620,[27] but a subsequent attack by 3/321 gained a foothold on the ridge farther to the north, and this time the Wildcats stayed there. (See below.) However, the 3d Battalion, 7th Marines, dug in that night on a front of 400 yards, facing eastward toward the heart of enemy pocket with the left flank deeply refused. Company I, which had borne the brunt of the day's fighting, was relieved on the left by Company L and passed into battalion reserve.[28]

If operations in this area proved somewhat confused and indecisive, the achievements of the 2d Battalion, 321st, appeared very promising indeed. With Company G at work consolidating defensive positions along the 0–4 line, a strong combat patrol supported by both Army and Marine tanks and Navy LVT-mounted flame-throwers was dispatched forward along the coastal flat to ascertain the strength and disposition of enemy defenses in that area. This force proceeded some 2,000 yards farther northward, to within sight of the large Japanese radio station, without encountering any notable opposition. A number of pillboxes, caves, and

---

[22] *Ibid.*, 17.

[23] The high ground in this area was not a well defined ridge system, although reports of all participating units so refer to it. Rather it resembles a natural coral formation pushed up from the ocean floor: a jagged jumble of unexpected heights and depressions extremely difficult to traverse, let alone assault.

[24] *Ibid.*

[25] "It was certainly not our mission to maintain the contact on the flat coastal road and turn the ridge over to the Japs. ... I watched the young major commanding make several gallant efforts to get his men back on the crest before finally becoming convinced that if friendly troops were going to control the ridge that night it would have to be our Company I." *Hurst.*

[26] 7th Mar *R–2 Journal*, Sheet #83. Also 3/7 *WD*, 11. No mention of this incident is made at division level in the reports of either 81st Div or 1st MarDiv.

[27] 7th Mar *R–2 Journal*, Sheet #86. Same entry mentions impending attack by 321st.

[28] 3/7 *WD*, 11, is authority for 400-yard front. There are many discrepancies in reports of situation evening of the 24th. 321st uses sketch map not easily oriented with Marine operations maps. This shows a continuous line along ridges, though other allusions indicate many elements still on road, and subsequent Marine overlays show no troops in positions indicated. Mar *R–2 Journal*, Sheet #87, carries entry dated 2025 that two Army platoons were on 3/7 left but that there was a gap of 100–150 yards between them and rest of their line. This writer has been unable to locate any 1st MarDiv overlays for this period.

entrenchments were observed, however, and their locations noted down for future reference.[29] This success strengthened the growing conviction that the enemy were determined to concentrate their strength in the high ground and would be unlikely to interfere seriously with troop movements elsewhere.

While this reconnaissance was taking place, Company E turned eastward along the trail which had been discovered earlier in the afternoon, now named in honor of the regiment: 321st Infantry Trail. This traversed a wide stretch of swampy land before beginning the climb of the ubiquitous coral

ridges. It was narrow and primitive in spots, but appeared readily convertible into a practicable communications route, which any sustained drive in this direction would sorely need.

Just as the coastal flat widened in this region, so did the ridge system become narrower and somewhat lower. The elevation which most directly dominated the trail, Hill 100, marked the northern extremity of that weird formation known as Umurbrogol Mountain, in which it was becoming increasingly evident that the main center of Japanese resistance was located. The tactical importance of Hill 100 was immediately apparent, and Company E, attacking with great determination, succeeded in seizing it

---

[29] 81st *OpnRpt*, II, 17.

before nightfall. Bulldozers of Company A, 306 Engineer (C) Battalion, commenced work on the 321st Infantry Trail at once.

Company I, foremost element of the 3d Battalion, attacked in conjunction with Company E, gained a foothold on the western rim of the ridge running south from Hill 100, and tied in with the latter unit's right. In the meanwhile, Company F had moved into position between Company E and Company G, thus completing the defense perimeter along the northern flank.

Thus, the tactical picture presented on the evening of 24 September was radically different from that of the morning. What had begun as a column advancing northward over the low ground was now a line facing eastward along the ridges, except for Company G anchored on the shore on the extreme left, and Company F whose front curved up from the flat to tie in with Company E on Hill 100.

The Japanese finally pulled themselves together and at about 1700 mounted a strong counterattack against the left (northern) flank of the new line. Advance elements of Companies G and F were forced back some 200 yards. However, the enemy failed to break through at any point, and the situation was soon rectified.[30] A second counterattack, discovered in process of organization at 1813, was dealt with effectively by artillery concentrations and never materialized. This abortive gesture signalized the final success of the day's operations.

The following day (25 September) saw some hard but inconclusive fighting on the part of RCT 321. To make all possible Army troops available to exploit the previous day's gains, 3/7 moved Company I from battalion reserve up on the left of Company L, extending the battalion's ridge-holding line an additional 250 yards northward. And the 1st Battalion, 7th Marines, was brought up the West Road for the purpose of supporting the eastward drive of 3/321, then to drive southward when opportunity afforded.[31]

On top of Hill 100, Company E, 321st Infantry, held what was obviously a key position. This assured control of that vital artery, the 321st Infantry Trail, and also looked down on the East Road which here passed through a saddle bounded on the east by a slightly higher and more formidable eminance detached from the main ridge system and known as Hill B. Because this dominated the road and abutted the swamp-lined eastern shore, its capture was clearly necessary if the peninsula were to be cut in two at this point.

Company E, moving out in assault, reached the East Road by 1030 against moderate resistance by rifle and machine-gun fire. However, it was now apparent that the enemy held Hill B in force, with well prepared defenses, and the company halted until such time as the 3d Battalion should arrive in position to make a coordinated assault possible.

But the 3d Battalion, attacking farther to the south, was getting nowhere against a combination of outlandish terrain and powerful Japanese resistance.

Strong enemy fire was encountered from a series of pillboxes and emplacements built on promontories and protected by steep walls and sheer cliffs. In an attempt to outflank these defenses, a gap developed between Co. I and Co. L which was filled later in the afternoon by Co. G. Gains for the day were unappreciable.[32]

---

[30] Available sources leave some doubt as to the exact situation on the left during the night of the 24th. 81st *OpnRpt* is authority for the 200-yard withdrawal, and adds: "The ground was promptly retaken." A message from CO 321 to CG, logged at 1700, states: "We have been driven back 50 yards. We have consolidated our positions." 7th Mar *R–2 Journal*, Sheet #86. Positions of 321st reported the following morning show a sizeable retrogression on the left (*Ibid*, Sheet #88) as compared to those defined the previous afternoon (1st MarDiv *D–3 Journal*, entry logged at 1630, 24 Sep).

[31] 1/7 *HistRpt*.

[32] 81st *OpnRpt*, II, 21. As nearly as it is possible to orient this action on the later sketch map, this area would appear to be that including what were subsequently known as Wattie Ridge and Baldy Ridge, where the 5th Marines came upon the bodies of a missing Wildcat patrol. See Chap. VII, footnote p. 160.

In contrast to the frustration encountered by the attempted break-through, developments to the northward were most encouraging. First thing in the morning, a strong combat patrol consisting of infantry, tanks and LVT flame-throwers was sent up the West Road to destroy the installations discovered by the reconnaissance of the previous day. This unit advanced 1,200 yards into what was technically enemy territory, wiping out four pillboxes and two supply dumps, but killing only 30 Japanese in the process. The weak nature of this resistance provided further substantiating evidence regarding the Japanese concentrations and intentions, and at 1530 advance elements of the 5th Marines began passing through the 321st's Garekoru positions in the initial step of the northward offensive, to be treated in detail in the next subchapter.

This new advance in force complicated a problem which had been difficult enough already. The West Road was now serving as the only and ever-lengthening supply and evacuation route for two regiments and part of another. Although this was the best thoroughfare found on Peleliu, it had been narrow to begin with and had been roughly handled by shell fire and a volume of traffic such as it had not been designed to accommodate. Again, the Army combat engineers of the 306th Battalion performed prodigies of widening, grading and surfacing, often obliged to resort to armored bulldozers on stretches still under fire from unsecured sections of the ridge. So the road sufficed; it had to.

Once off the highway and the 321st Infantry Trail, however, supply conditions were indescribable. Everything had to be manhandled from rock to rock, up and down the precipitous slopes: food and amunition up, the wounded down, often to their acute misery. It was this situation nearly as much as the tenacious resistance of the Japanese which so thoroughly bogged down the offensive of the 3d Battalion Wildcats.

The tempo of the fighting mounted on 26 September to what was to prove a successful crescendo, but the day began as inauspiciously as had the previous one.

Some new troop dispositions were made preparatory to launching the attack. The 2d Battalion, 7th Marines, was directed to extend its line to take over the sector held by Company K on the right of the 3d Battalion, K to move around the battalion's left, relieving the Army unit tying in there for the assault. Company B, 7th Marines, took over the sector of L/321 for the same purpose, while the rest of 1/7 prepared to advance in immediate suport of the offensive.

The plan of RCT 321 called for the 3d Battalion to attack on a narrower front, supported by fire from the 2d Battalion from its positions on and around Hill 100, still with the object of breaking through to the East Road in order to assault Hill B from the south and west. Jumping off at 0700, the advance elements gained a foothold on the first ridge, but progress was described as "slow and costly".[33] The 1st Battalion, 7th Marines, was to follow the advance at 200 yards,[34] prepared to exploit any breakthrough the Wildcats might achieve.

There was none. Company I, on the left, was stopped by rifle and automatic weapons fire. Company L, coming up on the right, was pinned down in turn by a concentration of mortar shells and eventually withdrew to allow its own mortars to bear. At 1244, after some hours of this fruitless struggle, a change of procedure was obviously in order.[35]

RCT 321 was now satisfied that there were no soft spots south of Hill 100, and plans were hurridely revised to effect a breakthrough at this point. The first attempt had failed, so: "When it became apparent that the 3d Bn would be unable to reach

---

[33] *Ibid.*, 23.

[34] Because of the inability of 3/321 to advance that far, 1/7 was not committed in this action and put in its time reconnoitering and filling gaps in the line caused by the alternate advance and recession of elements of 3/321. 1/7 *HistRpt. Gormley.*

[35] Dispatch CO 1/7, 7th Mar *R-2 Journal*, Sheet #98.

Hill B, the 2d Battalion was assigned the mission of seizing it." [36]

The change in plan was not effected quite that simply, however. To make 2/321 available for this new mission, the RCT's 1st Battalion, hitherto in reserve near the regimental command post, was brought forward to take over the extreme left flank in case the Japanese should take advantage of the action across the peninsula to stage a counter-attack of their own in this zone. And to support the 2d Battalion's attack from the west and south, a strong combat patrol was sent out by a round-about route in order to come down on Hill B from the north.

This interesting unit, designated the Neal Task Force,[37] consisted of seven medium tanks, six LVT's, one LVT flame-thrower, and 45 riflemen (from Company F). It moved northward on the West Road to Road Junction 15, where the disputed East Road, after angling across the low land above the central (Kamilianlul) ridge system, joined the main road a short distance below the radio station. This region had already been secured by the previously mentioned advance of the 5th Marines (dealt with in detail in next sub-chapter). The Neal Force reached the junction without incident, turned south on the East Road, and at 1500 had approached within 150 yards of its objective before the first feeble attempt was made to stop it: by a group of 15 Japanese, all of whom were killed.

Heavy artillery and mortar fires were massed on the objective preparatory to the final assault, and white phosphorus shells blanketed Hill B with smoke. The concerted attack jumped off at 1600. Resistance was stubborn on every front, but the advance was sustained and inexorable. At 1647 elements of Companies E and F reached the summit and set about the dirty job of making it tenable. As usual, the Jap-

anese defenders fought to the death,[38] but 20 Korean laborers were only too happy to surrender when given the opportunity.

By nightfall the positions on and around Hill B had been thoroughly consolidated. This achievement of the desired break-through greatly simplified the over-all tactical problem. The enemy pocket at the base of the peninsula was isolated, though its points of strongest resistance had yet to be defined. What lay in the region north of the break-through, the 5th Marines was then in the process of finding out. Orders were issued to RCT 321 to begin expanding its grip in both directions the following morning: one component pushing southward to compress the Umurbrogol Pocket, the other moving northward to cooperate with the 5th Marines. Study of the operations of these two units will be dealt with in detail in the second sub-chapter following.

DRIVE TO THE NORTHWARD

As has been noted briefly, the 5th Marines passed through the Garekoru lines of RCT 321 on the afternoon of D-plus 10 (25 September) and attacked toward the tip of the northwestern peninsula. Thus simply stated, this might appear a simple troop movement; actually, the promp assembly and displacement of this regiment was a remarkable and noteworthy accomplishment.[39]

---

[38] 81st *OpnRpt*, II, 25, states succinctly and without equivocation: "All Japanese defenders were killed." Yet when elements of 1/7 took over the position three days later, they were obliged to call in a special demolitions team to dispose of numerous lurking snipers who had deliberately allowed themselves to be overrun. 7th Mar *R-2 Journal*, Sheets #113, 115; 1/7 *Hist Rep*, entry dated 30 September. The Wildcats were to have similar experience in taking over positions from the Marines. See second sub-chapter following.

[39] Col Nakagawa did not appear greatly impressed by these goings on. Of RCT 321's struggle for Hill B, he reported: "On *Suifuzan* (a term evidently designating all of the Umurbrogol north of the Horseshoe) a small battle took place." Of the 5th Marines' advance: "Two infantry com-

---

[36] 81st *OpnRpt*, II, 23.

[37] So named for the group's commanding officer: Captain (later Major) George C. Neal. 81st *Unit History*.

DRIVE TO THE NORTH: 5th Marines move up West Road.

At the time the new plan was determined upon, the several elements of the 5th Marines were widely deployed across the region of eastern Peleliu which they had secured in performing their initial mission and organized against counterlandings: 1st Battalion in the Ngardololok RDF area, 3d Battalion (less Company L which was still tied-in with the 7th Marines east of the ridges) along Purple Beach, and 2d Battalion on the islands above the northeastern peninsula. The division order [40] covering the movement was not issued until 1030, the regimental order at 1100, yet so rapidly and smoothly was the new deployment effected that the 1st Battalion was in position to launch its attack at 1300. The 3d Battalion followed closely, and even the 2d Battalion, obliged to wade several hundred

panies (*sic*), tanks and alligators advanced to the northern area along the seaside road. *Tada Record,* 25Sept44.

[40] Field Order No. 3a–44.

yards of reef from the islands to Ngardololok, was tied-in with the rest of the regiment shortly after dark.

Resistance was stubborn where encountered, but it was discontinuous. Furthermore, the widening palm-grown flat now being traversed was admirably suited to the employment of tanks and LVT flame-throwers. Thus, the advance moved so swiftly that the forward elements had secured the northern Japanese radio station by dusk. The 2d Battalion, bringing up the rear, reached a point approximately 600 yards north of Garekoru. Colonel Harris wished neither to over-extend his lines nor to relinquish the afternoon's gains; therefore, he boldly broke off contact with the 321st and set up his own perimeter defense for the night, with both flanks resting on the beach.

The terrain in this region was comparatively low, forming a broad saddle that separated the central and northern ridge systems.[41] The 3d Battalion, occupying the center of the regiment's present formation, pushed inland against minor resistance and set up its perimeter athwart the East Road [42] which here angled across the saddle to join the main West Road at Road Junction 15, previously mentioned in connection with the 321st's operations of the following day. Thus, the 5th Marines' beachhead achieved considerable depth and tactical importance.

The night was quiet for all elements save the 1st Battalion. This unit's forward position lay only 300 yards from commanding high ground from which two enemy 70mm guns and numerous mortars poured in heavy harassing fire.[43] It had also come within range of mortars and 37mm guns mounted in caves on off-lying Ngesebus Island which exacted further toll. Small-arms fire converged upon the position from three sides, under cover of which three strong counterattacks were launched. These were beaten off without loss of ground, and at 0200 one platoon of Company C staged a night coun-

terattack of its own and destroyed two especially troublesome Japanese machine guns.

The attack was resumed by the center at 0600 the following morning, the 2d Battalion holding fast on the right. By 0830 the 3d Battalion had secured the high ground to its front, an elevation known as Hill 80, and reached the peninsula's eastern shore just beyond it, here indented by a deep swamp. Thus the northern tip of Peleliu was sealed off on the same day (D-plus 11—26 September) that the capture of Hill B by the 321st isolated the Umurbrogol Pocket.

The 1st Battalion, attacking at 0900, ran into a situation considerably tougher. To understand what happened, some description of this terrain is necessary.

Peleliu's northernmost hill system, Amiangal "Mountain," is roughly L-shaped. Begining at the shore just below Akarakoro Point, the island's northern tip, a series of narrow ridges follows the axis of the peninsula to the southwest for a distance of nearly 1,000 yards. Here it changes direction at nearly right angles and runs crosswise nearly the entire width of the peninsula in an uncharacteristic formation to which the 321st Infantry, on which the final mopping-up devolved, applied the apt descriptive name, "Hill Row." This consisted of a line of four high, steep-sided, semiseparated knobs, called for convenience Hills 1, 2, 3 and Radar Hill,[44] the last named rising sheer and round-topped from the low flat close to the eastern shore. Highest of the four, wholly detached, and site of the enemy's radar installations, it constituted one of the most prominent features of the Peleliu profile as viewed from the sea.

Driving northward, Boyd's battalion very soon came under heavy fire from enemy positions on, and in, Hill 1: 75mm and 37mm fire, as well as mortars and automatic weapons. Although tanks and LVT flame-

---

[41] The high ground of Peleliu's northwestern peninsula broke down conveniently into three components, each labeled on the map by its native name. Southernmost and most formidable was Umurbrogol Mountain ("mountain" is a misnomer in each case). Adjoining this about midway along the peninsula was Kamilianlul Mountain, a continuation of the same formation, but lower, narrower, and less rugged. The broad saddle separated this from Amiangal Mountain, the northernmost formation.

[42] Testimony to the swiftness and efficiency of the regiment's advance was furnished by a group of Japanese who strolled noisily down the road into the midst of a group of Marines without suspecting their presence. *Crown.*

[43] There was serious concern over the feasibility of holding the exposed forward position under such a volume of fire. In an effort to reduce it, Marine artillery employed a somewhat unusual technique. "One battery fired on map or photo selected positions from which enemy fire could be originating. If reduced enemy fire resulted, continuous fire, at a slow, irregular rate, was employed on the target throughout the night. By repeating the process, and by utilizing the fire power of all field artillery battalions except 1/11, enemy fire was greatly reduced and the forward positions maintained." Ltr Maj D. R. Griffin to CMC, 13Mar50.

[44] Nomenclature was not uniform at the time, and most contemporary reports identify these hills by the target squares in which they are located: #1—156 H & I; #2—156 N; #3—156 T; Radar Hill—156 Y.

throwers were available, that stubborn, 140-foot, cave-pocked elevation refused to succumb to frontal assault, and forward movement came to a halt.

On the right (east) Company B enjoyed better success against Hill 2, securing this less formidable height by 1400. This provided a position on the flank of Hill 1. Before the day was over, the Marines had succeeded in knocking out one 75mm and two 37mm guns, but Company C, which had got part way onto Hill 1 before dusk, had to be withdrawn in order to set up tenable night defensive positions.

While this fighting was going on, the 2d Battalion had remained uncommitted on the southern flank of the perimeter throughout the morning and early afternoon. At 1600, with the advance otherwise stymied, it was ordered forward, passed through the left of the 1st Battalion, bypassed Hill 1 on the west, and continued northward. The going was not easy. There were strong emplacements on the low ground, and plunging fire lashed at the troops from the ridge line to their right, a formation that angled closer and closer to the shore as the advance progressed. And as though they did not have enough troubles already, they came under increasing fire from Ngesebus, on their left. Concentrations of artillery fire proved effective in reducing the volume of this, but the battalion was in far from a happy state.

The regimental front as it was defined that night presents an odd appearance on the situation overlay. Owing to its forward progress and the intervention of that pestiferous Hill 1, the 2d Battalion was out of contact with the 1st, and Major Gayle set up a little perimeter of his own with both flanks on the beach. The 1st Battalion lay partly athwart Hill Row and was tied-in with the 3d Battalion on the right, but had only a refused flank to the northward where its left looped around the summit of Hill 2. The situation appeared somewhat less than reassuring, and the 3d Battalion, posting Company I to hold the high ground captured early in the morning, was assembled

in position to move to the support of either or both of the other battalions.

What was not fully appreciated at the outset was that these ridges and hills of northern Peleliu contained some of the most elaborate caves on the entire island. Not that there were not hints aplenty: as the 5th Marines *Regimental Narrative* puts it, in a tone of some frustration, ". . . tank guns, firing point-blank directly into caves and tunnels, did not even *temporarily* cause the enemy therein to cease fire." Repeatedly in daily entries in various unit reports certain caves are listed as having been reduced, only to have those identical caves reappear in subsequent days' entries as having to be reduced all over again. Indeed, one of these frequently "reduced" caves was not finally liquidated until the following February: by the Island Command, months after the assault troops had departed Peleliu. (See Appendix D.)

The truth, as subsequently discovered, was that what were taken to be individual caves more frequently than not were multiple entrances leading to tortuous passageways within a single enormous tunnel system where the occupants could find any number of safe refuges. For this zone had been designated originally for defense by Japanese naval contingents, which included the 214th Naval Construction Battalion, made up of miners and mining engineers who had given it the full treatment. Wherever practicable, caves were prepared not only with numerous mouths but on two or more staggered levels. Thus, Marines victoriously ensconced on a hard-won summit would often be irritated by the smell of cooking rice and fish wafted up to their nostrils from three or even four layers of Japanese resting comfortably underneath them and ready to sally forth in a counterattack when someone among them thought that might be a good idea. Here was a "defense in depth" in a more literal sense than that term is usually applied.

However, the hill system in this region lacked the lateral depth which was to make

the Umurbrogol Pocket, with its multiple mutually supporting positions, so appalling. Furthermore, some of the defenders here appeared to lack the fighting tenacity of their brethren to the southward, and they lacked entirely the firm direction of the stout Colonel Nakagawa. Thus, it took a single regiment only four days to seize the entire area, as contrasted with the weeks stretching into months which it would take five regiments working in relays to secure the Umurbrogol.

D-plus 12 (27 September) was a day of crisis for the 2d Battalion. This unit had advanced painfully along a narrowing open flat under sustained fire from Japanese caves in the face of a steep ridge on the right, to have its progress halted the previous evening at a large antitank ditch. This had been constructed to bar the approach to a defense installation of formidable proportions: the reinforced concrete foundation of the demolished phosphate plant, which the enemy had converted into a reasonably accurate facsimile of a blockhouse. With the fire from this work combined with plunging fire from hidden caves in the high ground, the position was obviously unassailable by infantry without armored support.

While a tank-dozer (i.e., a medium tank equipped with a bulldozer blade) [45] labored

----

[45] Of three tank-dozers originally landed with the 1st Tank Bn, this was the only one remaining

PRIVATE FIRST CLASS WESLEY PHELPS, posthumously awarded the Medal of Honor, rolled on an enemy grenade in order that his companion's life might be spared.

to fill in the deep trap that prevented Marine armor from closing, Company E, the rearmost element, sent patrols probing into the high ground to the east. The crest of this proved to be defended in no great strength, and the entire ridge top in this sector was soon occupied, although Japanese out of reach in the precipitous slope remained troublesome for some time to come.

The armored dozer completed its work about 0830, and the tanks got across. Under cover of the fire of their 75's and the weapons of the supporting infantry, an LVT flame-thrower closed to effective firing range and worked the improvised blockhouse over with leisure and efficiency. More than 60 Japanese dead were counted in the ruins, and the advance rolled on to northward,

---

operative at this stage. Its work here was made extremely difficult by accurate and well controlled enemy fire, which knocked out its periscope once and pinned down the officer directing its labors from the outside. *Brant.*

both along the road and atop the ridge line which here closely abutted it.

Company F, in the lead, found progress anything but easy. From the outset all elements of the battalion had been harassed by heavy mortar and artillery fire, some coming from beyond the ridges on the right, some from Ngesebus [46] across the water on the left. Now they found the low ground infested with bunkers and pillboxes, plus cave positions in the base of the hills, here pressing ever closer against the road and the shore, from which small arms and automatic weapons poured a galling fire. The tank-dozer could have rendered yeoman service in dealing with these, but that useful machine had been sent back to the 1st Battalion which needed its approaches cleared before being able to attack. So the 2d Battalion was obliged to spend the rest of the morning at the slow, dangerous work of destroying the enemy installations individually by hand.

Then, about 1200, all forward movement was rudely halted when the advance came up against what was subsequently discovered to be perhaps the largest and most elaborate cave on all of Peleliu, garrisoned at one time by more than 1,000 Japanese. [47]

This extraordinary example of the mining engineer's art occupied the entire nose of Peleliu's nothernmost ridge. Its seaward tip loomed directly above the road, here so cramped between the hill and the shore line as to be barely wide enough for the passage of a single tank, and dominated completely

---

[46] Both aircraft and Marine artillery tried repeatedly to silence the fire from Ngesebus but without permanent success. After the island's capture, the weapons were found to be emplaced in caves in the low ridge west of the fighter strip. *Walt.*

[47] This is the cave described, and its main level diagrammed, in Appendix D. Because the intricacy of its construction exceeded anything they could imagine, the Marines at first fell into the error of mistaking its multiple entrances for the mouths of individual caves and were repeatedly bewildered by the refusal of these to remain knocked out. After its true nature was recognized, many men on the scene believed it to be a disused phosphate mine, and it is so designated in some reports.

by the cave mouth which faced in this direction. The first tank to attempt getting around the nose was promptly hit, and though it was not knocked out, indications were that a worse fate might await any others so rash as to attempt the passage until some remedial steps could be taken.

The problem of what steps to take was a poser. Under the existing situation, no heavy weapons were in position to deliver direct fire where it was needed most, and manifestly anything short of direct fire would be valueless. Infantry attempting to operate against the position from the low ground not only came under fire from the many cave mouths themselves, but were clear targets for those enemy weapons on Ngesebus and Kongauru which had been inflicting increasing casualties on the battalion for the past two days. Those elements which had advanced along the ridge crest, and taken some severe losses doing so, were able to get on top of the nose, directly above the cave system itself. But this served mainly to place them in the way of friendly supporting fires without giving them any advantageous means of getting at the Japanese holed in below them.

Yet it was tactically essential to the operation planned for the following day (28 September) that the low ground be secured and the cave (or caves) at least partially neutralized. Faced with this urgency, the regimental command of the 5th Marines worked out a method which has been cited since as an outstanding example of the ingenious and skillful employment of a combination of weapons and resources. Fifth Marines *Unit Reports* describes how it was done as follows:

Artillery laid a continuous barrage on Ngesebus. Naval gunfire was laid on Kongauru. Nine medium tanks pulled up to 158 X [along the shore below the phosphate plant] and fired smoke shells on the beach of Ngesebus. . . . Every fourth artillery shell was smoke on Ngesebus. 5 LVT(A)'s (75mm) then pushed out in the channel and reached a point 159 G [on the reef about 300 yards due north of the ridge nose]. From here they poured shells into the mouth of the cave. The tanks then moved up the road supported by G Co. and got by the cave.

An LVT flame-thrower was used on the cave. The lines of the 2d Bn consolidated this gain and dug-in for the night.[48]

The 1st Battalion spent most of this day (27 September) securing Hill 1, which proved to be a maze of caves and tunnels. Owing to the difficult terrain of the approaches, the attack had to be delayed until the tank-dozer which was operating with the 2d Battalion should be released for service in this sector.

During this wait, a patrol from Company C was sent southeastward along a secondary road, or trail, which ran parallel to the base of Hill Row. This unit encountered no resistance but found a number of Japanese dead, evidently the result of the artillery concentrations which had been poured into the area in an effort to check the persistent mortar fire which had been harassing the advance farther to the west from the defilade of the hills. The road was discovered to be heavily mined, and early in the afternoon a squad of engineers went out to clear the way for further operations in this direction which were planned for the following day.

With the tank-dozer available at last, the assault on Hill 1 jumped off at 0930 with Companies B and C closing in from two directions. Progress was exasperatingly slow. Without the support of direct fire of heavy weapons, the advancing infantry was extremely vulnerable and could make little decisive impression on Japanese positions so strongly armed and well concealed. And clearing approaches for the tanks was a laborious process. It was accomplished,

---

[48] 5th Mar *War Diary* describes this incident in similar terms with only minor changes in wording, and *Regimental Narrative* presents the same essentials in summary form. The wording above would indicate that the impression still prevailed that the Marines were contending with one or more small caves with individual mouths instead of a single enormous one with nine entrances. According to *Walt*, three of these were discovered to be facing seaward, and all had to be temporarily neutralized by the LVT(A)'s to allow the tanks to pass.

however, and the men on foot moved in for the bloody business of reducing individual installations in turn. Four 75mm and a like number of 37mm guns were destroyed during this action in addition to an oversize quota of automatic weapons. At 1700, while Company C was consolidating night positions on top of the hill, engineer demolitions teams set about a systematic program of sealing every opening they could find which bore the most remote resemblance to a cave mouth.[49]

The 3d Battalion played no part in this day's fighting. Instead, the units still remaining on the line were relieved by elements of the 321st Infantry (see sub-chapter following), and the whole battalion was assembled near Road Junction 15 (West and East Roads) to await further orders. There: "Late in the afternoon word came that the battalion would land on Ngesebus Island at 0900 the following morning."[50]

The overlay as of nightfall of 27 September shows a somewhat healthier situation than had been the case the previous evening, but still something short of ideal. From the seemingly precarious left flank, anchored on Peleliu's northern shore beyond the ridge nose, the 2d Battalion's line followed the axis of the high ground in a southwesterly direction. Its right, however, had only remote visual contact with the left of the 1st Battalion atop Hill 2, owing to the intervention of a jumbled, steep-sided ravine which cut through between the ridge and the hill at this point.[51] From athwart the center of Hill Row, the 1st Battalion's line followed favorable terrain contours to where Company A tied in on the right with the newly arrived 321st Infantry which, in turn, had its right anchored on the swamps that fringe the peninsula's eastern shore. Thus, the enemy on northern Peleliu were compressed within a pocket slightly more than 2,000 yards in length and consisting almost entirely of low, flat land save for the two still uncaptured elevations which comprised the southern half of Hill Row, and the slopes of the northern ridges whose crests were occupied by the Marines.

NGESEBUS TO RADAR HILL

D-plus 13 (28 September) saw several notable developments which cleared the way for the final mopping up of northern Peleliu. Of these, the most spectacular was the assault and seizure of Ngesebus Island, 500 to 700 yards away across shallow reef. This attack was planned as a simple, straightforward shore-to-shore operation, utilizing all available supporting arms. Because it promised to provide a good show, high officers from the various elements, including the transports, command ships and fire support vessels, were invited to view it from a vantage point which provided safety and even a certain amount of comfort.[52] They were not disappointed.

Because the executive officer of the 5th Marines was closely associated with the operation and an eyewitness to much of it, what took place may well be described in his own words.[53]

The Division Commander issued a verbal order to the Regimental Executive Officer at 1600 [on 27 September] at the Regimental CP [CO was away from CP on reconnaissance] to attack Ngesebus at 0900 the following morning with 3/5 in assault and 1/7[54] in reserve. A warning order was immediately issued to these battalions. Also, in direct sup-

---

[49] 5th Mar *WD*.

[50] 3/5 *Record of Events*.

[51] 1/5 *Bn–3 Journal* states: "C Company on the left flank tied into the beach at 156 C." This information does not appear on the regimental situation overlay. The then CO of Co. C states that his flank was atop Hill 2 that night. Ltr Maj J. H. McLaughlin to CMC, 8Mar50, hereinafter cited as *McLaughlin*.

[52] "After the third day (28 September) the Regimental CP was almost constantly filled with at least a general or an admiral." Ltr Maj D. A. Peppard to LtCol G. D. Gayle, 13Nov49, hereinafter cited as *Peppard*.

[53] *Walt*, 7–10.

[54] This battalion was assembled and stood by in reserve but was not employed. Subsequently the reserve function passed to Company E, 5th Marines, which committed one platoon on the island during the mopping-up phase. 3/5 *Record of Events*.

NORTHERN RIDGES, showing blasted entrance to one of the huge artificial caves constructed by Japanese naval personnel.

port of the operation was one battleship, one cruiser, two destroyers, division and corps artillery, one company of tanks,[55] one company of LVTA's and one company of LVT's. Representatives of all units were assembled at the 5th Marines CP, and the attack order was issued orally at 1700.

The general plan of the attack was as follows: One hour of naval gunfire, air and artillery preparation commencing at 0800; the last 200 yards advance of the assault wave to the beach to be covered by continuous strafing by Marine Corps fighter planes [56] parallel to and directly on the landing beach; the landing force to be led by the Sherman tanks, flanked on either side by LVTA's and followed by LVT's loaded with the troops of the assault wave; the entire battalion to be loaded in LVT's and the waves to land successively at two minute intervals.

The attack took place on schedule . . . except that the three leading Sherman tanks swamped [57] and

---

[55] The 1st Tank Battalion had 19 Shermans operative at this time. Three of these continued with the 5th Marines elements still fighting on Peleliu, and three others drowned out during the reef crossing (see below). Thus, a total of 13 actually participated in the securing of Ngesebus.

[56] From VMF 114, which had based on the Peleliu airfield only two days previously. Their presence

---

was a source of great satisfaction to all hands not only because of the magnificent performance they turned in, but because this was the first instance in the war where air support for a Marine landing was furnished exclusively by Marine Corps planes. It was not the first instance of such planes participating in such an operation, however, as erroneously stated in 1st MarDiv *SAR* and widely quoted elsewhere.

[57] This possibility had been foreseen and H-Hour set to coincide with the lowest ebb of the tide in order to minimize the danger. At this time the

the tank company commander was forced to reconnoiter a route across, which took some time. The LVTA's led the attack and attempted to carry out the tank mission of furnishing supporting fires into the beach to cover the landing as well as their own mission of placing supporting fire on the flanks of the beach.

The landing was highly successful. Some 50 of the enemy were killed or captured in the pill boxes on the beach without having so much as a chance to fire a shot at our approaching waves. The fighter planes did a remarkable job of strafing the beach up to the time our leading wave was 30 yards from the water line. A Japanese officer captured in the beach positions stated that the strafing was the most terrifying experience he had been through and that they had been allowed no opportunity to defend the beach. . . .

The 3d Battalion had no casualties in the landing but lost a total of 28 men during the remainder of the operation. Perhaps the low casualty figure and the short period involved caused higher headquarters to belittle this operation. From my own personal survey of the battle ground the following day I felt 3/5 had done a remarkable job and that a less capably handled force would have taken from two to three days and probably would have lost better than a hundred men.

In the paragraph above Colonel Walt reveals a difference in viewpoint existing between regimental and higher levels: between the men who were on the scene and those who formed their judgments at a distance or through hearsay. Reports of higher echelons [58] abound in such terms as "light", "slight", and "meagre" in describing the opposition encountered on Ngesebus. This reflects the view obtaining at the division command post at the time and filtered upward from that point and which has thereby been perpetuated. Actually, 3/5 accounted for 463 [59] (23 prisoners) fighting Japanese on Ngesebus, nearly all of them in caves and strongly prepared positions: hardly "light" opposition for a single infantry battalion already badly depleted. The truth is that a skillful adaptation of tactics and weapons to terrain, plus unusually fine teamwork, caused a potentially difficult operation to be carried through so quickly and effectively as to appear easy. [60]

The scheme of maneuver called for landing Company K on the left, Company I on the right and Company L in reserve. The assault wave jumped off at 0905 [61] and crossed the reef in six minutes. By 0930 all tanks, troop carriers and LVT(A)'s were ashore, and from that point on infantry and armor performed with a ruthless efficiency unequalled in any previous Pacific operation.

The only terrain with any claims to formidability lay in the zone of Company K: a cave-pocked ridge along the island's western shore which provided a small-scale replica of conditions in the high ground on Peleliu. As the advance swept northward, one platoon of Company L, supported by two tanks and three LVT(A)'s, wheeled to the east and secured the semi-connected island of Kongauru and the unnamed islet beyond it.

---

tanks could be only partially water-proofed, the fording kits used for the initial landing on D-Day having been damaged beyond further usefulness. *Stuart.*

[58] 1st MarDiv *SAR*, II, 11. CTF 32 *OpnRpt*, 72. TF 36 *OpnRpt*, Enc A, PerRpt #8, 2.

[59] Nor were these all of the Japanese on the island. While conducting final mopping up after relieving 3/5, the 2d Battalion, 321st Infantry, reported a "considerable number" still holding out on 30 September, and noted killing ten more on 2 October. 81st *OpnRpt*, II, 35, 37.

[60] "Major Gustafson and the officers under his command used excellent tactics and made maximum use of supporting arms." *Walt.* "It should be emphasized that with the terrain most suitable for an infantry-tank attack, with both elements coordinating perfectly, the operation was made to appear easy. . . . The tanks should get a great deal of credit. On the other hand, the tank commanders later said that they had never experienced such coordination from infantry." *Gustafson.*

[61] At this point a hitch in the plans occurred. The command ashore had planned the assault in the manner of land warfare, with H-Hour designating the time of crossing the line of departure. But naval and air elements, thinking in terms of an amphibious operation where H-Hour is time of landing, lifted supporting fires at the moment the LVT's were beginning the perilous reef crossing. No serious consequences ensued, however, as the aircraft, in plain view of the situation, quickly resumed their support in advance of the leading waves. TF 36 *OpnRpt*, Enc A, PerRpt #8, 2. *Coleman.*

By 1700 all of Ngesebus had been overrun except for an area a few hundred yards in extent at the extreme northern end, though a few caves in the ridge remained to be demolished.

The 3d Battalion completed the seizure the following day (29 September—D-plus 14). In the process tanks knocked out a large naval gun and a 75mm artillery piece which had opened point-blank on the approaching infantry. Ngesebus was declared secure [62] at 1500, and an hour later the 2d Battalion, 321st Infantry, in accordance with orders issued the previous day, commenced relief [63] of the assault troops for the final mopping-up. That night 3/5 was safely bivouacked in the Ngardololok RDF area with an excellently performed job to its credit.

One aspect of the operation proved disappointing, however. The Japanese fighter airstrip, capture of which had been originally the main objective of this little foray, proved to be surfaced with sand so soft as to render it useless. Thus, the most substantial achievements were the elimination, once and for all, of that harassing fire into the rear of troops operating on northern Peleliu, and denying the Japanese further use of what could have been a valuable staging point for reinforcements moving down from the central Palaus.

Simultaneously with the Ngesebus landing, the 1st Battalion, 5th Marines, continued its slow, stubborn operations against Hill Row. The primary objective was Hill 3, which could now be approached from two directions: north from captured Hill 2 and west from the parallel trail seized the previous day. Both approaches were naturally difficult, and Japanese, firmly entrenched in the honeycomb cave system, made them hazardous as well. Bazooka men and demolition teams crept forward under cover of infantry fire. A Sherman tank got into the area and made some valuable contributions, but it had to be maneuvered backward into a depression and thus canted at an angle in order to gain the necessary elevation to bring direct fire to bear on caves higher up the slope.

An attempt by the enemy to reinforce the position was broken up by mortar fire in the early afternoon, and the securing of the hill, at 1600, had the tactically invaluable effect of isolating its intrinsically more formidable but detached neighbor: Radar Hill, immediately to the south.

In the 2d Battalion area Company G, which had rounded the northern ridge nose with such difficulty and spent a perilous and uncomfortable night exposed to attack from practically every direction, now began reaping the reward for the previous day's tribulations. Attacking at 0630 with the support of three tanks, the forward elements quickly secured the whole northern tip of the peninsula and deployed for a drive southward against the flank of Hill Row, the opposite flank of which was under attack by the 1st Battalion.

The terrain on this side of the ridges was a widening flat and more or less open: coconut groves giving way to a strip of swamp along the eastern base of the high ground. The area was infested with the Japanese, many of them in prepared positions where they fought to the death. But, somewhat surprisingly, few of them fought with the skill and determination which the Marines had learned to expect from Japanese combat infantrymen of the 14th Division.[64] While a few surrendered,[65] the majority

[64] Subsequent intelligence indicates that most of the Japanese killed here were personnel from the naval construction battalions. However, in a contemporary report to Koror, Col Nakawaga estimated army strength in northern Peleliu at about one battalion, over and above the naval complement. *Tada Record*, 28Sept44.

[65] The 5th Marines captured 45 POW's (23 on Ngesebus) on this day, as contrasted to a total of 8 taken by the regiment during the 13 days preceding. 5th Mar *War Diary*.

[62] As in the case of Angaur, losing contact with his troops in the north did not deter Col Nakagawa from reporting to Koror as "my guess" that heavy fighting continued there. The Marines and Wildcats organized Ngesebus as the closest equivalent to a rest area possible on Peleliu.

[63] 1st MarDiv *SAR*, II, 13; 81st *OpnRpt*, II, 33; 3/5 *RofE*.

simply hid, abjectly awaiting death with little effort either to defend themselves or to injure their attackers, a point which the Marines were nothing loath to appreciate. Company G swept on southward across the flat until reaching a point where Radar Hill could be brought under fire by infantry weapons, and here a perimeter defense was set up for the night.

While this advance was in progress, Company F, occupying the line of the ridgetop, and those elements of Company E not committed on Ngesebus, busied themselves at the slow, exasperating work of sealing up the innumerable cave openings in both faces of the ridge. In the afternoon a platoon of the latter company moved onto the flat to mop-up behind Company G. During the process, one detail flushed a group of 70-odd Japanese who attempted to make a break across the reef. Three LVT's carrying personnel of Company F easily overtook them, and those of the now helpless enemy who refused to surrender were adequately disposed of.[66]

The 1st Battalion spent 29 September working on Radar Hill with flame-throwers, bazookas and demolition charges. The capture of Hill 3 had isolated the strategic elevation, but so intricate and strongly manned was its cave system that reducing it proved an all-day job, plus. While the rest of the battalion was thus engaged, Company B sent out patrols through the wooded flat to the northward in an effort to make contact with Company G, known to be moving in this direction. When no contact had been achieved by late afternoon, the 1st Battalion withdraw to its previous position for the night.[67]

In the 2d Battalion area east of the ridges, Company G continued mopping-up operations, harassed now by fire from caves high up in the precipitious slopes above the phosphate plant, with which the Marines were unable to close because of the intervening swamp. Tanks posted in the coconut grove placed direct 75mm fire in the most troublesome cave mouth, without perceptible effect. Company F, working on the ridgetop against caves on both slopes, succeeded in sealing up four openings, only to have the Japanese inside blast them open again in a short time and resume their harassing operations.

The men of Company G encountered further tribulations when the enemy suddenly began firing into their rear from positions near the northern tip of the peninsula which had been thoroughly worked over the previous day. Once again a mopping-up platoon of Company E moved into the area, and with the same result: the positions were reduced and their occupants chased out on the reef, where armored amtracks made short work of them. No doubt this combination of divertisements was largely responsible for the failure of Company G to make contact with the 1st Battalion patrols, although the company reached its assigned objective line.

D-plus 15 (30 September) saw all of northern Peleliu secured, organized resistance [68] declared at an end. Both the 1st and 2d Battalions had been alerted to expect relief that morning by elements of RCT 321, to which final mopping-up had been assigned, and bright and early they set about putting the area in order.

Patrols from the 1st Battalion scaled Radar Hill and operated on its summit without opposition, although it was known that live Japanese still occupied a large cave beneath them.[69] Pushing northward through scrub jungle and coconuts, other patrols

<hr>

[66] *Ibid.*

[67] 1/5 *Bn–3 Journal.* 5th Mar *War Diary* states that the 1st Battalion seized Radar Hill on this day.

[68] Another instance where the term "organized resistance" is apt to be deceptive. By the time they finished mopping-up this area, relieving elements of RCT 321 were convinced that they had been through a major battle. See 81st *OpnRpt;* also sub-chapter following.

[69] LtCol R. W. Boyd, CO of 1/5, interviewed 2Mar50, described the cave mouth as protected by a large stone and log revetment. Unable to attack this frontally, the Marines scaled the hill and sealed the cave entrance from above by using shaped charges to create a sizeable landslide. The Japanese, however, dug their way out during the night.

RADAR HILL looms above dense mangrave swamp. Remainder of Hill Row at left.

soon made contact with elements of Company G which had been working toward them, mopping-up as they came. Only scattered sniper fire was encountered, and this had been silenced by the time, about 1000, when both units were ordered to withdraw to the vicinity of the radio station preparatory to their relief.

Second Battalion elements on the ridgetop were drawn back from their positions in order to get out of the line of fire of a 155mm gun which had been brought forward to bear directly on particularly troublesome cave openings above the phosphate plant which had been inflicting casualties along the West Road for the past two days with apparent impunity. By now it had become something more than a suspicion that the presence of so many openings on both flanks of this same ridge was not mere coincidence; that the survival of their occupants after repeated direct hits and the tender attentions of flame-throwers was no accident. Therefore, on the theory that this position comprised a single enormous cave rather than a collection of small individual ones, Com-

pany E placed a detail armed with machine and submachine guns safely in defilade from friendly fire to cover the eastern face of the ridge under attack.

Sure enough, no sooner did the big 155mm shells begin exploding inside the western cave mouth than Japanese began scurrying out through half a dozen openings on the east, where the Marines were waiting for them. After this had gone on for a while, sealing the entire ridge proved a comparatively simple matter, though how many survivors were sealed inside of it, and how permanently, could never be determined with any conclusiveness.

This novel and ingenious employment of a large artillery piece for direct fire is worthy of some elaboration, if for no other reason than that it represented the first of several similar cases of effective adaptation of weapons to missions which must have been far from their designers' minds. Weapon and crew were from the 8th 155mm Gun Battalion and were commanded by Major George V. Hanna, Jr. It was set up on the beach under heavy small arms and ma-

155mm **GUN IN POSITION** to place direct fire into caves in northern ridges.

chine-gun fire that killed two and wounded three of the gunners before they could get it emplaced and the position sandbagged. The range was so short—less than 200 yards—that the crew had to take cover from the fragmentation of their own bursts.[70] As one eyewitness has described the action:

Nips could be seen trying to crawl out through the rubble knocked down by the shell bursts. One round set off a munitions cache inside the cave system which blew out through the principal cave mouth in three successive blasts, the last with a large smoke ring. Ammunition was mixed, with WP, delay, superquick and AP used.[71]

Although the latest available intelligence indicated an estimated 500 Japanese in the northern ridges on 27 September,[72] the 5th Marines and their supporting elements had

eliminated a total of 1,172 [73] during the three succeeding days (28–30 September inclusive). Not without reason could the 1st and 2d Battalions believe that they were leaving northern Peleliu secure, as trucks and DUKW's and amtracks hauled the weary men to rejoin the previously relieved 3d Battalion for a "rest" in the Ngardololok defense area.

FURTHER OPERATIONS OF RCT 321

In order to deal with the securing of northern Peleliu, this narrative left RCT 321 posted athwart the ridge and firmly ensconced on Hill B, capture of which on the afternoon of 26 September (D-plus 11) had sealed off the enemy's Umurbrogol Pocket. Beginning the following morning, this combat team was assigned a dual mission: (1)

---

[70] *Harrison.*

[71] MS. Corrections and Comments, Col E. L. Lyman, Mar50.

[72] *Prisoner of War Interrogation #15.*

---

[73] This figure includes casualties on Ngesebus. It breaks down to 1,070 killed (estimated) and 72 prisoners of war. 5th Mar *War Diary.*

To compress the Pocket further by driving southward to a new phase line, 0–X, laid arbitrarily across the entire width of the peninsula; (2) To sweep northward through the central ridge system (Kamilianlul Mountain on the maps) which had been by-passed by the 5th Marines on that regiment's swift advance to the end of the island.

The first phase was assigned to the 2d Battalion, to which Company K was operationally attached. Companies G and E remained on Hill 100 and Hill B respectively from which supporting fire could be placed on objectives to the south, and the remainder of the 3d Battalion held fast to the western rim of the ridge system to cope with any enemy attempts to reinforce their defensive zone in front of the 2d Battalion.

D-plus 12 was a day of sustained hard fighting for the units on the offensive in this area. Company K jumped off at 0700 and commenced its tortuous southward advance down the parallel lines of ridges: rugged, broken, up-ended terrain where the holed-up enemy had every advantage. Progress was slow, and the heavy casualties sustained included the company commander.

Company F, supported by the Neal Task Force, advanced along the East Road, plagued by heavy fire from the ridge and from caves cut into the face of the cliff wall that dominated the open low ground. The terrain here made possible the employment of tanks and flame-throwers, and these knocked out many enemy positions. Many others, however, proved wholly inaccessible. At 1200 the column was still 200 yards short of 0–X, and further advance appeared inadvisable.

Because of the impossibility of digging in securely in the hard coral-limestone, a withdrawal for the night was ordered. Company F and the Neal group fell back to the protection of Hill B and formed defensive positions at its base. Company K withdrew to the westward and entered the perimeter sector occupied by Company I. The following day, because of the severe casualties which this unit had suffered, Company K

was removed to the comparative safety of Hill B where it relieved Company E.

For the next day's attack (28 September) Colonel Dark threw together a composite battalion under command of CO, 3/321. Company I took over the central ridge sector, while Company E moved down from Hill B and resumed the advance along the East Road, supported by Company A, 710th Tank Battalion, with Company F in battalion reserve.

The fighting on D-plus 13 in general repeated the pattern of the previous day: hard, sustained and unspectacular. Company L contributed its bit by swinging southward from its position on the western ridge line and tying in with the right of Company I. This time the forward momentum carried successfully to the 0–X line by nightfall. And there was no withdrawal: the composite battalion was still holding firm to its well consolidated position the following morning when it was relieved by the 1st Battalion, 7th Marines.

In the meanwhile, the 1st Battalion had been carrying out the northward sweep which comprised the second phase of the regiment's current mission. The battalion advanced at 0700 on 27 September with two companies abreast, one in reserve. Company C, on the left, moved athwart and along both flanks of the Kamilianlul Mountain ridges. Company A followed the East Road with Company B immediately behind it.

The high ground in this region was less formidable than either the Umurbrogol or that to the extreme north, and it soon became apparent that the Japanese had given priority to defense of those other sectors. The advance was unopposed.[74] However, to describe any Peleliu terrain as "less formidable" is to use a purely comparative term. The ridges in the center and swampy ground on the right made progress slow and difficult. It was 1700 by the time Company A passed beyond the northern extremity of the ridge where it came under heavy fire from a pillbox at a point where the road

---

[74] 81st *OpnRpt*, II, 27. See footnote p. 132.

looped sharply to the west. Lateness of the hour dictated a halt to set up night defenses.

This occurred on D-plus 12 (27 September), the day that the 3d Battalion, 5th Marines, was withdrawn from that regiment's perimeter in preparation for the Ngesebus assault. As early as 1235 orders had been received for 1/321 to move elements as far as Road Junction 15 (East-West Roads) in order to fill the gap thus created. No sooner had Company A been halted by the fire of the pillbox at the road loop than Company B, hitherto in reserve, began its swift march around the left flank of Company C and forward to the designated spot, a movement accomplished successfully before nightfall.

At this point certain elements of confusion enter the picture as it emerges from the action reports of the two regiments. The pillbox in front of Company A lay some distance below where 3/5 had reached the eastern shore the previous morning, but long before Company B reached Road Junction 15 it entered territory over which Marine units had been operating for the past two days. Of this fact the officers of the 321st appear to have been unaware. Thus, henceforth until the end of operations in northern Peleliu, that regiment's reports contain frequent allusions to the "capture" of positions which the 5th Marines had already seized and moved beyond, perhaps without mopping-up thoroughly, as is often the case with troops in assault.

A case in point is that of the elevation known as Hill 80, located in the saddle between the northern and central ridge systems. Fifth Marines *Unit Reports*, entry for 26 September, has this to say: "At 0830 L Co secured hill in square 152 A, F & K." The following is quoted verbatim from 81st Division *Operation Report* for 28 September: "In the center of the line Co B captured the hill in TX 152 F, G and organized it for defense." As a glance at the target square map will show, the latter designation represents a segment of the identical hill the 5th Marines had reported as "se-

cured" two days before.[75] The operational overlay for the 5th Marines on 28 September shows the front line in that sector as lying along Hill Row, nearly 1,000 yards in advance of the "captured" position.

The obvious inference is that 1/321 was engaged in large scale mopping-up rather than actual assault, as its officers seem to have believed—and not without some reason. That they should have been wholly ignorant of Marine operations a thousand yards to their front might appear extraordinary by the standards of "The Book"—but not to anyone who had to cope with the problems presented by the terrain of Peleliu: not only the broken nature of the high ground to the north, but in this particular case a large, deep swamp imposed between the Marine and Army positions.[76]

While Company B was mopping-up Hill 80, Company A succeeded in liquidating that troublesome pillbox, and by 1600 the 1st Battalion, 321st, controlled the northern stretch of the East Road save for one small pocket which was eliminated the following day. Early the next morning (29 September) the two battalions which had been working against the Umurbrogol pocket were relieved of responsibility for central Peleliu and ordered to make the necessary dispositions for relieving all elements of the 5th Marines in the north, an operation for which RCT 321 had been alerted on the evening of the 27th.

---

[75] Company I, 5th Marines, had occupied this position, abutting the east shore swamp, for two days as right flank anchor of the regimental perimeter, prior to its withdrawal the previous evening preparatory to the Ngesebus operation. Quite possibly infiltrating Japanese moved back in during the brief period it was unoccupied.

[76] The foregoing elaboration has been propounded in an effort to explain an apparent conflict in what must necessarily be considered the primary historical sources for the campaign. This should be accepted as inference and deduction on the part of the author, based on some personal knowledge of the terrain and problems involved, and partially substantiated by interviews with officers who took part.

"A NEW HIGH IN TANK-INFANTRY COORDINATION was achieved," as one authoritative witness stated.

The 2d Battalion, as previously noted, concentrated at Garekoru preparatory to relieving 3/5 on Ngesebus. Orders to effect this move were received at 1410 following word that the smaller island had been secured, and 2/321 departed at once, taking along a platoon of tanks to assist in the final mopping-up.

The 3d Battalion advanced northward over the same ground traversed by 1/321 two days previously, combing the area for any Japanese who might have been missed by its predecessors. A number of such were found and put out of the way.[77] Proceeding with that systematic thoroughness characteristic of all 81st Division units on Peleliu, the battalion paused to blow in every cave the men were able to discover, as a precautionary measure against reoccupation

by infiltrating Japanese. This slowed progress notably. The 3d Battalion had moved only about 200 yards beyond the 321st Infantry Trail by nightfall and was to continue engaged in this work for the next three days.

The 1st Battalion received orders on the morning of 29 September to effect the relief of the 1st and 2d Battalions, 5th Marines, the following day. These units, as previously related, had closed in on Hill Row from the west and north and seized the high ground by dint of some hard fighting. Radar Hill, deprived of its mutually supporting positions, had fallen comparatively easy prey to 1/5. All of its defense installations were reported knocked out with the exception of one large cave,[78] and Marines had occupied its summit without encountering any further resistance.

By noon of the 30th (D-plus 15) 1/321 had completed reconnaissance of the ground it was to take over. However, the remain-

---

[77] 81st *OpnRpt*, II, 31. Here is another example of Japanese allowing themselves to be overrun in order to get in American rear, since the 1st Battalion had traversed this same ground two days earlier without encountering any of the enemy. *Ibid*, 27.

[78] 1st MarDiv *SAR*, II, 13.

ing cave on Radar Hill was huge and well populated. No sooner had the unfortunate members of Company B [79] begun moving into position than, as the 81st Division *Operation Report* (p. 39) puts it: "Japanese swarmed from Radar Hill to attack our troops ascending the slope. A major skirmish ensued in which tanks and mortar fire had to be employed to drive the Japanese back into their cave. The company was unable to take the hill before dark and organized a perimeter defense for the night on the low ground at its base." [80]

Here, then, was another example of the difficulty of thorough mopping-up in terrain of this nature. Nor was this the only one. Company A encountered a similar situation in the ridge just east of the West Road and secured the position that evening only after hard fighting. Company C, operating in the extreme north, killed 40 Japanese who had evidently infiltrated to reoccupy captured caves and emplacements which it had not appeared necessary to destroy the previous day, and disposed of another 40 under similar circumstances the following morning.

Company B assaulted Radar Hill again on 1 October, and the area of main enemy resistance was localized. At 1600 a rifle platoon and an engineer demolition squad attempted to storm this, but a Japanese counterattack again drove them from the hill.

---

[79] This force was a single platoon. It was en route to the position when it encountered Co C, 5th Mar, which had just left the hill. The CO of the latter unit was dubious of the ability of so small a force to hold the position should the Japanese be able to dig out of their blasted cave and volunteered to carry word to that effect to the platoon leader's battalion operations officer. By the time this could be done, however, the platoon had already run into trouble. *McLaughlin.*

[80] "Before the Regimental CP (5th Marines) had moved out of the area, the 321st had been forced to evacuate Radar Hill and had brought up their M-10 tank destroyers which were working over that area. They were also verbally working over the Marines." *Peppard.*

The unexpected difficulties being encountered on northern Peleliu led to a call for reinforcements. Company G of the 2d Battalion, then completing the mop-up of Ngesebus, was brought over to the main island on the morning of 2 October to support the attack on Radar Hill. Company B assaulted again from the south and west at 1000. Using flame-throwers and heavy demolition charges, the attack was successful this time. All resistance had ceased, on the hill and throughout the entire zone, by 1700. Examination of the main cave area revealed approximately 100 dead Japanese therein.

With the completion of mopping-up on the northern peninsula, the 321st assumed what was to be mainly a passive role for the next two weeks: organizing defensive areas against possible landing attempts by Japanese from the central Palaus, and clearing up the debris left in the wake of battle. During this period the regiment was also called upon to undertake several secondary offensive operations, which will be dealt with elsewhere, before resuming a major part in the final conquest of Peleliu.

OTHER DEVELOPMENTS AND FIRST RELIEFS

On 24 September (D-plus 9) the 1st Marine Division Command Post displaced forward and set up in what was left of the former Japanese administration building, a short distance north of the airfield. The signs of crumbling enemy resistance everywhere except in the thoroughly isolated Umurbrogol Pocket were now unmistakable, and the U. S. flag was raised here with simple ceremonies at 0800 on D-plus 12. To most witnesses this event appeared to signalize the beginning of the end, as indeed it did. It was perhaps fortunate for such optimism as remained in the division that none could foresee the tortuous road which remained to be traveled before this end would be achieved.

Although portions of the Umurbrogol Pocket remained within mortar range of the airfield, and the enemy occupied lofty observation posts [81] affording a clear view of all southern Peleliu, they made no serious efforts to interfere by this means with operations there. Once he had determined on a last ditch defense, Colonel Nakagawa apparently saw no point in revealing his well concealed positions in what could be nothing more than a futile gesture and conserved his ammunition for more immediate targets. He did send out suicide squads of varying size heavily laden with demolition materials in attempts to infiltrate to the field and do as much damage as possible. But none of these managed to get through, so work on the strips progressed rapidly and satisfactorily.

As early as D-plus 3 a Navy TBF plane was able to make an emergency landing and take off successfully the following day. On D-plus 4 two artillery observation planes from VMO 3 landed ashore, and from 20 September on the entire squadron operated from the field. With the fighter strip serviceable for 3800 feet, [82] ample dispersal areas available, and everything made ready for them by their ground crews, the first Marine fighter planes flew in to base on the field on 24 September: an advance echelon of four night fighters (F6F's) from VMF(N) 541, the remainder of the squadron arriving on 1 October. VMF 114, flying Corsairs (F4U's), followed intact on the 26th and supported the Ngesebus landing as previously narrated. This new strength made it possible to dispense with further naval air support as of 1800 that day. Arrival of VMF 122 (F4U's), also on 1 October, filled the complement of MAG 11 assigned to Peleliu.

---

[81] This was believed at the time and subsequently proved to be true. As an indication of how narrowly distance was contracted in this area, during the first air strike against the pocket by land-based planes, fragments of a 1,000 pound bomb striking in the enemy-held ridges carried all the way back to the airfield from which the plane that dropped it had taken off.

[82] With repairs and extension of the bomber strip completed on 5 October, the field was capable of accommodating any plane short of a B-29. As early as 23 Sep a PB4Y (Navy version of the B-24) was able to land on two dead motors, effect repairs and take off. CTF 32 *OpnRpt*, 8. For further detail regarding aviation activities on Peleliu, see Appendix E.

MARINE CORSAIRS on Peleliu Airfield, equipped with belly tanks for a napalm strike against Japanese-held ridges.

With land-based air support well established, the danger of counter-invasion from the north was greatly reduced. Thus, it became possible to take steps toward evacuating the 1st Marines to the division base in the Russell Islands, and Movement Order No. 3–44 was issued on 28 September to effect this. As noted previously, this regiment had been occupying Purple Beach and the northeastern defensive zone after excessive casualties had necessitated its withdrawal from the lines. With completion of the northern operations, elements of the 5th Marines relieved the 1st in position, and the latter commenced loading on 29 September.

The weather hampered this work, as it now hampered all operations on the island. Rain had been falling more or less steadily for the past two days. At first this had been welcomed as a break in the oppressive tropical heat which had persisted since D-Day,[83] but as the rains continued, borne in on winds of increasing velocity, serious problems began to arise. As events were to prove, this storm was actually the edge of a major typhoon which piled LST's on the reef, wrecked the pontoon causeway running seaward from Orange 3, and rendered the western beaches unusable for several days. Even on Beach Purple, on the lee side of the island, unloading operations were so hampered that it was necessary to put the troops ashore on two meals a day. Before the emergency was over, vital supplies had to be brought in by air[84] owing to the continuance of high seas even after the wind had died down and the weather cleared.

Most of the 1st Marines were safely embarked by the evening of 30 September, but complications resulting from the weather delayed departure of the convoy until 2 October. With the regiment went various of the reinforcing elements which comprised the combat team, and a sizeable detachment from division headquarters.[85] The constriction of the enemy-held area eliminated massed artillery fires as dangerous to friendly troops, so it was considered expedient to relieve the two pack howitzers battalions of the 11th Marines (1/11 and 2/11). The exhausted platoons of the 1st Tank Battalion were also shipped back at this time. Both the men and machines of this unit had seen much rough and strenuous service and the nature of the terrain in the remaining enemy pocket made it appear that tanks would be of little use henceforth. This proved to be an unfortunate misapprehension.[86]

Thus, the end of September saw all of Peleliu conquered save for a single pocket of rough, hilly terrain. This conquest had cost the reinforced division 843 killed, 3,845 wounded, and 356 missing: total casualties of 5,044.[87] On the credit side of the ledger, an estimated total of 9,076 Japanese had been killed and 180, mostly Koreans and Okinawans rather than first line troops, taken prisoner.

---

[83] The holed-up Japanese, who had been running seriously short of drinking water, welcomed these torrential rains even more eagerly, if for a different reason.

[84] Approximately 75 C–46 and C–47 aircraft were employed for this purpose during the height of the emergency. *Benedict.*

[85] Including 1st Plat., 1st MP Co. "With it went any hope of successfully performing our assigned tasks of traffic control, security watches, guarding POW's and maintaining a straggler line." Ltr Maj F. H. Scantling to CMC, 11Mar50, hereinafter cited as *Scantling.* See discussion of souvenir hunters and death of Col Hankins, Chap. VII.

[86] O. P. Smith *PerNar.* During their remaining operations on Peleliu, the Marines were dependent for tank support on the 710th Tank Battalion, attached to the 81st Division. These men and machines turned in an outstanding job of supporting the Marines and, especially later when they were working with their own troops, their contribution to the final subjugation of the Japanese on Peleliu would be difficult to overestimate.

[87] 1st MarDiv *SAR*, II, 13. Like mid-operation casualty figures previously quoted; these were compiled amid the confusion of battle and without complete returns. Figures on men missing in action are especially misleading.

CHAPTER VII

The Umurbrogol Pocket: D-plus 14-D-plus 30
(29 September—15 October)

In the minds of the men who fought there, the exotic-sounding name "Umurbrogol Mountain" became associated with some of the most unpleasantly exotic terrain on the face of creation. Marines had been fighting in this outlandish high ground since D-plus 2, and some attempt has been made to describe it. But words are inadequate, photographs not much better. One has to see it fully to believe it.

The generally accepted geological explanation is that Peleliu was once a part of the ocean floor which, thickly encased in coral growth, had been forced above the surface by subterranean volcanic action. Many areas of the island still retain a semblance of the natural submerged coral formations to be seen on any tropical reef. But where the pressure had been strongest, the ground had buckled and cracked to form a maze of ridges and defiles, the whole littered with jagged boulders and rubble which had been torn adrift by the violent action. This pressure accounts for the elevations attaining no great height before splitting apart. It also accounts for the broken nature of the terrain and the extreme steepness of most of the slopes, many of them sheer cliffs. The thin topsoil above this bedrock had been capable of sustaining scrub jungle just dense enough to screen the contours from aerial photography, thereby rendering the preliminary maps of this particular region so egregiously inaccurate in detail.

The same pressure which caused these weird surface contortions had created innumerable underground faults in the coral limestone; cracks and fissures in the solid rock, many of which had been further enlarged by erosion into natural caves, cluttered with the stalactites and stalagmites characteristic of caverns in all varieties of limestone. Since rock faults seldom follow any traceable patterns, these natural caves occurred in all shapes and sizes, and at every conceivable level from the floors of valleys, up the faces of sheer cliffs to the tips of craggy pinnacles. It was the Japanese exploitation of these natural features which caused the fighting in the Umurbrogol Pocket to develop as it did.

The terrain within the Pocket, as defined at the end of the third operational phase (1 October), differed only in degree from that in the Kamilianlul and Amiangal systems to the northward: the ridges were higher, longer, and packed more closely together in greater depth. The highest elevation achieved an altitude of only about 300 feet, but that was almost straight up. No caves here were as large and elaborate as some of the engineering feats encountered

STALACTITE FORMATION in natural cave "improved" by the Japanese and "revised" by the Americans.

in the northernmost ridges—but there were a lot more of them.[1]

Natural caves, of course, did not always occur in positions of tactical importance, and a number of them were taken without great difficulty or abandoned by the enemy. A case in point was Colonel Nakagawa's original command post, located in a "balcony"[2] cave well to the south of the final Pocket. This boasted most of the comforts and conveniences of permanent quarters: wooden decks, electric lighting, communication facilities, a well equipped galley, partitioned quarters with built-in bunks. Yet because he rightly judged its approaches to be indefensible, the colonel evacuated it on D-plus 2 and retired without haste to that inaccessible position which was destined to be the last hard core of organized resistance on Peleliu.

However, where a natural cave did possess tactical importance, especially if it were adaptable to the emplacing of heavy weap-

---

[1] See Appendix D for further description of caves and their utilization.

[2] A type of natural hillside cave with an extremely wide horizontal mouth, partially obstructed by stalactites and stalagmites, which it was all but impossible to seal. On the other hand, such an open- ing provides far less cover than a small one. Many caves of this type are extremely large, this one extending, with some improvement on nature, entirely through the ridge and out the other side on a different level. *Japanese Military Caves on Peleliu.* ·CinCPac-CinCPOA Bulletin 173–45, 27–33.

ons, the Japanese went to great lengths to improve it. Blast walls, or revetments, of logs, coral-filled oil drums and reinforced concrete were placed to protect the entrance, or entrances, from direct fire or the force of nearby explosions. A few were even equipped with doors of steel armor plate which could be swung open in order to run out artillery pieces, mortars or automatic cannon, then closed again to provide cover and concealment after a few rounds had been fired. Elaborate communication equipment was subsequently discovered in several of these.

All approaches were protected with great shrewdness by the construction of artificial, or semi-artificial, caves so placed as to bring mutually supporting and interlocking fires to bear against the flanks or rear of attackers. In this respect there were limiting factors in the amount of work required and shortage of labor personnel.[3] As a result, many such were so small and simple as to prove death traps once the Marines were able to get to them.

But many others proved quite the opposite. They assumed a number of shapes and sizes, depending on local conditions. Wherever possible, bays and ells were blasted or chiseled in which the occupants could take refuge from direct fire through the cave's mouth. The ultimate desideratum was another entrance, or entrances, on the opposite side of the ridge or out of view of the attackers around a shoulder, through which the defenders could duck out for a safe cigarette or two during such time as the Marines were earnestly blasting and burning their empty refuge. In that region of jumbled razorback ridges, construction of multiple entrances proved practicable in a surprising number of cases. Thus, during the earlier stages of the operation, there were repeated instances of caves being declared

secure in all good faith, whereas in actuality they were reoccupied by their unharmed defenders within minutes of the time the attack ceased and the whole business would have to be done all over again.

But if the Marines learned the hard way, at least they did learn. As the fighting developed in the Umurbrogol, it became standard procedure to search out and seal every opening bearing the remotest resemblance to a cave mouth, regardless of whether there was reason to believe it occupied. No doubt much energy and high explosive were wasted in this manner, but by the time a systematic job had been completed, attacks proceeded much more smoothly. There was simply no easy, inexpensive way.

The impossibility of judging the nature of a cave or the number of its defenders from the outside doubtless led to some exaggerated estimates of enemy casualties. But sometimes this had the opposite effect. There is one authenticated case of eight Japanese being reported killed defending the mouth of what appeared a smallish cave, which on subsequent investigation proved to be an enormous cavern containing the bodies of 80.

Greatly enhancing mutual support of enemy positions was the generally parallel orientation of the ridges. Following the peninsula's northeast-southwest axis, they faced one another, often at very close range, across a succession of gullies, draws, box canyons and miscellaneous declivities; steep-sided, fissured and strewn with those ubiquitous boulders and coral outcrop. Thus, Marines on one narrow, open ridge crest were vulnerable to fire from concealed Japanese in the faces of the flanking ridges, even though there might be friendly troops atop those ridges, too, prevented by the steepness of the slope from getting at the enemy below them. There were numerous instances of such troops lowering explosives over the cliffs on ropes in an effort to explode them in the cave mouths below—and of the Japanese reaching out and cutting the ropes.

---

[3] Japanese Navy elements on Peleliu used artificial caves almost exclusively and had what amounted to a monopoly on the skilled labor available. See Appendix D. Army people did not find their sister service's ideas of cooperation especially amusing. See Appendix F.

From the infantryman's point of view, perhaps the greatest curse of this evil ground was the limitations it imposed on the effectiveness of supporting arms. Flat trajectory naval gunfire had proved valueless against invisible targets impervious to anything short of a direct hit, and most of them in defilade, anyhow. Massed artillery fires were useful in keeping the enemy holed up when that suited the attackers' purpose, but any permanent effect it had was wholly a matter of luck.[4] And with constriction of the Pocket, massed fires had to be abandoned to avoid danger to friendly troops.

Direct fire by individual heavy weapons could be extremely effective,[5] but all too often no amount of labor or ingenuity sufficed to get such weapons into the desired positions. Tanks were invaluable wherever they were able to operate; but in such up-ended terrain, this excluded many of the most critical areas. The same applied to the LVT-mounted flame-throwers, and prodigious time and labor were expended bulldozing routes for both types of machine into some highly improbable territory. But in the end the business of reduction usually resolved itself into the infantryman struggling in across all but impassable ground with such weapons as he could carry on his back.

The air arm helped, or tried to. Five hundred and 1000-pound bombs made an impressive display and doubtless rattled the teeth of many underground Japanese, but caused no visible slackening in enemy resistance. Napalm fire bombs were tried. Later, in order to minimize danger to friendly troops in the constricted Pocket, unfused belly tanks filled with napalm were dropped to saturate a chosen target area which was then ignited by lobbing in white phosphorus mortar shells. There is at least one substantiated report of the intense heat driving a small group of Japanese into the open where they could be destroyed. But perhaps the most useful purpose served by napalm was burning away what vegetation remained, thereby depriving the enemy of concealment and occasionally revealing positions heretofore unsuspected.[6]

The Umurbrogol Pocket, as defined at the time responsibility for its reduction passed to the 7th Marines (29 September), has been described as roughly 900 yards long by 400 yards wide.[7] Certain of its southern features have been touched upon in passing in Chapter IV, but may be reviewed briefly in connection with the accompanying maps and photographs.

The valley known as the Horseshoe [8] offered what appeared the most practical avenue of ingress into the heart of the Pocket from the southeast. This was bounded outboard by the elevation which came to be called Walt Ridge, which formed the Pocket's eastern wall in this area; inboard by a generally parallel formation: the Five Brothers. Ringing it to the north, three other major elevations frowned down into the valley at various angles: Hill 140, Ridge Three and Boyd Ridge, the latter also part of the eastern wall and separated from Walt

---

[4] "From the light artillery standpoint, the most emphatic lesson of Peleliu was that 75's fired futilely at Jap caves. 1/11 fired 20,000 rounds at one two hundred yard area in front of the 1st Marines without disturbing appreciably anything below the foliage and topsoil." Ltr Maj J. R. Chaisson to CMC, 8Mar50.

[5] Employment of a 155mm gun against the northern ridges was described in Chapter VI. This gun was later emplaced to angle direct fire in through the mouth of the Horseshoe. There was one somewhat bizarre incident, well authenticated, of its gunner sighting in on an individual Japanese and picking him off at 300 yards like a clay pipe in a shooting gallery.

[6] "The enemy plan seems to be to burn down the central hills post to ashes by dropping gasoline from airplanes." *Tada Record*, 7Oct44.

[7] Exact distances in this region cannot be gauged accurately as the three different maps used at one time or another are not in scale with each other. Insofar as it is possible to orient terrain features on the standard 1:20,000 map, length of the Pocket at this time would appear to be closer to 1,200 yards.

[8] Appearing in reports of the 81st Division as "Mortimer Valley." Place names used herein, unless otherwise noted, are the ones applying at the close of Marine action at Peleliu.

UMURBROGOL POCKET from the southeast, Walt Ridge center foreground, Boyd Ridge to its right north of draw. Smoke rises from western face of Five Brothers, north of which lie Hill 140 and Ridge 120. Five Sisters at left, abutting China Wall in background. Swamp-surrounded inlet in foreground prevented approach from eastern peninsula.

Ridge by a steep-sided draw. The East Road, approaching from the south parallel to the extension of Hill 200 (see Chapter IV), angled sharply eastward near the base of towering Hill 300 and crossed the swamp at the mouth of the Horseshoe on the causeway previously described, just beyond which a secondary road branched off to a dead end inside the valley.

West of the Horseshoe and separated from it by the Five Brothers lay a generally similar valley at a somewhat higher elevation subsequently christened "Wildcat Bowl." [9] Bounding this on the west, in turn, was the towering, butteressed China Wall,[9] a double-crested ridge extending northward from the Five Sisters. The latter formation, together with Hill 300, partially closed the Bowl to the south, while an unnamed transverse ridge closed it completely on the north. The narrow, rough defile known as Death Valley skirted the western base of the China Wall, separating it from the serried high ground of jumbled coral formations which reached almost to, and dominated, the West Road.

North of the Horseshoe the ridges were piled closer to one another, and the defiles were narrower: Wattie Ridge, Baldy, Baldy Ridge, Ridge 120, the Three Knobs (see Map 14). Here was concentrated some of the heaviest and utlimately most successful Marine action.[10]

When Colonel Nakagawa chose to fight a defense to the death in prepared positions in the Umurbrogol, he automatically sacrificed anything resembling mass mobility for his force.[11] Thereafter the Japanese potential for jeopardizing island security on any considerable scale ceased to exist. The sole object became to make the conquest as costly and time-consuming as possible: to kill for the mere sake of killing, and to pin down U. S. troops against their employment elsewhere.

---

[9] Both of these names were applied by the 81st ("Wildcat") Division and constitute exceptions to the rule cited in previous footnote. They are used herein in the interests of easier orientation, inasmuch as Marine reports have no standardized terms for them. A few units referred to the Bowl as "Peleliu Pocket." Aviators, to whom terrain appears much different than it does to ground troops, called it the "Little Slot," as differentiated from the "Big Slot," their name for the Horseshoe.

[10] This would appear to be the area lumped together in Japanese reports under the inclusive designation *"Suifuyama"*, or *"Suifuzan"* (suffixes *yama* and *zan* are interchangeable, both meaning "mountain").

[11] In a report just prior to the period under discussion, Nakagawa estimated Japanese strength in the Umurbrogol as "about 2½ battalions put together," with "the main body of 2d Bn, 2d Infantry and part of 2d Bn, 15th Infantry, not yet under our control." *Tada Record*, 28Sept44.

THE HORSESHOE as it appeared during the later stages. Five Brothers (left), Walt Ridge (right), Hill 140 (center background).

To this end, the defenders followed the general policy of obliging the Marines and soldiers to come to them, often exercising an extraordinary degree of fire discipline to avoid giving away their positions. One could stand at the Horseshoe's mouth in broad daylight and study at leisure the precipitious slopes and sheer cliffs that wall it in, almost physically aware of the weightless impact of scores of hostile eyes. Yet there would be no sign of the enemy: no movement, no shots; only a lonely silence. Occasional small patrols operated there, and in similar spots elsewhere, with impunity. But let an important position be approached, or a sufficient force be committed to furnish a profitable target, and a fury of fire of all varieties would be angled in from every direction and every altitude the hills provided.

Nights were something else again. Infiltrating Japanese, as in all Pacific operations, constituted a continuous nuisance and minor menace. Mass mobility might be no longer possible, but small-scale activity and limited counterattacks were the rule throughout the Pocket. Lurking in concealment by day, with the coming of darkness the little men swarmed out of their holes like so many gophers, bent on raising hell. No doubt, some of their actions were dictated by the whims of individuals, but there was ample evidence that many parties were acting under orders in carrying out predetermined missions.

As always, the infiltrators' object was to cause all possible damage and confusion in the Americans' rear areas. They went about this in two principal ways.

Individuals and small groups sought to reoccupy positions previously taken, as was noted previously in connection with earlier phases of the operation. Owing to their complete familiarity with the region, they usually knew exactly where they wanted to go, the best route for getting there, and the nature of the particular installation they wished to use. Moving under cover of darkness, through weirdly jumbled terrain of the ridges, they often reached their destinations despite all efforts to intercept them. Once ensconced in their chosen hideouts, they would snipe at targets of opportunity until their inevitable destruction, often manging the business so shrewdly that they remained undetected for days.[12] Conversely, of course, the more cautiously they operated, the less damage they managed to do. It is an ironic commentary on the effectiveness of infiltration as a tactic that most of their few victims were noncombatant souvenir hunters who were turning out in such hordes as to constitute nearly as great a nuisance as the Japanese infiltrators.

The presence of so many of these gentry was largely the result of the inability of the military police company to maintain an effective straggler line through having been weakened by evacuation of one of its platoons with the 1st Marines. While a few 1st Division Marines no doubt were guilty of this practice, mostly it was confined to aviation ground personnel, sailors ashore from the transports, and miscellaneous service troops with nothing better to do.[13] Disgusted front line Marines did not much care whether these people got themselves hurt or not. The trouble was that every time one was wounded, good men had to expose themselves to the same peril in order to rescue him.

In justice, however, it should be recorded that not all of the men who had no business being forward were motivated solely by souvenir hunger or morbid curiosity. As the struggle dragged on and casualties mounted, a feeling of unrest and insufficiency developed among troops in the rear areas. Many such who could get away from their assigned duties came forward with no other object than to lend a hand to their embattled comrades: bringing up supplies, serving as stretcher bearers, helping man the containing lines. Writes the battalion commander of 2/7: "I believe that . . . the unknown officers and men from the Marine air units who slipped away from the field and plagued me daily to let them participate 'in any way' should be mentioned."[14]

The second objective of Japanese infiltration was potentially more serious. Groups laden with demolition charges repeatedly attempted to penetrate the lines, evidently with the intention of getting through to the airfield and destroying planes and installations there; or, failing that, to blow up any artillery, tanks or other vehicles encountered along the way. Although they did some trifling damage, none ever reached the air-

---

[12] This writer had the experience of coming under fire from a cave in the nose of a ridge which had been secured and thoroughly explored more than a week previously. The incident occurred just at dusk, at a range of approximately 300 yards, making it all but impossible to determine the exact source of the shots. Although the sniper had betrayed his general location, most of the next day was required to find and destroy him. Had he chosen a nearer target or an hour of better visibility, he would have been located with little difficulty, but might have done more damage.

[13] "These souvenir hunters and the morbidly curious were mostly service troops and aviation personnel on their first operation and had apparently been given a thorough 'snow job' in some rear area to the effect that all Japs died with a jeweled sword in hand. . . . An effective straggler line would have saved many lives." *Scanlling.*

[14] *Berger.*

field.[15] Most such parties were stopped short of the lines, many being blown to kingdom come by their own explosives. While this kept U. S. nerves on edge, it was certainly an easier method of destruction than mining them out of the ridges and canyons.

Reduction of the Pocket evoked a high degree of the proverbial Yankee ingenuity and brought into play, at one time or another, every weapon at the Marines' disposal, plus a few improvised for the occasion. And when the job devolved on the 81st Division, the Wildcats not only improved on some of their predecessors' techniques but dreamed up a few new ones of their own. Many of the lessons learned here would be found useful in subsequent operations; but if Peleliu, Iwo Jima and Okinawa proved anything at all, it was that there is no single over-all tactical solution to Japanese cave fighting: no easy way.

The story of the Umurbrogol comprises the sum of the stories of the units which operated there, and will be developed here in connection with each of these in turn. To understand the nature of the fighting, it will be well to note at the outset that it was conducted for the most part by small units: "With the exception of a very few cases, most of the objectives were taken by platoons or squads of men, for as a whole the fronts were small and the terrain too irregular for company operation and maneuver."[16] Note, too, that by now the toll of casualties had reduced the Marine units far below T/O strength: the terms squad, platoon, company, battalion did not designate the same number of men they had two weeks earlier.

---

[15] At least, none of which U. S. troops were ever aware. However, by dint of what must be construed as wishful thinking, Colonel Nakagawa was able to inform his superiors: "One part of our unit infiltrated into the air base on the night of the 5th and threw the enemy into confusion and at the same time they set fire to the air base between 0030 and 0250 on the 6th." *Tada Record,* 6Oct44.

[16] Ltr Maj A. J. Doherty to CMC, 15Feb50.

HILL 200: Marines on top were unable to get at holed-up Japanese in the precipitous slopes below. Airfield in background.

OPERATIONS OF THE 7th MARINES

As recorded in Chapter IV, the 1st Battalion, 7th Marines, relieved those elements of RCT 321 facing the northern perimeter of the Pocket on 29 September, at which time responsibility for operations throughout the Umurbrogol passed to 7th Marines command.

This date found the depleted regiment deployed thinly to encircle the Pocket on three sides, the dense swamp containing it on the east as effectively as any number of troops could have done. The western ridges were lower and less well defined than those surrounding the Horseshoe and Wildcat Bowl. In many places they could scarcely be called true ridges, being rather coral high ground, pitted, creased, broken into a score of crazy cross-compartments, box canyons, sump holes and low but sharp precipices. It was recognized from the first as the most impractical terrain in the entire region over which to attack, and the line established here was pushed inland just far enough to safeguard the West Road against enemy fire. Thereafter until almost the end of Marine participation action here was purely defensive, and the line remained largely static.

It may be noted in passing that this particular line was by no means so sharply defined as the maps might indicate. Some sectors were manned in strength only at night. At one time or another, for various reasons, portions of it came down out of the hills altogether and were positioned along the West Road. Mapped locations are intended to be only approximate, or indicative.

On 29 September the greater part of this line was held by the 3d Battalion where it had extended the front up the peninsula behind the advance of the 321st. But, as will be seen, within a few days this area was turned over to detachments from various supporting arms in order to make all possible assault infantry available for offensive operations.[17]

The mission of containing the Pocket to the south had been assigned to the Regimental Weapons Company, which also acted in support of the several offensive drives from this direction. This unit took up a position facing the mouth of the Horseshoe across the swamp, its left extending in front of the bases of Hill 300 and the Five Sisters, at a respectful distance. This area was the scene of the enemy's strongest and most persistent infiltration attempts, both because its terrain was adapted to such tactics and because it provided the most direct route to the airfield, the infiltrators' main objective. To cope with this, personnel from Regimental Headquarters and Service Company, detachments from other units, and individual volunteers were brought up to reinforce the line at night.[18]

The 2d Battalion was atop the ridge on the Weapons Company's left, a northerly extension of Hill 200, in which the Japanese were still holed up in some strength and expended much time and energy attempting to infiltrate. The line followed this crest to a point where Colonel Berger's command post faced the Five Sisters and China Wall at a range of 25 to 40 yards across the mouth of Death Valley. Beyond here it angled off across the coral badlands toward the West Road to tie in with the right of the 3d Battalion. The 2d Battalion had occupied this position since 21 September, playing what was intended as a relatively inactive role; yet some indication of the peril prevailing in this area is conveyed by the fact that in the nine days preceding its relief, 2/7 sustained 149 battle casualties.[19]

The initial offensive plan of the 7th Marines for reduction of the Pocket called for the 1st Battalion to drive southward along the East Road and the ridges immediately adjacent to it, with elements of the 3d Battalion cooperating on the right. To make this last possible, it was necessary to stretch the containing line still thinner (the battalion front covered 1150 yards at this time) and for a short period to divide 3/7 into two separate task forces: one to defend, facing east; the other to attack southward.

---

[17] Characteristic of the Corps tradition which considers every Marine basically an infantryman, secondarily a specialist, and trains him accordingly. LVT personnel became increasingly available as landing facilities were developed, artillerymen as constriction of the Pocket precluded massed fires, pioneers on relief from shore party duties. Engineers subsequently assumed some of this duty, but operated mostly with the combat teams to which they were attached. Before the end, details were drawn from every Marine ground unit on the island, including Division Hq Bn and 16th Field Depot.

[18] Major Joseph E. Buckley, CO of the Weapons Company, had his own method for obtaining "volunteers." As previously noted, souvenir hunters had become a wholesale nuisance. Any men found in Buckley's area without good reason for being there were promptly seized, handed weapons and placed in the line, where they were held by force if necessary. If they behaved themselves, he notified their unit commanders of their whereabouts and employment; otherwise he did not bother, and they were carried as AWOL for as long as Buckley chose to hold them.

[19] 33 killed, 116 wounded. *Berger.*

In the 1st Battalion Zone, Company B jumped off on schedule at 0800 on the morning of 30 September, and by 1025 had accomplished its mission: seizure of a high ridge west of the road. Here it was in position to support an attack down the road by Company A, which was to leapfrog at this point in order to secure the next ridge to the south.

However, heavy rain and low-lying fog made visibility so poor that the second phase of the attack was delayed until 1245. The intervening time was utilized by an engineer demolition team in sealing all caves in the overrun territory. As soon as visibility permitted, a mortar barrage was laid on the second objective, and Company A, supported by a tank and an LVT flame-thrower, attacked down the East Road to such good effect that an advance of 300 yards to the south and 150 yards inland was achieved. Company C moved in to help hold the captured territory, and a platoon of engineers was sent forward to aid in preparing it for defense.

A side light on this action offers ground for interesting conjecture regarding the enemy's plans and motives.

During this advance [of Company A] enemy troops were observed running down the southernmost valley . . . in small units of four to eight men. . . . Subsequent knowledge of the general situation as of D+15 indicates that our forces had reached the northern outposts of the enemy final defensive area. The attempted movement of enemy troops north during A–1–7's attack was probably from a central reserve, portions of which were committed to counter our encroachment anywhere on their perimeter.[20]

The attack group of the 3d Battalion had been extending eastward throughout the morning in order to narrow the front of the 1st Battalion for the latter's attack. But the same atrocious weather conditions which delayed 1/7 had the effect of causing the two units to lose physical contact. Company L sent one patrol groping through the rainy fog in an effort to tie in once more. Another, moving forward farther to the west, came face to face with a formidable obstacle, christened descriptively "Baldy Hill": a rocky eminence rising like a high wart on the northern nose of a long, narrow ridge. As they explored possible approaches for an attack, members of the patrol sighted a number of Japanese on the hill and shortly thereafter were brought under heavy mortar fire. With failing visibility and the lateness of the hour dictating an end to the day's operations, both patrols were withdrawn for the night.

There was no notable advance the following day (1 October). The 3d Battalion group, with Company L in assault, moved out bright and early (0720) with the aim of rectifying the lines prior to an attack on Baldy. But the forward movement had progressed no more than 75 yards before the men came under such a heavy volume of rifle and machine gun fire from that formidable hill as to indicate the inadvisability of frontal assault. A supporting 155mm barrage had to be called off because of fragmentation falling in the lines.

Nor did it prove possible to establish physical contact between the battalions. As one observer noted: "The terrain in the gap was very rocky with numerous sheer cliffs and difficult draws."[21] Visual contact was reported at 1034, and that had to suffice.

On its own part, the 1st Battalion was in no shape to be of much help. A check-up showed only 90 riflemen remaining fit for duty.[22] These held a front extending into the swamp on the left, across the road and approximately 150 yards inland over the southern nose of the unnamed ridge immediately north of Boyd Ridge and separated from it by a deep draw. Clearly incapable of further offensive action, the battalion was overdue for relief, and steps were taken to effect this the next day.

The fact is that the entire 7th Regiment was in deplorable condition, with casualties

---

[20] Ltr Maj D. P. Wyckoff to CMC, 13Mar50.

[21] 1/7 *HistRpt.*

[22] "At this time diarrhea was prevalent; many men could barely walk as a result of this malady." *Gormley.*

approaching the ruinous percentage which had necessitated evacuating the 1st Marines from the island. Even Major Hurst's 3d Battalion, which had suffered least to date, reported combat efficiency below 50 percent for the first time during the campaign. Lieutenant Colonel Berger reported his 2d Battalion's combat efficiency at 30 percent, adding gloomily, "The men are very tired."[23] Yet these weary, battered remainders gathered themselves for one last all-out effort which provided the 7th Marines' greatest contribution to the pinching out of the Umurbrogol Pocket.

In order to make "fresh"—if you could call them that—assault troops available, some extensive regrouping was necessary. Detachments of artillerymen—"Infantillery", they liked to call themselves—took over those sectors of the containing lines held by 3/7. This latter unit was reinforced for the occasion by a platoon of the Weapons Company, Company C, 1st Engineer Battalion, and 52 men of the 1st Amphibian Tractor Battalion, and relieved 1/7 on the latter's newly acquired front. The 3d Battalion, 5th Marines, now available after completing the mop-up of Ngesebus three days before, was attached operationally to the 7th Marines and relieved 2/7, which moved to a bivouac area south of the Weapons Company sector for a night's rest preparatory to the coming attack.

The plan for 3 October called for a series of coordinated efforts aimed at one main objective: seizure of the remaining enemy-controlled stretch of the East Road and the ridges which dominated it, in order to gain staging points from which flank attacks could be launched against the strongholds which had checked the drives from the north and south.

Furthermore, the fighting on the northern perimeter had given the East Road a new importance. So long as the enemy controlled this lower stretch, all supplies brought into that sector and all wounded evacuated from it had to travel north on the West Road as far as Road Junction 15, then turn southward along the upper portion of the East Road where it angled across the peninsula: a trip of several miles to cover a distance which could be measured in hundreds of yards.

The main effort called for a converging attack to seize the remaining ridges which dominated the road. The 2d Battalion would attack from the south with Walt Ridge as its objective, the 3d Battalion from the north to capture Boyd Ridge.[24] Once the crest lines had been occupied and the units had made contact, they would face westward along the newly established front against the heart of the pocket. To avoid the danger of colliding head-on since the two forces would be moving straight toward each other, the attacks were to be successive rather than simultaneous: 3/7 would not jump off until 2/7 had achieved maximum penetration and could mark its flank with smoke.

In coordination with these movements, 3/5 was to attack the Five Sisters and extend eastward in order to strengthen the line on the south, and the Weapons Company, in conjunction with Army tanks, would support the attacks by moving both into the Horseshoe and up the East Road. To make this unit available for these missions, its static defensive line was taken over by the weary 1st Battalion.

The attack from the south jumped off at 0703 in the wake of an intensive barrage by 155's and the concentrated 81mm mortars of five battalions, the latter throwing

---

[23] "By juggling men from Headquarters Company and from E Company, some balance had been achieved and rifle company strengths read as follows: E Company 67, F Company 60, G Company 82. . . . These figures . . . (were) much lower than Regiment had reported to Division . . . and I am afraid the result did not exactly endear me to Regiment." *Berger.*

[24] It should be remembered that these particular place names had not been applied at this time. In the 2/7 *Journal* (but nowhere else) "Walt" is referred to as "Hill X", and definitely located by listing of the target squares in which it lay. "Boyd" is unnamed in any reports of this particular action and designated only by its target squares.

SEVENTH MARINES HALF-TRACKS advancing toward Horseshoe. Japanese in Hill 300 (right background) were not ousted until 2 November.

smoke during the closing stages in order to screen the advance. From his position so long held atop the flanking ridge, the commanding officer of 2/7 had been a distressed witness to the bloody repulses suffered by 2/1 and 1/7 before this same objective. Now that his own battalion's turn had come, he had made his preparations with great care, using both air and ground reconnaissance. The approach route selected followed the trail through the swamp [25] over which Captain Pope had withdrawn nearly two weeks before. Resistance was light, and so rapid was progress that the leading platoon of Company G, in assault, reached the top of Walt Ridge at 0730, the rearward elements following closely. Up to this point the battalion had suffered no casualties,[26] but all hands knew from bitter experience that this happy condition would not obtain for long. Sure enough, as the company carried out its mission by expanding its gains, the men came under a savage cross fire from the Five Brothers, facing them across the Horseshoe, and from the heights to the northward. And the regimental command

---

[25] *Berger.*

[26] The bodies of many dead Marines were found scattered about the ridgetop, however, sad reminders of Captain Pope's gallant stand there throughout the night of D-plus 4 (see Chapter IV)—Oral statement of Capt. F. T. Farrell, 20Apr49.

post began to receive increasingly urgent calls to send up stretchers.[27]

Tanks and halftracks from the Weapons Company moved into the Horseshoe to cope with enemy installations which were harassing the sweep of Company G along the axis of the ridge's military crest. Also, mortar fire was called down on the fourth of the Five Brothers which was proving especially objectionable.

In the meanwhile, elements of Company G, on top of the ridge, were obliged to face in two directions: west, to cope with the flanking fire pouring in from that direction, while the drive endeavored to move northward along the crest. Company E was ordered up with the mission of passing through Company G's right and continuing the attack to the north. At 0900, however, progress was halted by "a slight saddle at this point which was covered by a murderous cross fire [from the Five Brothers]. Two out of every four men attempting to get across were hit."[28] It was necessary to wait until ropes and ladders could be brought up, and until the engineers could blast a covered approach along the east face of the ridge at the top of a 90-foot vertical cliff.

While Company E waited for ropes and the tanks for ammunition, Company F moved up the road to assault the ridge still farther along. The leading elements had progressed part way up the slope when they were ordered to halt, then to withdraw in order to be available for a subsequent mission. With no way of telling when the advance could be resumed, 2d Battalion elements along the ridge crest were directed to consolidate their positions and mark the northernmost flank with purple smoke as a signal for the 3d Battalion to begin its attack southward.

The 3d Battalion sighted Company G's smoke and jumped off at 1020. All went well until the advance elements reached the draw separating the unnamed ridge which they occupied from the objective ridge (Boyd). The foremost squad of Company K[29] got past this, perhaps because the enemy were not yet aware of attackers' intention. But the remainder of the platoon was promptly pinned down by fire funneled through the draw from the high ground farther inland, thereby holding up the rest of the company. Tanks which had been supporting the stalled attack of the 2d Battalion[30] moved forward to help beat down the volume of fire. In this they were not wholly successful, and a new means was sought for placing Company K on its objective.

Company K got the remainder of its personnel to the summit[31] of Boyd Ridge by the expedient of detouring the draw through the swamp which lay just east of the road. This provided excellent concealment and some defilade, but the dense growth and wet underfooting made for slow progress. It was not until nearly 1530 that the mission was accomplished. However, so practical had this resort proved that steps were taken

---

[27] 2/7 *Journal.*

[28] 2/7 *WD.*

[29] This squad consisted of nine men commanded by Lieutenant Charles R. Hickox, Jr., one of the company's platoon leaders. The presence of this small force on the north face of the objective proved far more valuable than an otherwise discouraging situation would indicate. Lt. Hickox was in continuous radio contact with the battalion commander and was able to place his men in position to be of great assistance to the subsequent attack. *Hurst.*

[30] Two tanks and an LVT flame-thrower had been detailed to support 3/7 that morning, and had to travel up and down three-quarters of the peninsula to reach the battalion. This subsequent reinforcement from the south stands out as the first successful attempt to use the direct line of communication along the East Road. 3/7 *WD.*

[31] The terms "summit" and "top" as they appear in the reports are apt to be deceptive. Boyd Ridge is a narrow razorback, its topographical crest bare and untenable by troops. The rifle units of Company K carried it in one rush, without artillery preparation but covered by machine-gun fire. With seizure of the objective, the company was deployed across the eastern slope with leading elements on the military crest where they remained "for two days and two nights, swapping hand grenades with the Japs on the western slope." *Hurst.*

at once to pass Company I over the same route, and around the next draw in an effort to tie in with the 2d Battalion to the south.

During this time 2/7 had continued its efforts to expand its hold on Walt Ridge. At 1550, Company E finally got over the covered trail blasted by the engineers. Now Company F, previously withdrawn, was committed to close the gap between the two battalions by making contact with Company I. Patrols of these two units, moving toward each other, met in the swamp facing the draw between the two ridges shortly after 1600.

This patrol contact, of course, was merely preliminary to closing a solid front. In order to achieve this final step, Company F pushed its left up the slope of Walt Ridge to tie in with the right of Company E, which move was reported accomplished at 1750.[32] Simultaneously Company F extended its own right northward while tanks attempted to neutralize the draw with covering fire. Company I acted in a similar manner in the 3d Battalion zone, and was reported tied-in with F at 1730.[33] However, subsequently it proved necessary to break this physical contact in order to remain tied-in with Company K on Boyd Ridge, and Company I refused its left flank, maintaining only visual contact with F.[34]

In the meanwhile, the weary men of Company G had been relieved on top of Walt Ridge by Company B and passed into battalion reserve. Thus, the regimental position as defined that evening shows Companies B, E, and F in line (left to right) along the crest of Walt Ridge, with the latter echeloned down the slope where it tied-in, to all practical purposes, with the 3d Battalion left. On its part, the 3d Battalion had Com-

panies I and K in line (l to r), curving back from where the former, facing generally south, had visual contact with Company F, up Boyd Ridge where K faced west along the ridge's military crest. Company L, uncommitted that day, remained in 3/7 reserve.

Colonel Nakagawa evidently got out his rose-colored glasses to view this particular action. According to the version received at Koror: "At 0730, 110 tanks [35] and about two infantry battalions began to attack the central hills from north and south. Our garrison units repelled them and withdrew. . . . In this district about 100 enemy troops infiltrated our front line secretly but were exterminated during the evening." [36] An interesting sidelight on these unequivocal statements occurs in an entry dated eight days later: *"Higashiyama* [Walt Ridge] is still in enemy hands."

While these events were taking place on the eastern perimeter, the 3d Battalion, 5th Marines, attacked the Pocket strongly from the south. This thrust was mainly supporting in nature, designed to distract the enemy's attention from the operations of the 7th Marines, deter any attempts to reinforce the eastern perimeter, and if possible gain positions from which the main attack could be supported by direct fire. The battalion's objective was the Five Sisters, that gaunt palisade which had checked all northward advance since the 1st Marines had come up against it two weeks earlier.

The approach was exceedingly difficult, paralleling the ridge on the left in which

---

[32] *2/7 Journal.*

[33] *3/7 Journal.*

[34] *3/7 WD.* Company F also refused a flank to the edge of the swamp. Since the draw was not much more than 50 yards wide, actual physical contact was not considered essential. *Hurst.*

[35] The Japanese were capable of some amusing deviations from the hard facts of life, but this extraordinary figure would appear the result of inaccurate translation.

[36] *Tada Record,* 3Oct44. This report concludes with an interesting example of Japanese intelligence work: "Judging from the enemy's organization, equipment, tactics and action, units . . . were believed to be Marines with one part of the Australian Army. Their strength was estimated at about five infantry battalions."

many Japanese were still holed up.[37] With Company L mopping-up behind it, Company K pushed forward and reached the base of the objective about noon. Here Company L moved up abreast, passing over the mopping-up job to Company I, and the two companies in assault ascended Sisters Number 1, 3, 4 and 5 (numbering from west to east). On the extreme left, one platoon of Company K, supported by a tank, moved into the ravine known as Death Valley, in an effort to get at Sister Number 2, which lay slightly to the north of the others.

A combination of difficult terrain and enemy resistance prevented the latter unit from making any important penetration, but the main assault carried to the jagged summits. No doubt, this success could be attributed in part to the steady attrition of the past two weeks which had knocked out supporting positions and installations in the Sisters themselves one by one. However, later in the afternoon the men of 3/5 began to come under an increasing volume of effective small arms fire from positions which they were unable to locate. Actually, this could have, and probably did, come from every direction save their immediate rear. The narrow crest was wholly devoid of cover save for occasional accidents of terrain, and the adamant coral, as everywhere inland of the beaches, defied efforts to dig in. Discreetly the battalion withdrew and set up a defense line for the night only a hundred yards or so in advance of the line from which it had jumped off that morning.[38]

While many enemy installations had doubtless been liquidated, the Japanese in the area were still capable of reacting with such determination that the bodies of 21 would-be infiltrators were found, mostly within the forward lines, at dawn next day.

The Weapons Company, 7th Marines, having accomplished its support mission, withdrew from the Horseshoe according to plan. Thus, night of 3 October found the containing lines in just about the same position they had been that morning, save for the significant gains accomplished by the 7th Marines atop Boyd and Walt Ridges along the eastern perimeter.

On this same day (3 October) the division was saddened by the death of Colonel Joseph F. Hankins, one of its best liked officers and the highest ranking casualty sustained on Peleliu: an event especially tragic in that some surviving accounts made it appear unnecessary.

Hankins, a battalion commander in the 1st Marines at Cape Gloucester, had been appointed provost marshal and commander of the big, unwieldy Division Headquarters Battalion upon his promotion to full colonel. In the former capacity he was responsible, among many other things, for the security of the West Road. During the day or two preceding, this vital artery had been brought under particularly troublesome fire from a Japanese sniper, or snipers, posted in the high ground dominating a stretch of evil repute known as "Dead Man's Curve." The Military Police Company, in its attenuated form, was unable to cope with the situation; so, at about 1600 on the afternoon in question, Colonel Hankins, a member of several famous Marine Corps rifle teams, armed himself with an M–1 and a pair of binoculars and announced that he was going to do a little countersniping.[39]

Whatever the colonel's plans on setting out, the situation discovered on the scene quickly changed them. The following account by an officer of the 1st Motor Transport Battalion represents the correlated versions of several eyewitnesses:

---

[37] This ridge was the northerly extension of Hill 200, on top of which 2/7 had been posted for so long without being able effectively to get at the Japanese below. Flanking fire from these positions had played an important part in the repulse of all previous attacks moving in this direction. The thorough job of cave sealing performed by 3/5 on this day nullified fire from this particular ridge as a major tactical factor henceforth. *Berger.*

[38] "The enemy unit that attacked *Kansokuyama,* our main post in the southeast central hills, was its best picked company. However, more than half of them were killed." *Tada Record,* 3Oct44.

[39] O. P. Smith *PerNar.* "The Old Breed", 337.

Colonel Hankins appeared at the curve in the road where the Military Police were regulating the one-way traffic. An LVT had become immobilized across the road directly in the open and two or three trucks were jammed up in the near proximity of this LVT. The men, under the heavy fire of small arms from the nearby cliff had deserted their vehicles and taken refuge on the reverse slope of the road. Colonel Hankins proceeded to the middle of the road in order to restore traffic to normal condition and had actually gotten the crews back on the vehicles when he was struck by a sniper's bullet and killed instantly.[40]

To avenge Colonel Hankins and eliminate the danger once and for all, the commanding general ordered up a company from 2/5, then in division reserve. After a study of the situation the battalion commander sent Company E into the general area of the high ground dominating Dead Man's Curve. Though it could not be known at the time, this grotesque jumble of broken coral formations constituted one of the approaches to Colonel Nakagawa's command post and in consequence was held in some strength. In the fighting that ensued, the company pushed about 75 yards inland to secure the military crest, and 150 to 200 yards northward to occupy all of the area from which it had been determined that the fire on the road had originated. Holding detachments from the 11th Marines followed the assault troops to organize the new positions, and Company E was relieved upon completion of its mission.[41] From then onward the West Road was free of sniper fire during the remaining time the 1st Marine Division operated on Peleliu.[42]

The day following Colonel Hankins' death (4 October), saw the last offensive efforts of the 7th Marines, as a regiment. For the 3d Battalion, it brought unmitigated tragedy.

The two tactically important ridges which bounded the Pocket on the east were now securely in the Marines' grip, and the day was spent in expanding and consolidating the positions there. However, the East Road remained a perilous passageway so long as the Japanese continued able to interdict it with fire funnelled through three major gaps: The Horseshoe, the draw separating Walt and Boyd Ridges, and the narrower draw between Boyd and the unnamed ridge to the north of it.[43] Clean-up of the two latter was the chore which fell to the 3d battalion, and a bloody business it turned out to be.

Company I undertook mop-up of the southern draw, that between Walt and Boyd Ridges, with collaboration of Company F, on the right of the 2d Battalion. Here tanks could be employed with some effect, but the job proved tedious, nerve-racking and costly. However, it was done to such effect that the two battalions were able to tie in physically that night, though some fire continued to be received from the high ground inland.[44] Two officers were killed in the process, and Company I emerged from the action with only one officer and 31 men fit for duty.[45]

Although what befell Company L rates only as a small unit action, it will be related here in some detail as exemplifying a number of characteristic aspects of the fighting in the Umurbrogol.

As the accompanying sketch shows, the high ground from which the Japanese could fire most directly down the northern draw included three semi-isolated hills or knobs. These were steep and rugged, varying in height from 60 to 90 feet, and rose just

---

[40] *DeBell.*

[41] 5th Mar *WD*, 4Oct44.

[42] O. P. Smith *op.cit.*

[43] By now the lower East Road was being used successfully for supply and evacuation. Fire coming through the draw was partially thwarted by interposing moving tanks as shields for the traffic: supply and ammunition vehicles coming up, and stretcher parties evacuating the wounded.

[44] Later, after the 81st Infantry Division had taken over the final mopping-up of the Pocket, engineers bulldozed a tank route through this draw to provide ingress to the Horseshoe from the north. This proved of great value, as the Japanese were discovered subsequently to have both a 75mm field piece and a 47mm antitank gun bearing on the mouth of the valley from excellent concealed positions in caves.

[45] 7th Mar *R–2 Journal.*

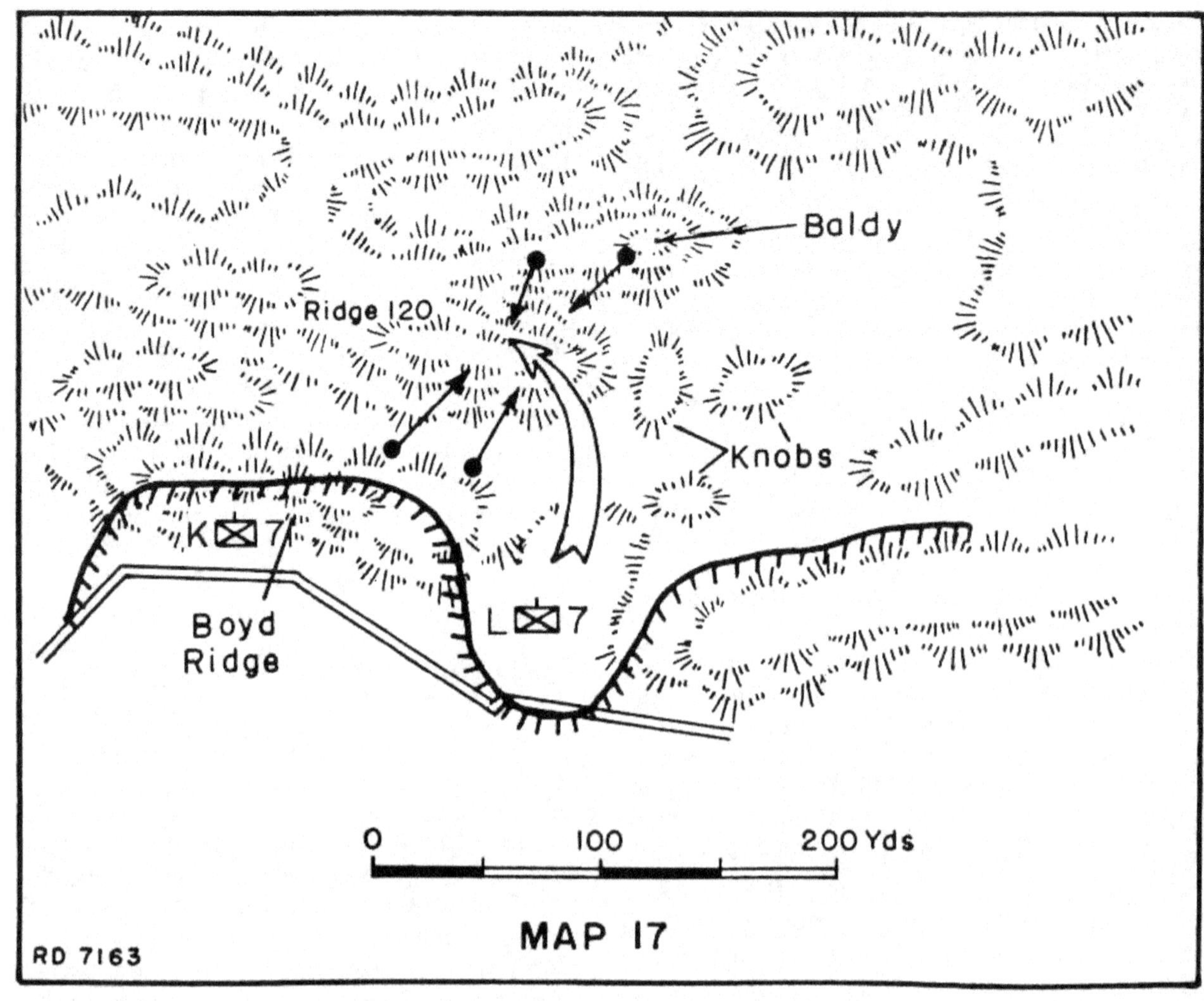

ACTION OF COMPANY L; 7th MARINES, on 4 October 1944.

north and northeast of Ridge 120, a steep-sided razorback running parallel to Boyd Ridge from which it was separated by a gorgelike valley. On the west of Ridge 120 and dominating it lay the height known as Baldy, which had frustrated attacks from the north for the past several days. So closely packed-in were all tactical features of the Peleliu landscape that the nearest knob was a scant hundred yards from the road, while the ridge was less than 150 yards in.

It should be borne in mind, too, that, while Company K was firmly ensconced on Boyd Ridge and had mopped-up its eastern slope in order to control the road, no effort had been made by infantry to enter the valley beyond, though tanks operating in the vicinity of the knobs had pounded Japanese installations in the ridge's western face which Marines on the summit were unable to reach.

Company L was ordered into the draw at 1430 with the mission of seizing the three knobs. This was accomplished by 1515 without loss and in the face of resistance so light as to astonish all hands. There, according to the original plan, the day's work would have ended. But Major Hunter Hurst had reason to feel that he had gained a great advantage. Just ahead lay Ridge 120, an ideal jumping off place for an attack against the flank and rear of that troublesome Baldy.[46] Moving in Company C, 1st Engineer Battalion, to hold the captured knobs, he ordered the attack continued.

Again resistance was surprisingly light. By 1605 an entire platoon had mounted the northern nose of Ridge 120. Here several enemy positions were destroyed, and the men began a slow, systematic movement south along the ridge's axis, parallel to the front of Company K, facing them less than a hundred yards away across the narrow gorge.

At 1645 [47] the platoon on the ridge began receiving fire from Baldy. There were several casualties, and the men moved quickly into defilade on the eastern military crest. This brought them into a clear line of fire of the enemy still holed up, with automatic weapons, in the lower slopes of Boyd Ridge, who proceeded to cut loose with everything they had.

Only then did the whole brutal truth become evident. Maintaining their excellent fire discipline, the Japanese had refrained from showing their hand until the maximum of U. S. troops had been irrevocably committed. Now, for the men caught in this savage cross fire, that coverless ridge crest became a death trap.

And there were other Japanese emplaced in the lower slopes of Ridge 120 and the captured knobs, covering the only possible line of retreat: down the cliffs and out through the draw.

What followed had the aspects of a protracted nightmare.[48] The enemy were now using everything that the constricted space permitted, and from every angle: small arms, automatic weapons, 20mm machine cannon, mortars. The senior non-commissioned officer on the scene, Gunnery Sergeant Ralph Phillips, was one of the first hit, shot dead by a machine gun burst. Two others were killed in a matter of minutes, and there were wounded all over the place. The three Navy corpsmen who had accompanied the platoon performed prodigies in caring for these, but two of them were killed before it was over.

One of the worst features was that the steepness of the slope made evacuation of helpless men nearly impossible. The platoon leader, Second Lieutenant James E. Dunn, was hit while lowering himself over the cliffside in an effort to lead his men to comparative safety and fell to his death on the jagged coral of the ravine floor.

The men on the ridge fought desperately. But so well concealed and so strong were the Japanese positions that the Marines were seldom able to see their enemies or to inflict serious damage when they did. On the floor of the draw Captain James V. Shanley, commander of Company L, viewed their predicament with increasing dismay. He ordered a tank up the narrow defile. The jumbled terrain checked it before it could reach a position where its guns would bear effectively, but at least it was far enough forward to provide cover of a sort for the command post and a rallying point behind which the wounded could be carried, once they could be got out. Then he called for smoke, and the battalion commander ordered Company K to blanket the area accordingly to screen the evacuation.

Frustrated heretofore in their efforts to furnish substantial aid to their comrades on the opposite ridge, the men of Company K responded energetically, hurling white phosphorus grenades down into the gulch. Fortunately, the wind was just right, and eddying smoke commenced to blot out the scene. Under its cover the few remaining able-bodied men began the backbreaking, heartbreaking job of getting the wounded down the precipitous slopes and to the cover of the tank. Although the Japanese were

---

[46] As will be seen, this was essentially the tactic used subsequently for the successful capture of Baldy and the ridge leading south from it, of which Ridge 120 was actually a spur.

[47] This is the hour recorded by 3/7 *War Diary*, 15.

[48] Many details of this action, subsequently verified, derive from an account by T/Sgt. Jeremiah A. O'Leary, a Marine Corps Combat Correspondent, written shortly after the event and published in *True Magazine*, October, 1945.

now firing blindly most of the time, men continued to be hit.

Nearly all of those still alive had made it, when Captain Shanley, peering out through the thinning smoke, saw two wounded Marines staggering toward him, clinging to each other for mutual support while bullets kicked up spurts of powdered coral about them. Some 30 yards away their strength gave out, and both fell. Springing forward, crouched low, the captain ran to them. He carried the first man to safety in the lee of the tank, and returned for the other. A mortar shell burst immediately behind him, and he went down mortally wounded.[49] The acting company executive officer, Second Lieutenant [50] Harold J. Collis, charged into the smoke to help him, only to fall at his side, killed instantly by a Japanese anti-tank gun.

It was over by 1820. All of the wounded who had survived to get as far as the tank had been safely evacuated. But of the 48 Marines who attempted to seize Ridge 120, only five emerged from the draw unscathed. With Company L reduced to the strength of a single platoon and Company I down to 31 men and one officer, the 3d Battalion was now about on a par with the other two as regards combat efficiency.

In the other sectors 4 October was uneventful by comparison. The 3d Battalion, 5th Marines, repeated its moves of the previous day against the Five Sisters and Death Valley, with almost identical results: some notable advances made which it proved impracticable to hold. The 2d Battalion, 7th Marines, attempted to move men and tanks up the East Road across the mouth of the Horseshoe, only to have two tanks knocked out and the men pinned down by a rejuvenated volume of enemy fire pouring from that dangerous defile; so devoted most of the day to consolidating positions along the crest of Walt's Ridge. Elements of the 3d Armored Amphibian Tractor Battalion reported as reinforcements to 1/7, and some elements of that unit retired to a bivouac area behind the lines.

The 7th Marines was now through as an assault unit on the regimental level, and its relief by the 5th Marines began the following day (5 October). The 1st Battalion and Regimental Weapons Company went out first. The battered 3d Battalion continued its efforts to mop-up the draws to the north and south of the Boyd Ridge position. During the afternoon it was thought advisable to withdraw depleted Company I, so Company F took over this sector, extending the line of 2/7 from Walt up onto Boyd Ridge, which was held through the night.

The final relief was completed on 6 October, with both of these battalions departing to join the other elements of the 7th Marines in bivouac in the Ngardololok area. Aside from a few limited combat missions (to be discussed hereinafter), they were destined to remain in general reserve, saddled with no more onerous duties than static beach defense.

The regiment had richly earned this rest.

FINAL DRIVE OF THE 5th MARINES

Bearing in mind that the 5th Marines had been fighting almost continuously for nearly a month under some of the worst combat conditions encountered anywhere in the Pacific, an apt foreword to any account of the last major effort of the 1st Marine Division on Peleliu is contained in a letter from an officer who was present:

I don't think that there can be any true picture of that final drive without some description of the great weariness of the Marines who participated in it. The Division had optimistically said that the 5th would be one of the first outfits to leave Peleliu, yet after securing the northern end of the island everyone knew that we would be committed again. Now the 1st and 7th Regiments were for the most part gone, but the 5th was back at it again. The men and officers were superb during this last phase

---

[49] Captain Shanley had been awarded the Navy Cross during the Cape Gloucester operation. For his action on this day he received, posthumously, a gold star in lieu of a second Navy Cross. He died that evening.

[50] Collis's promotion to First Lieutenant had been received at regimental headquarters that morning, but he never learned about it.

"MEN AND OFFICERS were superb during this last phase but very, very tired."

but very, very tired. . . . I have never forgotten Major Gayle's answer, when questioned as to how the fighting men were doing, as it typified the character and ability of all those who remained of the 5th: "Every Marine fighting in those hills is an expert. If he wasn't, he wouldn't be alive." [51]

As related in the previous section of this chapter, the 3d Battalion, 5th Marines, operationally attached to the 7th Marines, had been engaged in the Umurbrogol since 2 October and had already made two assaults on the Five Sisters. This unit reverted to parent control on the morning of 6 October when the 5th Marines, as a regiment, completed relief of the 7th in the drive to reduce the Pocket.

The tactical concept with which this regiment approached its new assignment is best explained in the words of its commander, Colonel Harris: "The 5th Marines, after careful air and ground reconnaissance, reversed the direction of all prior attacks and made the main drive down from the north.[52] The methodical reduction of enemy positions was possible in driving southward due to the compartmentation of the terrain. It was this slow but steady eating away of the Jap defenses that gave the real payoff. Too

---

[51] *Peppard.*

[52] It may be noted that both RCT 321 and the 7th Marines had attacked from the north. However, in both cases the main efforts were concentrated against the enemy's eastern perimeter with the aim of gaining control of the East Road.

much credit cannot be given for the splendid support furnished by our artillery, tanks, engineer company, and LVT flame-throwers." [53]

According to orders, the 1st Battalion relieved 2/7 and the 2d Battalion took over the positions held by 3/7. The commanding officers of these two units had reconnoitered the ground the previous afternoon. However, the regimental overlay for the first day shows a situation somewhat different from that existing on disastrous 4 October. Following the debacle of Company L, Major Hurst had found it expedient to evacuate the not readily tenable summits of the three

captured knobs and further to shorten his line by withdrawal of badly battered Company I. Thus, the front taken over by 1/5 included both Walt and Boyd Ridges, and the already depleted battalion was spread thinly over some 1200 yards.

On the north, 2/5 faced Baldy Hill and its supporting network of ridges and knolls from a respectful distance. On the south, 3/5 had been withdrawn to a bivouac area following its second attack on the Five Sisters, preparatory to new offensive efforts from this direction.

The containing line on the west remained essentially unchanged, manned by supporting troops. In its northern sector Major

---

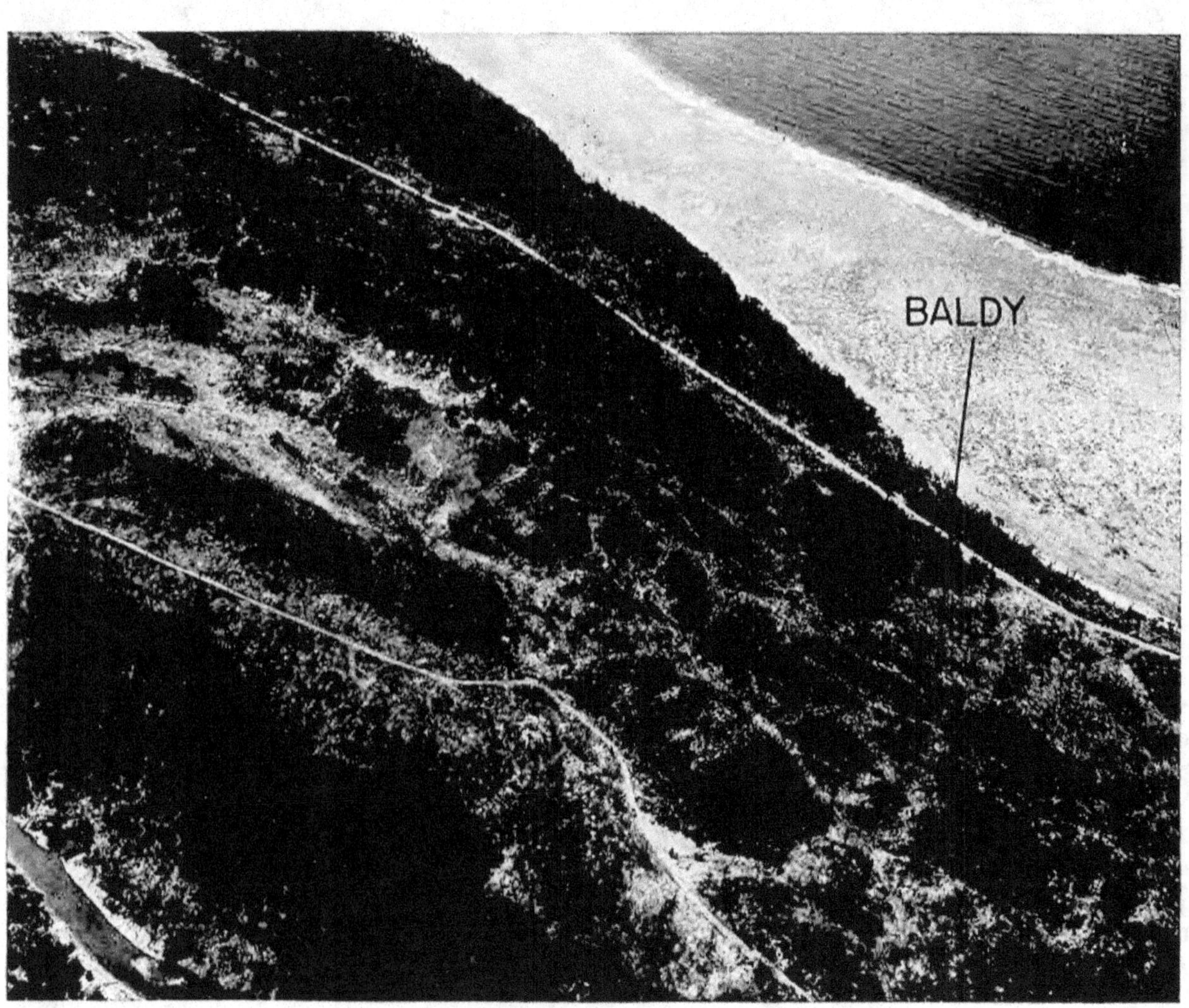

POCKET viewed from northeast. Boyd Ridge at jog in East Road (foreground). Paralleling it (right to left) are Ridge 120, Ridge Three and Hill 140. Immediately to right of 120 lies Baldy, with Wattie Ridge beyond it.

---

[53] Harris comments on preliminary script.

Harold T. A. Richmond, executive officer of 1st Battalion, 5th Marines, commanded a group made up mostly of detachments from the 1st Pioneer Battalion. On his right lay Lieutenant Colonel Richard A. Evans' group of "Infantillery": detachments from the corps artillery and 11th Marines, stiffened by volunteers from miscellaneous units. Closing the *cordon sanitaire* at the south were men of the amphibian tractor battalions. As these sectors were destined to continue static for several days longer, immediate interest focuses elsewhere.

The 2d Battalion immediately encountered the same contact problem that had plagued the 7th Marines when operating in the same area the previous week. On the left, Company E, occupying the ridge paralleling the East Road north of Boyd Ridge (now actually occupied by Lieutenant Colonel Boyd's command), found itself separated by a long, steep canyon from Company G on the high ground to the westward, facing Baldy. For the first few days Company F in battalion reserve, was used to patrol this gap, setting up a defensive line at night to prevent infiltration. Otherwise the action in this zone was wholly aggressive.

Company E attacked within half an hour of arriving in position: at 0900 on 6 October. The direction of the push was westward, into the badlands where Captain Shanley's company had met disaster two days earlier. Two of the previously abandoned knobs were recaptured, but again the troops came under heavy and accurate fire from many of the same positions which had frustrated their predecessors. Not only was further advance impossible, but the men risked having their heads blown off if they so much as raised them above the knobs' crests. But their rear was secure for the moment, so there they stayed. Company E was destined to spend four days making this area sanitary, while bulldozers cut a track for tanks and flame-throwers toward hitherto inaccessible points still farther in, in preparation for the crucial drive southward.

Meanwhile Company G staged a frontal assault on Baldy. The line of advance lay through the same terrain where 3/7 had been turned back on 30 September and 1 October, and the attack was ordered only under pressure and with considerable reluctance.[54] However, even though lacking strong fire suport, a unit of approximately platoon strength reached the summit. This could not be reinforced for the simple reason that the occupied position would accommodate no more; nor was it possible to bring up there any weapon larger than a BAR. Baldy was considered untenable, and with the approach of night the assault platoon withdrew to the original jumping-off place.[55]

The offensive effort of 7 October was delivered from the southeast by the 3d Battaloin, supported by tanks—or vice versa. Following two and a half hours of intensive artillery preparation, six army tanks advanced to the mouth of the Horseshoe at 0900 and commenced firing into all enemy positions which could be located on either flank: the lower slopes of Walt Ridge on the right, and the Five Brothers on the left. Those elements of the 1st Battalion in position atop the former moved over the crest in order to bring their firepower to bear in support. Several of the tanks were hit by Japanese heavy weapons, but none was seriously damaged. Much encouraged, they withdrew at 1045 to replenish their fuel and ammunition, determined to return and give the Horseshoe the full treatment.

---

[54] Harris Interview. Officers from all infantry units who have been consulted speak of the constant pressure from above to speed up the action and get the operation over with.

[55] Authority for last statement is 5th Mar *War Diary*. The battalion commander (interviewed 28 June 1949) states succinctly of this position: "It didn't have any future." It was his contention that lines drawn on a situation overlay are meaningless, per se: that the only position worth risking men's lives to hold is one capable of emplacing weapons with which to support a further advance. Since this one obviously was not, he preferred to withdraw and probe elsewhere in hopes of finding a better one.

The second attack jumped off at 1215 with a fire team of Marines protecting each tank, supported by two LVT flame-throwers and a platoon of the 1st Engineer Battalion for demolitions work and mine removal. Again heavy fire was received from the dominating terrain. Company L, on the left, attempted to drive into the declivity, later known as Wildcat Bowl,[56] which angles westward a short distance within the mouth of the Horseshoe through a narrow pass between the Brothers and the Sisters, bounded on the west by the as yet untested buttressed ridge later christened the China Wall. This combination was simply too much, and the attackers were stopped before being able to make any significant penetration.

Company I, attacking up the main valley, did somewhat better, advancing as far as the terrain permitted tanks to travel at this time: about 200 yards. Men and machines attacked numerous caves with every means available and killed many Japanese. Altogether, this was the largest single dose of destruction the Horseshoe defenders had received to date. But, again, once the tanks had run out of ammunition, the position became untenable for the infantry.[57] And so naturally powerful were the enemy positions that it was another ten days before U. S. troops and tanks attempted again to operate in those confines; nearly the end of October before the Horseshoe could be called anything approximating secured.

The 2d Battalion spent this day (7 October) paving the way for events to come: locating the enemy's strongest positions and taking the preliminary steps toward destroying them. The success of Company G's patrol the previous day indicated that Baldy Hill served the Japanese mainly as as observation post. The same did not apply, however, to the ridge extending southward from it. The crest and flanks of this were still wooded, and Marines attempting to advance anywhere within range invariably drew heavy fire from hidden positions somewhere along its axis.

Much the same could be said of other spurs of the ridge system. It was determined, therefore, to destroy this cover systematically in order to reveal the enemy positions before launching an infantry attack. Once LVT flame-throwers could be bulldozed within range, the vegetation could be burned off with comparative ease. While engineers labored toward this end, mortars were set up wherever they could be brought to bear. A single 60mm mortar on the ridge north of Boyd, for instance, fired 3,000 rounds during this phase.

Patrols from Company E came down from the knobs and operated with bazookas against a number of caves which had been located in that area: in the lower slopes of the ridges and of the knobs themselves. In the Company G sector, small patrols moved to the front, probing for a soft spot to the west which would provide access to the high ground and make possible an attack on Baldy Ridge from the rear. This was the same basic objective, it will be recalled, that had motivated Captain Shanley's ill-fated effort from the east three days earlier.

These activities continued for the next two days, as a trail was worked farther and farther up the gorge in order to bring tank guns to bear on both Ridge 120 and the western face of Boyd Ridge. There was no hurry now. The tactical situation [58] called

---

[56] This declivity could be classed as possibly the worst death trap on the island. Not until more than six weeks later, after the Sisters, the Brothers, and the Horseshoe had all been secured, were 81st Division units, which had relieved the Marines, able to operate effectively within the Bowl. Colonel Nakagawa's CP was located in a deep dual cave in the China Wall near the northwestern end of the gulch. (See Chapter VIII.)

[57] This sortie was made for the sole purpose of knocking out caves suspected of containing the heavy weapons which were firing on the airfield and southern perimeter lines. In this it was entirely successful, as no further fire of this nature was received. There was no intention of retaining a foothold within the Horseshoe at this time. Harris Interview.

[58] The containing lines had rendered the Japanese so ineffectual outside of the Pocket that there was pseudo-serious talk of simply setting up barbed

for thoroughness rather than haste, and Colonel Harris resisted all pressure [59] to speed things up at the cost of unnecessary losses.

There was no activity in the other sectors so far as the infantry was concerned. The 3d Battalion remained in reserve in its bivouac area to the south, and along the eastern ridges the 1st Battalion contented itself with countersniper fire. Pressure against the Pocket was maintained by artillery fire from both north and south, and on 8 October Marine Corsairs delivered two air strikes against the Five Sisters, Five Brothers, and the ridges beyond, using 1,000-pound bombs and napalm.

Near the 2d Battalion command post, then located hard by the West Road about on a line with the Japanese northern perimeter, heavy weapons were being positioned to support this unit's impending attack. Fired point-blank into the sheer cliff that barred approach from this angle, the powerful shells pulverized the coral until the face of what had been a precipice began to assume the aspect of a steeply inclined ramp, greatly simplifying the problem of gaining access to the high ground.[60]

Attacking on the morning of 9 October, a platoon of Company G, commanded by Second Lieutenant Robert T. Wattie, scaled

TANK-INFANTRY SORTIE attacks Japanese positions in the Five Brothers.

this new approach and succeeded in reaching the top of the narrow ridge which forms the western spur of Baldy. This was a position of tactical importance for two reasons: (1) It commanded a clear field of fire to the West Road and constituted a potential danger so long as it remained in enemy hands; (2) About midway of its length it connected with Baldy Ridge, thereby providing direct access to that primary objective. It was promptly named in honor of the platoon leader who had captured it and appears as "Wattie Ridge" on subsequent maps and reports.

Lieutenant Wattie led his men southward along the crest for about 100 yards, knocking out several Japanese positions. But at this point the platoon came under heavy fire from the ridge to the east and from a large cave situated at the head of the dead-end gulch that separated the two, and he withdrew his men to more tenable ground to the northward to give supporting weapons a chance to work over the enemy positions.

---

wire around the whole area, classifying it as a prisoner of war enclosure and ceasing all further assault operations.

[59] "Sometimes, if a pressure is not exerted, a battle may be allowed to deteriorate into a stalemate simply because of the peculiarities of mass inertia. On the other hand, unreasonable goading . . . may breed a resentment which . . . may result in an effect just the opposite of the one desired. . . . This sensitiveness on the part of the commander is the mark of a great commander as distinguished from one who is merely good. In this particular instance . . . I am certain that no pressure was received by Corps from Commander Expeditionary Troops and Landing Force and that none was upon the Division by the Corps Commander." *Wachtler.*

[60] Subsequently the engineers improved this and constructed two additional ramps of a similar nature which gave ingress to LVT flame-throwers into the western ridges. Harris Interview.

By this time the LVT flame-throwers had been bulldozed within range and had ample time to burn off the concealing vegetation from the crest of Baldy Ridge and the jumble of razorbacks to the east of it. An attempt was made to subdue that troublesome cave in the gulch by air attack, but it proved so located as to make a bombing strike dangerous to friendly troops nearby. The direct fires of the supporting artillery were then concentrated on the area. A lucky shot, or shots, precipitated a most satisfactory landslide, with such good results that wary infantrymen approaching to finish the job next morning found the cave entrance sealed as effectively as they could have done it with demolition charges applied by hand.[61]

A battery of 105mm howitzers, an Army M-10 mounting a 76mm, and a 37mm were now available to support the 2d battalion's attack. On the morning of 10 October (D-plus 25) the southward push jumped off in earnest, with Companies G and E both in assault.

In the former unit's zone Lieutenant Wattie led his men back over the ground they had relinquished the previous day, proceeded beyond, and commenced to move over to Baldy Ridge. Here they ran head-on into some Japanese who had different ideas. A sharp skirmish ensued, with both sides using small arms and hand grenades in considerable quantities. Then the Marines gathered themselves together and carried the enemy position with a rush. From this point they swept northward along the crest against only scattered opposition, burning out or blasting every installation encountered. By noon they had secured the entire ridge and the formidable heights of Baldy itself from the rear, in accordance with the original plan.

---

[61] Patrols operating in this gulch came across the decomposing bodies of 12 U. S. soldiers, grisly reminders of the 321st Infantry's grim efforts to find a practicable route of attack across the peninsula in order to isolate the Umurbrogol Pocket, more than two weeks before.

Seizure of this dominating terrain secured Company E's right flank against the deadly cross fire that had previously trapped Captain Shanley's company. This unit's own operations of the past three days, plus the advent of tanks and LVT flame-throwers in the draw, had already secured its left. Thus, Company E, launching its assault at 1215, was able to secure the full length of Ridge 120 with comparative ease.

In conjunction, other elements of Company G secured Ridge 3, a semi-detached razorback south and slightly to the east of Baldy Ridge. When the 2d Battalion halted to consoidate the new positions, the situation overlay showed the line pushed well forward on the left over some of the most difficult and stubbornly contested terrain in the entire Umurbrogol Pocket. The two companies were tied-in only by fire, however, owing to a steep gulch between them, and one platoon of Company F was moved forward and attached to Company G as a special reserve to cope with this situation.

Next morning (11 October) the 2d Battalion resumed its drive on what had been selected as its final objective: Hill 140, a position of the utmost tactical importance, situated just north of the Five Brothers, from which it was separated by a sheer, narrow declivity. A heavy weapon emplaced here would be capable of placing direct fire not only into the nearest of the Brothers and part of the Horseshoe, but down the draw between Walt and Boyd Ridges, dominating this and quite possibly converting what had been a potent peril to the East Road into a practical route of entry into the very heart of the Pocket.

The battalion commander was convinced that Hill 140 would provide a fine position for at least one such weapon for the support of future operations. Major George E. Bowdoin, executive officer of the 4th Battalion, 11th Marines, had been considering the possibility of getting artillery pieces into the hills to provide direct fire. He believed that the 75mm pack howitzer would prove wholly practicable for this purpose and already had taken steps to see that several such were made available.[62]

Company G continued southward along Baldy Ridge, and progressed satisfactorily until reaching the ravine which separated the southern end of that elevation from Hill 140. Company E attacked on a parallel line on the left, sweeping along the eastern slope of Ridge 3 until stopped short of the objective by a heavy volume of small arms fire from the front and right; i.e., the northern face of Hill 140 and the slope of Baldy Ridge. Elements of Company G moved down from their vantage point on the high ground to help eliminate fire from the latter position, while forward elements of both companies endeavored to neutralize the enemy to the front with their own fire. At this point Company F, the remainder of which had been brought forward in close reserve at the beginning of the attack, passed through Company E, moved up the ravine, and carried the objective positions by assault from farther to the west.[63]

Hill 140 was announced secure at 1500. The remainder of the afternoon was spent in consolidating the new position and mopping-up enemy caves which had been overrun in the advance or which lay within reach in other directions. In the course of this work an LVT flame-thrower which had managed to work its way up the draw within range detonated a 12-inch naval shell in one of the occupied caves, with a resultant blast that blew away a large bite of the hillside. Fortunately, this unlooked-for event caused only one Marine casualty. Altogether, so thorough had been the preparation and so well executed the attack, capture of one of the most important single positions in the whole Umurbrogol had cost the 2d Battalion only two killed and ten wounded.

Apparently the significance of this fighting was not immediately apparent to the Japanese. On 10 October Nakagawa reported: "There were no large battles during the day and no changes in the front lines." And again on the 11th: "All through the day there were no heavy engagements," adding, "Areas which are secured by our garrison are *Oyama*, *Suifuzan*, *Kansokuyama*, the main districts in the central hills," though conceding at last the loss *Higashiyama*;[64] a definition of position which squared quite accurately with that shown on Marine situation overlays of the period.

On the 12th, however, a note of concern crept in. Evidently dealing with events of the previous day and night, the colonel informed headquarters: "The enemy seems to have made *Suifuzan* their main objective. They attacked *Suifuzan* and the west hill of *Suifuzan* [translation not entirely clear] with flame-throwers. The enemy penetrated our front lines but were repelled by night attack."[65]

The Japanese did indeed stage a counterattack on Hill 140 that night. But the position was admirably suited to defense, and 2/5, unaware that it was in the process of being "repulsed," beat off the enemy without undue difficulty. None penetrated the line, and their final dispersal marked the

---

[62] The two pack howitzer battalions of the 11th Marines had been evacuated several days before, but fortunately the heavy seas raised by the near-typhoon had prevented loading of their guns aboard ship.

[63] Verbal statement of Lieutenant Colonel Gayle interviewed June 1949. 5th Mar *War Diary* states that Company G's attack carried to the objective and "secured Hill 140". No hour is given, but farther on the same account states: "By 1500 F Co had secured Hill 140."

[64] *Tada Record.* Exact orientation of these Japanese place names is difficult, as the sketch map showing them is completely out of scale with any U. S. maps. "*Oyama*" is the area of Nakagawa's CP and would appear to include both the China Wall and Five Brothers, together with immediate approaches from north and west. "*Suifuzan*" is an inclusive term embracing all of the Umurbrogol system north of *Oyama*, most of which was in U. S. hands by this time. "*Kansokuyama*" is Hill 300, possibly including the Five Sisters. "*Higashiyama*" is Walt Ridge, perhaps Boyd Ridge as well. See Map 14.

[65] *Ibid.*

TACTICAL CONFERENCE. Strain of the protracted campaign stamped on their faces, three Marine commanders study situation map. Left to right: General Geiger, Colonel Harris, General Rupertus.

end of the 2d Battalion's active participation in the Peleliu campaign. At 0930 on 12 October, relief of the weary men was begun by the only slightly less weary 3d Battalion, and they came down out of the hills for a well-earned rest.

There was little activity in the other sectors during the 2d Battalion's drive. The 1st Battalion's mission had been simply to hold its line along the eastern ridge, countering random enemy fire and sealing up such undestroyed caves as could be found in its area. Colonel Boyd improved this time by tightening the containing cordon on the south: moving the line facing the Horseshoe's mouth from the far side of the swamp to the lee of the causeway, tying in on the right at the base of Walt Ridge. On the morning of 10 October 1/5 had been relieved by the 2d Battalion, 7th Marines, and moved into a bivouac area to the south. As the latter unit had previously occupied the same line, officers and men were entirely familiar with the positions, and the relief

was completed without casualties or notable incidents. Thus, 2/7 had been on the left of 2/5 throughout the two final days of the latter's attack, but had been no more active there than had its predecessors.[66]

Following its sortie into the Horseshoe on 7 October, the 3d Battalion had been in regimental reserve near the command post. On 10 October Company K had been sent up into the hills to eliminate some enemy snipers who had become unexpectedly active in caves located in an area far behind the present front lines which the 1st Marines had overrun and believed secured as early as D-plus 3.

Whether these Japanese had lurked undiscovered in these supposedly cleaned out caves all this time, or had infiltrated from the Pocket to reoccupy them, was anybody's guess. But they were there, firing down a draw at troops passing along the main road and generally making a nuisance of themselves. And so craftily did they play their little game that the men of Company K never did find them, though they received some rifle fire and five mortar shells in the process of trying. They blasted shut every cave opening they could find and returned the next day to finish the job. They were successful in that somewhere along their methodical course they put an end to the sniping, but in all of their two days work there they glimpsed not a single live Japanese.

Any resemblance between the uneventful relief of the 1st Battalion and that of the 2d, two days later, was purely coincidental. Instead of moving into a comparatively quiet sector already familiar to the relieving unit, the 3d Battalion was taking over a front which had been seized only the previous afternoon and with which even the troops being relieved had had small chance to become acquainted. And it was anything but "quiet", comparatively or otherwise. Before the day's doings were over, 22 Marines

---

[66] The depleted battalion suffered 31 additional battle casualties during this period, however, and its total strength was down to 277 on 14 October.

of the two battalions had become casualties.

The line [67] held by the 2d Battalion on the morning of 12 October was in the form of a deep salient, nowhere achieving any great width. At the apex Company F, facing southward, had no friendly troops on its immediate left, where the side of Hill 140 fell away in a sheer cliff into the northern end of the Horseshoe. Company E was echeloned rearward along the eastern slopes of Ridge 3 and Baldy Ridge, in visual contact with elements of 2/7 on Boyd Ridge across the narrow canyon. On the right, Company G was bent back almost as sharply along the opposite slope of Baldy and over onto Wattie Ridge.

According to the 3d Battalion plan, Company L relieved Company F on Hill 140. Since the narrow canyon in Company E's sector could be controlled by patrols operating from Boyd Ridge, there was no need to continue this front in any force, so the remaining two companies of 3/5 were placed in position on the right preparatory to straightening out the front by a push southward pivoting on Hill 140: Company K tying in with Company L, and Company I extending the flank westward across Wattie Ridge.

There was trouble in all sectors. The commanding officer of Company K found the troops he was to relieve so thoroughly pinned down by enemy fire that the machine gunners were sighting along the under side of their weapon's barrel. A stranger in some of the strangest territory in the world, he raised his head in an attempt to orient himself—and was killed instantly by a Japanese bullet.

Over to the westward things were just as bad. Late the previous day, in an effort to rectify the line, a reserve platoon of Company F had pushed forward into the high ground above the West Road. Heretofore this region had been kept under control, more or less, by concentrations of interdicting artillery and mortar fire. With friendly troops in actual occupancy, this fire had to be called off. The Japanese, reacting promptly, reoccupied the area in some force. Exercising their excellent fire discipline, they kept their presence hidden until a platoon of Company I moved in; then, taking advantage of the inevitable confusion attendant on performing front line relief, they cut loose with heavy rifle and machine gun fire from positions enfilading both platoons. This was a situation calling for discretion, and the troops were drawn back under smoke grenade concealment to allow new concentrations of mortar fire to work over the area again.

This day, 12 October (D-plus 27), saw two other significant developments.

First, was issuance of a new map which at last undertook to show the terrain of the Pocket as it actually was rather than as it had appeared in preliminary aerial surveys when overgrown with vegetation. This was a hurried sketch job prepared by the Intelligence Section of the 5th Marines: inaccurate as regards relative elevations and with contour lines deceptive. However, it was reasonably accurate on the horizontal plane, and certainly a vast improvement over anything existing heretofore. With its advent, some uniformity in nomenclature began to appear in unit reports.[68]

The second event of importance was the emplacing of artillery in the high ground.

---

[67] It should be understood that this was not a "line" in any strict military sense; rather, a series of positions, held in no great strength and often in only visual contact with one another.

[68] As has been noted earlier, place names were improvised hurriedly and without due consideration as to whom should be so honored. Thus, when the mapping party found LtCol R. W. Boyd occupying the elevation seized a week earlier by Maj Hunter Hurst's 3d Bn., 7th Marines, it was tagged on the map "Boyd Ridge". Similarly, when LtCol L. W. Walt, executive officer, 5th Marines, was discovered inspecting positions on the ridge immediately to the south, where Capt E. T. Pope had won the Medal of Honor on D-plus 4, and which had been secured on 3 October by LtCol S. S. Berger's 2/7, it became "Walt Ridge" henceforth. A number of people were most unhappy about this—and still are.

It has been noted that the 2d Battalion especially wanted Hill 140 for this purpose, and even though this unit was in the process of being relieved, no time was lost in carrying through the plan. Tackle was rigged to swing a disassembled 75mm pack howitzer to the summit of Wattie Ridge, from which point it was manhandled to the forward position, reassembled, and set up behind sandbags to fire into the Horseshoe and the western base of Walt Ridge. A second one was similarly installed in the sector of the containing line held by the artillery-infantrymen, now commanded by Lieutenant Colonel Edson A. Lyman, 11th Marines, who had relieved Lieutenant Colonel Richard A. Evans, IIIAC Artillery, on 9 October.

This latter gun was destined to have a brief but colorful career. Colonel Lyman emplaced it on the western rim of Death Valley to bear on the Five Sisters and China Wall. The point directly across from it was believed to be Colonel Nakagawa's observation post from the fact that what were apparently high ranking Japanese officers,

wearing white gloves, had been seen there on occasion studying the terrain through binoculars; a supposition which the violence of enemy reaction seemed to bear out. The first rounds "routed out a covey of Nips," and shortly thereafter the crew was brought under heavy small arms fire at the deadly range of about 75 yards. By the time 40 rounds had been fired, one man was hit and "it was deemed expedient to secure." Two more were killed at daybreak by a hornet's nest of hidden enemy, and the position was considered too perilous for further artillery operations.[69]

Exactly who should be credited with carrying the first sandbag [70] into the Peleliu

------

[69] *Lyman.*

[70] Sandbags were ordered used by the 5th Marines in the attack on the northern end of Peleliu. First use was made in emplacing the 155mm gun in that area and subsequently on the 155mm and 105mm positions placed to angle fire into the mouth of the Horseshoe. At the time of the events here related, the positions atop Walt and Boyd Ridges were fortified with both sandbags and armor plate taken from disabled LVT(A)'s. The latter, how-

ridges has never been clearly established, but he started something which was to become increasingly important as the grim campaign of attrition rolled on its inexorable course. The lack of cover and impossibility of digging-in had repeatedly obliged attacking troops to relinquish hard-won gains as untenable. Obviously, the sandbag provided an answer of a sort, and many were in use at this time in more or less permanent positions, such as the gun emplacement on Hill 140 was intended to be.

But so long as the operation remained essentially one of movement, the problem of sandbagging successive positions on any large scale presented formidable difficulties. Nowhere was there any sand inland of the beaches, which meant that the heavy bags had to be carried into position already filled, no small undertaking in that crazily upended country. It remained for the 81st Division, following relief of the Marines, to develop a technique with such ingenious refinements as to make the sandbag into something closely resembling an offensive weapon, in which capacity it played a crucial part in the final reduction of the Pocket.

The 1st Battalion, 5th Marines, remained inactive in its bivouac area throughout the day of 12 October, but at 1900 one element moved out in a novel attempt at counter-infiltration by placing Marines in concealed positions on the Five Sisters. The force was a small combat patrol from Company C, led by First Lieutenant Roy O. Larsen, Assistant R–2, and its approach was covered by a diversionary shelling within the Horseshoe. As the *Regimental War Diary* records: "The plan was to get on top of these hills and dig in during the remainder of the night." The men managed to climb to the saddle between Sisters number 1 and 2, where they encountered a group of about 35 Japanese who dropped a grenade in their midst, scattering them so that "full control was never regained." The *War Diary*

---

ever, proved too heavy and too awkwardly shaped to be adaptable on any wide scale. Harris Interview.

account adds, somewhat picturesquely: "There were a great many more Japs in these hills as they could be heard talking and sliding around in the coral." Larsen discreetly withdrew.

Morning of 13 October found the 3d Battalion the only unit of the 5th Marines still on the lines, and the only unit of any regiment with immediate orders for resuming the offensive. Hereafter its main efforts would be concentrated to the westward, with the dual purpose of straightening out the salient formed by Hill 140, and providing greater security for the West Road by constricting the Pocket further from this direction.

It will be recalled that the terrain here was considered impractical for attack by either party, and by a sort of tacit mutual consent had been a quiet sector ever since the Pocket had been isolated. The containing lines against sporadic Japanese infiltration, fully manned only at night, followed the most defensible contours, in some places being withdrawn altogether from the high ground during the day to the low ridge just seaward of the West Road. Now 3/5 began probing southward into the flank of the ground in front of the containing lines.

Under cover of artillery and mortar barrages, a patrol from Company K pushed forward 75 yards into the jumbled terrain without encountering any resistance, destroying some Japanese rifles and ammunition discovered during the process. On its right, a similar patrol from Company I penetrated 150 yards, also without resistance, and preparations were made for a serious advance the following day.

At 0600 a napalm strike by aircraft against the region into which it was proposed to attack ushered in the morning of 14 October. Two hours later Company I jumped off in the wake of a heavy mortar preparation. This time resistance was encountered, described in the *Regimental War Diary* as "severe enemy sniper fire." The methodical advance continued nevertheless, and when the men halted at 1630 to prepare positions for the night, they had made a gain of approximately 250 yards.[71]

Simultaneous with this advance by Company I, what was left of the 1st Battalion, 7th Marines, which had been brought up from a rest area for the purpose, attacked northward from the southern perimeter in a converging movement, gaining 125 yards before being halted by enemy fire. A further advance of 150 yards during the next two days completed the job.[72] Since both of these operations had been moving across the front of the old containing lines, these had only to displace forward in order to consolidate the territory thus gained. When this had been done, the new lines were as much as 200 yards deeper into the high ground and something like 400 yards shorter from north to south than they had been nine days earlier.[73] The West Road was not subjected to sniper fire again during the time the Marines remained in occupancy.

By now, even Japanese optimism was wearing a bit thin. Describing an attack on "the western districts of *Suifuzan* yesterday," Nakagawa for once refrained from making claims of victory: "A powerful unit of our garrison force in a daring night attack attacked the enemy in this area. At present a fierce combat and severe artillery fire is taking place, with results unknown." And on the next day: "A unit of the enemy penetrated into *Suifuzan* and western part of *Higashiyama*.[74] Our units holding the southern part of *Suifuzan* together with another strong raiding unit are repulsing the enemy. . . . The enemy intercepted our movements in the western part of *Higashiyama* with a mortar attack which lasted all through the night. They also attacked with flame-throwers attached to tanks."[75] And with that last somewhat puzzling statement ended Japanese cognizance of Marine operations on Peleliu.

The other two companies of 3/5 confined their 14 October activities to improving their positions, sealing caves, patrolling. Company L brought up additional sandbags to Hill 140 and laid concertina wire around the position beyond grenade range which was instrumental in thwarting a Japanese infiltration attempt later that very night. And that was the last gasp of the Peleliu campaign so far as these units were concerned. By 1100 the following morning (15 October), their relief by elements of the 321st Infantry had been completed and they were on their way to a rest in the northern defense zone. The positions which they turned over, and from which the Army regiment commenced its attritional operations against the Pocket, are indicated (approximately) on Map 19.

As early as 27 September, the U. S. flag had been raised at the 1st Marine Division command post to symbolize that Peleliu was secured—as indeed it was to all practical purposes, though it could not be so

---

[71] The inadequacy of such maps as are available of the Pocket area makes exact orientation of positions exceedingly difficult. Those indicated on the accompanying maps are intended to be no more than approximate. According to 3/5 *Record of Events*, Company I's advance carried to Target Square 140–T. This would appear to place it abreast of the Five Brothers and 150–200 yards west of the China Wall. Although the *Regimental War Diary* refers to an overlay, none concerning this movement can be found in the records. It would be inconclusive in any event since the China Wall, as such, is not definitely located on the map it was designed to overlie.

[72] The 1st Battalion, 7th Marines, was attached operationally to the 5th Marines for this action. The route of its first day's attack took it past the western flank of the Five Sisters. On the second day the battalion attempted to penetrate Death Valley but was able to gain only about 50 yards. The mission was completed on the third day by advancing up the next draw to the westward. 1/7 *Historical Report*.

[73] It was estimated that these several operations reduced the area of the Pocket by 30% to 40%. It now measured roughly 400 yards x 500 yards. O. P. Smith, *Personal Narrative*. Here again distance is impossible to scale accurately owing to map variations.

[74] These allusions to *Higashiyama* are not clear, as the Japanese had conceded its loss several days previously and made no claims to having retaken it.

[75] *Tada Record*, 14, 15Oct44.

termed officially. On 12 October,[76] as 3/5 was beginning its final push, the "Assault Phase" of the operation was declared at an end.

This perhaps unfortunate phrase was used at the time and occurs in the official reports of IIIAC (p. 11), 1st Marines Division (II, p. 18), and 81st Infantry Division (II, p. 47). It gave rise to some pungent comment among the Marines still very much in assault in the Umurbrogol ridges, and the 81st Division Wildcats, for whom six weeks of hard fighting remained.

Actually the term had technical significance in that it signalized a transfer of command functions from the assault forces to the Central Pacific administrative echelons: Forward Area (Vice Admiral J. H. Hoover), Western Carolines Sub Area (Rear Admiral J. W. Reeves, Jr.), and Island Command (Brigadier General H. D. Campbell).[77] Admiral Fort in his report used the term "Attack and Occupation Phase"[78] and explains further:

I was directed by Admiral Halsey to turn over command of the Palaus to Vice Admiral Hoover, who was in command of the Forward Area, when the Attack and Occupation Phase terminated. This was when the islands had been occupied and when Base Development had been initiated and could proceed without enemy interference, and when the Assault Troops could be relieved by the Garrison Forces. This phase was completed on 13 October 1944, and I transferred command to CTF 57, Vice Admiral Hoover, at 1200 on 14 October, 1944.[79]

So at long last a turning point had arrived, and it was possible to initiate steps for evacuating the rest of the 1st Marine Division to the doubtful charms of its "re-habilitation" base. But even Pavuvu would look good now.

RELIEF AND DEPARTURE OF 1st MARINE DIVISION

The operation which the commanding general had predicted would be over within four days had now lasted a month—and was still going on. It has been seen how the 1st Marines had been evacuated after that regiment's over-all strength had been cut by 58 per cent in a week of what was possibly the most savage fighting the campaign produced. Succeeding weeks had whittled away the 7th and 5th Marines in turn until their casualties began to approximate that ruinous figure. Furthermore, these two regiments had had a far more protracted dose of war in Peleliu's debilitating heat, soggy rains and backbreaking terrain, and their assault potentials had been as seriously impaired. The troops stood in great need of rest and rehabilitation, and now, at last, their turn was coming.

The permanent relief of the 1st Marine Division by the 81st Infantry Division began on the morning of 15 October when the 2d Battalion, 321st Infantry, took over the area held by 3/5 across the northern end of the Pocket: the Hill 140 salient and the line extending westward from it. The following day the infantry regiment's 1st Battalion relieved 1/5[80] atop Walt and Boyd Ridges and facing the mouth of the Horseshoe. At about the same time elements of the 323d Infantry, newly arrived from the successful seizure of Ulithi, completed taking over the southern and western containing lines, and at 1245 on 16 October command of operations in the Umurbrogol passed officially to the commanding officer, 321st Infantry.[81]

---

[76] Coincidentally, IIIAC command post was set up on shore at 0800 on this date. IIIAC *OpnRpt*, Enc B, 11.

[77] Mission of the Island Command as defined in Western Carolines Sub Area Order #2–44, 2Nov44: "Maintenance of an air base for offensive and defensive use; defense of the Command." This group assumed responsibility for unloading and construction on 28Sept, prisoners of war on 21Oct, and air defense on 10Dec. It did not assume responsibility for ground defense until 13Jan45.

[78] CTS 32 *OpnRpt*, 95.

[79] *Fort.*

[80] This battalion had relieved 2/7 in these positions on 14 October but had remained on the defensive during these two days.

[81] To which the 1st Bn., 323d, was attached operationally at this stage. It should be noted, however, that over-all command of the attack remained in the hands of the 1st Marine Division for another four days, pending the arrival and establishment of the 81st Division CP on 20 Oct.

BATTLE WEARY MARINES could be relieved at last.

This completed relief of the 5th Marines, the 2d Battalion having moved out four days earlier. But the regiment was destined to spend two more weeks at Peleliu in the capacity of general reserve, occupying positions designed to defend against possible Japanse counterlanding: the 2d Battalion on Ngesebus, Kongauru, and Garekayo;[82] the 1st Battalion along the northern extremities of the long peninsula; and the 3d Battalion deployed along the East Road, facing seaward. This defensive conception was a bit euphemistic, as everyone was pretty well convinced that the danger of counterlandings was long since past;[83] so, although they went through a few perfunctory military motions, the troops managed to rest.

The 7th Marines remained committed longer but got away from the island more quickly. Movement Order No. 4–44, dated 16 October, directed embarkation of the regiment for return to base in the Russells as soon as this could be managed, and elements commenced moving to Purple Beach to commence loading operations.

At the time that command passed to the 321st Infantry, 1/7 was still engaged in its northward drive to make possible advancement of the containing lines from the west, and its immediate relief was not thought ex-

---

[82] A smaller island lying northeast of Ngesebus. For its seizure on 9 October see Chap. VIII.

[83] Further evidence of the futility of relying on reason when fighting the Japanese was furnished during the dark morning hours of 18Jan45, when the enemy actually did stage a counterlanding on

Peleliu. By that time most of the 81st Division, in turn, had left the island. With the coming of dawn those elements remaining combined with units of the Island Command to hunt out the intruders with no great difficulty, killing 71 and capturing two. 81st *Unit Hist*, 200.

pedient. Upon completion of its mission later that afternoon, however, the unit was relieved in position by Company B, 323d Infantry, and returned to its bivouac area where it reverted to parent control at 0800 on 17 October. Shortly thereafter the battalion moved in turn to Purple Beach and was embarked in the transport *Sea Sturgeon*.

The 3d Battalion had been ordered into division reserve on 14 October and remained in that capacity for five days without actually being employed in the lines. Company K was attached to the 1st Battalion on the 15th and supported that unit's push, but reverted to parent control before sundown. Then, on the 17th and 18th, the battalion attained the dubious distinction of being the last 1st Division unit to see action on Peleliu.

This was directed against a group of Japanese infiltrators who had reoccupied caves in the area of Company E, 1st Medical Battalion, a short distance south of the Pocket, where they indulged in some lively sniping. The action began at 1840 on 17 October. Company I moved up and engaged the enemy in a short, sharp fire fight but was unable to reduce the positions before dark. The following morning Company L relieved Company I and resumed the attack, only to discover the Japanese present in considerably greater strength than previously estimated. A tank came forward in support but had the misfortune to strike a large land mine and was very thoroughly blown up. The company commander [84] had been directing the tank's fire and was killed, together with three crew members, two others being wounded. Resistance still existed in the area at nightfall, but 81st Division elements relieved Company L the next morning, and the weary battalion reverted to regimental control.

---

[84] Captain H. W. Jones, formerly CO of the Battalion Headquarters Company, had taken over this command only a short time before, following the death of Captain Shanley. The 3d Battalion was especially hard on rifle company commanders: of four who served in that capacity during the Peleliu operation, three were killed in action and one wounded. *Hurst.*

PRIVATE FIRST CLASS RICHARD E. KRAUS earned the Medal of Honor when he intentionally smothered an exploding grenade with his own body thus saving the lives of three men.

Company K had been sent to the beach the previous day to lend a hand at loading ship, and on the morning of the 20th the rest of the battalion arrived at the same destination, where by 1730 all hands had joined the 1st Battalion aboard *Sea Sturgeon*. Loading was completed the following day, and the ship shoved off on 22 October, arriving at Pavuvu on the 30th.

The 2d Battalion, which had been engaged in some patrolling in the northeastern islands, did not commence loading until 26 October. The men thereupon ran into unexpected complications of a somewhat bizarre nature, which the battalion commander describes as follows:

The *Sloterdyke* was a Dutch merchantman (under a Dutch captain with a polyglot crew) leased by the Army with an Army TQM and a Navy armed guard aboard and was carrying a skeleton Marine infantry battalion and a Marine artillery battalion (4/11). By dint of the Marines manning the winches and booms, we were able to load and depart on the 30th.[85]

The good ship *Sloterdyke* (or *Sloterdyck,* or *Sloterdyk*—sources vary as to the spelling) with her colorful complement arrived "home" at Pavuvu on 7 November in the convoy bearing the 5th Marines and its reinforcing elements.

This combat team had been organized as a task force under Brigadier General O. P. Smith, assistant division commander, attached operationally to the 81st Division. The force was not employed in the active fighting, however, the several battalion units remaining in the defensive positions previously described, except for a few minor changes, until 26 October. On that date 81st Division Field Order No. 23 directed their relief by Army elements, which was accomplished by 1200. On the 27th trucks became available and began shuttling the troops from northern Peleliu to Purple Beach.

Lack of suitable shipping delayed embarkation. No regular personnel transports were available, and most of the freighters which were used as resupply ships lacked both accommodations for troops and the loading devices necessary to handle some of the heavy equipment. Even after an adequate ship had been found (transport *Sea Runner*),[86] loading out was seriously complicated by rough seas. In the end it proved necessary to leave some of the equipment behind with a detail of men to take care of it.[87] Not until 30 October did the weary Marines see the last of that island for which they had fought so long and so bloodily.

Some sour punster dubbed it "Nothing Atoll".

---

[85] *Berger.*

[86] Most 5th Marines personnel were embarked in *Sea Runner,* but at least two other vessels took part in this movement. *Benedict.*

[87] A detail of 13 men with 15 vehicles of 1st MT Bn. They left on or about 13Nov44. Ltr 1stLt J. B. Darnell to CMC, 13Mar50.

CHAPTER VIII

The Wildcats Take Over
(15 October–27 November)

Except for personnel and machines of the 710th Tank Battalion acting in support of the Marines in the Umurbrogol, RCT 321 had taken little active part in the Peleliu fighting since completion of its mission in the north on 2 October. Yet the men kept busy at useful tasks: building defense installations against possible counterlanding, burying enemy dead, clearing up the inevitable debris of battle. And, lest their part appear wholly passive, in one four-day period (4–8 October) they managed to kill 171 Japanese.[1]

On 7 October, the 2d Battalion, stationed on Ngesebus and Kongauru, began a series of minor amphibious operations along Peleliu's northern approaches. A number of small islands lay in this region, leading like stepping stones into the central Palaus, with the enemy quite possibly in occupancy. With the idea of finding out, Company F, reinforced, boarded LVT's on the early morning of 9 October and crossed the few thousand

yards of reef to Garakayo, the nearest and largest. The troops encountered some machine-gun fire from a ridge overlooking the southern beach and from the neighboring island of Cordoray, but succeeded in securing it by 1500. Five Japanese were killed in the process and five more during the following night.

On the 10th Company G replaced F and set about platoon reconnaissance of the other nearby islands named with such characteristic Palaus tongue-twisters an Ngemelis, Arimasuku and Garyo. Whenever they were so fortunate as to find an island not already named, the soldiers happily christened it after one of themselves, with the result that their special map shows Murphy, Galligan and Turner among all the Ngargersiuls and Gorokottans. They found no more Japanese, however.

As preparations progressed for evacuation of the 7th Marines, the 321st occupied that regiment's defense sector as well as its own, and on 13 October the assault battalions were ordered to relieve the 5th Marines in the Umurbrogol on the 15th and 16th. All these dispositions threatened to spread the regiment rather thin, but this was somewhat compensated for by arrival and attachment of the 1st Battalion, RCT 323, from Ulithi, with the other two battalions scheduled to follow shortly.

---

[1] 81st *OpnRpt*, II, 45. Many of these had been lurking in caves which had been overrun, but others, discovered on the beaches evidently trying to escape from the island, were believed to have infiltrated from the pocket. Such would-be deserters turned up in increasing numbers as the long grind wore on, their occurrence probably symptomatic of the deterioration of Japanese morale under the remorseless pressure.

With completion of the relief and assumption of command, the assault units of the 321st were deployed around the Pocket as follows: 3/321 held the eastern perimeter with positions along the crests of Walt and Boyd Ridges and extended below the mouth of the Horseshoe; 2/321 was atop Hill 140 and extending west from there, with the 1st Battalion on its right to the southward; 1/323 held the south-southwestern zone, facing the Five Sisters and Death Valley.

For two days (16 and 17 October) elements of the 2d Battalion tried vainly to get from Hill 140 to the top of No. 1 of the Five Brothers. The ravine between was too narrow, the ascent too steep, cover too scarce in view of the heavy and accurate fire from the enemy's commanding positions. On the battalion's right, 1/321 made an advance of 200 yards on the 17th but was stopped cold on the following day and commenced to sandbag its position and bring up pack howitzers.

The tactical importance of gaining a foothold on the summit of the Five Brothers was self-evident to all hands; and RCT 321 was especially anxious to have such an achievement to its credit by the time the 81st Division assumed command. Authority was therefore obtained from the 1st Ma-

TANK-INFANTRY ACTION inside the Horseshoe.

rine Division (which, as has been noted, retained over-all command until 20 October) to stage an all-out effort on the 18th.[2]

To support this assault, tanks and LVT flame-throwers entered the Horseshoe over a track which had been bull-dozed through the draw north of Walt Ridge where they could bear directly on many of the Japanese positions capable of angling fire against the narrow, exposed crest of the Brothers: from the lower slopes of Walt Ridge, Hill 300 and the Five Sisters. Then heavy concentrations of 81mm and 4.2 inch mortar fire were placed on the Brothers themselves.

Under cover of this Company E succeeded in scaling Brother No. 1 at 1100, and 45 minutes later took No. 2. In an effort to exploit these gains while the enemy was still off balance, Company F passed through Company E and was established on the summit of No. 3 by 1315.

At this point, however, success came to an end. On that narrow crest the men were frightfully exposed, with Japanese on three sides of them and no time for the laborious process of bringing up sandbags. Before Company F could consolidate its position, the men found themselves pinned down by a vicious cross-fire from enemy emplacements which the tanks in the Horseshoe

---

[2] O. P. Smith *PerNar*.

were unable to get at. Under cover of this, the Japanese staged a strong counterattack from the two southernmost Brothers and by 1700 succeeded in driving the men of the 2d Battalion from all three of the seized crests.[3]

With establishment of the 81st Division command post on 20 October, the top Marine echelons departed at once by air: General Geiger and the corps staff that morning, General Rupertus and the division staff at 2300. In parting, CG, 1st Marine Division, paid tribute to the Army unit which had fought with him so long and so well in the following terms:

"The performance of duty of the officers and men of Regimental Combat Team 321, throughout the assault phase on Peleliu, Ngesebus and the northern outpost islands warrants the highest praise. It was a pleasure to have this unit serve as part of my command during this extremely difficult operation, and I express the sentiments of every officer and man of the 1st Marine Division in wishing them good luck in future operations against the enemy. In the eyes of the entire 1st Marine Division they have earned a 'Well Done.'"

With his assumption of command, Major General Paul J. Mueller announced that he proposed undertaking a major seige operation, and that was precisely what he did. During the initial phases of an amphibious operation, time is so all-important that often heavy losses must be sustained in order to capitalize it. But this period was long since past on Peleliu. From now on there would be no more ambitious but premature assaults such as that on the Five Brothers. Reduction became a step-by-step business; grim, methodical, inexorable; characterized more by hard work than hard fighting. Not a life would be lost that could possibly be spared.

The number of Japanese remaining in the Pocket was unknown, of course, and estimates varied widely. Asked by the 81st Division for a tentative figure, the 1st Division staff guessed roughly 500, raised by other guessers to a maximum of 1200, "a figure which was subsequently ascertained to be underestimated."[4] At the end of the operation the 81st reported: "Over 1500 Japanese were known to have been killed and fifty-eight captured",[5] an estimate which would appear to disregard the possibility that a few of these might have been disposed of by the Marines during the month they had fought over this terrain. But three days after the Wildcats took over, Colonel Nakagawa, whose reports were seldom exactly pessimistic, informed his superiors on Koror: "Our total garrison units number about 700 soldiers, including the slightly wounded;" and six days later: "Garrison units number about 500 still able to fight."[6]

Whatever their numbers, fight they did, and in the best Japanese tradition.

Although many Marines[7] remained on the island following termination of Marine Corps command, their part was minor. After 20 October the story of Peleliu is the Army's story. Army agencies have told it elsewhere and told it well. It will be only summarized here in order to round out the picture.

The 81st Division employed only two of its regimental combat teams on Peleliu. The 322d Infantry remained mopping up and in garrison on Angaur, though as matters straightened out on that island most of its reinforcing elements were detached and transferred to the scene of the main fighting. All elements of RCT 323, less a small detachment left to garrison Ulithi, had arrived by 26 October, on which date they

---

[3] The narrowness of these razorback crests made it impossible either to fight effectively or to withdraw in an orderly manner. BrigGen O. P. Smith witnessed this action through glasses from below and records: "All of the men did not withdraw north up the ridge, but many of them slid down the steep slopes of the Brothers into Horseshoe Valley below." Smith *PerNar*.

[4] 81st *OpnRpt*, II, 6.

[5] 81st *UnitHist*, 200.

[6] *Tada Record*, 23Oct, 26Oct44.

[7] Notably the aviation units operating from the airfield, service troops attached to the Island Command, two battalions of artillery (4/11 and 3d 155mm Howitzer Bn.) and crews of the LVT flamethrowers.

relieved the weary 321st, less 3d Battalion which remained on the now comparatively inactive eastern perimeter.

Thereafter these four battalions carried on the Pocket battle to the bitter end a month later, though 81st Cavalry Reconnaissance Troop participated in two more island seizures to the north: Gorokottan on 11 November and Ngeregong on the 15th. The latter island had been seized previously by personnel from the LCI gunboats operating in the region, but these had been chased out by an enemy counterlanding. The Reconnaissance Troop went in prepared for any contingency, with artillery and air preparation and LVT(A)'s and LCI's for direct support. But only three Japanese were found, all of them dead.

Back in the Pocket the methodical attrition continued. No one was in any hurry, and the Wildcats' caution was exceeded only by the thoroughness with which they did the job. Mortar concentrations and napalm air strikes prepared the way for each major attack, and extraordinary labor was undertaken to bulldoze routes for tanks and LVT flame-throwers to inaccessible enemy strong points. At times a satisfactory day's advance measured ten to fifty yards, and there were cases of men crawling ahead on their bellies pushing sandbags in front of them with poles. If any one implement could be said to have done more than any other to seal the fate of the Japanese in the Umurbrogol, it would be the humble sandbag.

The Marines' idea of emplacing heavy weapons in strategic high ground for direct fire support was elaborated and ramified by the 81st. There seemed no limit to the Wildcats' ingenuity, especially that of the engineers. When no amount of labor would suffice to get LVT's into one particularly troublesome area, they rigged up what must stand as one of the most unique flame-throwers in anybody's war: a 300-yard pipe line leading to the target from a fuel truck parked on the West Road, complete with booster pumps to insure pressure and equipped with a nozzle which enabled the

TWIN VALLEYS THAT WERE DEATH TRAPS: Horseshoe (left) and Wildcat Bowl, walled in by Walt Ridge, Five Brothers and China Wall. Japanese command post near northern end of the latter.

operator to play flame on the Japanese positions like water from a hose.

A battery of flood lights was mounted so as to focus on the pond within the Horseshoe which served as the enemy's only stable water source. And near the end the 306th Engineer Battalion built a coral ramp that enabled tanks to get from the floor of Wildcat Bowl to the summit of the rugged China Wall. Some of the conveyor systems developed to get supplies up into the ridges and to evacuate the wounded looked like pure Rube Goldberg.

The seige developed according to a traceable design but seldom exactly according to plan. The first heavy pressure was applied from the north and northwest. Elements of 2/321 got back to the top of Brother No. 1 three days after they had been thrown off: on 21 October. This time they had seen to it that ample sandbags were readily available; these were passed to the crest hand-to-hand via human chain, and the position was secured. The following day No. 2 was taken and sandbagged in turn, and on 23 October Nos. 3 and 4 got the same treatment. No. 5, lower in elevation, was dominated by strong positions still enemy held and hence let alone for the time being.

On 22 October elements of 3/321 came down from Walt Ridge and sandbagged a line of defense on the floor of the Horseshoe from which they were never driven, thereby shortening the perimeter considerably on the east. But with the attack stalled in the west and northwest by a combination of terrible terrain and strong resistance, interest next shifted to the south.

Rain and poor visibility stopped offensive operations for the first few days after RCT 323 took over, but on 2 November that regiment's 2d Battalion, attacking in the wake of napalm and mortar preparation, seized the Five Sisters and Hill 300 [8] with comparative ease, sandbagged them and hauled up pack howitzers. But an attempt to move a tank-infantry patrol up Death Valley was repulsed the following day.

Attrition continued to gnaw away, hampered by the weather [9] as well as the Japanese. Armored bulldozers concentrated on the approaches to the two main declivities, and on 13 November tanks and an LVT flame-thrower, supported by infantry, made the first successful sortie into Wildcat Bowl.

This was part of an all-out push from every direction and succeeded so well as a diversion that Company G was able to get from the Sisters onto the southern end of the China Wall against light opposition. This curious formation was really a double ridge, the serried pinnacles along either flank separated by a narrow, jumbled gulch which required something approximating alpine tactics merely to negotiate. By the time the men had toiled and scrambled 75 yards along this, they came under heavy fire from positions farther northward, and the invaluable sandbags were brought up.

A similar gain was made by Company B, attacking from the west, but the advance of the 3d Battalion from the north could be measured in feet, when it could be measured at all. The terrain here was very bad, but certainly no worse than atop the China Wall, and the opposition determined. The reason was surmised at the time and later verified: nearby lay the hard core of all Japanese resistance, the CP of the doughty Nakagawa, who was not a man to neglect defense of his approaches.

The rest of the story is one of unceasing pressure from the north, south and west, with the resulting gradual attrition. Units in assault were relieved at short intervals, and the sandbags continued creeping forward. The action was grinding and monotonous, with few highlights.

By 17 November, tanks had worked onto the southern portion of Death Valley with the aid of armored bulldozers, and by dint of great exertion commenced slugging their way northward from there. Tank-infantry patrols operated virtually at will within Wildcat Bowl, with results that must have been highly discouraging to the enemy. By 21 November it became apparent that the Japanese, moving under cover of darkness, had withdrawn altogether from their remaining caves in the western flanks of the Brothers to concentrate for a last stand in the seemingly impenetrable China Wall.

By taking quick advantage of this development, the Wildcats achieved their most sig-

---

[8] Here that bugaboo of variant place names arises again. The Marines thus called this elevation and considered it a part of the Five Sisters formation though it was separated from the others by a fairly wide saddle. The Wildcats called it "Old Baldy", and it so appears on all their maps, which gives rise to confusion with the Marines' "Baldy Hill" nearly 1,000 yards to the north. Other names applied by the 81st were Wildcat Bowl, China Wall and Grinlinton Pond, none of which had been named previously. They also renamed the Horeshoe Mortimer Valley in honor of Captain Joseph F. Mortimer of the 323d Infantry who was killed in action there. But where the Marines had operated before the new names were applied, this account will continue to adhere to their terminology.

[9] Rain accompanied by the edge of a typhoon halted offensive action altogether 4 to 9 November, and repeated spells of foul weather constituted a minor nuisance until the end of the campaign.

nificant gain of the past two weeks. With advance of the 3d Battalion from the north still held up by impossible terrain and desperate resistance, Company F, supported by tanks and LVT flame-throwers, commenced a sortie up the length of the Bowl at 0700 on 22 November. Forty-five minutes later the foremost elements reached the northern extremity and commenced the precarious ascent of the China Wall itself. By the time the Japanese discovered what was up and were able to react, the company was consolidating a tactically important position on the high ground immediately south of the 3d Battalion lines, trapping those enemy remaining in the area between the two units and imperiling those holding up the drive from the west: above and beyond Death Valley.

Simultaneously with this action, Company H attacked through Company G in the 2d Battalion's position atop the China Wall to the south and sandbagged a 75 yard gain from this direction. And then, as though to prove the validity of the new development, Company I secured the last of the Five Brothers without encountering any opposition. This permitted the containing line to close across the saddle between the Brothers and Sisters, greatly reducing its length.

At last the pattern of Victory was taking shape for the final kill. With a foothold secured at the northern end of the China Wall, Company A, 306th Engineer Battalion, commenced construction of that remarkable coral ramp from the floor of the Bowl to the crest of the double-pinnacled ridge as a means for bringing flame and armor against the enemy's last and heretofore inaccessible strong points.

During that night (24–25 November) 45 Japanese,[10] including two officers, were killed in what proved to be the dying convulsion of organized resistance on Peleliu. The story was obtained from a prisoner captured at about 1100 the following morning. According to his account, Colonel Nakagawa and Major General Kenjiro Murai[11] had ordered this last attack in an effort to break through the beseiging cordon and conduct guerilla warfare against the rear areas. They had then notified headquarters to the effect that the end had come, burned the regimental colors,[12] and ceremoniously shot themselves.

Although no other witnesses remained to verify the suicides, the rest of this characteristically Japanese scene is substantiated by the opening phrases of the last message received from the Peleliu garrison: "Our defense units were on the verge of being completely annihilated; therefore, the unit destroyed the 2d Infantry Regiment flag which they had in their possession. . . . All documents were burned."[13]

Throughout the day of the 25th the circling lines continued their inexorable closing, moving slowly, searching the jumbled ground with infinite care to insure that not a single enemy be overlooked. The 1st Battalion, advancing from the west, flushed 30 Japanese and captured the prisoner referred to above. Twenty-one more were killed during the night in what appeared to be individual attempts to escape rather than concerted action.

The 306th Engineers' ramp was completed late that afternoon, and first thing the

---

[10] There were doubtless a few isolated individuals still holding out in the region, but the garrison commander reported only 56 men under a Capt Nemoto as of 1700 on 24Nov. *Tada Record.*

[11] This was the only intelligence obtained during the entire operation which placed General Murai on Peleliu. The Japanese CP occupied a deep, two-chambered cave 40 feet down a vertical shaft near the northern end of the China Wall, but this was not fully explored until the bodies it contained had decomposed beyond positive identification. For further elaboration on this minor mystery, see Appendix F.

[12] In Japanese military tradition, the burning of any unit's colors signified that that unit had ceased to exist and should be stricken from the Army lists.

[13] *Tada Record,* 24Nov44. Text of the message as eventually relayed to Tokyo read: "The splitting of the men into 17 teams was completed at 1700 hours. Following the commander's wishes, we will attack the enemy everywhere. This will be the last message we will be able to send or receive."

NAPALM STRIKES, such as this against the Five Sisters, were spectacular, but, as the Japanese commander reported, "Since perfecting our defenses against fire, we suffered no losses."

following morning tanks and an LVT flamethrower began the tricky negotiation of this route to the ridge's summit. Otherwise action on 26 November was a repetition of the previous day's, with the strongest resistance still encountered in the area at the head of Death Valley.

No fireworks, literal or metaphorical, signalized the end of one of the most stubbornly contested campaigns in the history of this or any other war. The units in assault jumped off in all zones at 0700 on 27 November. As the 81st Division *Operation Report* puts it succinctly: "Resistance to this multisided attack seemed to disintegrate completely." At 1030 elements of the 2d Battalion, moving northward along the China Wall, came face to face with their comrades of the 3d Battalion, working southward. Across the few yards intervening, they could see men of the 1st Battalion perched on the rim of Death Valley. For long moments the weary Wildcats looked at one another in an uncanny silence, trying to realize that this was all there was; there wasn't any more.

At 1100 Colonel Arthur P. Watson, commanding RCT 323, reported officially to General Mueller that the Peleliu operation was over. "The enemy had fulfilled his determination to fight to the death." [14]

---

[14] 81st *OpnRpt*, 97.

CHAPTER IX

Conclusion

The Peleliu operation closely resembled no other in the Pacific war in which Marines participated; yet in no respect was it wholly unique. In a sense it was a repeat performance of Tarawa and the Marshalls, with overtones of Saipan and Guam; and it presaged the pattern of things to come on under-tunnelled Iwo Jima and, perhaps more particularly, in the high ground of Okinawa.

Although many of its aspects were dramatic and spectacular in themselves, the operation produced no important features which were entirely novel when the war is viewed in perspective. Several, however, are of interest to the student of warfare.

Perhaps the most significant of these on the historical level was the unequivocal demonstration of the value of sea power [1] in effecting economy of manpower. The forces defending the Palaus were notably superior in numbers to the land forces attacking; yet because the latter were able to concentrate their full striking power against the vital objective while the U. S. Navy denied the Japanese the sea lanes necessary to pour in substantial reinforcements, effective control of the entire island group was achieved by commitment of a fraction of the assault troops which would have been required had command of the sea been less absolute.

That doubt should be cast on the strategic importance of this seizure [2] is unfortunate to the memory of the men who fought and died there. And that is a matter on which no definite conclusion can be reached: because the conquest was a *fait accompli* prior to the invasion of the Philippines, no one can state with full certainty what would have happened had it not taken place. What is known is that Peleliu, together with air facilities subsequently developed on Angaur, proved exceedingly useful as a support and staging point for the Philippines throughout that lengthy campaign. Equally important, the Japanese were denied the whole Palaus chain as a base and staging area for attacks on U. S. naval shipping and lines of communication supporting the Philippines invasion.

On the tactical level, Peleliu was notable as a complete vindication of the essential amphibious doctrines developed by the Ma-

---

[1] Including naval aviation. Because the enemy's air potential had already been destroyed, U. S. air power, as such, played a purely supporting role during the assault phase of the operation.

[2] This doubt, together with the misapprehension regarding the nature and probable duration of the operation which was implanted in the minds of newspaper representatives, and by them transmitted to the U. S. public, resulted in the Peleliu operation being among the least known and least understood in the entire war.

CORPORAL LEWIS K. BAUSELL won the Medal of Honor on D-Day for his heroism in smothering a greneade's explosion with his own body.

rine Corps through two decades of peacetime study and perfected in the crucible of combat on the long road from Guadalcanal to the fringes of the Japanese Empire. This was demonstrated by the quick and efficient securing of a beachhead against the heaviest kind of resistance by an assault force considerably smaller proportionately than prescribed by doctrine to insure success in a landing of this nature. That subsequently the operation proved long-drawn-out and costly is attributable to factors extraneous to the purely amphibious aspects: the nature of the terrain, and the determination and resourcefulness of the enemy.

For Peleliu was also notable in demonstrating that the Japanese, too, had learned by experience. One thing they had learned was to minimize their losses from naval gunfire.[3] And they had gained security consciousness. In marked contrast to recent goings-on in the Marianas, U. S. troops noted a dearth of captured operational maps,

[3] See Appendix C.

orders and miscellaneous documents packed with useful information, a dearth astonishing to intelligence officers whom long experience had taught to take such sources for granted. As had been noted in passing, there were no frantic, futile *banzai* charges to simplify the attackers' problem; for the first time in the Marines' experience in the Pacific, the Japanese made good their tactic of exacting a maximum toll of their enemies in fighting to the death. Though it could not be foreseen at the time, these seeming phenomena were to characterize enemy procedure from this time onward.

Two new Japanese weapons made their appearance, which were also destined to be encountered again.[4] One was a highly effective 150mm mortar, resembling a king-size 81mm, with a tube more than six feet long and a base plate so heavy as to render it primarily a static rather than a mobile weapon. The second was a homemade rocket, improvised by attaching a propellant charge to the base of a 200mm naval shell. This detonated with a terrific concussion—when it detonated at all. What little information was gleaned concerning this came from examination of the several duds which fell within the lines, for no launching device was ever found, nor was any prisoner taken who would admit knowing anything about it. Evidently it could not be aimed but was simply launched in the general direction of American-held territory. Lacking stabilizing fins, it usually made its descent as described by one eyewitness, "end over end, like a badly punted football." Ineffective as this was on Peleliu, it was to prove but the crude forerunner of the infinite variety of self-propelled missles which were destined to lend variety, if little feeling of security, to life on Iwo Jima a few months later.

On the U. S. side, the most important new weapon to make its initial apearance

[4] Also found were several 200mm permanent mount naval guns with sawed-off barrels, the exact purpose of which was never determined as those captured were incompletely mounted and inoperative.

was the long-range flame-thrower. This performed yeoman service, yet the vulnerability of the LVT as a carrier for a purely offensive weapon proved a limiting factor throughout the operation. This came as no great surprise; the amtrack was simply the most practical vehicle to which this new device could be adapted in the short time available. With development of a mount suitable to the Sherman tank, the long-range flame-thrower went on to play its highly useful part in subsequent operations.

That naval gunfire preparation proved inadequate for its mission has been touched upon in passing. The fact is that local conditions made this mission impossible of anything resembling complete fulfillment by any techniques then in practice.[5] And there was an additional limiting factor: the protracted bombardment of Guam had caused a shortage of ammunition which could not be fully replenished in the short interval between the two operations.[6]

There is no place in a monograph of such limited scope for debate on the pros and cons, potentialities and limitations, of naval gunfire as a supporting arm. At corps and division levels, the essential fact was that, for whatever reasons, enemy installations enfilading both flanks of the landing beaches were still operative when the assault waves went in and inflicted casualties to personnel and materiel so severe as to hamper seriously the first day's operations. Nor had any effective plans been made to utilize naval gunfire to preclude or interdict attack by Japanese tanks known to be on the island.[7]

---

[5] "The caves encountered on both islands presented a problem that so far has not been successfully solved by any supporting arm." IIIAC *OpnRpt*, Encl G, 4.

[6] *Fort. Oldendorf.* Owing to the defeat of the Japanese fleet in the Philippines Sea and the delay in the Guam invasion, it was possible to subject that island to 13 days of pre-landing bombardment, with exceptionally good results.

[7] "Peleliu indicated that tanks could survive a preparatory bombardment, and that NGF and air were at that time of little effectiveness in prevent-

NEW JAPANESE WEAPON. This king-size 150mm mortar made its first appearance at Peleliu. Projectile lies on base plate.

On the credit side, however, the volume of fire actually delivered did achieve two highly useful results: it sheared away much of the covering vegetation, thereby revealing the true contours at last and reducing the enemy's concealment; and it partially neutralized the high ground during the initial landing to the extent that the shelling encountered by assault troops crossing the reef, bad as that was, proved less severe than what was to be encountered in some later phases. And once the Marines were ashore and able to pin-point profitable targets, fire missions delivered on call were nearly always accurate and effective.

To a greater extent than any other Pacific operation, Peleliu pitted U. S. troops in the open against a devilishly concealed and fortified enemy. That bedrock of adamant coral limestone underlying the island's thin soil made digging in impossible with the means available to troops in assault, whereas the Japanese had had time to drill and blast out their defensive positions. During the early phases, the attack moved mainly across open terrain dominated by high ground; later the high ground itself proved a maze

---

ing hostile tanks from closing on the landing force." *Stuart.*

DEDICATING PELELIU CEMETERY. General Rupertus near center with cane; Colonel Puller on his right. Group on extreme right: General O. P. Smith, Colonel Harrison, Colonel Harris.

of fire-swept razorback ridges and barren declivities devoid of natural cover.

Here, if ever, was essentially an infantry battle, with all supporting arms and troops concerted to help the man on foot in their several ways and with varying degrees of effectiveness, again mainly as dictated by terrain conditions.

During the initial phases, their parts were the conventional ones they had been trained to perform. But once the fighting entered the ridges, more particularly after resistance was localized within a constricted pocket, the battle became one of improvisation: traditional Yankee ingenuity and the will to live pitted against Japanese preparation and the fanatic will to die; with each offensive thrust, often each individual cave, presenting problems peculiar to itself.

It is this feature, perhaps more than any other, which characterizes the Peleliu operation in the minds of those who partici-

pated or who have studied it. To the combat engineers, this meant greatly increased burdens and responsibilities; to the artillery, an early end to massed fires and the adaptation of individual weapons to direct fire missions. To the air arm, it meant a greatly curtailed field of usefulness and, because of the nature and location of enemy defenses, greatly reduced effectiveness despite the daring and ingenuity displayed. The tanks and LVT flame-throwers played their valuable parts to the bitter end, under difficulties never anticipated and rarely encountered elsewhere. But in the final analysis it was the man on foot with a weapon in his hand who took that evil ground and held it.

Because the fighting dragged on to such seemingly interminable length, it is easy to lose sight of the important fact that the basic mission of the entire operation was accomplished within a week. The airfield had been secured and was becoming fully operational, all the beaches necessary for the landing of supplies were in use, and base development was in full swing. Two months before the last wretched Japanese combatant was exterminated in the Peleliu ridges, capture of the Palaus in the strategic sense had become an accomplished fact, with upward of 25,000 enemy troops to the northward left to wither on the vine, as useless to the defense of the Empire as though they were stationed at the South Pole rather than within 500 miles of the Philippines.

With capture of the high ground immediately dominating the airfield, the campaign degenerated into what was in effect guerrila warfare of a type peculiar to no people other than the Japanese. The defenders' potential for tactical action on any effective scale had been destroyed, and they were cut off from support and reinforcement. From that point onward, they killed solely for the sake of killing, without hope and without higher purpose.

The operation was a costly one by any standards. Latest available check up [8] gives total Marine Corps casualty figures of 6,526, of whom 1,252 are listed as dead (killed in action, died of wounds and missing presumed dead). An indication of how heavy a share was borne by the assault infantry appears in a report shortly following the action which breaks down total regimental casual-

PRIVATE FIRST CLASS CHARLES H. ROAN was awarded the Medal of Honor for throwing his body upon an enemy grenade, thereby saving the lives of four men.

ties as follows: 1st Marines—1,749; 5th Marines—1,378; 7th Marines—1,497.[9]

In addition, the 81st Infantry Division, Reinforced, lost 1,393 officers and men on Peleliu, 208 killed in action, plus 1,676 (196 killed in action) on Angaur.[10]

Victory over dug-in Japanese never did come cheap.

---

[8] Figures certified and released by USMC Personnel Accounting System, 1Jun50.

[9] 1st MarDiv *SAR*, II, Annex G, 2. These figures should be taken as approximate and indicative rather than accurate in detail. Owing to a change in the methods of casualty accounting, no up-to-date breakdown by units is available at this writing.

[10] Figures from 81st *Unit Hist*, 1948.

Bibliography

Primary sources used in compiling this monograph are the official reports, by whatever title, submitted by units which participated in the Palaus operation. Necessarily, these vary widely in completeness and reliability, necessitating painstaking evaluation in each individual case. This has required a good deal of flexibility in the handling. In only one particular has a hard and fast policy been followed: Wherever practicable, reports of the echelon most immediately concerned with the events discussed have been guided on in cases where evidence appeared to conflict.

Thus, as the operation broke down increasingly into actions by smaller and smaller units, battalion reports, perhaps scribbled in pencil on soiled paper, are cited in preference to the often voluminous and nicely bound studies turned in by division, corps or task force; this on the principle that there can be no more "basic" source on any particular fight than the men who did the fighting. In combat, reports seep upward, losing detail and reality in the process. The higher the echelon, the farther removed it was from the scene of action. It has been this writer's experience that reports on those levels, besides having fundamentally different interests, tend to perpetuate rather than screen out the inevitable inaccuracies which sometimes occur.

To supplement the basic sources, preliminary drafts of this monograph were distributed to individual participants who occupied key positions during the campaign, soliciting comments, corrections and elaborations. Notes and interview transcripts resulting are now on file in the records of the Historical Division, U. S. Marine Corps. Such material cited in the text has been carefully checked against the official reports and any discrepancies noted. In this manner much additional detail has been gained, and it has been possible to elaborate many necessarily terse official entries. Only in a very few instances not adequately covered in any extant reports have statements of individuals been accepted as primary source material, simply because otherwise these facets of the operation would have been impossible of any treatment whatsoever. Recognizing the fallibility of the human memory five years after the event, the reader is asked to accept such passages as what they purport to be: informed conjecture, or studied surmise.

Documents consulted in the preparation of this work, though not all of them are cited therein, are listed below, progressing downward by successive echelons, except in the case of battalion reports which are grouped under the respective regimental heads. Unless otherwise noted, these are on file in the records of the Historical Division, Headquarters U. S. Marine Corps.

DOCUMENTS

Combined Chiefs of Staff. Specific Operations for the Defeat of Japan. Serial CCS 397 (Revised); SEXTANT Conference, 137th meeting, 1st and 2d Plenary meetings. Office of Naval Records and Library.

Joint Chiefs of Staff. Directive to CinCPOA and CinCSoWesPac. Serial JCS 713/4, dtd 12Mar44. Office of Naval Records and Library.

CNO (F–111). STALEMATE. Chronological Resume of Operations. File contains dispatches (incoming and outgoing), maps, and a daily estimate of the situation.

CNO (Air Intelligence Group). Air Group 16 (USS *Lexington*) action report, 30, 31 March and 1 April, 1944. Serial Op–16–V–E–MEM; dtd 2Jun44.

CNO (Air Intelligence Group). Excerpts from USS *Bancroft* action report. 30 March 1944 to 1 April 1944. Serial 16–V–E–LSM; dtd 19Jun44.

CNO (Air Intelligence Group). Excerpts from CTU 58.2.2 action report for 29–31 March 1944. Serial Op–16–V–E–MEM; dtd 18May 44.

CNO (Air Intelligence Group). Excerpts from Task Group 58.2 action report for 30 March–1 April 1944. Serial OP–16–V–E–ITZ; dtd 5Jun 44.

CNO (Air Intelligence Group). Excerpts from narrative of action of USS *Petrof Bay* and USS *Savo Island*, 12–30 September 1944. Serial Op–16–V–E/JSA/MEM over 276; dtd 14Nov44.

CNO (Air Intelligence Group). Excerpts from action report of CTU 32.7.2. Serial Op–16–V–E/AMG/MEM over 302; dtd 6Dec44.

CNO (Air Intelligence Group). Material Excerpts From Action report of CTU 32.7.1. Serial Op–16–V–E–AMG/bjn over 305; dtd 25Nov44.

CNO (Air Intelligence Group). Navy Department Comments on action report of Commander, Air Group 13. Serial Op–16–V–E/EW/MEM over 307; dtd 25Nov44.

CINCPAC (OpInfoSec). Report of Operations USS *Bunker Hill*, 30–31 March and 1 April 1944. Serial EWM/dmt; dtd 19May44.

CINCPAC-CINCPOA. Photographic Intelligence Reports. Serials vary with each document; dates are date of report. Cover period 16Apr–8Aug44.

CINCPAC-CINCPOA. Translations of Captured Japanese Documents. Serials vary with each document; dates are date of translation and publication. Cover period 15Aug–5Sep44.

CINCPAC-CINCPOA. GRANITE Campaign Plan. No serial; dtd 27Dec43. Office of Naval Records and Library.

CINCPAC-CINCPOA. Outline Campaign Plan, GRANITE II (with nine appendices). Serial Pac–132–asc over A16/GC over 00071; dtd 3Jun44.

CINCPAC-CINCPOA. Bulletin Number 114–44. "Tables: Tides, Currents, and Daylight and Dark (Marianas, Western Carolines and certain of Philippines)."

CINCPAC-CINCPOA. Bulletin Number 120–44. "Anchorages and Harbor Facilities for Carolines, Luzon, Formosa, Pescadores and China Coast."

CINCPAC-CINCPOA. Bulletin Number 124–44. "Southern Palau Information Bulletin." No serial; dtd 15Aug44. Supercedes JICPOA Bulletin Number 87–44.

CINCPAC-CINCPOA. Bulletin Number 129–44. "Palau Gazetteer."

CINCPAC-CINCPOA. Bulletin Number 136–44. "Northern Palau-Information Bulletin."

CINCPAC-CINCPOA. Bulletin Number 173–45. "Japanese Military Caves on Peleliu—Know Your Enemy!" No serial; dtd 23Jul45. A reprint and expansion of Peleliu IsCom study prepared by Lt. W. C. Phelan, USNR.

CINCPAC-CINCPOA. Item Number 11,190, translation of Japanese training order for Palau Sector forces. Serial 0680 (4th MarDiv); dtd 7Nov44.

JICPOA. Bulletin Number 17–44. "Palau Information Bulletin."

JICPOA. Bulletin Number 17A–44. "Palau Air Target Folder."

JICPOA. Bulletin Number 31–44. "Tables—Carolines and Marianas (Tides, Daylight and Dark)".

JICPOA. Bulletin Number 87–44. "Palau Information Bulletin."

JICPOA. Bulletin Number 87T–44. "Palau—Target Analysis."

JICPOA. Change and Addition Bulletin Number 87A–44. "Palau—Babelthaup and Koror—Air Target Folder." With supplements.

JICPOA. Change and Addition Bulletin Number 87B–44. "Palau—Peleliu and Angaur—Air Target Folder." With supplements.

Amphibious Forces, Pacific Fleet. Anti-Invasion Mines on Peleliu (enclosing report of UDT Number 6). Serial CAF/S76 over 001011; dtd 5Nov44.

Third Fleet. Action Report (with three enclosures). Serial A16–3/(16) 0090; dtd 14Nov44.

Third Fleet. Comments on Operation Report of III Amphibious Corps. Serial A16–3/(02) over 00174 dtd 28Dec44.

FMFPac. First endorsement on 3d Amphibious Force Operation Report (Enclosed III PhibCorps 2d endorsement to basic document). Serial 1870 over 0253/210 over 001081; dtd 3Nov44.

Third Amphibious Force. Report on STALEMATE II Operation (with ten enclosures). Serial FE25/-A16–3(3) over 00314; dtd 11Nov44.

Western Pacific Task Forces. Operation Plan No. 14–44. Serial A16–31(16) over 0030; dtd 1Aug44.

Task Force 32. STALEMATE II Operation Plan A501–44. Serial Gr5A/A4–3 over 00026; dtd 2Sep44.

Task Force 32. STALEMATE II Movement Order No. A503–44. Serial Gr5A/A4–3 over 00018; dtd 24Aug44.

Task Group 32.1. STALEMATE II Training Order No. A504–44. Serial Gr5A/A4–3 over 00010; no date.

Task Group 32.1. STALEMATE II Attack Order No. A502–44 (with 2 enclosures). Serial Gr5A/-A4–3 over 00019; dtd 23Aug44.

Task Force 33. STALEMATE II Attack Plan A303–44. Serial FE25/A16–3 (1); dtd 25Aug44.

Task Force 34. Operation Order ComBatPac No. 10–44. Serial FF12–2/A16–3(5) over 0064; dtd 26Aug44.

Task Force 57. Operation Plan CmFwdArea No. 6–44. Serial A4–3(1)/FF12/25–dch; dtd 18Aug-44.

Amphibious Group 5 (Task Force 32). Amphibious Operation—To capture Peleliu and Angaur (with twelve enclosures). Serial Gr5A/A9–8 over 0054; dtd 16Oct44.

Task Group 32.19. Training Order ComLSTFlot 13 No. 3–44. Serial A16–3/A4–3–m; dtd 24Aug44.

Western Landing Force Task Group 36.1. Operation Plan 1–44, STALEMATE II. Serial 14–DWF-jfm; dtd 31Jul44.

Western Landing Force Task Group 36.1. Administrative Order 1–44 to accompany Operation Plan 1–44 STALEMATE II. No serial; dtd 27Jul44.

Task Group 38.3. Operation Order, ComCarDiv 1 No. 1–44. Serial FB2–1/A16–3/dp; dtd 25Aug44.

Battleship Division Seven. Operation Order Com-BatDiv 7 No. 2–44. Serial A16–3/FB 1–7 over 0001; dtd 29Aug44.

Transport Division 6, Amphibious Forces, USPac Fleet. Operation Report of Assault and Occupation of Peleliu. Serial CTD6 over A16–3/A9–8 over 0116; dtd 2Oct44.

Transport Division 26. Action Report—Assault landing on Angaur (with 1 enclosure). Serial FB7–26/A16–3 over 0129; dtd 1Oct44.

LST Flotilla 13. Attack Order ComLSTFlot 13 No. 8–44. Serial A16–3/A4–3 over 0009–44; dtd 30Aug44.

USS *Centaurus*. Action Report, 14 August–10 October 1944. No serial, dtd 25July45.

USS *Du Page*. Operation Memorandum 9–44. No serial; dtd 10Sep44.

USS *Fayette*. Action and Operation Report 15–20 September 1944. Serial APA 43/416–3/A9–8/hj over 049; dtd 21Sep44.

USS *Harris*. Action Report 15–25 September 1944 (with two enclosures). Serial APA2/A16–3 over 036; dtd 8Oct44.

USS *Leedstown*. Action Report on Occupation of Peleliu Island, 15–20 September 1944 (with 3 enclosures). Serial APA56/A16–3(Cy) over 0112; dtd 22Sep44.

USS *Sumter*. Action Report, Landing on Angaur Island, 17–23 September 1944 (with 4 enclosures). Serial APA52/A9–8; dtd 24Sep44.

USS LCI(G) 452. Action Report, 4 September–5 October 1944. No serial; dtd 23Feb45.

Task Unit 10.15.3, Island Command, Peleliu. War Diary, September 1944. No serial or date.

Task Unit 57.14.1, Island Command, Peleliu. War Diary, October 1944. No serial or date.

Island Command, Peleliu. Jap military caves on Peleliu (a photographic study prepared by Lt. W. C. Phelan, USNR). Serial 3252 over G–2: WCP–rtd; dtd 20May45. Later reprinted and expanded in CINCPAC-CINCPOA Bulletin Number 173–45.

Island Command Peleliu. Operation Plan No. 1–45. No serial; dtd 5Mar45.

Island Command. Operation Plan, ComMarianas No. 6–45. Serial 03643; dtd 14Nov45.

Island Command. Operation Memorandum No. 3–45, Standing Operating Procedure for Defense of Southern Palaus. Serial 3252; dtd 13Jan45.

V Amphibious Corps. War Diary, October 1944 (with 8 enclosures). Serial 1975–50 over 0129/-192 over 000122; dtd 7Nov44.

Expeditionary Troops, Third Fleet. Special Action Report (with ten enclosures). Serial 00155; dtd 12Oct44; Palau Island A1–2.

Expeditionary Troops (Task Force 36). Operation Plan 1–44, STALEMATE II. Serial JOB/jfm; dtd 2Sep44.

Expeditionary Troops (Task Force 36). Administrative Order 1–44 to accompany Operation Plan 1–44, STALEMATE II. No serial; dtd 22Jul44.

III Amphibious Corps. Operation Report, Palau Operation (with thirteen enclosures) Serial 5/187-whf over 00883–1; dtd 24Oct44.

III Amphibious Corps. C–2 Reports 15 September–19 October 1944. 35 Reports. No serial; dates are date of individual reports.

81st Infantry Division. Operation on Peleliu Island, 23 September–27 November 1944 (in three phases with a pictorial supplement). Serial RS–3–1538; dtd c. 9Feb45.

81st Infantry Division. The Capture of Angaur Island, 17 September–22 October 1944 (in three phases). Serial RS–1–109; dtd 26Dec44.

81st Infantry Division. Operation Reports. No serial; dtd 21Sep44–4Jan45.

4th AAA Battalion. War Diary, October 1944. Serial RTG/efp over (051); dtd 20Nov44.

7th AAA Battalion. War Diaries for September and October 1944. Serial B15044 and B15944 respectively; dtd 1Oct44 and 1Nov44 respectively.

7th AAA Battalion. War Diary, September 1944 (with 3 enclosures). Serial HRP/rm over B15144; dtd 1Oct44.

7th AAA Battalion. War Diary, October 1944 (with 3 enclosures). Serial B15044; dtd 1Nov44.

7th AAA Battalion. Report of Operations (with forwarding endorsements). Serial HRP/bfs over B15644; dtd 27Oct44.

7th AAA Battalion. Report of Operation. Serial 2295–10 over 0212/220 over 001053; dtd 18Nov44.

7th AAA Battalion. Combat Reports (accounts of three antiaircraft actions forwarded under two separate letters). Serial HRP/wts dtd 7Oct44.

7th AAA Battalion. Operation Plan 1–44. Serial HJI/gcc; dtd 26Aug44.

12th AAA Battalion. War Diary, September 1944. Serial 2385–15 over JRH/eks; dtd 1Oct44.

12th AAA Battalion. War Diary, October 1944. Serial 2385–15/HHM/eks; dtd 1Nov44.

3d 155mm Howitzer Battalion. War Diary, October 1944. No serial; dtd 12Dec44.

8th 155mm Gun Battalion. War Diary, 1 September–10 December 1944. Serial 2295/GVH-wwl; dtd 18Jan45.

8th Amphibian Tractor Battalion, III Amphibious Corps. Report of Operation. Serial 471/380; dtd 27Sep44.

4th War Dog Platoon, III Amphibious Corps. Combat Report. Serial 3/000 over 13/237–wha over 001165–1; dtd 9Dec44.

5th War Dog Platoon, III Amphibious Corps. Combat Report. Serial 30,000–05 over 13/237–lac over 001142–1; dtd 24Nov44.

1st Marine Division. Special Action Report, Palau Operation (in two phases with 17 annexes and additional maps and overlays enclosed; endorsements of III PhibCorps and FMFPac, attached). Serial 01019; dtd 16Nov44.

1st Marine Division. War Diary, September 1944 (with 1 enclosure, 5 annexes). Serial 458/390 over 1990–5–80 over AE0003; no date.

1st Marine Division. War Diary, October 1944 (with 13 annexes). Serial 0779 over 1990–5–80 over 458/396; no date.

1st Marine Division. Operation Plan 1–44 (with 14 annexes and three addenda). Serial 0003 over 1990–5–80 over 458/332; dtd 15Aug44.

1st Marine Division. Administrative Order 1–44. Serial 1990–25 over 106/286 over 0003; dtd 7Aug44.

1st Marine Division. Special Action Report. Serial 0775 over 1990–5–80; dtd 13Sep44.

1st Marine Division. Intelligence Journal of Peleliu Operation (with one enclosure). Serial 00062 over 475/397; dtd 22Feb45.

1st Marine Division, Intelligence Section. Peleliu, Its Terrain and Defenses. Serial 00161 over 475/-355; dtd 14Dec44. A collection of photographs of terrain features and specific defenses. Pictures were taken on the ground during the operation, and are printed in conjunction with excerpts from aerial photos taken before the operation.

1st Marine Division. Preliminary Interrogation Reports. No serial; dates are date of individual reports. Includes 53 reports covering period 16 September–16 October 1944.

1st Marine Division. D–2 Periodic Reports. No serial; dates are date of individual reports. Includes 29 reports covering period 18 September–19 October 1944.

1st Marine Division. Compilation of captured Japanese documents (translated and assembled in a single jacket). Undated; no serials. Japanese or translation dates apply.

1st Marine Division. Miscellaneous intelligence correspondence (many originals) received by 1st MarDiv from Third Fleet and X-Ray Corps. Covers period 17 July to 14 August 1944.

1st Marine Division. D–3 Journal. No serial; dates are date of individual report. Covers period 26 August–7 November 1944.

1st Marine Division. Field Order No. 5–44. Serial 1990–5–80 over 458/332; dtd 5Oct44.

Rear Echelon, 1st Marine Division. Movement Order No. 1–44. Serial 410/388; dtd 23Oct44.

1st Amphibian Tractor Battalion. Activities of Navy Flamethrower Detachment. Serial 1975–50; dtd 18Dec44.

1st Engineer Battalion, 1st Marine Division. Relief Mapping Unit Operation Report—Peleliu (with photographs of relief maps). No serial; undated, but prepared prior to 12Dec44.

1st Engineer Battalion. C–4 Periodic Report, Supply and Evacuation. No serial; dates are date of individual report. Includes 10 reports covering period 13–18 October 1944.

1st Marines. History of 1st Marine Regiment, 26 August–10 October 1944. No serial; (12Oct44).

1st Marines (Intelligence Section). Intelligence Action Report. No serial; dtd 27Oct44.

1st Marines (Intelligence Section). Recommendations concerning regimental and battalion intelligence sections. No serial; dtd 11Nov44.

1st Battalion, 1st Marines. Unit History. No serial; dtd 23Nov44.

3d Battalion, 1st Marines. Record of Events, 26 August to 10 October 1944. No serial; dates are date of individual entry.

5th Marines. Field Order No. 1–44. Serial AE00122 over 1990–5–80 over 434/283; dtd 5Oct44.

5th Marines. Movement order No. 1–44. No serial; dtd 24Oct44.

5th Marines. Casualty Reports. No serial or dates. Includes three reports covering period 15 September–25 October 1944.

5th Marines. Unit Reports (covering period 23 September to 25 October 1944). No serial; dates are date of individual reports.

5th Marines. R–2 Reports (covering period 16 September to 17 October 1944). No serial; dates are date of individual report.

5th Marines. R-3 Daily Log, 23 August to 5 November 1944. No serial (a handwritten notebook); dates are date of entry.

1st Battalion, 5th Marines. Bn-3 Journal (covering period 15 September to 16 October 1944). No serial; dates are date of individual entry.

2d Battalion, 5th Marines. Journal (covering period 15 September 1944 to 19 January 1945; entries not continuous). Handwritten. No serial; dates are date of individual entry.

3d Battalion, 5th Marines. Record of Operations (covering period 26 August to 7 November 1944). No serial; dates are date of individual entry.

7th Marines. Administrative and Warning Orders for Peleliu (with annexes, addenda, and modifications). Various serials and dates.

7th Marines. R-2 Journal of Peleliu Operations (covering period 15 September to 19 October 1944). No serial; dates are dates of individual reports.

1st Battalion, 7th Marines. Historical Report (actually a journal covering period 15 September to 30 October 1944). No serial; dates are chronological arrangement of entries.

1st Battalion, 7th Marines. Bn-2 and Bn-3 Journal (covering period 15 September to 18 October 1944). No serial; dates are dates of individual entries.

2d Battalion, 7th Marines. War Diary (covering period 25 August to 26 October 1944). No serial; dates are date of each entry.

2d Battalion, 7th Marines. Unit reports (with overlays attached covering period 21 September to 5 October 1944). No serial; dates are dates appearing on the four reports.

2d Battalion, 7th Marines. Unit Journal (covering period 25 August 1944 to 4 February 1945). No serial; dates are dates of individual entries.

3d Battalion, 7th Marines. War Diary for Peleliu Operation (covers period 24 August to 30 October 1944). No serial; dtd 18Nov44.

3d Battalion, 7th Marines. Unit Journal (covering period 23 August to 30 October 1944). No serial; dates are date of each entry.

3d Battalion, 7th Marines. Operation reports (with two enclosures). No serial; dtd 11Oct44.

3d Battalion, 7th Marines. Estimate of the Situation. No serial or file; dtd 21Aug44.

3d Battalion, 7th Marines. Operation Plan 1-44. Serial 0001/44; dtd 21Aug44.

11th Marines. Operation Report. No serial; dtd 10Nov44.

2d Battalion, 11th Marines. Special Action Report. No serial; dtd (unknown).

4th Battalion, 11th Marines. War Diary for period 25 August to 7 November 1944. Serial 1975; dtd 10Nov44. This document has unit journal sheets appended for the period 22-27 October 1944.

4th Battalion, 11th Marines. Unit Journal (covering period 15 September to 22 October 1944). No serial; dates are dates of individual entries.

MAG-11. Report on Palau Operations (with 4th MAW comments thereon and forwarding endorsements). Serial KV11/A16-3/ (jrw) over (00123); dtd 22Dec44.

MAG-11. War Diary, 1-30 September 1944. No serial or date.

MAG-11. War Diary. 1-31 October 1944. No serial or date.

Service Squadron, MAG-11. War Diary, 1-30 September 1944. No serial; dtd 26Oct44.

VMF-114. Revised War Diaries, August, September and October, 1944. Serial A9-4/RFS/jwb over (28-45); dtd 17Jan45.

VMF-121. War Diary, 1-30 September 1944. No serial; dtd 3Nov44.

VMF-121. War Diary, 1-31 October 1944. No serial; dtd 4Nov44.

VMF-122. War Diary, 1-30 September 1944. No serial or date.

VMF-122. War Diary, 1-31 October 1944. No serial or date.

VMF(N)-541. War Diary, 1-30 September 1944. No serial or date.

VMF(N)-541. War Diary, 1-31 October 1944. No serial or date.

VMTB-134. War Diary, 1-30 September 1944. No serial; dtd 1Oct44.

VMTB-134. War Diary, 1-31 October 1944. No serial; dtd 1Nov44.

VMR-952. War Diary, 1-31 October 1944. No serial or date.

VMR-952. War Diary, 1-30 September 1944. No serial or date.

PRIMARY SOURCES

King, Admiral Ernest J. *U. S. Navy at War, 1941-1945; Official Reports to the Secretary of Navy.* Washington: United States Navy Department, 1946.

Marshall, General George C. *The Winning of the War in Europe and the Pacific; Biennial Report of the Chief of Staff of the United States Army, July 1, 1943 to June 30, 1945, to the Secretary of War.* New York: Simon and Schuster (for the War Department), 1945.

United States Strategic Bombing Survey. *The Campaigns of the Pacific War.* Washington: Government Printing Office, 1946.

United States Strategic Bombing Survey. *Interrogations of Japanese Officials.* 2 volumes, Washington: Government Printing Office, 1946.

SECONDARY SOURCES

Boyd, Lt. Col. Robert W. "1st Battalion, 5th Marines, 1st Marine Division in the Palau Operations. A summary of Offensive Action." Quantico, Va.: Marine Corps Schools, Amphibious Warfare School, Senior Course, 1948–49. A historical tactical study, with 36pp typed, and four photostatic maps.

Boyer, Lt. Col. Kimber H. "The 3d Armored Amphibian Battalion, Palau Operation—15 September to 20 October 1944." Quantico, Va.: Marine Corps Schools, Amphibious Warfare School, Senior Course, 1948–49. A historical tactical study of 18pp typed.

Halsey, Fleet Admiral William F. and Lieutenant Commander J. Bryan, III. *Admiral Halsey's Story.* New York: McGraw-Hill Book Company, Inc., 1947.

Hoffman, Carl W. *Saipan: The Beginning of the End.* Washington: Government Printing Office, 1950.

Hunt, George P. *Coral Comes High.* New York: Harper and Brothers, 1946.

McMillian, George. *The Old Breed: A History of the First Marine Division In World War II.* Washington: Infantry Journal Press, 1949.

Mueller, Major General Paul J., Chairman, 81st Wildcat Division Historical Committee, *et al. The 81st Infantry Wildcat Division in World War II.* Washington: Infantry Journal Press, 1948.

Pratt, Fletcher. *The Marines War—An Account of the Struggle for the Pacific from Both American and Japanese Sources.* New York: William Sloan Associates, Inc., 1948.

Robson, R. W. *The Pacific Islands Handbook, 1944.* New York: The MacMillan Company, 1945.

SCAP (First Demobilization Bureau). Central Pacific Operational Record, Volume II, *ms.* Field in WDSS Historical Division. This record was drawn up by the former Chief of Staff of the 14th Division (IJA), Colonel Tada, with the assistance of former staff officer, Colonel Nakagawa. Diaries and memoranda of both officers plus other materials were used as references for the drafting of this record. The translations are not final and are subject to change. Cited in this monograph as *Tada Record.*

Smith, Maj. Gen. Oliver P. "Personal Narrative." An original typed copy of General Smith's personal journal. Inclusive dates: 28Jan44–1Nov44. Covers New Britain, Russells and Peleliu. 215pp.

Wood, Lt. Col. Noah P. "Field Artillery Support of the First Marine Division, Peleliu, 15 September to 20 October 1944. A study of Artillery Support of a Marine Division in an Amphibious Attack." Quantico, Va.: Marine Corps Schools, Amphibious Warfare School, Senior Course, 1948–49. A historical tactical study, with bibliography, one appendix and one photostatic map. Typed.

PERIODICALS

Army and Navy Register, 30 September 1944. "Cave Fighting on Peleliu."

Leatherneck, August 1945. "Peleliu Today" by Sgt. Duane Decker.

Leatherneck, May 1945. "Tough Going for Easy Company" by Sgt. Joseph P. Donahue.

Marine Corps Chevron, 22 July 1944. "Islands in the News."

Marine Corps Chevron, 16 September 1944. "Palau Hit by Marines."

Marine Corps Chevron, 23 September 1944. "Toughest Terrain."

Marine Corps Chevron, 30 September 1944. "Peleliu Cleared up by Battling First Division."

Marine Corps Chevron, 7 October 1944. "Writer Describes Battle for Toehold on Beach."

Marine Corps Chevron, 7 October 1944. "The First Two Days of Hell on Peleliu."

Marine Corps Chevron, 14 October 1945. "Amtracs Assigned Most Varied Tasks Yet in Peleliu Battle."

Marine Corps Chevron, 14 October 1944. "Flame Throwers Attacking Mt. Umurbrogol."

Marine Corps Chevron, 28 October 1944. "Japs Still Holding Out in Peleliu."

Marine Corps Chevron, 4 November 1944. "Tokyo Radio Claims Japs Landing on Peleliu."

Marine Corps Chevron, 18 November 1944. " '75's Moved Piece by Piece up Cliff's Side."

Marine Corps Chevron, 25 November 1944. "The Battle of Suicide Ridge."

Marine Corps Chevron, 2 December 1944. "Marines Use Fists and Rocks in All-Night Fight for Hill."

Marine Corps Chevron, 16 December 1944. "Fighter Plane Strike Scatters Japs."

Marine Corps Gazette, December 1944. "Battle for Peleliu" by Maj. David M. Schmuck.

Marine Corps Gazette, December 1944. "Battle for Peleliu." A staff prepared map.

Marine Corps Gazette, January 1945. "Infantillery on Peleliu" by LtCol R. A. Evans.

Marine Corps Gazette, January 1945. "Point Secured" by Capt George P. Hunt.

Marine Corps Gazette, February 1945. "Marine Aviation at Peleliu" by Capt Donald A. Stauffer.

Marine Corps Gazette, September 1946. "The Closer the Better" by Lt Col Lewis W. Walt.

Time, 16 October 1944. News report by Robert Martin.

True Magazine, October 1945. "Hell in the Umurbrogol" by Jeremiah A. O'Leary.

Stalemate II and
the Philippines Campaign

As he relates in his book *Admiral Halsey's Story*, the Commander III Fleet had inclined toward a dim view of the whole Western Carolines project from the time it was first broached to him in early May at a conference with Admirals King and Nimitz in San Francisco. Thus, when the Joint Chiefs of Staff queried the feasibility of by-passing certain of these objectives, he favored striking directly at the Philippines and by-passing all of them with the possible exception of Ulithi, which offered a fine anchorage and was believed garrisoned lightly, if at all. Yap, he contended, could be of use only as a minor staging point for aircraft. The Palaus constituted a threat to the New Guinea-Philippines route and possessed valuable air and anchorage facilities, but he believed that the cost of taking them would be excessive in relation to the advantages gained. He was alone in this opinion, however, and the final conception of STALE-MATE II emerged as something of a compromise.

The need for a large land mass on which to mount an all-out assault on the Japanese home islands was recognized by all, but there was little unanimity of opinion on what this should be. Admiral King favored Formosa, Admiral Spruance and others various areas along the coasts of China and Korea. Admirals Nimitz and Carney agreed with Halsey that it should be the Philippines, which General MacArthur was determined to take for sentimental and political as well as strategic reasons.

Admiral Halsey had long held the belief that at some point in the war Japanese resistance would begin a swift collapse, and that when this occurred every advantage should be pressed vigorously. The unexpectedly weak opposition he encountered when striking at enemy air bases in the Philippines as part of the covering action for STALEMATE II convinced him that this time had come. Accordingly, on 13 September he dispatched to CinCPOA the following drastic recommendations: (1) That STALEMATE be cancelled immediately; (2) that the ground troops already mounted for that operation be turned over to General MacArthur; (3) that MacArthur revise his own plans in order to invade the Philippines at the earliest possible moment.

Admiral Nimitz replied that with commitments already made, Phase I must go through as planned, but that Phase II would be submitted to immediate review.

MacArthur's plans, as then set up, called for an invasion of Mindanao, the big southern island, on 15 November, to be followed by an assault on Leyte, in the central Philippines, on 20 December. On the day that the Marines hit the Peleliu beaches, a dispatch in his name [1] expressed willigness and ability to shift the sequence of these operations and to strike at Leyte as early as 20 October, provided the immediate services of the XXIV Corps could be obtained.

Word to this effect was immediately relayed to the Joint Chiefs of Staff, then in Quebec with President Roosevelt for the OCTAGON conference. So impressed were they by this dramatic agreement between the top Pacific Theater commanders that ninety minutes after the dispatch was received they were able to flash their approval. Thus the XXIV Corps departed the Central Pacific to play its important part in the dramatic "liberation" campaign.

---

[1] But without his knowledge. As General George C. Kenney describes the situation at the time this dramatic decision was made: "MacArthur was on a cruiser off Morotai, with radio silence being preserved. There was no way of getting in touch with him, but a decision had to be made and an answer sent to the Joint Chiefs immediately." George C. Kenney, *General Kenney Reports*, New York, 1949.

Japanese Defensive Concept

A clue as to why the Japanese defenders of Peleliu behaved so differently in some respects than had their compatriots in previous island operations is furnished by a captured document entitled: "Palau Sector Group Training for Victory."[1] This was issued at Group Headquarters on 11 July 1944, over the signature of Lieutenant General Sadai Inoue, over-all commander, but internal evidence, substantiated by post-war interrogations, indicates that it was mainly if not entirely the work of Inoue's chief of staff, Colonel Tokechi Tada, generally regarded as one of the most capable staff officers of the Imperial Army.

This document is of special interest in revealing certain departures from previous Japanese military thinking and as the first tangible intelligent effort to profit by past experience. The portion dealing with basic tactics and initial defense is quoted here, omitting extraneous matter and the inevitable bombast which Japanese officers appear to consider necessary for inspiring their troops.

. . . Victory depends on the officers and men of the entire army concentrating . . . on our thorough application of recent battle lessons, especially those of Saipan.

The ultimate goal of this training is to minimize our losses in the severe enemy pre-landing naval and aerial bombardment and, on the very night of the enemy landing, to take advantage of the fact that their equipment is not yet fully consolidated, to destroy their bridgehead in one blow. . . .

Compared with our "short sword" the Americans have a "long spear" with which to do battle. . . . We must first resolutely penetrate to the enemy and then we shall display our short swords and slash to the very marrow of his bones. . . .

We must recognize the limits of naval and aerial bombardment. Every soldier and civilian employee . . . will remain unmoved by this, must strengthen his spirits even while advancing by utilizing lulls in enemy bombardment and taking advantage of the terrain according to necessity—without incurring damage or exposing other areas too quickly or thoughtlessely. . . .

We are ready to die honorably. . . . (But) even if we die delivering our territories into the hands of the enemy it will not necessarily contribute to the opening of a new (and favorable) phase of the war and how can we carry out our mission? (TN: That is, mere dying is not enough). . . .

We must preserve personnel and ordnance-psychological and material strength. . . . We must detect the opportunity for opening up accurate fire and recognize that it is unavoidable for the enemy either to increase his range or move his target, as his landing craft approach. . . .

It is most advantageous to be able to repel groups of landing craft before their arrival at the beach by means of strongly prepared beach positions but we cannot expect to accomplish this completely. . . . Moreover it is most urgent, in addition to attempting to destroy and confuse enemy landing craft by means of these strong points, to lead the enemy to confusion and destruction by concentrating rapidly disappearing fire power from our strong points remaining in his midst, even though par-

---

[1] For reference purposes translation of this document is listed as CinCPac-CinCPOA Item #11,190.

tially trampled under foot by landings,[2] and to carry out strong counter-attacks from previously planned and prepared positions in order to destroy the enemy that has landed, by dawn of the next day.

In order to do this it will be necessary to carry out this counter-attack with men who have been withdrawn from non-active fronts or else to use as a nucleus well-selected reservists who have been previously withdrawn. . . .

Small sector unit COs and sector unit COs, if they are able to judge the enemy landing front with certainty, should seize the opportunity to move reserve troops to this front. . . .

In view of the tendency of the enemy . . . by means of an overwhelmingly superior naval and aerial bombardment to intercept and control our reinforcements . . . it is absolutely necessary that the movements of those aforementioned reserve units and troops drawn from other sectors should make practical use of terrain, natural objects, lulls in enemy fire, weather, atmospheric phenomena (especially squalls, clouds, mist, and smoke) in selecting their routes and, in addition that they plan

------

[2] This passage describes the tactic of "passive infiltration" (i.e., hiding out in overrun positions in order to be in the rear of U. S. troops) which played such a prominent part in the operation.

and prepare before hand all necessary equipment and works. There will be no rapid exhaustion of battle strength if we pay careful attention to these details. . . .

Without concerning ourselves with the great explosive bursts or the strong local effect of naval firing, the destructive power wrought upon personnel is not very great. Especially when we consider that originally the object of naval guns was to sink ships and that their shells possess the special quality of falling low, their physical power is not very great against men who are advancing at a crawl, utilizing terrain, natural objects, and shell holes.

Aerial bombardment is almost identical. . . . By observing very carefully the activity of enemy planes and the bombs while they are falling, avoiding thereby instantaneous explosions, and by taking advantage of gaps in bombardment in order to advance, it can cause no great damage. The only fearful thing next to great physical power is the psychological effect upon ignorant and inexperienced personnel. . . .

It is certain that if we repay the Americans (who rely solely upon material power) with material power it will shock them beyond imagination. . . .

Heavenly aid on the road to victory falls only to those commanders who have a thorough control of command. . . .

Japanese Caves

How many caves existed on Peleliu, and how many of these were utilized by the Japanese defenders, will never be known. After the conclusion of the land fighting, the Island Command undertook a comprehensive correlation of all intelligence on the subject, together with a painstaking on-the-scene survey of all caves still recognizable as such, which counted more than 500.[1]

An interesting aspect revealed by this study is the fundamentally different approach to cave utilization by Japanese Army and Navy elements. Perhaps characteristically, the Army's principal interest was adaptation of terrain to defensive combat. In contrast, the Navy, at least until shortly before the landings, appeared to regard caves mainly as shelters against attack by sea or air, their defensive possibilities purely incidental.

Thus, the Army made use of all the many natural caves in Peleliu's coralline limestone formations which possessed tactical value, improved on nature as necessary, and constructed their artificial caves as covering or mutually supporting positions. The latter occurred in a variety of forms, depending on local terrain conditions and tactical situations. Most of them were small, owing to limiting factors of time and labor available, so the larger natural caves were mainly adapted, often with great ingenuity, for the emplacement of heavier weapons.

Naval troops, on the other hand, almost entirely ignored natural caves, preferring to construct their own. In this, progress was facilitated by the presence of the 214th Naval Construction Battalion, a tunnel construction unit (*Suidotai*), made up of personnel who had been miners and tunnel workers in civilian life, commanded by civilian engineers. Their handiwork was characterized by professional competence. Passageways were of ample size and free of the cluttering stalactites and stalagmites inevitable to natural limestone erosion, with cross-tunnels and excavations opening off both sides for the convenience and protection of the occupants.

Most of the Navy caves were located near the northern end of the northwestern peninsula, though a few had been constructed adjacent to Army installations for liaison purposes. Although they were not designed primarily for combat, defensive tactics could be improvised readily, particularly in the larger ones which provided a high degree of interior security owing to the complex of passageways and bays. This was

---

[1] *Japanese Military Caves on Peleliu, "Know Your Enemy!"* CinCPac-CinCPOA Bulletin 173–45. This detailed and elaborately illustrated work provides the basis for most of the material incorporated herein.

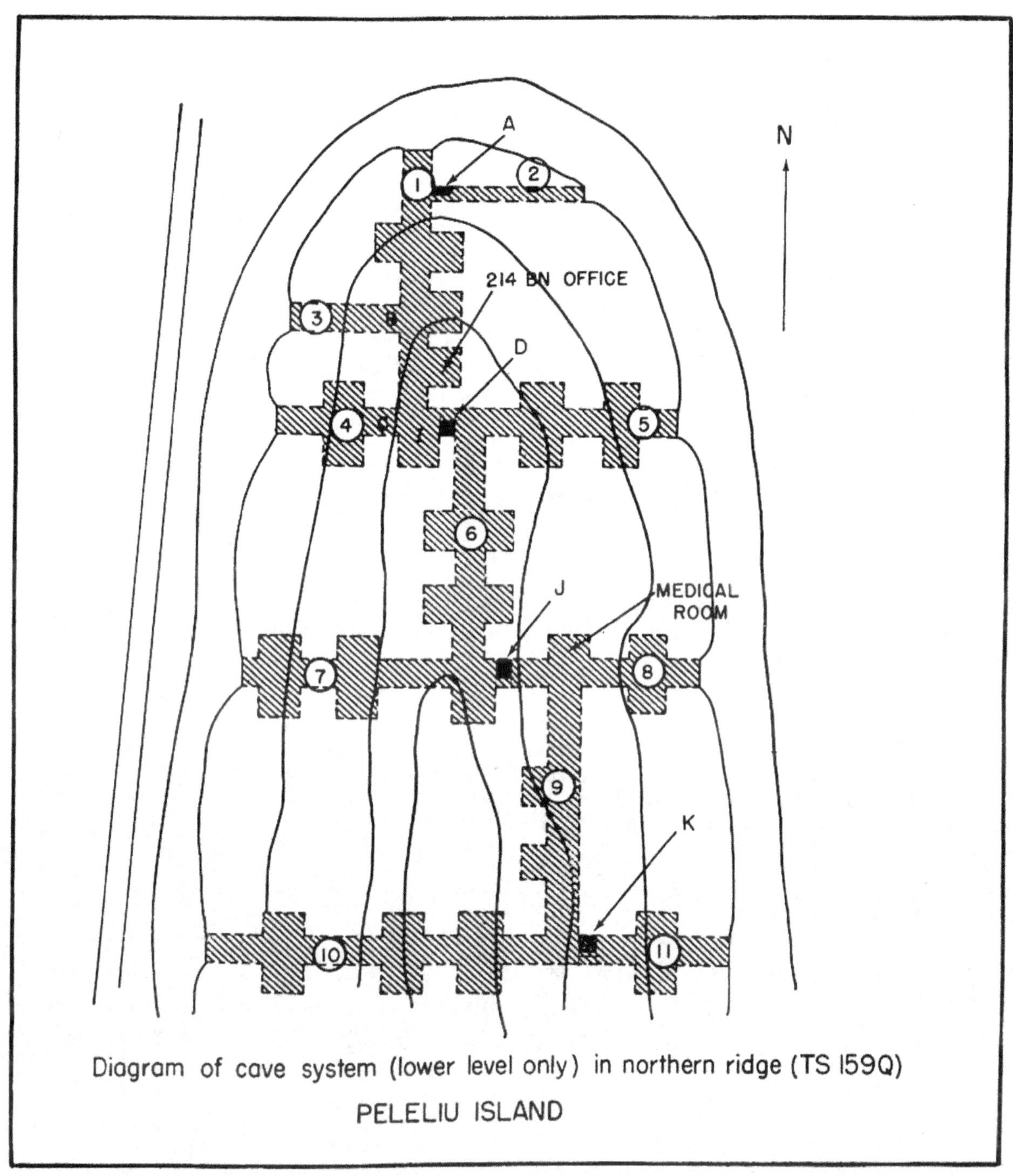

Diagram of cave system (lower level only) in northern ridge (TS 159Q)

PELELIU ISLAND

demonstrated by the trouble encountered by the 5th Marines in northern Peleliu. But the failure to integrate these positions into a system of mutually supporting defenses accounts for the comparatively quick securing of the Amiangal ridges in contrast to the long-drawn-out process of attrition which took place in the Umurbrogol.

The accompanying sketch shows the floor plan of the largest and most elaborate Navy tunnel system discovered on Peleliu; so elaborate that many Marines believed it to be the mine which supplied the raw material for the phosphate refinery, located nearby.[2] It is a cave (or caves) of what is defined as the "adjoining H's type," with multiple entrances facing in three directions from the nose of the northernmost ridge on the entire island. Dominating the West Road and the reef approaches to Ngesebus, it could be by-passed only by use of the extraordinary concentration of supporting weapons described in Chapter VI. Viewing its complex interior, one can understand more readily the plaint voiced in 5th Marines *Regimental Narrative* that: "Tank guns, firing point-blank directly into the caves and tunnels, did not even *temporarily* cause the enemy therein to cease fire."

How the enemy utilized this striking example of the miner's art has been reconstructed in some detail from the description furnished by a prisoner taken in February 1945: one of five living Japanese still lurking there three months after the last fighting had faltered out in the Umurbrogol.[3]

On 3 September when the prisoner first entered the caves there were over a thousand men in them. ... On 28 September 1944, (D-plus 13) all the military personnel were organized for an attack on the American forces who were holding the hill directly over the caves. They poured forth from all nine tunnels and attacked. He claims they drove the Americans off the hill but suffered many losses.[4] When they reassembled in the caves there were only about 50 military men left. ...

---

[2] Actually the abandoned phosphate diggings lay some distance to the south, in the vicinity of Asias village, where mining was by the open-pit rather than the tunneling method. *JANIS No. 103* Vol. I, p. VIII, 4.

[3] *Pelelin Island Command POW Interrogation Report #6.*

[4] No mention of this counterattack appears in any Marine operation reports at regimental or higher levels, and the participating battalion (2/5) turned in no written report of such counterattack. The CO of this unit recalls heavy fighting and casualties that night, but the Marines atop the hill (elements of Company F) most certainly were not driven off. Oral statement by LtCol Gordon D. Gayle, interviewed 17Feb50.

The survivors moved the wounded into tunnels 9, 10, and 11, the workers into tunnels 4, 5, 6, and 8, and the military personnel into tunnels, 1, 2, and 3. On the morning of 29 September our forces assaulted the entrance to tunnel #1 with a tank, machine guns and flame-throwers. The Japanese military personnel attacked through tunnel #1 and all the military were killed except the prisoner who remained behind an improvised barricade at "A" in tunnel #2, and six others who were in lower passages. The flame-thrower used by our forces penetrated to where he was and burned his left arm and leg. He claims the flame-thrower was our most effective weapon in this attack and that it reached point "A" where he was standing and points "B", "C" and "D" killing some of the workmen who were located in these areas. The tank and machine gun fire was only effective in the immediate tunnel it was firing into.

Later, tanks and flame-throwers were used on most of the entrances and when our forces withdrew there were only 30 remaining alive. The wounded in tunnels 9, 10 and 11 were all killed by our flame-throwers which penetrated the entire length of tunnel 7–8 and to points "F" in tunnel 9 and "G" in tunnel #6. Our flame-throwers also penetrated the entire length of tunnel #3 and tunnels #4 and 5 and around to points "N" in tunnel #6 and "H" in tunnel #1. Tunnel #2 was not subjected to the flame-thrower and most of those men who survived had taken refuge in it.

Our forces then closed all entrances and the Japs moved into tunnel #2 which was the most completely closed. They posted men at points "I" in tunnel #5, "J" in tunnel #8 and "K" in tunnel #11. These men were able to pick off a number of "Foolish Yankees" who wandered into the entrances of tunnels #10, 7 and 4 during November and December (TN: During this period American personnel were killed and wounded in and around this cave). According to the prisoner as soon as they fired at anyone they would withdraw into tunnel #2 and as many times as flame-throwers or demolitions were used on the various tunnels they were always safe because the entrance to this tunnel was completely covered and unrecognizable from the outside.

Prisoner states that about 1 January 1945, after they shot an American in tunnel #8, very large explosive charges were set off in all the entrances except tunnel #2 and that the force of these explosions was much more penetrative than the flame-throwers. They reached to every part of the cave and shocked those they did not kill. If charges had been put in tunnel #2 all would have been killed. However, 19 of the remaining 30 were killed and three more were badly injured. On 24 January

1945 American "Seabees" who were excavating in that area stumbled on two of the Japs at "A" in tunnel #2. The prisoner states that they then moved the three wounded into tunnel #6, left two men at "A" in tunnel #2 as guards, and the others went to tunnel #11, passing point "L" in tunnel #9 where our demolitions had caused the tunnel to partially collapse. The flame-thrower used on tunnel #2 at this time killed the two guards. (TN: Probably gasoline that was used by our forces in an attempt to burn out this cave at that time). The prisoner claims that on the night of 1 February 1945 the five Japs who were in good physical condition dug their way out of tunnel #8.

Aviation at Peleliu

Japanese air power in the Palaus had been very thoroughly knocked out long before the assault took place, and with the prompt capture of the main airfield at Peleliu whatever capacity the enemy might have had for sending in aerial replacements was effectively disposed of. Wreckage of 127 planes was found on Peleliu, most of it probably dating back to the powerful carrier strike of 30 March–1 April, when 168 Japanese planes were claimed destroyed either in the air or on the ground. Thereafter the task of keeping the secondary field on Babelthuap neutralized was a simple matter. Enemy air activity during the operation was confined to a few minor nuisance raids by individuals, believed to be float planes from Koror, which resulted in no reported casualties or damage.

U. S. air power proved effective in its basic mission of keeping the enemy neutralized. That it produced no more far-reaching results on the tactical level should be attributed to natural conditions rather than lack of skill or effort.

Air support prior to and for two weeks following the landing was furnished by the Navy: the carriers of Task Force 38 and Task Group 32.7 from D-minus 8 to D-minus 1; escort carriers of TG 32.7 augmented by units of TG's 38.4 and 38.2 from D-Day through D-plus 3; and by the escort carriers exclusively from that date until D-plus 13. Altogether more than 300 missions, planned and called, were flown during this period, dropping a total of 620 tons of bombs of all types, including Napalm.[1]

During the early phases of the assault, especially prior to setting up of artillery, air was used almost exclusively as a close support weapon. Here, where the terrain was more or less open and level, "In General, the regimental commanders expressed themselves as being well pleased with the air missions." There was much criticism, however, of the inefficiency of the strafing attacks owing to the pilots' practice of pulling out of their runs at an altitude of about 1,800 feet.[2]

Also notable at this time was the effect on the enemy of the ubiquitous aerial observers. So promptly were weapons positions spotted and brought under attack that the Japanese exposed themselves as little as possible, thereby reducing their volume of fire during a crucial stage of the operation.

Beginning with D-plus 2, however, the practice was to call close air missions only on targets denied the artillery, generally in defilade or on reverse slopes, and after D-plus 6, the Navy air arm was used almost

---

[1] 1st MarDiv *SAR*, II, Annex L, 1.

[2] *Ibid*, 4, 5.

exclusively as a deep support weapon. It will be noted that by this time the fighting had progressed well into the ridges: jumbled, jungled terrain where spotting friendly front lines was next to impossible and where coaching fliers onto specific targets was exceedingly dangerous owing to the inaccuracy of the operational maps. Since the location and nature of the great majority of Japanese installations on the northwestern peninsula rendered them impervious to effective air attack, even had it been possible to pin-point them, the tactical value of aviation approached negligibility.

The 1st Division's own observation planes (VMO–3) began operating from the Peleliu airfield on D-plus 4 and continued skillful direction of artillery fire until the enemy-held pocket became so constricted as to bar massed fires as dangerous to friendly troops.[3] Then, on 28 September Marine air units of MAG 11 based on the island assumed the support function, and the carriers were released for other missions. Striking changes in employment and methods became noticeable immediately.

Perhaps the most significant aspect of Marine aviation's participation in the Peleliu campaign was the opportunity afforded for perfecting the practice and techniques of that Corps specialty, close air support, which had been relegated to a secondary role owing to the protracted employment of the air arm in neutralization missions in the Solomons, Bismarcks and Marshalls.

The splendid close support which made the shore-to-shore assault on Ngesebus one of the most effective operations of its kind in the whole Pacific has been dealt with in passing. Dive bombing with pin-point precision, strafing at treetop level the pilots of VMF 114 so stunned the defenders that Japanese in well manned, well prepared beach installations were incapable of opposing the landing. Throughout all the subsequent fighting on Peleliu, the Marine fliers of all the squadrons continued to display great daring, ingenuity, professional skill and an eagerness to cooperate that raised the morale of the ground troops immeasurably:[4] not only the Marines, who were happy to be working with their own people, but the 81st Division Wildcats as well, who seldom made an attack without called air preparation.

Yet it would be difficult to substantiate a report that all of this fine work, with the conspicuous exception of Ngesebus, had any important tactical effect on the outcome of the campaign or the duration of the fighting. It was through no fault of the fliers that the underground enemy were simply proof against any methods of air attack yet developed.

---

[3] 1st MarDiv *SAR*, II, 4.

[4] MAG 11 *Report on Palaus Operation.*

The Mysterious Mission of Murai

Was Major General Kenjiro Murai on Peleliu during the U. S. assault? If so, why and in what capacity?

The Marines had no reason to suspect his presence during their participation in the operation. Nor did the 81st Division until the last enemy resistance had virtually flickered out: with the capture of the Japanese prisoner who described the general's suicide, as related in Chapter VIII. Subsequently a body, decomposed beyond recognition, was identified by the prisoner as that of Murai from personal effects found on it. When the 81st was in occupation in Japan, intelligence officers sought out Lieutenant General Sadae Inoue, commander of the Palaus Sector Group, who certified Murai's presence in the capacity of "tactical adviser." [1]

Many aspects of Japanese military procedure served to mystify American officers during the course of the war, the curious chain of command implied above not being the least of them. As noted previously, captured orders and prisoner of war interrogations indicated that the *de facto* commander was Colonel Kunio Nakagawa, 2d Infantry, IJA. Does it make good sense, militarily speaking, for a major general to act in a mere advisory capacity to an officer two grades his junior, especially when the size of the Japanese force on Peleliu raised it far above the level of a regimental command?

An effort to throw more light on the subject, on the basis of a preliminary draft of this monograph, was made in March 1950, by a Marine officer stationed on Guam: Lieutenant Colonel Waite W. Worden, who had served as executive officer, 1st Battalion, 7th Marines, on Peleliu. At that time General Inoue was still confined in U. S. Naval Prison, Guam, awaiting result of an appeal from a death sentence for war crimes. Evidence brought out through extensive interviewing by Colonel Worden tends to confirm Murai's presence in detail. [2]

Following his talks with General Inoue, Colonel Worden made a personal visit to the Palaus (Peleliu, Koror and Babelthuap) where he interviewed a number of natives who had been there before and during the operation. Excerpts from his report are presented herewith for such intrinsic inter-

[1] Ltr MajGen P. J. Mueller, USA, to BrigGen C. C. Jerome. 14Apr50.

[2] Further confirmed by report received by CMC from Japanese Ministry of Foreign Affairs, dated 15Apr50. This states that Japanese Army official records carry both Murai and Nakagawa as killed in action on Peleliu 31Dec44, evidently the date the fact of their deaths was accepted, and adds that each was raised to the grade of lieutenant general by special promotion order the same day.

est as they may contain, both in the case of General Murai and as showing some of the bizarre aspects of the Japanese military-naval establishments.[3]

Although Inoue has been confined for about six years, his memory is indeed very clear and accurate. He has recalled events and dates *exactly* as they have been recorded in your monograph. As a result, I have a high regard for the accuracy of his memory and will quote him freely. . . .[4]

Regarding the Jap 2d Battalion, 15th Infantry, General Inoue states that he himself sent it to Peleliu on the fifth night after the landing. . . . His reason for sending this battalion was "for the sake of the garrison at Peleliu and to bolster the morale of the troops there." . . . Inoue thinks they got ashore without loss . . . but perhaps the Peleliu commander chose not to tell Inoue of his losses. . . .

Inoue's belief that we would attack Koror and Babelthuap (when we had finished with Peleliu) kept him from attempting large scale reinforcements. It also kept him from attempting to supply his Peleliu forces with more ammunition. Had Inoue believed otherwise we might have had a much more difficult time on Peleliu.

Major General Murai *was* on Peleliu, stated Inoue, "to see that Colonel Nakagawa didn't make any mistakes." Asked if he considered Nakagawa to be a capable officer, Inoue stated that he was one of the best in the entire Japanese Army. . . . He also considered Murai to be a very capable officer. I stated to Inoue that to put a major general over such a capable colonel, without giving the major general the over-all command indicated that he either (1) didn't have full confidence in the colonel or (2) that he didn't have complete confidence in the major general. This amused him, and with the self-satisfaction of a practical joker who has had the last laugh, he said that he had put Murai there for two reasons: (1) as insurance, because he considered Peleliu to be so important to the military defense of Japan, and (2) because the Peleliu Navy garrison was commanded by a flag officer, Vice Admiral Itou, and Murai was to give the Army sufficient rank to cope with that of the

Navy. . . . The Jap Army and Navy on Peleliu were at bitter odds and treated each other with little respect and with no cooperation, in many instances. . . .

Nakawaga arrived on Peleliu in April 1944, states Inoue. This is confirmed by Peleliu natives. Peleliu natives also state that the Jap army worked furiously in the preparation of defenses. . . . Inoue stated that the Jap Navy had all the native labor tied up, and operated labor pools, from which it was practically impossible for the Army to get any labor. . . .

There were practically no caves developed for defensive installations. From April, therefore, until the Marine landing in September, the Jap soldiers and some civilians were driven hard to develop natural caves and to construct other emplacements, which they did by hand and by dynamite. Inoue stated that the Navy had some caves, but not very many . . . (and) the Navy refused to allow the Army to use the Navy caves, and the Navy tied up almost all the civilian labor. . . . (Inoue) sent his next senior officer, Major General Murai, to get the Navy off Nakagawa's back so he could do his job. Inoue stated that the Palaus had been a naval base for so long, and had been considered as Navy territory for so many years, that the sudden arrival of an Army division with a lieutenant general in command senior to all naval personnel was too much for the Navy to take lying down. . . . To the Navy it was an insult. . . .

It is apparent from the above that Inoue had only six months in which to prepare his defenses, and he stated that he fully believed that if he had had one year instead of six months, he could have completely repulsed us. . . . He further stated that he was *really* prepared for us in Koror and Babelthuap, and was positive he could have defeated us there. . . .

Inoue had *telephone* communication with Murai over a sub-oceanic cable. This cable has been seen by several of the Peleliu natives to whom I have talked. Inoue stated that they had no radio communication at that time. The telephone call sign used over this cable, both for Peleliu and Koror, was "SAKURA," the name of a city (Sakura, Ibaraki, Keng) in Japan. This name was used as we might use "Texas" or "Denver" as a switchboard designation. While the Peleliu operator, on 25 November, was calling "Sakura . . . Sakura . . . Sakura . . . Sak . . . ." his voice suddenly ceased and General Inoue on Koror heard no more from his Peleliu command. This interruption led Inoue to believe that the American Marines had blown up the Jap Peleliu command post, and also led him to believe that General Murai, Colonel Nakagawa, and his men (which he thought then numbered 150–200) had been wiped out by enemy action, and not by suicide. However, when I told

<hr>

[3] Ltr LtCol W. W. Worden to CMC, 8Apr50, with enclosures. This document, now in records of Historical Division, USMC, also contains new evidence regarding the death of LtCol A. E. Ellis, at Koror in 1923, which is not considered pertinent to this monograph.

[4] A Marine officer who was active in the arrest and interrogation of General Inoue has described him as an elderly man verging on senility whose real military brains belonged to his unusually capable chief of staff, Colonel Tokechi Tada. Oral statement by Maj J. A. Moriarty, 15Mar50.

him about the report we received from a Jap prisoner . . . of the burning the regimental flag and the suicides, he then stated, "I am sure that was done."

Asked how Toyko had received the [final Peleliu] message, General Inoue said "I reported it to Tokyo myself by radio from Koror."

It is possible that this monograph has done a grave injustice to the memory of General Murai in attributing the skillful Japanese defense of Peleliu entirely to Colonel Nakagawa. But, accepting the heavy weight of evidence that Murai actually lived and died there, the part he played remains obscure. And the only men who could bear authorative witness at this late date died in the Umurbrogol.

Marine Order of Battle for Peleliu

Over-all ground command of the STALE-MATE II operation was vested in Major General Julian C. Smith, Commander, Expeditionary Troops, Third Fleet. Direct command of Western Task Force (Southern Palaus) was exercised by III Amphibious Corps (Major General Roy S. Geiger), major components of which were 1st Marine Division (Peleliu) and 81st Infantry Division (Angaur). Corps troops committed, including garrison units in assault, were operationally attached to the 1st Marine Division and distributed throughout the various task units as indicated below. The addition of 10,994 Corps to the 17,490 organic to the 1st Division brought the total in assault on Peleliu to 28,484.

Task Organization—1st Marine Division

MajGen William H. Rupertus, Commanding

Combat Team 1 ("Spitfire")—Col Lewis B. Puller
1st Marines
Co A 1st Tk Bn
Co A 1st Engr Bn
Co A 1st Pion Bn
1st Plat 1st MP Co
Co A 1st Med Bn
1st Plat Ord Co 1st Serv Bn
Det S&S Co 1st Serv Bn
Det 4th JASCO

Combat Team 5 ("Lone Wolf")—Col Harold D. Harris
5th Marines

Co B 1st Tk Bn (less 1st & 4th Plats)
Co B 1st Engr Bn
Co B 1st Pion Bn
2d Plat 1st MP Co
Co B 1st Med Bn
2d Plat Ord Co 1st Serv Bn
Det S&S Co 1st Serv Bn
Det 4th JASCO

Combat Team 7 ("Mustang")—Col Herman H. Hanneken
7th Marines (less 2d Bn)
1st & 4th Plats Co B 1st Tk Bn
Co C 1st Engr Bn (less 2d Plat)
Co C 1st Pion Bn
3d Plat 1st MP Co
Co C 1st Med Bn
Det 4th JASCO

Armd Amph Trac Group—LtCol Kimber H. Boyer
3d Armd Amph Trac Bn (Prov)

Amph Trans Group—Maj Albert F. Reutlinger
1st Amph Trac Bn
6th Amph Trac Bn (Prov)
454th Dukw Co (U.S.Army)
454th Dukw Co (U.S.Army)
8th Amph Trac Bn (less Dets)

Arty Group—Col William H. Harrison
11th Marines
3d Bn III PhibCorps Arty (155mm How)
8th Bn III PhibCorps Arty (155mm Gun) (less Btry G)

AA Group—LtCol Merlyn D. Holmes
12th AAA Bn

Engr Group—Col Francis I. Fenton
  1st Engr Bn (less Cos A, B, & C)
  33d Nav Const Bn
  73d Nav Const Bn
Shore Party Group—LtCol Robert G. Ballance
  1st Pion Bn (less Cos A, B, & C)
  Garrison Beach Party
  1st MT Bn (less Dets)
Serv Group—Col John Kaluf
  1st Serv Bn (less Dets)
  16th Fld Depot

Corps Air Del Sect
Det 1st MT Bn
Res Group—LtCol Spencer S. Berger
  2d Bn 7th Mar
  1st Tk Bn (less Cos A, B, and tanks of
    Co C)
  Reconn Co Div Hq Bn
  4th JASCO (less Dets)
  2d Plat Co C 1st Engr Bn
  Det Co D 1st Med Bn
Med Group—Comdr (MC) Emil E. Napp
  1st Md Bn (less Cos A, B, C, & Det Co D)

Command and Staff

EXPEDITIONARY TROOPS

Commanding General — Maj. Gen. Julian C. Smith

Chief of Staff — Col. Dudley S. Brown

F–1 — Col. Harry E. Dunkelberger

F–2 — Lt. Col. Edmund J. Buckley

F–3 — Col. Robert O. Bare

F–4 — Lt. Col. Jessee S. Cook, Jr.

7th Antiaircraft Artillery Battalion [1]

Commanding Officer — Lt. Col. Henry R. Paige

Executive Officer — Lt. Col. Elmer C. Woods

Bn–3 — Capt. Hugh J. Irish

III AMPHIBIOUS CORPS

Commanding General — Maj. Gen. Roy S. Geiger

Chief of Staff — Col. Merwin H. Silverthorn

C–1 — Lt. Col. Peter A. McDonald

C–2 — Col. William F. Coleman

C–3 — Col. Walter A. Wachtler

C–4 — Col. Francis B. Loomis, Jr.

CORPS TROOPS

1st Amphibian Tractor Battalion

Commanding Officer — Maj. Albert F. Reutlinger (To 21 September)
Capt. Arthur J. Noonan (From 22 September)

Executive Officer — Capt. Thomas H. Boler (From 23 September)

Bn–3 — 1st Lt. Norman H. Bryant

6th Amphibian Tractor Battalion

Commanding Officer — Capt. John I. Fitzgerald, Jr.

Executive Officer — 1st Lt. Whitley A. Cummings, Jr. [2]

---

[1] This was a VAC unit which landed on Angaur on 21 Sept and remained as part of the garrison.

[2] Lt Cummings served also as Bn–3 as additional duty.

8th Amphibian Tractor Battalion

Commanding Officer	Lt. Col. Charles B. Nerren
Executive Officer	Maj. Bedford Williams
Bn–3	1st Lt. John R. Tull

3d Armored Amphibian Battalion

Commanding Officer	Lt. Col. Kimber H. Boyer
Executive Officer	Maj. Arthur M. Parker, Jr.
Bn–3	1st Lt. Marvin E. Mitchell

12th Antiaircraft Artillery Battalion

Commanding Officer	Lt. Col. Merlyn D. Holmes
Executive Officer	Lt. Col. Edwin A. Law (To 18 October) Lt. Col. Kenneth A. King (From 19 October)
Bn–3	Maj. Joseph R. Jacyno (To 10 October) Capt. Whitman S. Bartley (11–25 October) Capt. Henry H. McUmber, Jr. (From 28 October)

3d 155mm Howitzer Battalion

Commanding Officer	Lt. Col. Richard A. Evans
Executive Officer	Maj. Lewis A. Jones (To 25 October) Maj. Hunter C. Phelan, Jr. (From 26 October)
Bn–3	Maj. Daniel S. Pregnall

8th 155mm Gun Battalion

Commanding Officer	Maj. George V. Hanna, Jr.
Executive Officer	Maj. Robert F. Meldrun

Bn–3	Maj. Hunter C. Phelan, Jr. (To 25 October)

1st MARINE DIVISION

Commanding General	Maj. Gen. William H. Rupertus
Assistant Division Commander	Brig. Gen. Oliver P. Smith
Chief of Staff	Col. John T. Selden
D–1	Maj. William E. Benedict (To 23 September) Lt. Col. Harold O. Deakin (From 24 September)
D–2	Lt. Col. John W. Scott, Jr.
D–3	Lt. Col. Lewis J. Fields
D–4	Lt. Col. Harvey C. Tschirgi

Division Headquarters Battalion

Commanding Officer	Col. Joseph F. Hankins [3] (To 3 October) Lt. Col. Austin C. Shofner (From 3 October)

1st Tank Battalion

Commanding Officer	Lt. Col. Arthur J. Stuart
Executive Officer	Maj. Donald J. Robinson
Bn–3	1st Lt. Ernest A. Hayden, Jr.

1st Service Battalion

Commanding Officer	Col. John Kaluf
Executive Officer	Maj. Charles F. Rider

---

[3] Col Hankins was killed in action on date indicated. He served concurrently as Division Provost Marshall, as did his successor.

1st Motor Transport Battalion

Commanding Officer__ Capt. Robert B. McBroom
Executive Officer______ Capt. George G. DeBell
Bn–3 _________________ 1st Lt. Walter M. Greenspan

1st Pioneer Battalion

Commanding Officer__ Lt. Col. Robert G. Ballance
Executive Officer______ Maj. Nathaniel Morgenthal
Bn–3 _________________ Capt. Warren S. Sivertsen

1st Engineer Battalion

Commanding Officer__ Lt. Col. Levi W. Smith, Jr.
Executive Officer______ Maj. Theodore E. Drummond
Bn–3 _________________ Maj. Eugene T. Schoenfelder

1st Medical Battalion

Commanding Officer__ Comdr. (MC) Emil E. Napp

1st Marines

Commanding Officer__ Col. Lewis B. Puller
Executive Officer______ Lt. Col. Richard P. Ross, Jr.
R–1 _________________ 1st Lt. Frank C. Sheppard
R–2 _________________ Capt. James W. Horton
R–3 _________________ Maj. Bernard T. Kelly
R–4 _________________ Maj. Francis T. Eagan

1st Bn, 1st Marines

Commanding Officer__ Maj. Raymond G Davis
Executive Officer______ Maj. Nikolai S. Stevenson
Bn–3 _________________ Capt. James M. Rogers

2d Bn, 1st Marines

Commanding Officer__ Lt. Col. Russell E. Honsowetz
Executive Officer______ Maj. Charles H. Brush, Jr.
Bn–3 _________________ Capt. Robert W. Burnette
(To 18 September)
1st Lt. Bernard J. Baker
(From 19 September)

3d Bn, 1st Marines

Commanding Officer__ Lt. Col. Stephen V. Sabol
Executive Officer______ Maj. William McNulty
Bn–3 _________________ Maj. Jonas M. Platt

5th Marines

Commanding Officer__ Col. Harold D. Harris
Executive Officer______ Lt. Col. Lewis W. Walt
R–1 _________________ Capt. Alan F. Dill
(To 16 September)
Capt. Paul H. Douglas
(From 16 September)
R–2 _________________ Capt. Levi T. Burcham
R–3 _________________ Maj. Walter S. McIlhenny
(To 16 September)
Capt. Donald A. Peppard
(From 17 September)
R–4 _________________ Maj. Joseph S. Skoczylas
(To 30 September)

1st Bn, 5th Marines

Commanding Officer__ Lt. Col. Robert W. Boyd
Executive Officer______ Maj. Harold T. A. Richmond
Bn–3 _________________ Maj. Hierome L. Opie, Jr.
(To 15 September)

Capt. Edwin B. Glass
(From 16 September)

2d Bn, 5th Marines

Commanding Officer__ Maj. Gordon D. Gayle
Executive Officer______ Maj. John H. Gustafson
(To 15 September)
Maj. Richard T. Washburn
(From 16 September)
Bn–3 __________ Maj. Richard T. Washburn
(To 15 September)
Capt. James H. Flagg
(From 16 September)

3d Bn, 5th Marines

Commanding Officer__ Lt. Col. Austin C. Shofner
(To 15 September)
Lt. Col. Lewis W. Walt
(Night 15/16 September)
Maj. John H. Gustafson
(From 16 September)
Executive Officer______ Maj. Robert M. Ash
(To 15 September)
Maj. Hierome L. Opie
(From 16 September)
Bn–3 __________ Maj. Clyde A. Brooks

7th Marines

Commanding Officer__ Col. Herman H. Hanneken
Executive Officer______ Lt. Col. Norman Hussa
R–1 __________ 2d Lt. Richard F. Spindler
R–2 __________ Capt. Francis T. Farrell

R–3 __________ Maj. Walter Holomon
R–4 __________ Maj. Hector R. Migneault

1st Bn, 7th Marines

Commanding Officer__ Lt. Col. John J. Gormely
Executive Officer______ Maj. Waite W. Worden
Bn–3 __________ Maj. Lloyd W. Martin

2d Bn, 7th Marines

Commanding Officer__ Lt. Col. Spencer S. Berger
Executive Officer______ Maj. Elbert D. Graves
(To 20 September)
Maj. John F. Weber
(From 21 September)
Bn–3 __________ Maj. John F. Weber
(To 20 September)
Capt. Lee W. Langham
(From 21 September)

3d Bn, 7th Marines

Commanding Officer__ Maj. E. Hunter Hurst
Executive Officer______ Maj. Victor H. Streit
Bn–3 __________ Maj. William J. King

11th Marines

Commanding Officer__ Col. William H. Harrison
Executive Officer______ Lt. Col. Edson L. Lyman
R–1 __________ 1st Lt. Robert M. Alderson
R–2 __________ Capt. Richard W. Payne
(To 24 September)
2d Lt. Ralph W. Smith
(From 25 September)
R–3 __________ Lt. Col. Leonard F. Chapman, Jr.
R–4 __________ Capt. Lewis F. Treleaven

1st Bn, 11th Marines

Commanding Officer__ Lt. Col. Richard W.
Wallace
Executive Officer______ Maj. James H.
Moffatt, **Jr.**
Bn–3 ___________________ Maj. John R. Chaisson

2d Bn, 11th Marines

Commanding Officer__ Lt. Col. Noah P.
Wood, Jr.
Executive Officer______ Maj. Floyd C. Maner
(To 15 September)
Maj. John P. McAlinn
(From 16 September)

Bn–3 ___________________ Capt. David R. Griffin

3d Bn, 11th Marines

Commanding Officer__ Lt. Col. Charles M.
Nees
Executive Officer______ Maj. William J.
Hannan
Bn–3 ___________________ Capt. William R.
Miller

4th Bn, 11th Marines

Commanding Officer__ Lt. Col. Louis C.
Reinberg
Executive Officer______ Maj. George E. Bowdoin
Bn–3 ___________________ Maj. Elliott Wilson

THE SECRETARY OF THE NAVY
WASHINGTON

The President of the United States takes pleasure in presenting the PRESIDENTIAL UNIT CITATION to the

FIRST MARINE DIVISION (REINFORCED)

consisting of FIRST Marine Division; First Amphibian Tractor Battalion, FMF; U.S. Navy Flame Thrower Unit Attached; Sixth Amphibian Tractor Battalion (Provisional), FMF; Third Armored Amphibian Battalion (Provisional), FMF; Detachment Eighth Amphibian Tractor Battalion, FMF; 454th Amphibian Truck Company, U.S. Army; 456th Amphibian Truck Company, U.S. Army; Fourth Joint Assault Signal Company, FMF; Fifth Separate Wire Platoon, FMF; Sixth Separate Wire Platoon, FMF,

for service as set forth in the following

CITATION:

"For extraordinary heroism in action against enemy Japanese forces at Peleliu and Ngesebus from September 15 to 29, 1944. Landing over a treacherous coral reef against hostile mortar and artillery fire, the FIRST Marine Division, Reinforced, seized a narrow, heavily mined beachhead and advanced foot by foot in the face of relentless enfilade fire through rain-forests and mangrove swamps toward the air strip, the key to the enemy defenses of the southern Palaus. Opposed all the way by thoroughly disciplined, veteran Japanese troops heavily entrenched in caves and in reinforced concrete pillboxes which honeycombed the high ground throughout the island, the officers and men of the Division fought with undiminished spirit and courage despite heavy losses, exhausting heat and difficult terrain, seizing and holding a highly strategic air and land base for future operations in the Western Pacific. By their individual acts of heroism, their aggressiveness and their fortitude, the men of the FIRST Marine Division, Reinforced, upheld the highest traditions of the United States Naval Service."

For the President,

John L. Sullivan

Secretary of the Navy

Maps

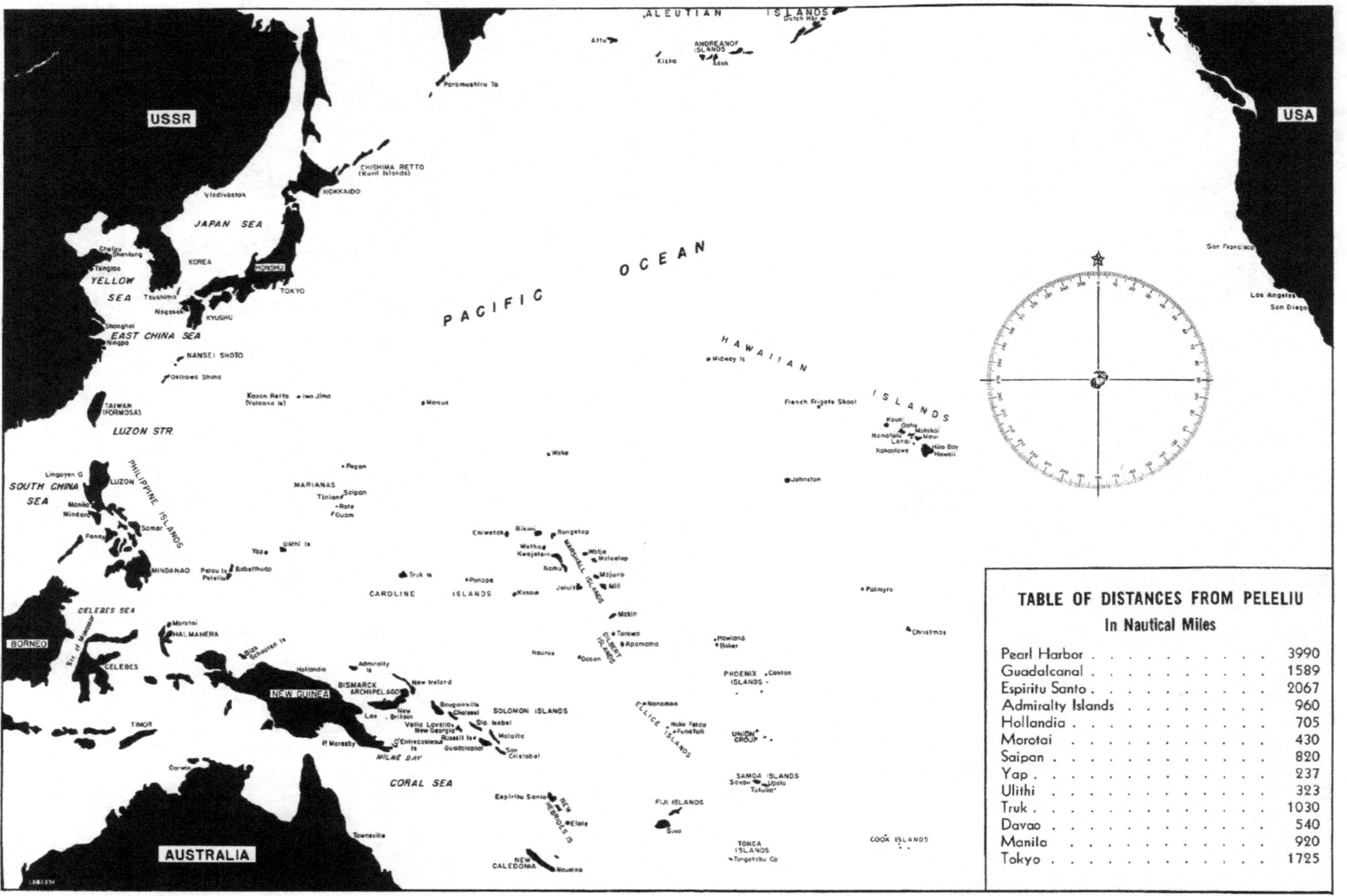

TABLE OF DISTANCES FROM PELELIU

In Nautical Miles

Pearl Harbor	3990
Guadalcanal	1589
Espiritu Santo	2067
Admiralty Islands	960
Hollandia	705
Morotai	430
Saipan	820
Yap	237
Ulithi	323
Truk	1030
Davao	540
Manila	920
Tokyo	1725

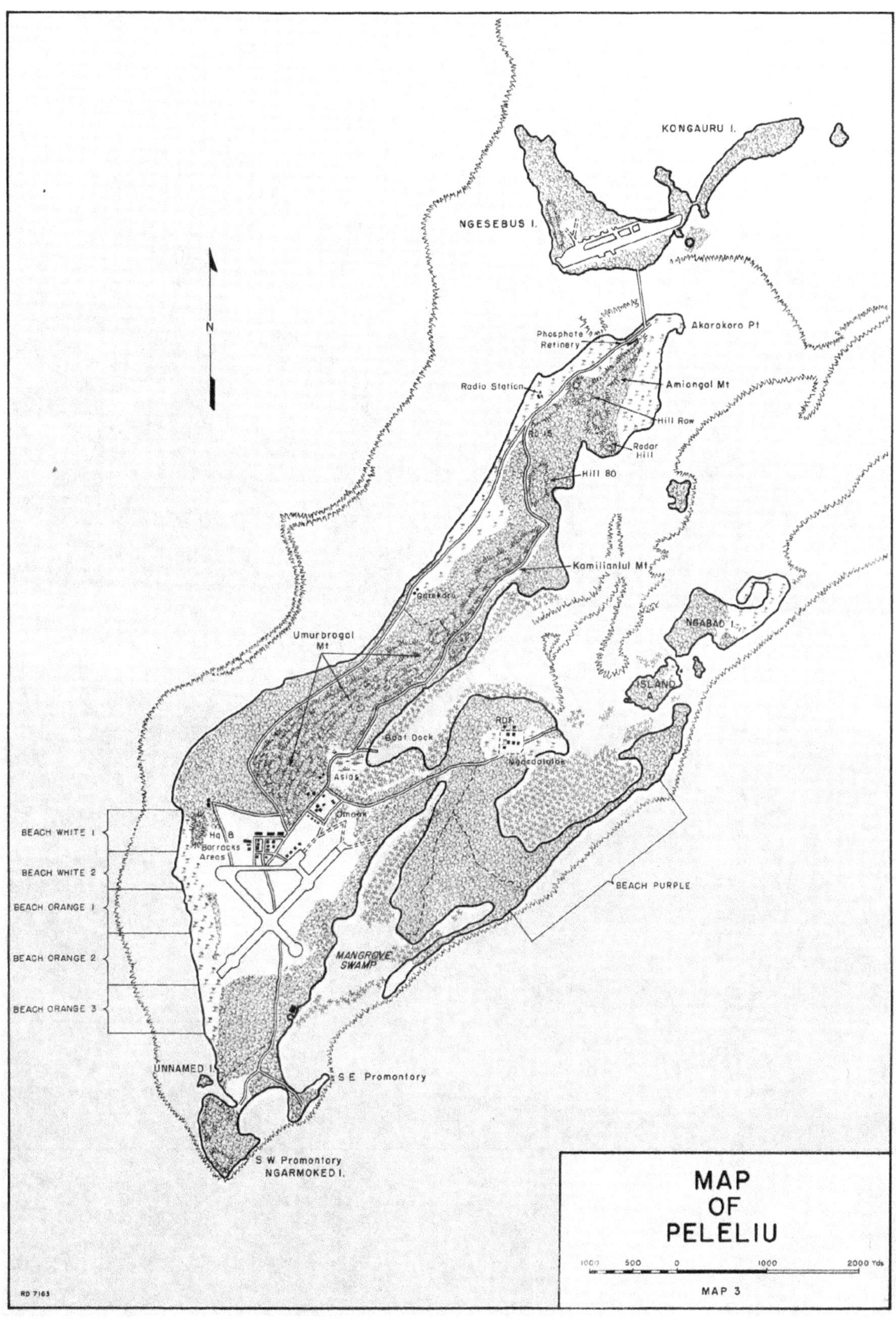

KONGAURU I.
NGESEBUS I.
Akarokoro Pt
Phosphate Refinery
Radio Station
Amiangal Mt
Hill Row
Rd 15
Radar Hill
Hill 80
Kamilianlul Mt
Garekoru
Umurbrogol Mt
NGABAD I.
ISLAND A
RDF
Boat Dock
Ngardololok
Asias
Omaok
BEACH WHITE 1
BEACH WHITE 2
BEACH ORANGE 1
BEACH ORANGE 2
BEACH ORANGE 3
Hq & Barracks Areas
MANGROVE SWAMP
BEACH PURPLE
UNNAMED I.
S E Promontory
S W Promontory
NGARMOKED I.
N
RD 7165
MAP OF PELELIU
1000 500 0 1000 2000 Yds
MAP 3

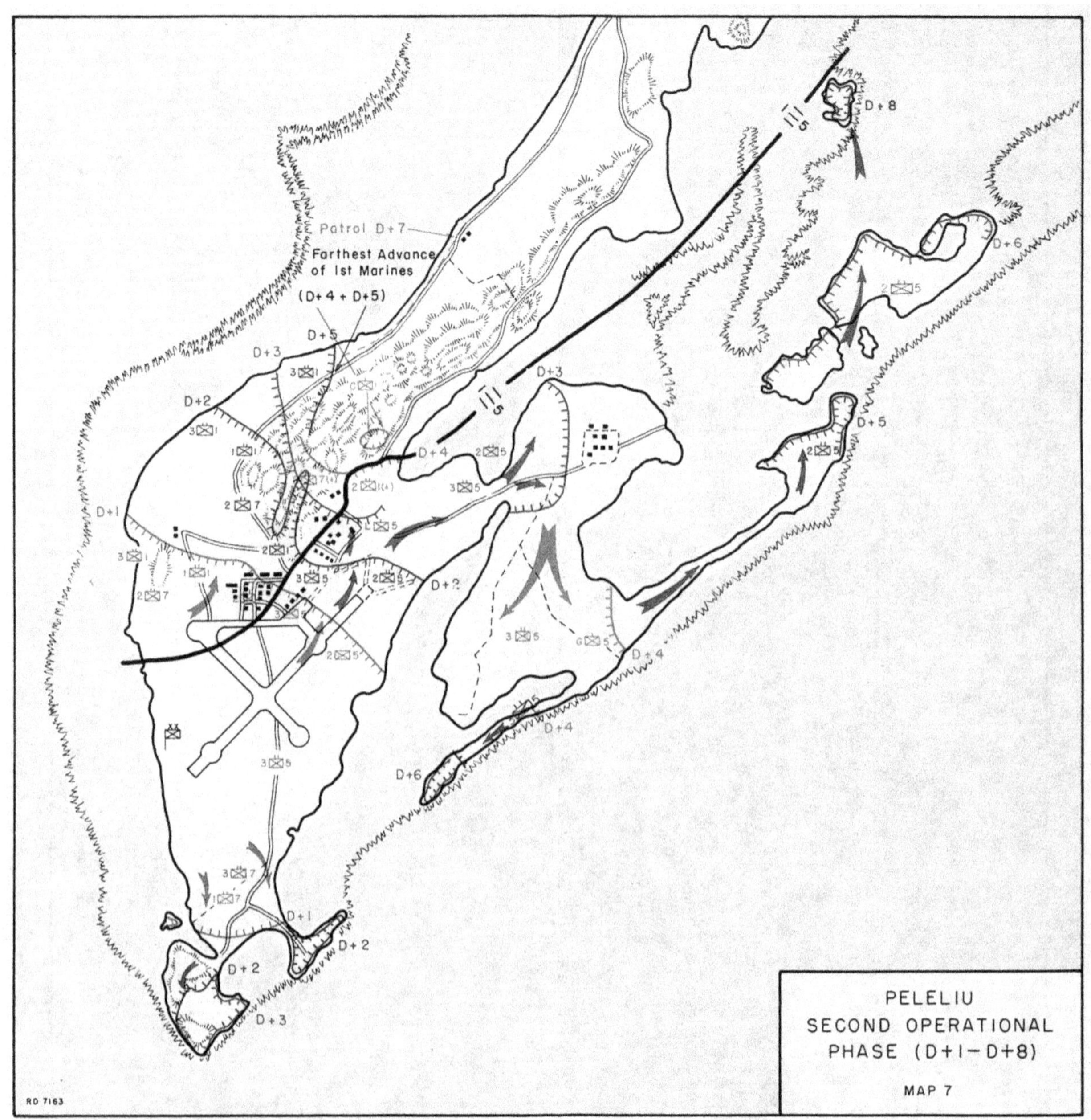

PELELIU
SECOND OPERATIONAL
PHASE (D+1—D+8)

MAP 7

RD 7163

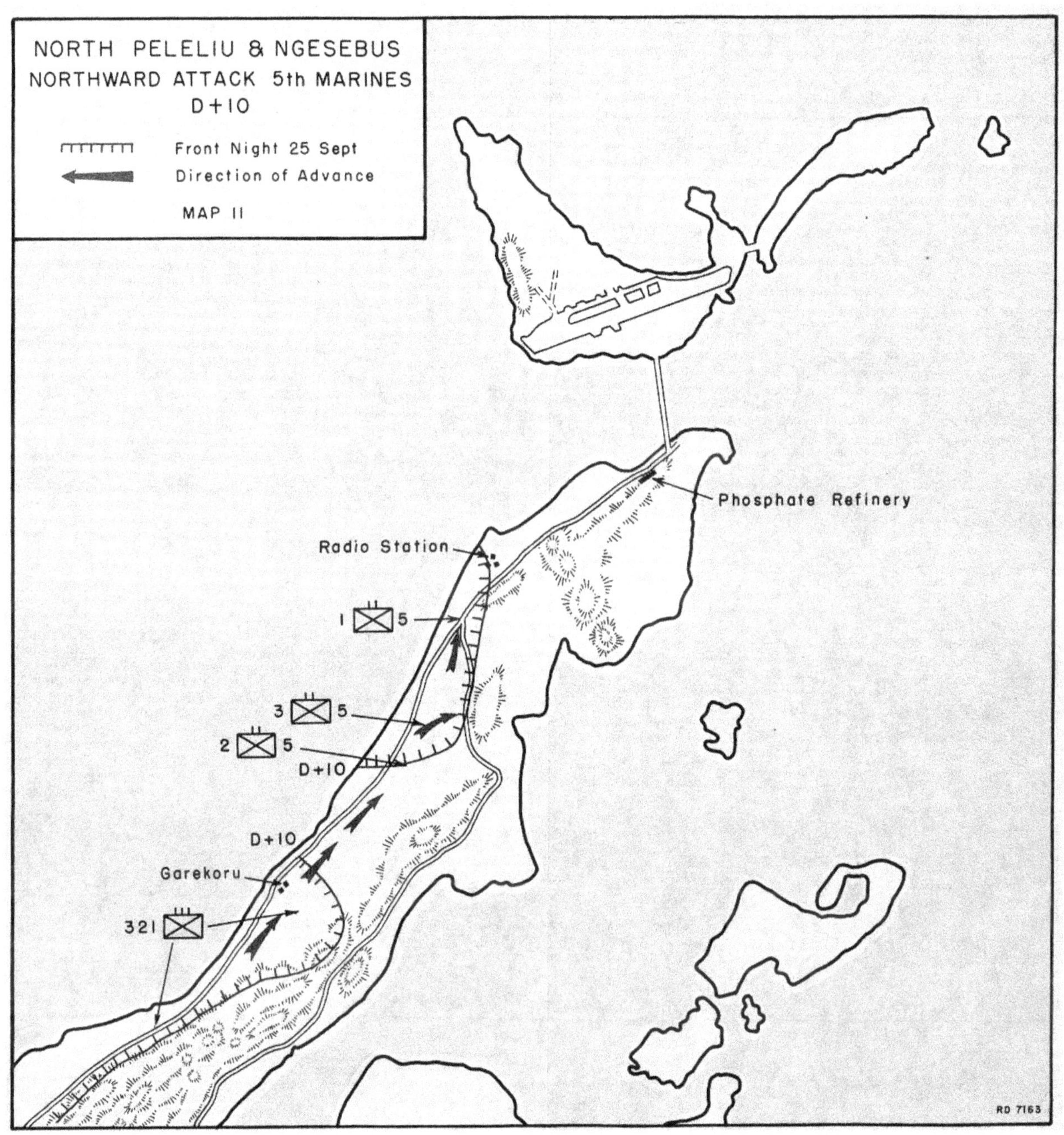

NORTH PELELIU & NGESEBUS
NORTHWARD ATTACK 5th MARINES
D+10
Front Night 25 Sept
Direction of Advance
MAP II
Phosphate Refinery
Radio Station
1 5
3 5
2 5
D+10
D+10
Garekoru
321
RD 7163

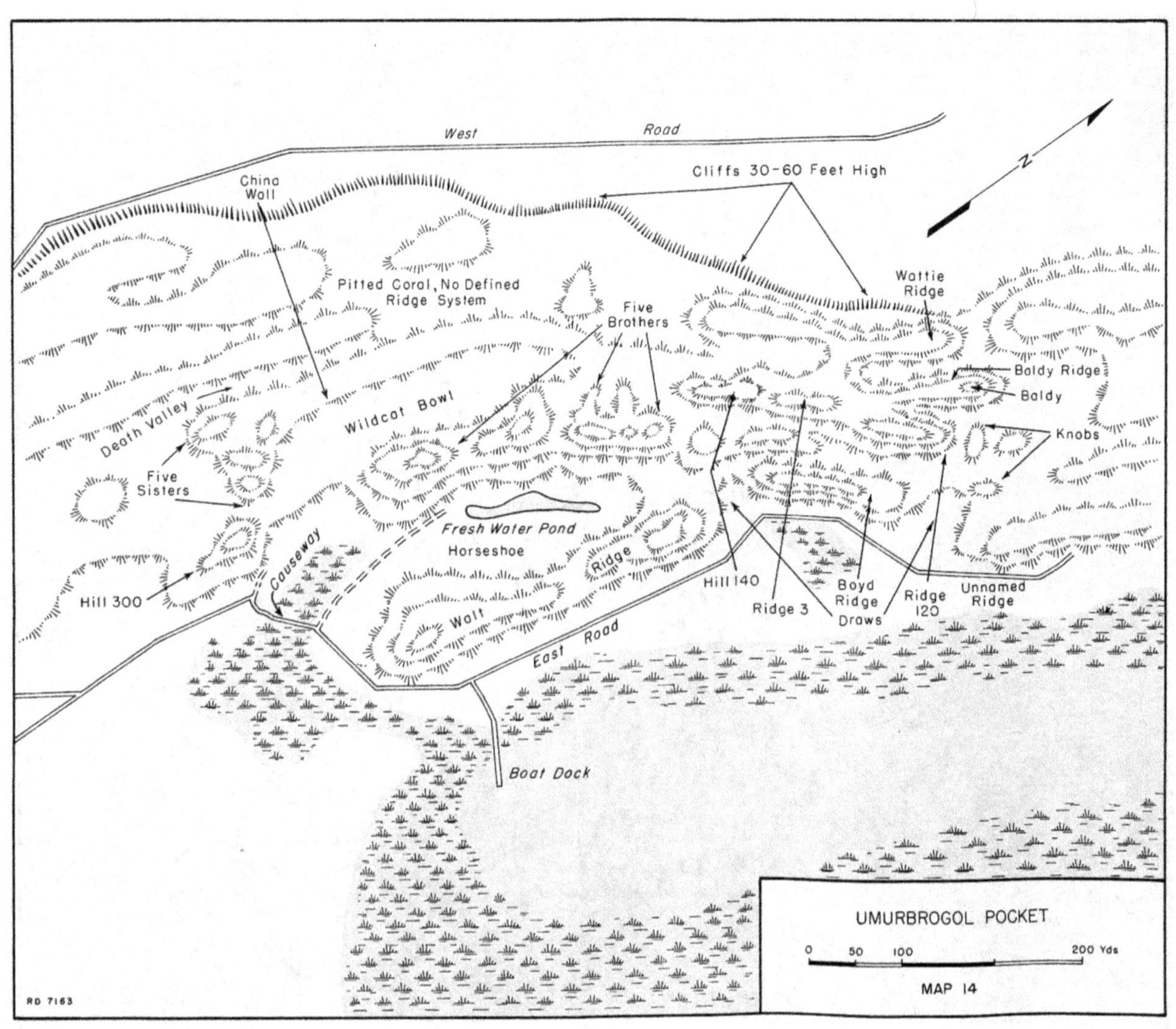

West Road
China Wall
Cliffs 30-60 Feet High
Wattie Ridge
Pitted Coral, No Defined Ridge System
Five Brothers
Baldy Ridge
Baldy
Death Valley
Wildcat Bowl
Knobs
Five Sisters
Fresh Water Pond
Horseshoe
Ridge
Causeway
Hill 300
Hill 140
Ridge 3
Boyd Ridge Draws
Ridge 120
Unnamed Ridge
Walt
East Road
Boat Dock
N
UMURBROGOL POCKET
0   50   100   200 Yds
MAP 14
RD 7163

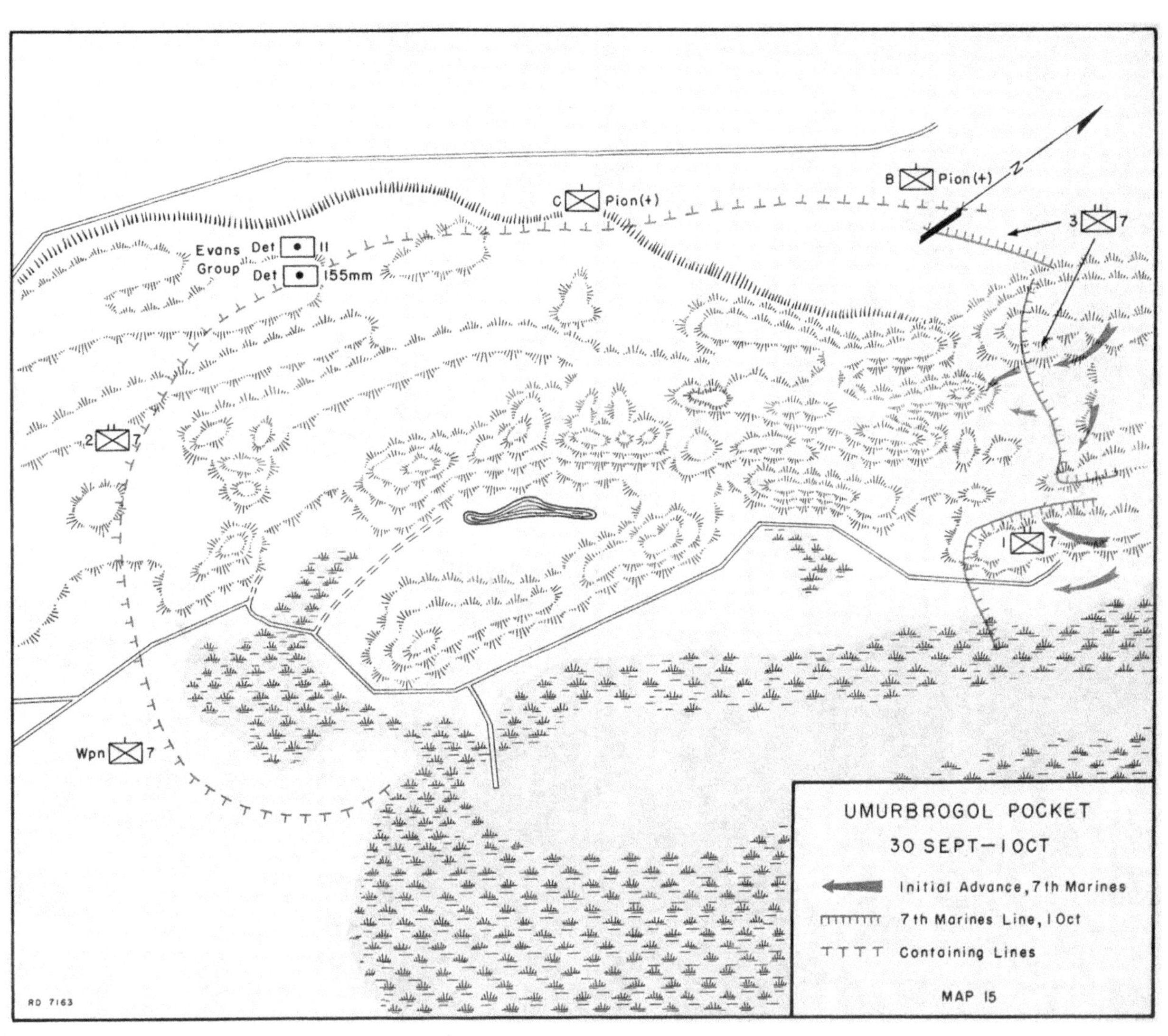

B Pion(+)
C Pion(+)
Evans Group
Det 11
Det 155mm
3 7
2 7
1 7
Wpn 7
UMURBROGOL POCKET
30 SEPT—1 OCT
Initial Advance, 7th Marines
7th Marines Line, 1 Oct
Containing Lines
MAP 15
RD 7163

Richmond Group
Det [X] I Pion (+)
N
2 [X] 5
1 [X] 5
Relieved By
2 [X] 7
E [X] 5
DRIVE FROM THE NORTH
Positions 6-8 Oct
Attack 9 Oct
Attack 10 Oct
Attack 11 Oct
Positions 2/5 Night 11 Oct
MAP 18
RO 7163

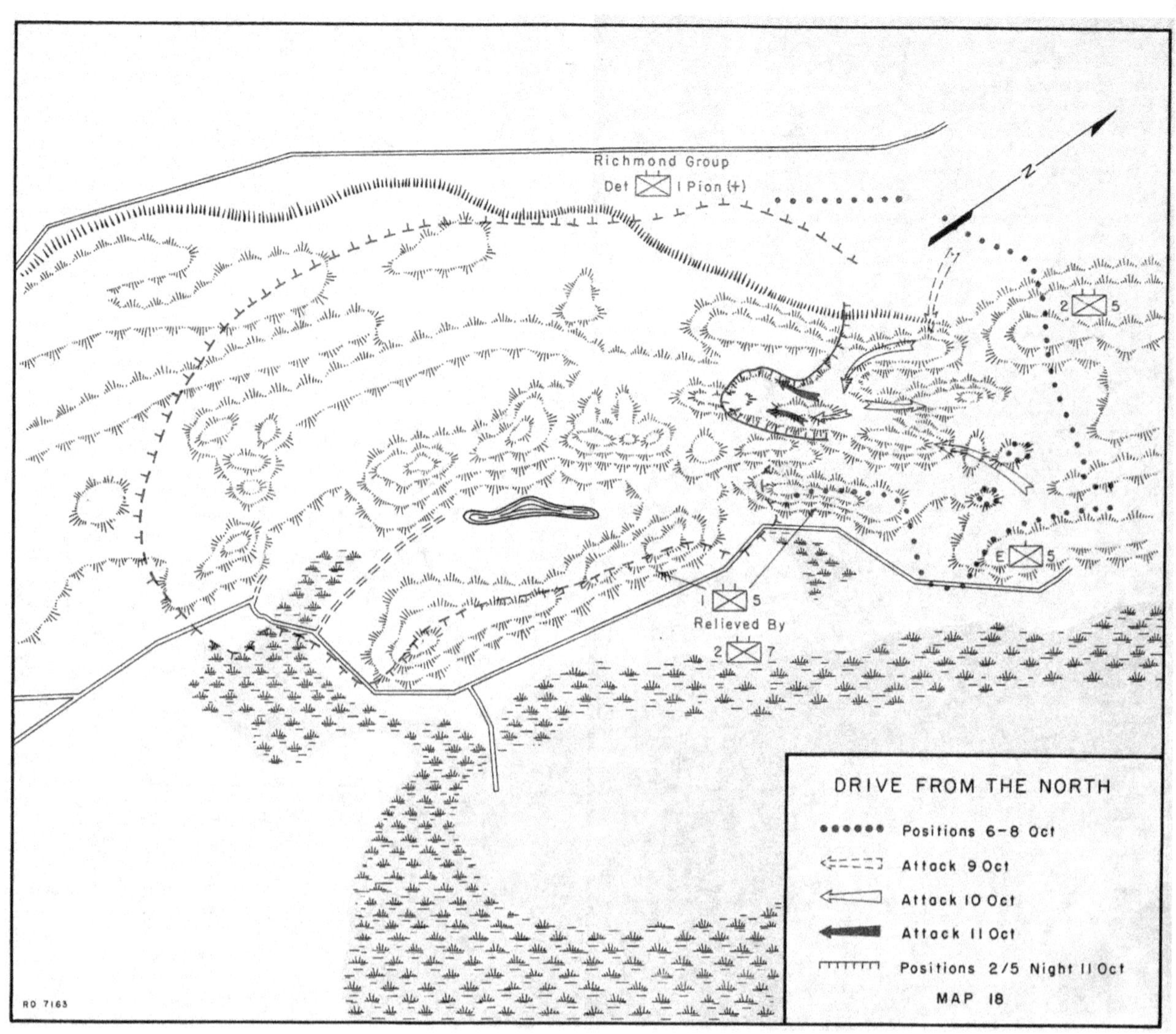

220

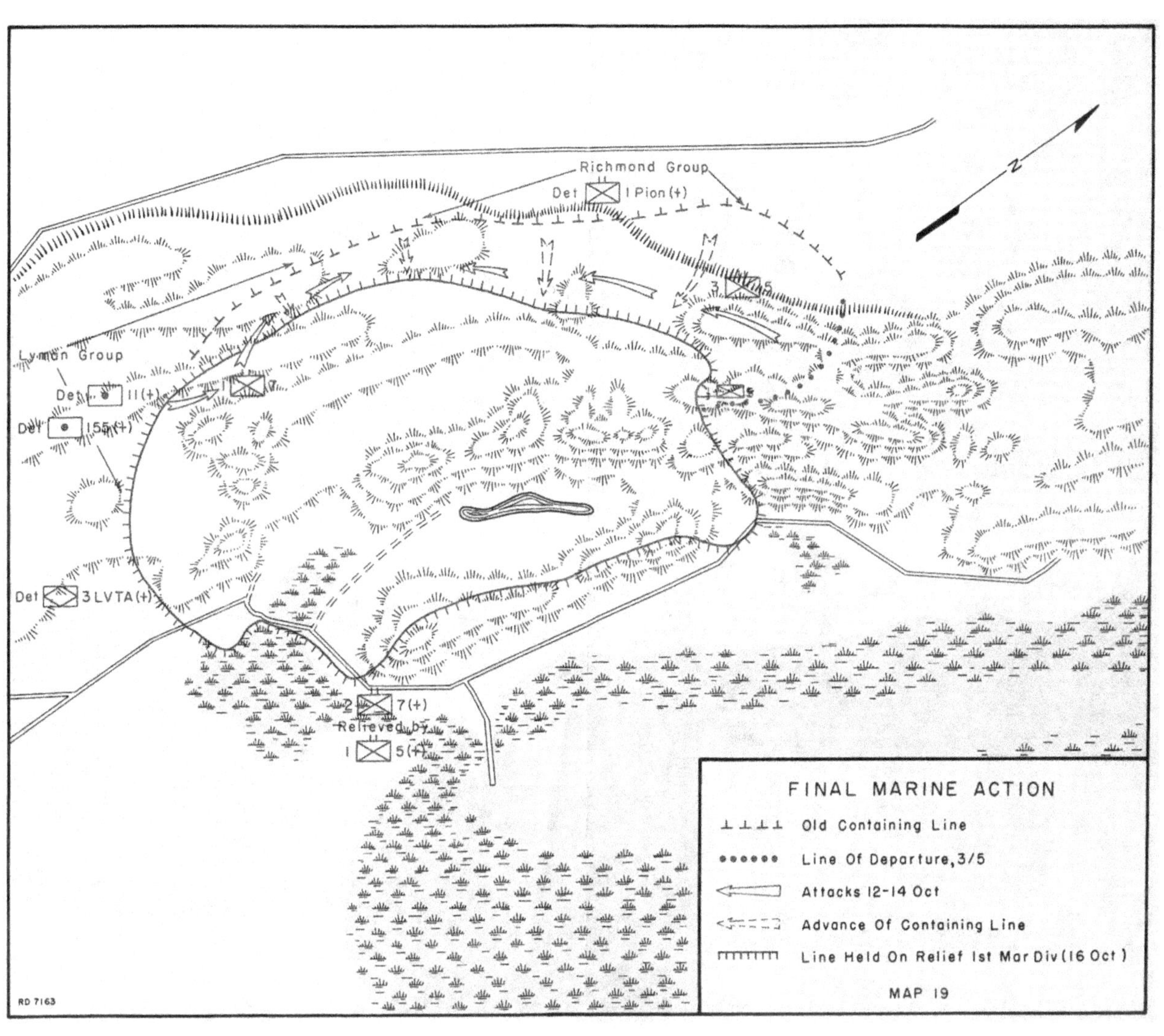

Richmond Group
Det 1 Pion(+)
N
Lyman Group
Det 11(+)
Det 155(+)
Det 3 LVTA(+)
2 7(+)
Relieved by
1 5(+)
FINAL MARINE ACTION
Old Containing Line
Line Of Departure, 3/5
Attacks 12-14 Oct
Advance Of Containing Line
Line Held On Relief 1st Mar Div (16 Oct)
MAP 19
RD 7163

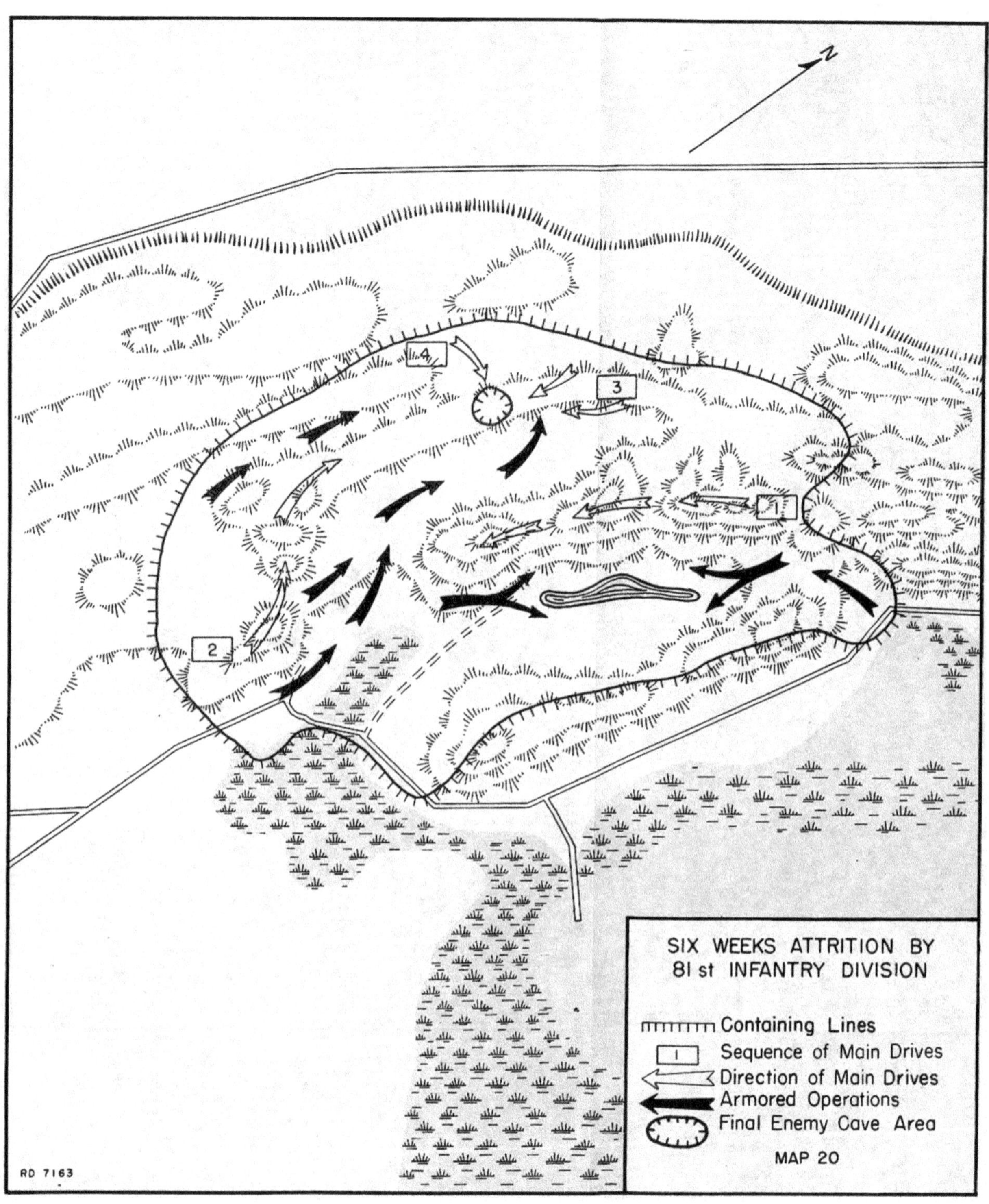

N
4
3
1
2
SIX WEEKS ATTRITION BY
81 st INFANTRY DIVISION
Containing Lines
Sequence of Main Drives
Direction of Main Drives
Armored Operations
Final Enemy Cave Area
MAP 20
RD 7163

www.ingramcontent.com/pod-product-compliance
Lightning Source LLC
Chambersburg PA
CBHW081142130726
47996CB00009B/2949